The Country Life Book of
GOOD COOKING

The Country Life Book of
GOOD COOKING

Marguerite Patten

COUNTRY LIFE
BOOKS

Picture acknowledgements

British Chicken Information Service 90, 91; British
Iceberg Growers Association 114; British Turkey
Federation 82 bottom; Hamlyn Publishing 183; National
Dairy Council 174–5 bottom; The Photo Source/
Colour Library International 139 bottom, 194 bottom,
195; Scotch Quality Beef and Lamb Association Ltd 58;
Syndication International 3, 6, 11 top, 11 bottom, 14, 19,
23, 26–7, 31, 34, 34–5, 39, 47 top, 47 bottom, 54
bottom, 58–9, 62–3, 67 top, 67 bottom, 71, 74 bottom,
82 top, 83, 87, 94, 95, 98, 103 top, 103 bottom, 107,
110–111, 115, 118, 119 top, 119 bottom, 122, 123 top,
123 bottom, 127, 130, 131 top, 131 bottom, 134 top,
134 bottom, 135, 138, 139 top, 143 top, 143 bottom, 146
top, 147, 150, 151, 154–5, 158, 159, 163 top, 163
bottom, 166 top, 166 centre, 166 bottom, 167, 170, 171,
174–5 top, 178, 179, 182 top, 182 bottom, 186, 190,
191, 194 top, 198 top, 198 bottom, 199, 202.
All other photographs by Chris King, copyright Newnes
Books.
All line drawings by Mei Lim, copyright Newnes Books.
The author and publisher would like to thank the
following for their help in providing props for colour
photographs: The Irish Shop, London; Acquisitions,
London.

Jacket photograph (left to right): Parsley pie (page 174),
Roast chicken (page 83), Brown and white rolls (page
144), Bread sauce (page 102), Meringue gâteau (page 166),
Spring crown of lamb (page 55), Seafood mousse (page
19), Summer pudding (page 126), Bakewell tart (page 133)
and Syllabub (page 140). Jacket photograph by Chris
King.

Published by Country Life Books,
an imprint of Newnes Books,
a division of The Hamlyn Publishing Group Limited,
84–88 The Centre, Feltham, Middlesex, England,
and distributed for them by
The Hamlyn Publishing Group Limited,
Rushden, Northants, England

First published 1984

ISBN 0 600 35837 2

Printed in Italy

Contents

Introduction

This cookbook has been written to gather together a wide range of practical and interesting recipes that make the very best use of our natural food resources. We are extremely fortunate in having such a wide range of ingredients from which to choose.

Our climate, about which we sometimes grumble, is variable, but temperate: the generous rainfall ensures lush pastures, so we have meats and dairy produce second to none together with a wide selection of first class vegetables, fruits and grain.

We have a long tradition of good food and cooking in this country and I have included some of the very best of the old recipes from England, Ireland, Scotland and Wales. Many of these have been handed down by generations of skilled cooks. In some cases, the original recipes have been adapted slightly to make them more appealing for today's menus.

Sometimes people are inclined to overlook our long and proud tradition of cooking. In Chaucer's Tales you will find praise for our good baking and pies. In the Tudor period the foods, dishes and banquets given were considered some of the most interesting and exotic in Europe. Good gardeners produced a range of herbs and salad ingredients to add flavour to dishes based upon meat and fish. The Royal parks and large estates had ample supplies of venison, hare, rabbit and game birds, which were enjoyed by the rich and the poorer families.

Merchant seamen have roamed the world for many centuries and among the treasures they brought back to Britain were spices and unusual foods that added variety to home-produced ingredients.

British families have enjoyed puddings and cakes for hundreds of years. It may be surprising to learn that as far back as the early 17th Century, ice creams and light fluffy desserts, such as syllabubs, were as popular in sophisticated households as the better known sustaining steamed puddings.

In addition to the older traditional recipes, you will find a wide selection of up-to-the-minute and original ideas and dishes. One of the interesting and exciting aspects of cooking is that there should be no monotony about the meals we serve, for the cook can develop and produce new dishes all the time.

I have thoroughly enjoyed working on this book for I have always been proud of the splendid foods available and of the skill and creative ability of the British cooks of the past and present.

Opposite: See chapter 'Good Baking', page 142

Useful Facts

The recipes in this book are given with metric, imperial and American quantities. Follow one set of weights or measures, they are not interchangeable.

MEASURES
1 standard imperial teaspoon is equivalent to a metric 5 ml spoon.
1 standard imperial tablespoon is equivalent to a metric 15 ml spoon.

Spoon measures should be level. In a few recipes the word 'level' is added, this is to point out the particular importance of careful measuring in that recipe.

1 standard imperial tablespoon is almost equivalent to 1½ American tablespoons, so when the recipe gives an American tablespoon, be a little generous with the amount of food. You will find that 2 imperial tablespoons are shown as 3 American tablespoons etc. in recipes. In the methods, the figures in brackets, eg. (3 tbsp) or (1¼ cups) refers to American measures.

An imperial pint, i.e. 20 fl oz, is equivalent to 584 ml – called 600 ml, but an American pint is 16 fl oz only.

WEIGHTS
In some recipes you will find a slightly different metrication weight given from the usual conversion, e.g. 110 g as compared with the usual 100 g as being equivalent to 4 oz. This is to provide the correct balance of ingredients.

OVEN SETTINGS
All oven positions and settings have been carefully tested but it is important to appreciate that individual ovens vary slightly. You should be guided by your own experience with your cooker and the manufacturers' instructions.

Oven positions are not important with a fan-assisted electric cooker, all positions give the same heat. Most people find it better to lower the oven setting slightly with this type of cooker, i.e. by 10°C or 25°F or 1 Gas Mark.

Use the sized tin(s) recommended to give the same cooking time as in the recipe.

CHOICE OF INGREDIENTS
In some recipes you will find a choice of ingredients, i.e. 'butter or margarine' or '2–3 onions'. I have put the ingredient or quantity I prefer first, but find the second ingredient or amount gives a perfectly satisfactory result.

In many recipes the type of flour to use is stated clearly, e.g. 'plain flour' (known as all-purpose in America). In some recipes though, e.g. in soups, sauces, etc., the word 'flour' only is used. This is because it is a small amount only and while plain flour is an ideal choice, it is relatively unimportant if self-raising flour is chosen.

As this is a book in which fresh ingredients are used to the best advantage, fresh herbs are given in practically all recipes. If you have to substitute dried herbs, use only half the amount as they have a stronger flavour, i.e. 1 teaspoon chopped fresh sage should be replaced by ½ teaspoon dried sage.

AMERICAN TERMS
The list below gives some American equivalents or substitutes for terms used in this book:

British	American
cake or loaf tin	cake or loaf pan
cocktail stick	toothpick
deep cake tin	spring form pan
dough or mixture	batter
flan or pastry case	pie shell
flan tin	pie pan
frying pan	skillet
greaseproof paper	wax paper
icing	frosting
knock back dough	punch down dough
pudding basin	ovenproof bowl or pudding mold
roasting tin	roasting pan
rub in	cut in
sandwich cake	layer cake
stoned	pitted
Swiss roll tin	jelly roll pan
very finely chopped	minced
whisk	beat

NOTES FOR AUSTRALIAN AND NEW ZEALAND USERS
In Australia and New Zealand metric measures are now used in conjunction with the standard 250-ml measuring cup. It is however important to remember that the Australian tablespoon (holding 20 ml) differs from the British (holding 17.7 ml) and American (holding 14.2 ml) tablespoons. The table below gives conversions to follow. A teaspoon holds about 5 ml in all three countries.

British	American	Australian
1 teaspoon	1 teaspoon	1 teaspoon
1 tablespoon	1 tablespoon	1 tablespoon
2 tablespoons	3 tablespoons	2 tablespoons
3½ tablespoons	4 tablespoons	3 tablespoons
4 tablespoons	5 tablespoons	3½ tablespoons

Star Coding
I feel it is helpful to see at a glance whether a recipe is quick and easy to make or whether you need to devote time and spend more money on the ingredients. The method of marking these recipes is as follows: Cooking times are given in all recipes.

*   dishes that are quick and easy to prepare generally of moderate cost

**   economical family dishes, the time for making varies

***   frankly luxurious dishes, the time of making varies.

Meal Starters

This has become one of the most interesting courses of a meal. Nowadays there are no 'rules' as to what one should serve as an hors d'oeuvre or meal starter. It is a case of choosing imaginative light dishes that complement the rest of the meal. These can be based upon seasonal fruits and vegetables; on light pastry dishes; potted foods and pâtés; well chilled salads and iced savoury sorbets. Smaller portions of the fish dishes in the chapter that begins on page 32 could be included; those based upon shellfish are particularly suitable. Smoked and soused fish make an ideal beginning to a meal.

Soup has always been one of the most popular ways in which to start a meal. There are unusual as well as traditional recipes for soups in the chapter that begins on page 20.

There may be occasions when you prefer to serve small appetizers with a pre-luncheon or pre-dinner drink and dispense with a formal first course. There are many suggestions for 'nibbles' on pages 175 to 177.

SERVING FRUIT AND VEGETABLES

Fruits or fruit juices make a simple and yet pleasant start to a meal. Be imaginative and mix fruits with salad ingredients to provide a colourful hors d'oeuvre, see pages 116 and 117 for ideas. The recipes on this page give an idea as to how dessert pears can be turned into a pleasing hors d'oeuvre and a simple way to combine fruit with green peppers.

PEARS WITH STILTON CHEESE

No Cooking   Serves 4   ✳

This is a 'made-in-a-minute' appetizer that makes good use of ripe dessert pears.

	Metric/Imperial	American
Stilton cheese	225 g/8 oz	½ lb
port wine	2 tbsp	3 tbsp
lemon juice	½ tbsp	½ tbsp
corn or olive oil	1 tbsp	1 tbsp
lettuce heart	1	1
small tomatoes, sliced	4	4
cucumber, sliced	small portion	small portion
large ripe dessert pears	2	2

Put the cheese into a bowl and add the port wine, lemon juice and oil. Stir briskly until like a very thick cream. Place the lettuce, tomatoes and cucumber on individual dishes. Peel, halve and core the pears just before the meal. Place a halved pear on each dish and top with the cheese mixture.

STUFFED PEPPERS

No Cooking   Serves 4   ✳

Sieve 225 g/8 oz (1 cup) cottage cheese. Blend with 2 peeled and diced dessert apples, 1 tablespoon lemon juice and 100 g/4 oz (1 cup) chopped mixed nuts.

Cut a slice from the top of 2 green peppers. Chop these slices and blend with the cheese mixture.

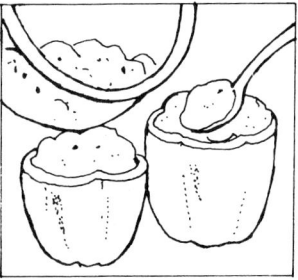

Remove the cores and seeds from the peppers. Fill the cavities with the cheese mixture.

Chill, then cut into slices. Serve on a bed of salad.

VEGETABLE APPETIZERS

It is interesting how vegetables have periods of being 'in fashion' or 'out of fashion'. The globe artichoke was a familiar vegetable in Britain until the 20th Century, since when it has become less readily available. This is a pity, for it is both easily grown and a delicious food. You will find directions for cooking globe artichokes on page 108. The hot vegetable can be served with melted butter or with a Cheese Sauce, as page 102. Globe artichokes are excellent as a cold dish; remove the centre choke after cooking, cool then fill the cavity with an oil and vinegar dressing or with Smoked Salmon Pâté or the Creamy Liver Pâté given on pages 17 and 15.

Asparagus, fortunately, has never been 'out of fashion'; it is ideal as a luxurious start to a meal. Serve hot with melted butter or hot butter mixed with a little lemon juice, salt and pepper. Cold asparagus can be wrapped in thin slices of smoked salmon or served with mayonnaise.

Stuffed cooked or raw tomatoes and dishes based upon mushrooms make excellent first courses. There are recipes on pages 114 and 109.

Globe Artichoke and Asparagus Appetizers

ROMANY MUSHROOMS

Cooking Time: 10 minutes   Serves 4   ❖❖

	Metric/Imperial	American
butter	50 g/2 oz	¼ cup
button mushrooms, sliced	225 g/8 oz	½ lb
salt and pepper	to taste	to taste
bacon rashers (slices)	4	4
double (heavy) cream	150 ml/¼ pint	⅔ cup
white wine	4 tbsp	5 tbsp
Cheddar cheese, grated	4 tbsp	5 tbsp

Heat the butter in a frying pan (skillet) and fry the mushrooms until soft; season lightly. Put into 4 heated individual flameproof dishes. De-rind and finely chop the bacon. Fry the rinds and bacon until just cooked; discard the rinds. Spoon the bacon over the mushrooms.

Whip the cream until stiff, season lightly then gradually beat in the wine. Spread over the bacon and mushrooms; top with the cheese. Place under a preheated grill (broiler) for 2 to 3 minutes until golden brown.

SAVOURY SORBETS

Fruit sorbets (sherbets) have been popular for generations, see page 139. Savoury ones are a comparatively modern taste but one that fast is becoming popular. Modern freezers and ice cream making equipment enable sweet or savoury mixtures to be prepared easily and quickly.

Savoury sorbets look attractive. Always add enough acid flavour (in the form of lemon or orange juice) to provide a refreshing taste. Take the mixture out of the freezer about 20 minutes before serving so it is not too cold and hard.

Carrot and Orange Sorbet

CARROT AND ORANGE SORBET

Cooking Time: 5 minutes   Serves 4–6   ✳✳

Choose really young carrots for this savoury ice. Peel and grate, rather than slice or chop them, so they cook quickly. The carrot curls that garnish the dish are made by cutting the raw carrots into long narrow strips that can be curled into shape.

	Metric/Imperial	American
oranges	2	2
carrots, grated	350 g/12 oz	¾ lb
small onion	1	1
salt and pepper	to taste	to taste
sugar	2 teasp	2 teasp
egg white	1	1
To garnish: carrot curls, see above		
watercress	few sprigs	few sprigs

Grate enough orange rind to give 1 teaspoon. Halve the oranges, squeeze out the juice. Put the carrots, peeled whole onion and orange rind into a little lightly seasoned boiling water and cook for 5 minutes. Strain and sieve or liquidize (blend). Blend with the orange juice and sugar. Freeze lightly; this takes about 40 minutes.

Whisk the egg white stiffly; fold into the half-frozen carrot mixture and freeze again until firm. Scoop or spoon out portions into chilled glasses.

Garnish with the carrot curls and watercress. Serve with plain biscuits (crackers). This sorbet is at its best if served within 24 hours of making.

CELERY AND CHEESE SORBET

Cooking Time: 10–15 minutes   Serves 4–6   ✳✳

Choose a really tender celery head (bunch); use just the more delicate stalks. A few leaves add colour and flavour to the mixture.

	Metric/Imperial	American
medium celery head (bunch)	1	1
salt and pepper	to taste	to taste
lemon juice	1 tbsp	1 tbsp
milk	300 ml/½ pint	1¼ cups
cream cheese	100 g/4 oz	½ cup
egg white	1	1
To garnish: chopped chives	1 tbsp	1 tbsp
celery leaves		

Chop the celery and leaves. Put into very lightly seasoned boiling water and cook until just soft. Strain well then rub through a sieve. Blend with the lemon juice, milk and cream cheese. It is, however, much easier to put the strained celery, lemon juice, milk and cream cheese into a liquidizer (blender) or food processor and switch on until smoothly mixed together.

Freeze the mixture for about 25 minutes. Whisk the egg white until stiff and fold into the half-frozen celery mixture. Freeze again until firm. Scoop or spoon out into chilled glasses.

Top with the chopped chives. Garnish with the darker celery leaves. Serve with stalks of celery and plain biscuits (crackers). This sorbet is at its best if served within 36 hours of making.

Celery and Cheese Sorbet

POTTED FOODS

Potted mixtures have been popular for generations. The texture and flavour is not unlike that of a pâté, although the ingredients used are generally more simple. In the past, potted cheese, fish, meat or poultry would be offered at breakfast-time as well as at other meals.

Potted foods can be served instead of pâté at the start of a meal. They are excellent with salad or as a sandwich filling.

When cooking the food, choose the method that retains the maximum flavour; do not overcook. Many potted mixtures have a smooth texture. This used to be achieved by pounding the ingredients with the help of a pestle and mortar. Nowadays the hard work of pounding is replaced by the speedy efficiency of a liquidizer (blender) or food processor. Do not liquidize or process for too long a period; stop the moment the mixture reaches the desired texture. Overhandling produces an unappetizing sticky mixture.

The covering of clarified butter or fat (shortening or drippings) not only keeps the potted mixture soft and moist but, by excluding the air, ensures that the mixture keeps well for up to 2 weeks in a refrigerator.

When the butter or fat is lifted from the potted food, it is highly perishable and should be eaten within 2 days. It is usual to prepare individual containers of potted food. Potted foods tend to freeze better than more elaborate pâtés. Potted cheese can be frozen for up to 3 months; potted fish and meats for up to 2 months.

Potted cheese, which follows, is an excellent dish for a cheese and wine party or it can be served for an unusual start to a meal or as an alternative to the cheese board with celery or radishes or nuts.

POTTED CHEESE

No Cooking   Serves 4–6   ❋❋

This is one of the traditional 'pâtés' or 'potted mixtures' so beloved of old cookery books. When the cheese is well pounded and the mixture stands for a while, it is possible to cut this into neat slices. It can be served with biscuits or bread, but old recipes often refer to this being served with fruit. The choice of cheese is entirely a personal matter, but I think a white Cheshire is best of all; for a really strong flavour a Lancashire is excellent or one can use a mild Cheddar. Try mixing several different cheeses together.

	Metric/Imperial	American
butter	150 g/5 oz	⅝ cup
Cheshire white cheese, or other cheese such as Cheddar or Lancashire	350 g/12 oz	¾ lb
mustard powder	1–2 teasp	1–2 teasp
dry sherry	2 tbsp	3 tbsp
dried, fresh or pickled walnuts (depending on flavour required)	75 g/3 oz	¾ cup

Cream 75 g/3 oz (6 tbsp) of the butter until very soft. Grate the cheese finely, then put it into a bowl and work well until like butter. In the olden day kitchens, a pestle

and mortar was used for this purpose, but a wooden spoon, used with energy, will give somewhat the same effect. Add to the creamed butter. Blend the mustard (the amount depends upon personal taste) with the sherry, then gradually mix this with the cheese.

Chop the walnuts very finely, if using fresh walnuts remove the skins; in my opinion fresh ones are the best to use since they do not detract from the colour or flavour of the cheese, but many people enjoy the 'bite' of the black pickled walnuts. Combine with the cheese mixture. Put into 4 to 6 small pots. Melt the remaining butter, allow to cool, then spoon over the top of each pot of cheese. Keep in a cool place. Serve with hot toast and crisp lettuce.

VARIATION
Potted Stilton: Follow the recipe for Potted Cheese, but crumble and then beat the Stilton and omit the walnuts. Port wine could be used instead of sherry. A good pinch of ground mace can be added for additional flavour.

Potted Fish

Many kinds of fish are suitable; the best known being small shrimps. Choose the method of cooking suggested in the various recipes in order to retain the maximum flavour.

To Cook Shrimps: Shrimps and prawns (shrimp) are cooked in salted water for just a few minutes until the shells change colour. Put the fish into boiling water to which you add a very little salt (this could be omitted if desired). Heat until the shells change colour. Small shrimp shells turn pinky-brown, the larger prawns bright pink.

POTTED SALMON

Cooking Time: few minutes   Serves 4   ❋❋❋

	Metric/Imperial	American
fresh salmon, cooked in foil as page 193	350 g/12 oz	¾ lb
butter, clarified as page 17	175 g/6 oz	¾ cup
grated or ground nutmeg	to taste	to taste
ground mace	to taste	to taste
salt and pepper	to taste	to taste
lemon juice or dry sherry	2 teasp	2 teasp

Flake the cooked fish. Heat the butter and blend half with the fish. Either pound until smooth or put into a liquidizer (blender) or food processor and switch on until smooth. Add the nutmeg, mace, salt, pepper and lemon juice or sherry. Mix well. Put into 4 individual containers; smooth flat on top. Cover with the remaining butter and allow to cool. Serve as Potted Shrimps.

VARIATION
Use other cooked fish, such as trout, salmon trout or kippers in place of salmon.

POTTED SHRIMPS

**Cooking Time:
few minutes
Serves 4** ❖❖

British shrimps are very small with a particularly delicate flavour. They are time consuming to peel (shell). You may therefore prefer to base the recipe on small prawns (shrimp).

It is advisable to peel shrimps or prawns while warm. If you have purchased the shellfish ready-cooked, place them in warm not hot water for 2–3 minutes. This loosens the shells and heads.

The butter need not be clarified if the potted shrimps are to be eaten within 1–2 days, but clarifying is advisable for longer storage. See instructions on page 17.

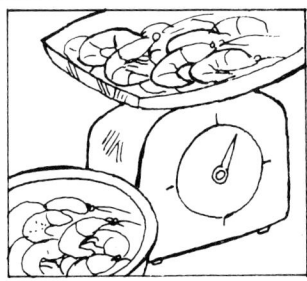

Peel (shell) 1.2 litres/2 pints (2½ pints) shrimps. These should be cooked as page 12 or see this page left.

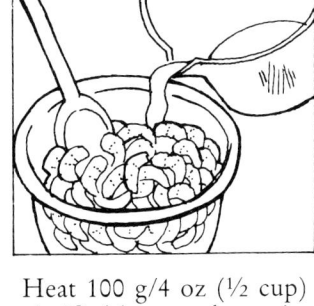

Heat 100 g/4 oz (½ cup) clarified butter, then mix half the butter with the shrimps.

Add freshly ground white pepper or a little cayenne pepper, a pinch of grated or ground nutmeg and a little salt if desired.

Spoon the mixture into 4 individual round dishes. Smooth flat on top.

Pour the remaining butter over the fish mixture. Allow to cool.

To serve potted shrimps, invert each container on to a small plate; garnish with lettuce and lemon wedges. Serve with hot toast.

Potted Meat, Poultry and Game

The recipes show the correct way to prepare potted meats of all kinds. It is an excellent method of using up small portions of cooked meat.

POTTED PHEASANT

Cooking Time: 3 minutes   Serves 4–6 ❖❖❖

	Metric/Imperial	American
roast pheasant, cooked as page 82, weight without skin and bone	350 g/12 oz	¾ lb
clarified pheasant dripping or butter	100 g/4 oz	½ cup
port wine	1½ tbsp	2 tbsp
ground mace	to taste	to taste
ground cinnamon	to taste	to taste
salt and pepper	to taste	to taste

Cut the flesh of the pheasant into pieces; either mince (grind) twice or chop in a food processor. Heat the dripping or butter and blend half with the pheasant. Add the port wine, spices and seasoning. Put into individual pots, top with the remaining dripping or butter. Chill well. Serve with hot toast and butter or use as a sandwich filling.

VARIATIONS
Grouse, pigeon or other game birds or venison can be used in place of pheasant.

● Chicken or turkey can be used instead of pheasant. Use half breast and half leg meat, and butter and dry sherry instead of dripping and port wine.
● *Potted Beef:* Use lightly cooked and minced (ground) roast beef instead of pheasant; add 1 to 2 teaspoons made mustard and a little garlic salt as well as other seasoning. Omit the mace and cinnamon from the recipe left. Blend with beef stock or brandy instead of port wine.
● *Potted Ham:* Use boiled bacon or ham in place of pheasant; omit the ground cinnamon. Flavour with made mustard and mace. Bind with dry sherry instead of port wine.

Hazelnut Terrine, Bacon and Chicken Pâté – recipe page 16, Creamy Liver Pâté, Orange Liver Pâté

MEAT APPETIZERS

Pâtés, as given on this and the next two pages, are a favourite way of serving meat as a first course. Some of the loaves and moulds in the meat, poultry and game sections of this book would be an ideal choice too. The more sophisticated pâtés and terrines that we enjoy today are really a development of the potted foods which you will find on the preceding pages. If one is being strictly accurate, the term 'pâté' should be used to describe a mixture encased in pastry, as the Game Pâté on page 97; whereas a terrine has no pastry. Nowadays though the two words have become interchangeable.

Most pâtés are better frozen for a short time, i.e. a maximum of 3 weeks, but if the recipe differs from this you will find the freezing time given.

HAZELNUT TERRINE

**Cooking Time:
2¼ hours
Serves 8** ✳✳✳

This terrine (a name given to many kinds of potted foods or pâtés) is made with an interesting blend of veal, chicken, liver and bacon together with firm hazelnuts (filberts).

	Metric/Imperial	American
For the liver layer:		
corn oil	2 tbsp	3 tbsp
butter	25 g/1 oz	2 tbsp
calves' liver, diced	350 g/12 oz	¾ lb
medium onion, chopped	1	1
garlic clove, crushed	1	1
chopped parsley	2 tbsp	3 tbsp
salt and pepper	to taste	to taste
mustard powder	1 teasp	1 teasp
brandy	1 tbsp	1 tbsp
grated or ground nutmeg	½ teasp	½ teasp
For the chicken and veal layer:		
raw veal fillet	350 g/12 oz	¾ lb
raw chicken flesh, weight without skin or bone	350 g/12 oz	¾ lb
ground mace	½ teasp	½ teasp
chopped rosemary	1 teasp	1 teasp
brandy	2 tbsp	3 tbsp
hazelnuts (filberts)	175 g/6 oz	generous 1 cup
To coat: streaky bacon rashers (slices)	350 g/12 oz	¾ lb
To garnish: rosemary sprigs	5–6	5–6
black (ripe) olives	4–5	4–5

Heat the oil and butter in a large frying pan (skillet). Fry the liver for about 2 minutes only, remove from the pan. Add the onion and garlic to the pan, fry for 5 minutes;

do not allow to brown. Put the liver, onion and garlic through a mincer (grinder) or chop in a food processor. Mix with the parsley, a generous amount of salt and pepper, the mustard powder, brandy and nutmeg.

Cut the veal and chicken into wafer thin slices or neat dice (depending upon personal taste). Put into a bowl. Add the mace, rosemary, brandy and unchopped hazelnuts, season lightly. Allow to stand for 20 minutes.

De-rind the bacon; lay the rashers (slices) on a board and stroke with a knife to make them as long as possible. Line the bottom of a terrine or other 900 g/2 lb ovenproof dish with some of the bacon; the rashers should just over-lap. Lay the remaining bacon up the sides of the dish; make sure there is sufficient bacon overhanging the top edges to eventually fold over the filling.

Arrange a thin layer of the chicken and veal mixture over the bacon on the bottom of the dish. Layer half the liver mixture in the dish. Top with a little chicken and veal mixture. Finally add the remaining liver and then the remaining chicken and veal mixture. Fold over the bacon rashers. Cover with the lid of the dish or lightly greased foil.

Stand the dish in a 'bain-marie' (tin of cold water) and bake in the centre of a very moderate oven, 160°C/325°F Gas Mark 3, for 2 hours.

Remove the lid or foil and place greaseproof (waxed) paper and a light weight on top of the mixture. Allow to cool. Remove any excess fat. Garnish with the rosemary and olives. This dish should be served with hot toast. Best eaten within 48 hours of cooking. It can be frozen for up to 1 month.

Creamy Liver Pâté

Cooking Time: 10 minutes   Serves 8   ❋❋❋

This liver pâté recipe is a splendid basic one. The cooking time is short, which retains the full flavour of the tender liver. This pâté, if covered with the butter, can be stored for up to 5 days in the refrigerator or up to 5 weeks in the freezer; so can the variations.

	Metric/Imperial	American
olive oil	2 tbsp	3 tbsp
butter	25 g/1 oz	2 tbsp
medium onion, chopped	1	1
garlic cloves, crushed	1–2	1–2
calves' liver, sliced	450 g/1 lb	1 lb
chicken livers, diced	350 g/12 oz	¾ lb
brandy	2 tbsp	3 tbsp
mustard powder	½–1 teasp	½–1 teasp
double (heavy) cream	4 tbsp	5 tbsp
salt and pepper	to taste	to taste
To coat: butter, clarified as page 17	100 g/4 oz	½ cup

Heat the oil and butter in a large frying pan (skillet). Add the onion, garlic and livers and fry steadily until just tender. Do not allow the ingredients to brown. Rub

through a sieve if you require a very smooth texture or put through the coarsest blade of a mincer (grinder) for a less fine pâté. If using a food processor, simply chop the ingredients to personal taste.

Put the liver mixture into a bowl, beat in the brandy. Blend the mustard powder with the cream and beat into the liver and other ingredients. As the mixture is beaten, the pâté will thicken. Lastly, add salt and pepper to taste. Spoon into an attractive dish; spread flat and coat with the butter. Chill well. Serve with hot toast and butter.

The pâté can be garnished before serving with green leaves (basil, mint, bay leaves, according to the season) and a fan of gherkin (sweet dill pickle).

VARIATIONS

Bacon and Liver Pâté: Fry 3 to 4 bacon rashers (slices) in the pan before adding the oil and butter. Chop very finely (do not sieve or put into the food processor). Blend with the other ingredients.

● *Economical Pâté:* Use 550 g/1¼ lb lambs' liver instead of 450 g/1 lb calves' liver. Reduce the chicken livers to 100 g/4 oz (¼ lb). Moisten 100 g/4 oz (2 cups) soft white or wholemeal breadcrumbs in 6 tablespoons (7 tbsp) beef or chicken stock. Omit the brandy and cream. Add to the sieved or processed liver and onion mixture together with ½ teaspoon ground cinnamon.

● *Herbed Liver Pâté:* Add 2 tablespoons (3 tbsp) chopped parsley, 1 teaspoon chopped lemon thyme to the mixture. Increase the garlic cloves to 3.

● *Orange Liver Pâté:* Finely grate the rind from 2 oranges (use only the top coloured zest and no bitter pith). Add this to the liver and onion mixture when frying. Omit the brandy and use orange juice instead. Garnish with cucumber and orange slices.

● *Piquant Liver Pâté:* Add 2 to 3 tablespoons diced gherkins (sweet dill pickle) and 2 to 3 teaspoons capers to the mixture after adding the cream.

Smoked Salmon Pâté – recipe page 17

BACON AND CHICKEN PÂTÉ

Illustrated in colour on page 14
Cooking Time: 1½ hours   Serves 8 ❊❊

	Metric/Imperial	American
bacon rashers (slices)	225 g/8 oz	½ lb
raw chicken, thinly sliced	350 g/12 oz	¾ lb
butter	50 g/2 oz	¼ cup
medium onion, chopped	1	1
garlic clove, crushed	1–2	1–2
lambs' liver, sliced	350 g/12 oz	¾ lb
salt and pepper	to taste	to taste
mustard powder	½ teasp	½ teasp
chopped sage	1 teasp	1 teasp
chopped thyme	½ teasp	½ teasp
double (heavy) cream	2 tbsp	3 tbsp
eggs	2	2
stuffed olives, sliced	100 g/4 oz	¾ cup
To garnish: chicken stock	225 ml/8 fl oz	1 cup
gelatine	7 g/¼ oz	1 envelope
dry sherry	2 tbsp	3 tbsp
stuffed olives, sliced	2	2
sage	sprig	sprig

De-rind the bacon; discard the rinds and cut the bacon into pieces the size of matchsticks. Cut the sliced chicken in matchstick pieces, too. Heat the butter in a large frying pan (skillet), fry the onion, garlic and liver together for 5 minutes. Put this mixture through a mincer (grinder) or chop finely in a food processor.

Blend the liver mixture with the bacon and chicken. Add salt, pepper, mustard, herbs, cream and eggs. Mix thoroughly then add the sliced olives; turn these carefully in the bacon and chicken mixture.

Spoon into a terrine or 900 g/2 lb ovenproof dish, smooth flat on top. Cover with a lid or buttered foil. Stand the dish in a bain-marie (tin of cold water) and bake in the centre of a very moderate oven, 160°C/325°F Gas Mark 3, for 1¼ hours. Remove the lid or foil and place greaseproof (waxed) paper and a light weight on top of the mixture. Allow to cool. Remove any excess fat from the top of the pâté.

Heat half the chicken stock in a saucepan, sprinkle the gelatine on top and stir to dissolve. Add the remaining cold stock and the sherry. Allow this jellied mixture to cool until it is the consistency of a thin syrup, then spoon over the pâté. Arrange the sliced olives and sage leaves on the half-set coating. Leave until firm. Serve with hot toast. This pâté should be eaten within 48 hours of cooking. It can be frozen for up to 1 month.

THREE-LAYER PÂTÉ

Cooking Time: 5 minutes   Serves 6–8 ❊❊

This simple pâté, very like potted meats, combines tongue, chicken and ham. It looks colourful and is a practical way of using relatively small amounts of cooked meat.

	Metric/Imperial	American
cooked chicken, weight without skin and bone	225 g/8 oz	½ lb
cooked tongue	225 g/8 oz	½ lb
cooked ham	225 g/8 oz	½ lb
butter	100 g/4 oz	½ cup
chopped rosemary	1 teasp	1 teasp
chopped chives	1 tbsp	1 tbsp
cream cheese	100 g/4 oz	½ cup
salt and pepper	to taste	to taste
tomato purée (paste)	1 tbsp	1 tbsp
double (heavy) cream	4 tbsp	5 tbsp
capers	2 teasp	2 teasp
dry sherry	1 tbsp	1 tbsp
grated or ground nutmeg	to taste	to taste

Cut the chicken, tongue and ham into pieces, then either mince (grind) or chop in a food processor. Keep each meat separate. Place the chicken and meats into 3 bowls. Melt the butter and pour an equal amount over each of the meats. Add the rosemary, chives, cream cheese and salt and pepper to the chicken and butter. Beat until smooth. Spread level in a 900 g/2 lb well-buttered terrine dish or loaf tin (pan).

Blend the ham and butter with the tomato purée (paste), half the cream, the capers and a good shake of pepper. Salt should not be required. Mix well and spread over the chicken layer.

Finally mix the tongue and butter with the sherry, nutmeg, remaining cream and a good shake of pepper. Mix well and spread over the ham layer.

Cover with buttered greaseproof (waxed) paper. Put a light weight on top of the mixture and leave for several hours until firm.

Turn out and serve with salad or with hot toast and butter. Cranberry Sauce is an excellent accompaniment to this pâté, see page 100.

FISH APPETIZERS

The recipes on this and the next two pages give a selection of fish dishes for the first course of the meal. In addition to these recipes, and those in the fish section, do not overlook the appeal of various kinds of shell and smoked fish. Dressed crab, lobster, prawns (shrimp) and mussels are all excellent ingredients for salads and fish cocktails.

WHITEBAIT

Cooking Time: 10 minutes   Serves 4   ✳✳

These tiny fish are the fry of herrings and sprats. When the fresh fish is not available, whitebait can be obtained in a frozen state.

	Metric/Imperial	American
whitebait	450–550 g/ 1–1¼ lb	1–1¼ lb
plain (all-purpose) flour	50 g/2 oz	½ cup
salt and pepper	to taste	to taste
cayenne pepper	pinch	pinch
To fry: deep oil or fat		
To garnish: lemon(s) quartered	1–2	1–2

Make certain that fresh whitebait is kept in a cold place until ready to cook, for it deteriorates badly. Wash in ice-cold water and pat dry very gently. Do not remove the heads. If using frozen whitebait, defrost sufficiently to separate the small fish.

Put the flour with a very good pinch of salt, pepper and cayenne pepper into a large greaseproof (waxed) paper bag. Drop some of the whitebait into the bag and shake gently until thinly and evenly coated with flour. Continue like this until all the small fish are coated; separate them before frying if they stick together.

Heat the oil or fat to 185°C/370°F, when a cube of bread turns golden brown within 1 minute. Put some of the fish into the frying basket, lower into the hot oil or fat. Fry for 2 to 3 minutes then lift out. Continue frying in batches. Place on a heated dish, covered with absorbent paper (kitchen towels), and keep hot in the oven. Serve while very hot with quarters of lemon, cayenne pepper and brown bread and butter.

SMOKED SALMON PÂTÉ

Illustrated in colour on page 15

No Cooking   Serves 4–6   ✳✳✳

This pâté is an economical way of using expensive smoked salmon; often fishmongers will sell 'trimmings' as well as slices of the smoked fish.

	Metric/Imperial	American
smoked salmon	225 g/8 oz	½ lb
unsalted butter	50 g/2 oz	¼ cup
corn or olive oil	1 teasp	1 teasp
lemon juice	2 teasp	2 teasp
cayenne pepper	pinch	pinch
dry sherry	2 tbsp	3 tbsp
double (heavy) cream	2 tbsp	3 tbsp

Cut the smoked salmon into very small pieces or put through a mincer (grinder). Cream the butter in a bowl, add the salmon and the remaining ingredients except the cream. If using a liquidizer (blender) or food processor, simply dice the fish, melt the butter, then liquidize or process until a smooth pâté. Add the cream, beat until the mixture thickens. Place into a container to set.

Garnish with lemon and parsley. Serve with thin brown bread and butter or hot toast and butter. This pâté can be frozen for up to 1 month.

FRIED EEL

Cooking Time: 10–15 minutes   Serves 4   ✳

This speedy dish is an interesting combination of fish and bacon. It is essential to buy quick cooking young eels.

	Metric/Imperial	American
fresh young eels or elvers	550–675 g/ 1¼-1½ lb	1¼- 1½ lb
bacon rashers (slices)	4–8	4–8
butter	25 g/1 oz	2 tbsp
To garnish: lemon, sliced	1	1
parsley sprigs	4	4

TO CLARIFY BUTTER

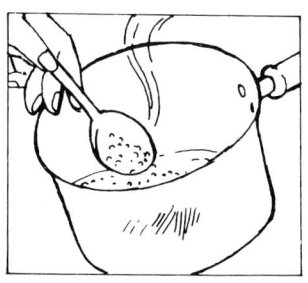

Heat the butter gently in a saucepan. Remove any foam from the top of the butter as it heats.

Allow the butter to stand for 6–7 minutes so the sediment sinks to the bottom of the pan.

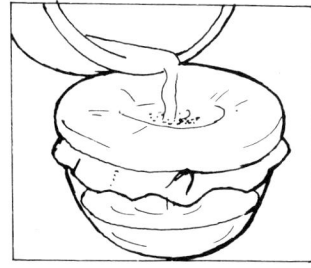

Strain the warm butter through muslin (cheese-cloth) then use. This is also the method used to make ghee for curries.

As the elvers are young, it is not essential to ask for the fish to be skinned. Cut the elvers into 2.5 cm/1 inch slices. De-rind the bacon, put the bacon and bacon rinds into a large frying pan (skillet) and fry lightly. Put the bacon rashers on to a heated dish and keep hot. Heat the butter in the pan, add the elvers and fry for 5 to 10 minutes or until tender and 'milky' in appearance.

Serve with the bacon, lemon slices and parsley.

FISH COCKTAILS

The following recipes each have one or more unexpected touches, which enhances the flavour of the fish. The fish mixture should be well chilled. It cannot be frozen.

PRAWN AND APPLE COCKTAILS

No Cooking   Serves 4   ✳✳

	Metric/Imperial	American
For the dressing: yoghurt	150 ml/¼ pint	⅔ cup
mayonnaise	2 tbsp	3 tbsp
tomato purée (paste)	1 tbsp	1 tbsp
lemon juice	½ tbsp	½ tbsp
dry sherry	1 tbsp	1 tbsp
Worcestershire sauce	1 teasp	1 teasp
For the cocktails: peeled prawns (shelled shrimp)	175 g/6 oz	1 cup
dessert apples, peeled and diced	2–3	2–3
celery stalks, finely chopped	2	2
lettuce heart, finely shredded	6 tbsp	7 tbsp
To garnish: lemon slices	4	4

Blend the ingredients for the dressing. Mix most of the prawns (shrimp), all the apples and celery with the dressing.

Divide the lettuce between cocktail glasses. Spoon the prawn mixture on the lettuce. Top with the remaining prawns. Garnish with lemon slices. Serve with brown bread and butter.

Prawn and Apple Cocktail

PIQUANT CRAB COCKTAIL

No Cooking   Serves 4   ✳✳

The creamy, yet flavoursome, dressing and unexpected crispness of the cucumber, spring onions (scallions) and red pepper, blend well with the crabmeat. Freshly cooked, frozen or canned crabmeat can be used.

	Metric/Imperial	American
For the dressing: double (heavy) cream	150 ml/¼ pint	⅔ cup
mayonnaise	2 tbsp	3 tbsp
lemon juice	1 tbsp	1 tbsp
Worcestershire sauce	½ teasp	½ teasp
Tabasco (hot pepper) sauce	few drops	few drops
tomato purée (paste)	2 teasp	2 teasp
For the cocktails: hard-boiled (hard-cooked) eggs	2	2
crabmeat, flaked	175 g/6 oz	1½ cups
cucumber, peeled and finely diced	2–3 tbsp	3–4 tbsp
spring onions (scallions), chopped	2–3 tbsp	3–4 tbsp
red pepper, de-seeded and finely diced	1	1
lettuce heart, finely shredded	6 tbsp	7 tbsp
To garnish: lemon slices	4	4

Whip the cream until it just holds its shape. Blend the mayonnaise and other dressing ingredients into the cream.

Halve the eggs, take out the yolks for topping the cocktails. Chop the egg whites, fold into the cream dressing with the crabmeat, cucumber, spring onions (scallions) and red pepper.

Divide the lettuce between cocktail glasses. Top with the crabmeat mixture.

Crumble or chop the egg yolks and spoon over the crabmeat. Garnish with the lemon slices.

FISH MOUSSE

A light and delicate mousse, based upon fish, makes an excellent start to a meal. Although the word 'mousse' is French, these light savoury mixtures have been popular in Britain and other countries since the Regency period.

To prepare a lobster, slit the cooked fish down the centre; discard the intestinal vein and remove the flesh from the body. Crack the large claws and remove the flesh.

SEAFOOD MOUSSE

Cooking Time:
15 minutes
Serves 6 ❋❋❋

Seafood Mousse

	Metric/Imperial	American
unpeeled prawns (unshelled shrimp)	450 g/1 lb	1 lb
small onion, halved	1	1
bay leaf	1	1
parsley	sprig	sprig
milk	450 ml/ ¾ pint	scant 2 cups
butter	40 g/1½ oz	3 tbsp
flour	40 g/1½ oz	6 tbsp
small lobster	1	1
white wine	4 tbsp	5 tbsp
gelatine	15 g/½ oz	2 envelopes
mayonnaise	150 ml/¼ pint	⅔ cup
tomato purée (paste)	1 tbsp	1 tbsp
salt and pepper	to taste	to taste
egg whites	2	2
To garnish: unpeeled prawns (unshelled shrimp)	8	8
chopped watercress or parsley	4 tbsp	5 tbsp
celery leaves		

Wash the prawns (shrimp) well. Remove the shells and put these into a pan with the onion, bay leaf, parsley and milk. Bring the milk to the boil, simmer for 5 minutes then strain; discard the shells, onion and herbs. The milk should now measure 300 ml/½ pint (1¼ cups) and it will have absorbed the various flavours.

Heat the butter in a saucepan and stir in the flour. Cook over a low heat for 2 to 3 minutes, then gradually blend in the milk. Stir as the sauce comes to the boil and thickens. Add the peeled prawns (shelled shrimp) to the sauce. (If these are large they can be halved or quartered.)

Remove the flesh from the lobster, see above; if a hen lobster take out the coral (roe) as well. Blend with the sauce.

Pour the wine into a bowl and place over a saucepan of hot water. Sprinkle the gelatine on top and leave until dissolved. Stir into the prawn and lobster mixture and allow to cool, but not to set.

Blend the mayonnaise and tomato purée (paste) with the cool lobster and prawn mixture, add seasoning to taste. Leave in the refrigerator until very lightly set. Whisk the egg whites until stiff, fold gently but thoroughly into the other ingredients.

Brush a 1.2 litre/2 pint (5 cup) mould with a few drops of olive oil or rinse in cold water. Spoon in the fish mixture. Allow to set. Turn out and garnish with the whole prawns (shrimp), chopped watercress or parsley and celery leaves. Serve with brown bread and butter.

This mousse freezes well for up to 6 weeks.

Soups

The soups in this chapter are both sustaining and varied. So many interesting ingredients can be used to make soup, ranging from familiar vegetables to ingredients such as cheese, fish and poultry.
Cold soups, though not as popular as hot ones, are well worth making. The modern idea of incorporating fruit flavours in some mixtures has been used in several recipes, see page 31.
Many soups depend upon good stock for flavour. In the section on poultry will be found advice on making first class stocks, see page 81.
When white or chicken stock is not available, use water with a chicken stock (bouillon) cube; similarly use a beef stock cube when you have no brown stock. Chicken stock, or the ingredients mentioned in the recipes, can be substituted if fish stock is not available.
Always taste soups during cooking and again just before serving. While you do not want to over-season the soup, an adequate amount of seasoning is important.
Garnishes for the soups are given in the individual recipes.
Modern liquidizers (also called blenders) or food processors save the effort of sieving ingredients, see pages 28 and 29. If the soup contains hard tomato pips or tough pieces of celery or tomato skin, you may find you need to sieve the mixture after liquidizing (blending) or processing. This is extremely simple when the mixture is relatively smooth.
This chapter contains satisfying soups, based mainly upon vegetables, continues with a selection of fish soups, several meat soups and ends with unusual fruit soups.

LA REINE SOUP

Cooking Time: 20 minutes   Serves 4–6   ✸✸

It is not unusual to find a French name in Scotland's menus, for the French had an influence on Scottish cooking. This soup is also known as Lorraine soup. The mixture of nuts with chicken is a very pleasant one.

	Metric/Imperial	American
chicken stock, see page 81	900 ml/1½ pints	3¾ cups
hard-boiled (hard-cooked) eggs	2	2
cooked chicken breast, finely diced	225 g/8 oz	1 cup
almonds, blanched and chopped	50 g/2 oz	½ cup
soft breadcrumbs	25 g/1 oz	½ cup
single (light) cream	150 ml/¼ pint	⅔ cup
salt and pepper	to taste	to taste
To garnish: chopped parsley	1 tbsp	1 tbsp

Heat the chicken stock in a saucepan. Shell and halve the eggs, remove the yolks. Chop these finely; save the egg whites for garnish. Put the chicken breast, almonds and breadcrumbs into a bowl; either blend a little hot chicken stock with these ingredients and beat until as smooth as possible, or put all the ingredients into a liquidizer (blender) or food processor and switch on until a very smooth thick purée.

Tip the purée and the cream into the pan containing the remaining stock. Add a little salt and pepper to taste. Heat gently, but do not boil.

Chop the egg whites finely. Garnish the soup with egg whites and parsley just before serving.

FREEZING SOUPS

Unless the individual recipes state otherwise, soups can be frozen for up to 3 months.

Allow the mixture to become quite cold before freezing. Always remove excess fat from the top of the cold soup prior to freezing.

Many thickened soups, particularly those that have been puréed, tend to separate out during the process of reheating. If that happens, whisk the mixture briskly. If this does not restore the original smooth texture, sieve the soup or put into a liquidizer (blender) or food processor.

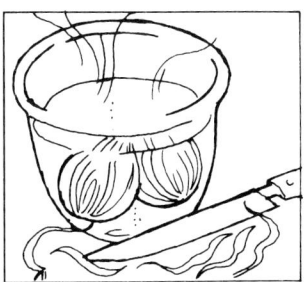

Peel and halve a medium onion; infuse in 600 ml/1 pint (2½ cups) hot chicken stock (or water and 1 chicken stock (bouillon) cube) for at least 1 hour.

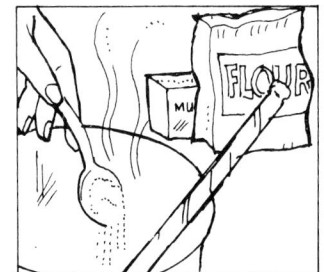

Heat 25 g/1 oz (2 tbsp) butter in a saucepan, stir in 25 g/1 oz (¼ cup) flour and 1–2 tablespoons mustard powder.

Gradually blend in 300 ml/½ pint (1¼ cups) milk, stirring. Whisk in the chicken stock, then add the onion halves. Bring to the boil, stir until thickened.

Blend the yolks of 2 eggs with 4 tablespoons double (5 tbsp heavy) cream in a bowl. Whisk on a little of the hot, but not boiling, soup.

MUSTARD SOUP

Cooking Time: 15 minutes   Serves 4   ✳✳

Mustard plants have been cultivated for over 2000 years; they were mentioned in many ancient writings. There are many kinds of mustard plants, some giving white and some black seeds. British mustard powder is prepared from the seeds of white mustard.

This unusual, but very pleasing, soup makes good use of mustard powder. When blended with other ingredients, such as stock and milk, the strong mustard flavour is much diminished.

Return to the saucepan, simmer gently for 4–5 minutes, then remove the onion halves.

Top each portion with whipped cream just before serving.

COCK-A-LEEKIE

Cooking Time: 1½ hours   Serves 4–6   ✳✳

	Metric/Imperial	American
prunes	12	12
water	300 ml/½ pint	1¼ cups
small chicken	1	1
chicken stock	1.2 litres/2 pints	5 cups
salt and pepper	to taste	to taste
leeks, cut into rings	450 g/1 lb	1 lb
To garnish: chopped parsley	1–2 tbsp	1–3 tbsp

Put the prunes into a bowl, cover with the cold water and leave overnight or for some hours to soak; unless they are the modern 'tenderized prunes', then this stage could be omitted.

Wash the chicken and put it into a large saucepan with the stock. The giblets of the fowl could be added, but omit the liver in this particular recipe as it darkens the stock. Bring the liquid to the boil, remove any grey 'scum', lower the heat, add salt to taste. Cover the pan and simmer gently for 1 hour until the chicken is tender. Lift the chicken out of the stock, strain the stock, pour back into the saucepan. If necessary, boil rapidly until reduced to 900 ml/1½ pints (3¾ cups).

Cut 225 g/8 oz (1 cup) meat from the chicken; dice this finely. Put the leeks into the chicken stock with the drained or tenderized prunes; cook for 30 minutes. Add the diced chicken and heat. Taste and season. Garnish.

FRIED CROÛTONS

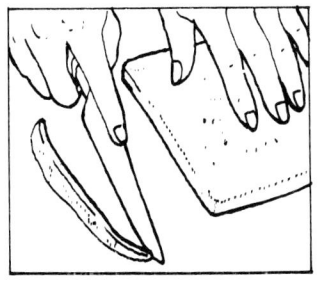

Cut the crusts from slices of bread. This is generally white bread but brown or wholemeal bread could be used.

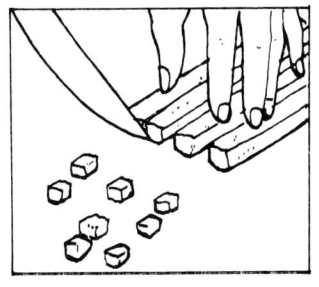

Cut the bread into small dice.

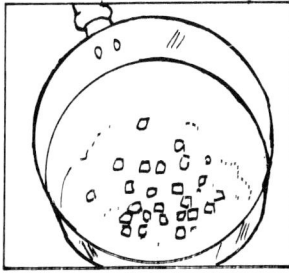

Either shallow fry in butter or oil, or deep fry in oil or fat (shortening), until golden brown.

Drain on absorbent paper (kitchen towels). Serve as a garnish for soup. Do not add to the soup until just before serving.

Above: Green Milk Soup. Right: Green Pea Soup

GREEN MILK SOUP

Cooking Time: 30 minutes   Serves 4   ❊❊

This Welsh soup is not unlike the French Vichyssoise. It is generally served hot but it is equally good if chilled; see Variations.

	Metric/Imperial	American
medium leeks, thinly sliced, see method	4	4
small onions, finely chopped	2	2
small potatoes, diced	2	2
mutton or lamb stock	450 ml/¾ pint	2 cups
butter	50 g/2 oz	¼ cup
flour	50 g/2 oz	½ cup
milk	600 ml/1 pint	2½ cups
salt and pepper	to taste	to taste
single (light) cream	4 tbsp	5 tbsp
To garnish: chopped parsley		

The vegetables should be prepared neatly since the soup is served without sieving, but see Variations. Shred a little of the tender green part of each leek to give colour to the soup.

Put all the vegetables into a saucepan with the well clarified stock, see page 81. Boil steadily until just tender, this takes approximately 20 minutes, do not over-cook. Meanwhile heat the butter in a large second saucepan, stir in the flour and cook for 2 to 3 minutes. Blend in the milk and stir or whisk until well thickened. Gradually add the vegetable mixture. Season well and reheat. Stir in the cream just before serving. Garnish with the parsley.

VARIATIONS

Creamy Green Milk Soup: Cook the soup as above, do not add the cream. Sieve or liquidize (blend) then return to the pan, reheat and add the cream just before serving.
● *Chilled Green Milk Soup:* Use chicken stock instead of lamb or mutton stock. Cook the soup as above, do not add the cream. Sieve or liquidize (blend) with 150 ml/¼ pint (²/₃ cup) single (light) cream. Chill well. Top with chopped chives and/or chopped parsley.

GREEN PEA SOUP

Cooking Time: 35–40 minutes   Serves 4–6 ❊❊

The tenderness of young green peas can be enjoyed both as a vegetable and a delicious soup. Thrifty cooks can use some of the tender green pea pods for extra flavour, provided they are willing to spend the time rubbing these through a sieve. It is not satisfactory to put them in a liquidizer (blender) or food processor. The pods must be very young and perfect.

	Metric/Imperial	American
butter	25 g/1 oz	2 tbsp
small onions, sliced	2	2
chicken stock	750 ml/ 1¼ pints	generous 3 cups
shelled green peas *or* peas with pods	350 g/12 oz 700 g/1½ lb	¾ lb 1½ lb
mint	sprig	sprig
salt and pepper	to taste	to taste
single (light) cream	300 ml/½ pint	1¼ cups
To garnish: chopped chives or parsley or mint		

Heat the butter in a pan and toss the onions in this. Add the stock, green peas or peas and pods (there is no need to shell the peas), the mint and a little seasoning. Cover the pan and simmer for 20 minutes if using peas only, or 25–30 minutes if using peas and pods. Remove the mint. Either rub through a sieve or, if using peas without pods, put into a liquidizer (blender) or food processor until small. If serving the soup hot, return to the saucepan, add the cream, bring to the boil, adjust the seasoning if necessary. Garnish with chopped chives or parsley or mint and serve. If serving the soup cold, chill the soup then whisk in the cream just before serving; adjust the seasoning if necessary.

VARIATION
Ham and Green Pea Soup:
Use stock from boiling ham or bacon instead of chicken stock. Garnish the soup with sippets (tiny pieces) of crispy fried bacon or cooked ham.

IRISH MILK SOUP

Cooking Time: 20 minutes   Serves 4–6 ❊

The Irish love of potatoes is reflected in this easy soup. Obviously the cooking time will be increased if you need to cook the potatoes especially for the dish.

	Metric/Imperial	American
butter	50 g/2 oz	¼ cup
flour	50 g/2 oz	½ cup
milk	1.2 litres/2 pints	5 cups
young kale, see method	350 g/12 oz	¾ lb
salt and pepper	to taste	to taste
medium cooked potatoes, finely diced	3–4	3–4

Heat the butter in a saucepan, stir in the flour and cook for 2 to 3 minutes. Add the milk, stir as this comes to the boil and thickens slightly. Choose only the youngest kale leaves; shred these very finely. Add to the sauce, together with salt and pepper. Cook steadily for about 6 minutes or until the kale is almost tender. Add the cooked potatoes and heat gently.

SORREL SOUP

Cooking Time: 30 minutes   Serves 4–6   ❊❊

Sorrel and rosemary are two of the herbs that have been used for generations; sadly sorrel is less grown and less seen nowadays than in the past. Sorrel is not unlike spinach, but it has a more bitter flavour. You can, however, use this recipe as a basis for other delicious soups, see under Variations. There is a saying about rosemary; it runs, 'If the rosemary bush flourishes in the garden, the woman is head of the house'. Rosemary is also quoted by Ophelia (in Hamlet) as being 'for remembrance'.

	Metric/Imperial	American
sorrel	450 g/1 lb	1 lb
butter	50 g/2 oz	¼ cup
medium onion, chopped	1	1
rosemary leaves, chopped	1 teasp	1 teasp
water	1.2 litres/2 pints	5 cups
salt and pepper	to taste	to taste
lemon juice	2 teasp	2 teasp
egg yolks	2	2
single (light) cream	150 ml/¼ pint	²/₃ cup

Wash the sorrel well, cut with a stainless knife into very thin shreds. Heat the butter in a saucepan, toss the onion in this. Add the sorrel and rosemary, blend with the onion. Bring the water to the boil in a separate container – this hastens cooking and makes quite sure the sorrel keeps a good colour. Pour over the ingredients in the saucepan. Add salt, pepper and lemon juice. Cook for about 20 minutes then sieve or liquidize (blend) the mixture. Return to the saucepan; heat, but do not boil.

Blend the egg yolks and cream together. Add a little of the purée soup to this mixture. Blend thoroughly, then whisk into the soup in the pan. Stir over a low heat for 4 to 5 minutes, but do not allow to boil.

VARIATIONS

If a slightly thicker soup is required, add several tablespoons of soft fine breadcrumbs with the egg and cream.

● *Cabbage Soup:* Choose young cabbage, that will become tender rapidly, in place of sorrel. Since cabbage has far less flavour than sorrel, use 2 to 3 onions, chicken stock or ham stock in place of water. Omit the rosemary leaves and add ½ teaspoon chopped sage instead. Cook the shredded cabbage for 10 minutes only, then proceed as for Sorrel Soup.

● *Cauliflower Soup:* Choose a cauliflower with plenty of fresh green leaves. Chop these and the stalks; simmer in salted water for about 25 minutes, strain and use this stock in place of the water in the Sorrel recipe. Divide the cauliflower head into neat florets. Toss the onions and florets of cauliflower in the butter, as described under Sorrel Soup, then proceed as for Sorrel Soup. Rosemary blends well with cauliflower.

● *Spinach Soup:* Use young spinach instead of sorrel or substitute cooked frozen spinach. Rosemary has rather too definite a taste to blend with the milder flavour of spinach, so use chopped thyme instead.

TOMATO AND MUSHROOM SOUP

Cooking Time: 25 minutes   Serves 4   ❊

'Love apples' is the name by which tomatoes were once known in Britain. It was believed they had to be cooked and not eaten raw, and that is why they were a favourite in soups and stews. It was not until comparatively recently that the good flavour of a raw tomato was appreciated.

	Metric/Imperial	American
butter or margarine	50 g/2 oz	¼ cup
medium onions, finely chopped	2	2
ripe tomatoes, skinned and chopped	675 g/1½ lb	1½ lb
chicken stock	600 ml/1 pint	2½ cups
button mushrooms, finely diced	100 g/4 oz	¼ lb
Worcestershire sauce	1–2 teasp	1–2 teasp
sugar	1 teasp	1 teasp
salt and pepper	to taste	to taste
To garnish: coarsely chopped parsley or basil	2–3 tbsp	3–4 tbsp

Heat the butter in a saucepan, stir in the flour and cook for 2 to 3 minutes. Add the milk, stir as this comes to the boil and thickens slightly. Choose only the youngest kale leaves; shred these very finely. Add to the sauce, together with salt and pepper. Cook steadily for about 6 minutes or until the kale is almost tender. Add the cooked potatoes and heat gently.

INCORPORATING EGGS AND CREAM

In some recipes for sauces or soups, see this page, eggs and cream have to be added to a mixture. The best way to do this to avoid curdling the mixture is as follows:

 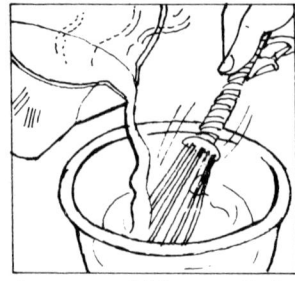

Beat the eggs and cream in a bowl.   Pour or whisk on a little of the hot liquid.

Return to the saucepan containing the rest of the hot, but not boiling, mixture and simmer gently, stirring well.

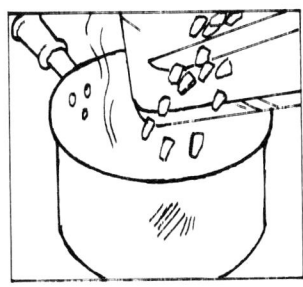

Peel and neatly chop 2–3 medium onions. Heat 25 g/1 oz (2 tbsp) margarine or butter in a saucepan, add the onions.

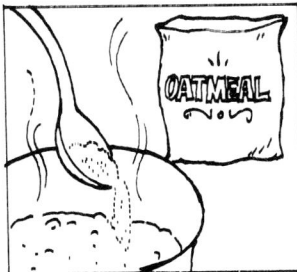

Cook the onions gently for 5 minutes; do not allow to brown. Blend 2 tablespoons (3 tbsp) medium or fine oatmeal with the onions.

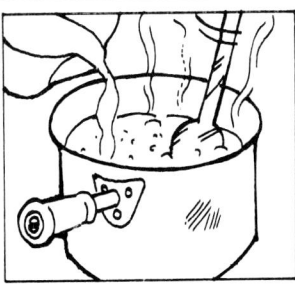

Pour in 600 ml/1 pint (2½ cups) chicken or ham stock, then 300 ml/½ pint (1¼ cups) milk. Stir as the liquid boils and thickens.

Add salt and pepper to taste. Cover the pan and simmer for 45 minutes, stir from time to time.

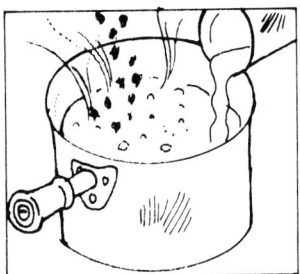

Blend in 150 ml/¼ pint (²/₃ cup) single (light) cream and 1 tablespoon chopped parsley. Heat for 2-3 minutes.

Serve topped with crisp croûtons and more chopped parsley.

OATMEAL SOUP

Cooking Time: 1 hour   Serves 4–6   ✱

Oatmeal has long been an established and popular food, particularly in Scotland. In the past, it was used as the basis for porridge and many people still like to use it instead of the more modern quick-cooking rolled oats.

Medical opinion strongly recommends the use of oatmeal or rolled oats in all forms of cooking, since it adds soluble fibre to the diet.

This soup is warming and satisfying, and ideal for cold days. It can be varied in flavour and texture. If you use quick-cooking rolled oats, reduce the cooking time in stage 4 to 15 to 20 minutes.

In addition to the onions given in the basic soup, you can include finely diced carrots and/or sliced leeks.

DRIED PEA SOUP

Cooking Time: 1¾-2¼ hours   Serves 6–8   ✱

This is one of the old traditional soups, for drying vegetables like peas and fruits was one of the ways of preserving summer foods for winter use, and dried peas make a delicious soup. Dried pea soup was called 'London Particular' by Dickens in one of his novels, since he felt it bore a likeness to the 'pea soup fogs' that were a particular feature of London in the old days. Bacon or ham stock is the perfect liquid in which to cook the peas.

	Metric/Imperial	American
dried peas	350 g/12 oz	¾ lb
ham or chicken stock, see method	2.4 litres/4 pints	10 cups
bacon rashers (slices)	2–3	2–3
large onion, sliced	1–2	1–2
pepper	to taste	to taste
large carrots, sliced	2	2
milk, optional, see method		
salt, optional, see method		
To garnish: fried croûtons, see page 21		

Soak the peas in the stock overnight to hasten cooking. De-rind the bacon and chop the bacon into small pieces.

Put the bacon rinds and bacon into a saucepan, fry until crisp. Discard the rinds and put the bacon on one side for garnish.

Add the onion(s) to the pan and gently fry for 5 minutes, then tip in the peas and stock. Add pepper only and the carrots. Cover the pan and simmer for 1½ to 2 hours. Sieve the soup or put into a liquidizer (blender) or food processor until a smooth purée. Return to the pan and reheat. The soup may be a little too thick, if a good proportion of liquid has evaporated, so add more stock or milk to give the desired consistency. Taste and add a little salt if necessary. Garnish with fried croûtons and the fried bacon.

VARIATION
Lentil Soup: Use split lentils in place of peas. There is no need to soak these and the simmering time is only about 1¼ hours. A small peeled and diced apple can be cooked with the other ingredients.

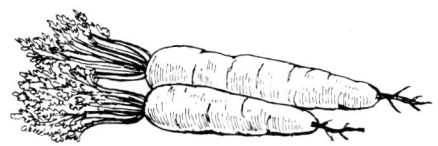

THICKENING SOUPS
The thickening in a soup is given by the ingredients themselves (as in the case of soups containing starchy vegetables) or by using flour or cornflour (cornstarch). You need twice as much flour as cornflour to achieve the same consistency.

WATERCRESS CREAM SOUP

Cooking Time: 15 minutes   Serves 4   ❄

Watercress is a salad ingredient that is grown and flourishes in clear cool water; that is why it is difficult, or almost impossible, to obtain in hot climates. Do not overcook the soup when the watercress has been added, for this would spoil the taste and colour. The basic recipe can be given additional flavour by the addition of fish, ham, eggs or cheese; see under Variations.

	Metric/Imperial	American
watercress leaves, finely chopped, see method	100 g/4 oz	2 cups
milk	150 ml/¼ pint	²/₃ cup
butter or margarine	50 g/2 oz	¼ cup
flour *or* cornflour (cornstarch)	50 g/2 oz 25 g/1 oz	½ cup ¼ cup
chicken stock	750 ml/ 1¼ pints	generous 3 cups
single (light) cream	150 ml/¼ pint	²/₃ cup
egg yolk	1	1
lemon juice	1 tbsp	1 tbsp
salt and pepper	to taste	to taste
To garnish: watercress	few sprigs	few sprigs

Chop the watercress leaves very finely with a sharp knife, or do this in a liquidizer (blender) or food processor with a little of the milk. Heat the butter or margarine in a saucepan, stir in the flour or cornflour (cornstarch). Stir over a low heat for 2 to 3 minutes, then blend in the stock, milk and cream. Whisk or stir as the mixture comes to the boil and thickens. Add the chopped watercress leaves and heat for 2 to 3 minutes.

Blend the egg yolk and lemon juice in a bowl. Whisk a little of the hot, but not boiling, watercress soup into this, then pour into the soup in the pan. Heat gently, but do not boil. Add seasoning to taste and serve as soon as possible. Top with the sprigs of watercress.

VARIATIONS
Watercress and Cheese Soup: Add 75 g/3 oz (¾ cup) finely grated cheese to the soup just before serving. Stir to melt this. Top each portion of soup with small balls of cream cheese.
● *Watercress and Egg Soup:* Add a second egg yolk to the soup. Top with 2 chopped hard-boiled (hard-cooked) eggs.
● *Watercress and Fish Soup:* Add 100 g/4 oz (½ cup) flaked cooked salmon or cooked shellfish together with a little extra lemon juice.
● *Watercress and Ham Soup:* Use ham stock in place of chicken stock. Add approximately 100 g/4 oz (½ cup) finely diced lean cooked ham to the soup.

SPICED CUMBERLAND SOUP

Cooking Time: 30 minutes   Serves 4   ❄❄

	Metric/Imperial	American
bacon rasher (slice)	1	1
butter	25 g/1 oz	2 tbsp
small onion, chopped	1	1
small carrot, chopped	1	1
small mushrooms, chopped	2	2
small tomatoes, skinned and chopped	2	2
beef stock	600 ml/1 pint	2½ cups
red wine	2 tbsp	3 tbsp
allspice	1 teasp	1 teasp
salt and pepper	to taste	to taste
orange juice	150 ml/¼ pint	²/₃ cup
redcurrant jelly	3 tbsp	4 tbsp
To garnish: orange(s)	1–2	1–2

MUSSEL CREAM

Cooking Time: 25 minutes   Serves 4–6   ❋❋

Although 'cockles and mussels' are generally associated with the well-known Irish ballad, these shellfish are obtainable in many countries. This is a delicately flavoured soup.

	Metric/Imperial	American
mussels	2 litres/3 pints	7 cups
small onion, chopped	1	1
water	150 ml/¼ pint	²/₃ cup
white wine	150 ml/¼ pint	²/₃ cup
parsley	sprig	sprig
butter or margarine	75 g/3 oz	6 tbsp
flour *or* cornflour (cornstarch)	50 g/2 oz / 25 g/1 oz	½ cup / ¼ cup
milk	600 ml/1 pint	2½ cups
single (light) cream	150 ml/¼ pint	²/₃ cup
salt and pepper	to taste	to taste
small mushrooms, sliced	100 g/4 oz	¼ lb
peeled shrimps or small prawns (shelled shrimp)	100 g/4 oz	¾ cup
To garnish: parsley or fennel	sprig	sprig

Scrub the mussels in cold water, discard any that do not close when sharply tapped. Put into a saucepan with the onion, water, wine and parsley. Place the saucepan over a low heat until the mussels open; cool slightly. Lift the fish from the liquid, remove from their shells; discard any mussels that have not opened completely. Strain the liquid and put on one side.

Heat 50 g/2 oz (¼ cup) of the butter or margarine in a saucepan, stir in the flour or cornflour (cornstarch) and cook gently for 2 to 3 minutes. Gradually blend in the milk, cream and mussel stock. Stir as the liquid just comes to the boil and thickens (do not boil quickly), season lightly.

Meanwhile, heat the remaining butter or margarine, fry the mushrooms until soft. Add to the soup with the mussels and shrimps or prawns. Heat for a few minutes only. Top with a sprig of parsley or fennel or other green herb.

VARIATION
Mussel Brose: Open the mussels as in the recipe above, but use all water and omit the wine. Take the fish off the shells. Strain the liquid, put on one side. Put 25 g/1 oz (¼ cup) rolled oats or oatmeal on to a flat baking sheet. Place in a moderate oven, 180°C/350°F Gas Mark 4, for 10 minutes or until golden brown. Heat 25 g/1 oz (2 tbsp) butter in a saucepan, fry 1 to 2 finely chopped small onions until soft. Add 600 ml/1 pint (2½ cups) milk and the oatmeal or rolled oats. Stir as the mixture comes to the boil and thickens slightly. Simmer for 10 minutes, then add the mussel liquid, the mussels, 1 tablespoon chopped parsley, salt and pepper to taste. Heat for several minutes then serve.

Watercress Cream Soup, Apricot and Apple Soup – recipe page 31, Mussel Cream, Spiced Cumberland Soup

De-rind and chop the bacon. Put into a saucepan with the butter, add the vegetables and fry gently for 5 minutes. Add the stock, cover the pan and simmer gently for 20 minutes. Rub through a sieve or put into a liquidizer (blender) or food processor. Return the soup to the pan, add the wine, allspice, a little salt and pepper, the orange juice and redcurrant jelly. Heat until the jelly has melted. Serve hot or chill well.

Cut away the peel from the orange(s), then cut the fruit into thin rings. Add to the soup just before serving.

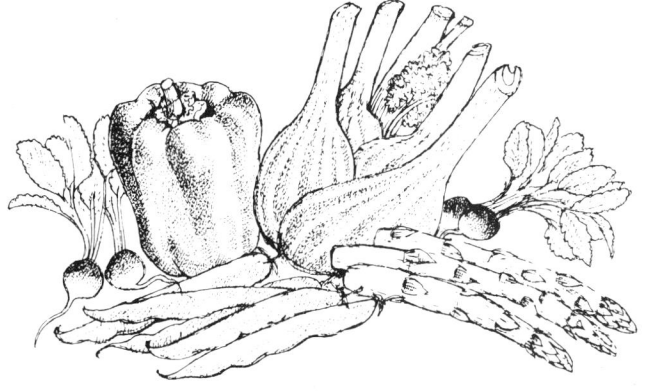

The recipes on this page, and the Mussel Cream on the preceding page, cover a range of fish soups. Do not over-cook a fish soup, for this would spoil the flavour and texture of the fish.

OYSTER SOUP

Illustrated in colour on page 218
Cooking Time: 1½ hours   Serves 4–6   ❉❉❉

The Welsh name for this delicious soup is Cawl Wystrys.

	Metric/Imperial	American
scrag end of neck of lamb or mutton, chopped	225 g/8 oz	½ lb
lamb or mutton bones	few	few
water	1.8 litres/3 pints	7½ cups
medium onions, peeled and whole	2	2
blade of mace *or* powdered mace	1 pinch	1 pinch
pepper	to taste	to taste
butter	50 g/2 oz	¼ cup
flour	50 g/2 oz	½ cup
small oysters	16–24	16–24
To garnish: leek, finely sliced or chopped	1	1

Put the lamb or mutton with the bones, water, onions, mace and pepper into a saucepan. Do not add salt, as the oysters provide a 'salty' taste and this can be adjusted before serving. Bring the liquid to the boil, remove any slight 'grey' scum. Cover the pan, simmer for approximately 1 hour or until a good flavoured stock is produced. Strain carefully through muslin (cheesecloth) or a fine sieve to give a clear stock. If necessary, boil the stock for a time in an open pan until it is reduced to 750 ml/1¼ pints (3⅓ cups).

Heat the butter in a pan, stir in the flour and cook gently for a few minutes until golden in colour. Blend in the stock, bring to the boil and stir over a low heat until smooth and thickened. Remove the oysters from their shells, add any liquid on the shells to the soup. Bring to the boil, taste and add seasoning if required. Put the oysters into bowls or soup plates, pour on the soup. Garnish with wafer thin strips of raw leek.

VARIATIONS
The oysters are generally left unheated, but if preferred they may be warmed in the hot soup before serving. DO NOT cook for any length of time as this would toughen the shellfish.
● To add more flavour to this soup, a very good shake of cayenne pepper and a little lemon juice may be added.

PARTAN BREE

Illustrated in colour on page 214
Cooking Time: 30–35 minutes   Serves 4–6   ❉❉❉

The word 'partan' is Scottish for a crab.

	Metric/Imperial	American
medium crab	1	1
long grain rice	75 g/3 oz	½ cup
milk	600 ml/1 pint	2½ cups
fish stock, see page 82	600 ml/1 pint	2½ cups
anchovy essence	½ teasp	½ teasp
salt and pepper	to taste	to taste
single (light) cream	150 ml/¼ pint	⅔ cup
To garnish: fried croûtons, see page 21 chopped parsley (optional)		

Remove all the flesh from the crab body and claws (see page 44, discard inedible parts). Put 2 tablespoons of white crabmeat and 1 tablespoon dark meat aside for garnish.

Put the rice, milk and stock into a saucepan; simmer gently for 20 to 25 minutes until the rice is tender. Stir in the anchovy essence and salt and pepper; use salt sparingly. Add the crabmeat, stir well until thoroughly blended. Heat, but do not cook for any length of time as this makes crabmeat dry and tough. Just before serving, stir in the cream. Put into very hot soup bowls or plates and top with the reserved crabmeat. Add the crisp croûtons immediately before serving.

VARIATIONS
When fish stock is not obtainable, use chicken stock.
● Instead of fresh crab, use 300 to 350 g/10 to 12 oz (1¼ to 1½ cups) canned or frozen crabmeat.

USING A LIQUIDIZER FOR SOUP

Check there are no tiny pieces of bone in the soup, if based upon meat or poultry.

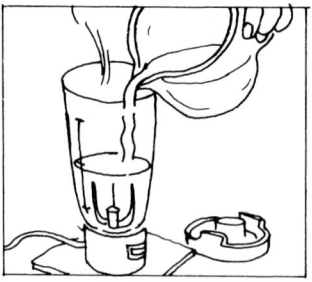

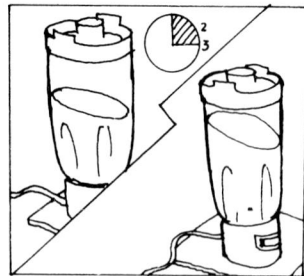

Pour the soup into the liquidizer (blender) goblet. Only half fill this, as the mixture rises drastically during the process of liquidizing.

Switch to low speed for 2–3 seconds, then to a higher speed until a smooth purée.

If you require tiny particles of vegetable or other food, switch on for 3 to 4 seconds only. Switch off and then on again for a further 3 to 4 seconds, or until the ingredients are as finely chopped as required.

SALMON SOUP

Cooking Time: 1 hour   Serves 4–6   ✳✳✳

	Metric/Imperial	American
head of salmon	1	1
fresh salmon	225 g/8 oz	½ lb
water	1.5 litres/ 2½ pints	6¼ cups
salt and pepper	to taste	to taste
bouquet garni	1	1
cod or fresh haddock, diced	225 g/8 oz	½ lb
small onions, coarsely chopped	2	2
small carrots, coarsely chopped	2	2
old potatoes, finely diced	2	2
butter	25 g/1 oz	2 tbsp
double (heavy) cream	150 ml/¼ pint	⅔ cup
To garnish: chopped parsley	1 tbsp	1 tbsp
coarse brown breadcrumbs	2 tbsp	3 tbsp

To make the fish stock, put the well washed salmon head into a saucepan. Cut away the skin and bone from the portion of salmon, add this to the salmon head together with the water, salt and pepper, bouquet garni, diced cod or haddock, onions and carrots. Simmer gently for 30 minutes. Strain the stock carefully.

To make the soup, pour the fish stock into the saucepan, add the diced potatoes and butter. Cook for 10 minutes or until the potatoes are soft. Sieve or liquidize (blend) and return to the pan. Cut the salmon into very small neat dice and add to the pan. Simmer for 10 minutes, then stir in the cream. Heat thoroughly, but do not boil. Add extra seasoning, if required. Serve topped with the parsley and breadcrumbs.

VARIATION
Salmon trout could be used instead of salmon.

SMOKED HADDOCK SOUP

Cooking Time: 15 minutes   Serves 4–6   ✳

Finnan haddie, the name given to smoked haddock, makes a delicious fish soup. The smaller and delicately flavoured Arbroath smokies give an even more delicious soup.

	Metric/Imperial	American
whole smoked haddock *or* haddock fillet	550 g/1¼ lb 350 g/12 oz	1¼ lb ¾ lb
milk	1.2 litres/2 pints	5 cups
pepper	to taste	to taste
hard-boiled (hard-cooked) eggs	2	2
To garnish: chopped parsley		

Cut a larger smoked haddock or fillet into smaller portions. Place in a saucepan with the cold milk, add a good shake of pepper, but no salt. Bring the milk to boiling point, lower the heat and simmer for 10 minutes or until the fish is tender. Remove the fish from the milk. Discard the skin and bones; flake the fish.

Shell the eggs, chop and pound with the flaked fish, or put the fish and eggs into a liquidizer (blender) or food processor with some of the milk and switch on until a thick smooth purée. Blend with the rest of the milk, add seasoning to taste and heat for a few minutes. Top with the parsley.

VARIATION
For a richer soup, use slightly less milk and substitute single (light) cream.

USING A FOOD PROCESSOR FOR SOUP

Check there are no tiny pieces of bone in the soup, if based upon meat or poultry.

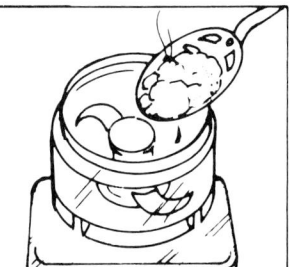

A food processor is more efficient with less liquid mixtures, so spoon the vegetables or pieces of meat or poultry out of the soup into the processor bowl, add a very little liquid. Use the metal cutting blade.

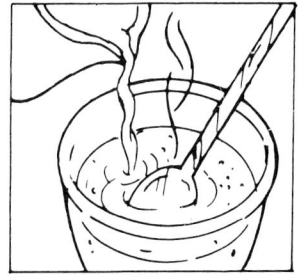

Fix the lid and switch on for a few seconds or until a smooth purée, then blend with the remaining liquid.

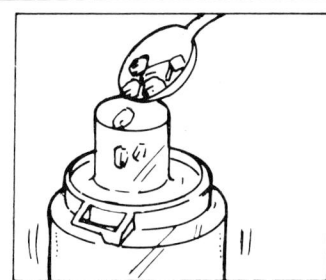

If you require small pieces of vegetable, meat or poultry, drop these through the feed tube with the machine in operation.

MEAT SOUPS

The soups on this page depend upon the good quality of stock for flavour.

WINDSOR SOUP

Cooking Time: 2½ hours   Serves 6   ✳✳

There is a tendency to call many brown soups 'Windsor', but often they do not taste at all like the soup below. This soup is very similar to one called 'mock turtle', since it has the same slightly 'sticky' texture, which one associates with real turtle soup.

	Metric/Imperial	American
stewing beef, diced	225 g/8 oz	½ lb
beef bones	2–3	2–3
calf's foot	1	1
water	1.8 litres/3 pints	7½ cups
bouquet garni	1	1
salt and pepper	to taste	to taste
Madeira wine	150 ml/¼ pint	²/₃ cup
To garnish: see method		

Put the beef, well washed bones and calf's foot into a large saucepan with the water, bouquet garni, salt and pepper to taste. Bring the liquid to the boil and remove any 'scum' from the top. Lower the heat, cover the pan and simmer gently for 2½ hours. Strain the liquid carefully; reheat this. Add the wine and extra seasoning as required. Pour into soup cups and top with the selected garnish, as below.

GARNISHES FOR WINDSOR SOUP
The simplest garnish is chopped parsley.
   Tiny profiteroles, made as page 157, are an excellent choice.
   Small pieces of lobster or crayfish or chopped well drained canned anchovy fillets were often chosen in the past.

VARIATION
To save cooking time, prepare the initial clear soup in a pressure cooker. Allow 30 to 45 minutes at HIGH/15 lb pressure. Use only 1.2 litres/2 pints (5 cups) liquid.

MULLIGATAWNY SOUP

Cooking Time: 1 hour   Serves 4   ✳✳

This curry flavoured soup is a reminder of the days when trading first began between Britain and India. Representatives from the East India Company brought back both oriental spices and Indian recipes.

	Metric/Imperial	American
lamb or mutton stock	1.2 litres/2 pints	5 cups
fat (shortening) or dripping	50 g/2 oz	¼ cup
apple, diced, see method	1	1
carrot, diced	1	1
onions, diced	2	2
flour	25 g/1 oz	¼ cup
curry powder	1 tbsp	1 tbsp
chutney	1 tbsp	1 tbsp
sugar	pinch	pinch
sultanas	25 g/1 oz	3 tbsp
salt and pepper	to taste	to taste
lemon juice or vinegar	½ teasp	½ teasp

The stock for this soup is traditionally made with lamb or mutton bones or a small lamb's head. Heat the fat (shortening) or dripping in a saucepan; put in the apple (this can be cored but not peeled if sieving the soup. It should however be peeled if using a liquidizer (blender) or food processor), then add the vegetables. Fry the apple and vegetables for 5 minutes – do not allow to brown. Stir in the flour and curry powder; blend with the ingredients in the pan. Add the remaining ingredients. Cover the pan and cook for 45 minutes. Sieve or liquidize (blend). Return to the saucepan and reheat; add extra seasoning if necessary.

VARIATION
Chilled Mulligatawny: Cook the soup as above; chill well. Sieve or liquidize with 150 ml/¼ pint (²/₃ cup) yoghurt; garnish with finely diced red and green peppers.

Mulligatawny Soup

ALMOND AND CHICKEN SOUP

Cooking Time: 45 minutes   Serves 4–6   ✳✳

	Metric/Imperial	American
chicken stock	1.2 litres/2 pints	5 cups
medium onions, chopped	2	2
celery stalks, chopped	2–3	2–3
carrots, chopped	2	2
ground almonds	100 g/4 oz	1 cup
salt and pepper	to taste	to taste
single (light) cream	150 ml/¼ pint	⅔ cup
To garnish: paprika	sprinkling	sprinkling
fried croûtons, see page 21		

Put the stock, onions, celery and carrots into a saucepan. Cover the pan and simmer for 30 minutes. Stir in the ground almonds with salt and pepper to taste. Simmer for 10 minutes. Sieve or liquidize (blend) the soup. Return to the pan; add the cream and reheat. Garnish with the paprika and croûtons.

FRUIT SOUPS
Fruit soups come from several European countries, where they have long been traditional favourites. Gradually, all countries are beginning to appreciate their refreshing taste.

APRICOT AND APPLE SOUP
Illustrated in colour on page 27
Cooking Time: 20 minutes   Serves 4–6   ✳✳

	Metric/Imperial	American
cooking (baking) apples, weight when peeled and sliced	350 g/12 oz	¾ lb
apricots, halved and stoned (pitted)	225 g/8 oz	½ lb
lemon juice	1 tbsp	1 tbsp
water	600 ml/1 pint	2½ cups
sugar	to taste	to taste
To garnish: dessert apple, sliced	1	1
soured cream	4 tbsp	5 tbsp

Put the apples, apricots, lemon juice and water into a saucepan. Simmer until the fruit is just soft. Remove a few apricot halves, slice these and put on one side for garnish. Taste the fruit mixture and add a little sugar. A fruit soup should not be too sweet. Rub the fruit through a sieve or put into a liquidizer (blender) or food processor to make a smooth purée. Chill very well. Garnish with the apple and apricot slices. Top with the soured cream.

Orange Soup

ORANGE SOUP

Cooking Time: 15 minutes   Serves 4   ✳

This is one of the best soups for hot summer days. It is deliciously refreshing.

	Metric/Imperial	American
oranges	4	4
chicken stock	600 ml/1 pint	2½ cups
salt and pepper	to taste	to taste
yoghurt	150 ml/¼ pint	⅔ cup
To garnish: orange slices	4	4
small lettuce heart, shredded	1	1

Grate the rind from 3 oranges; take only the top golden 'zest'; the white pith would spoil the flavour of the soup. Put the rind into a saucepan with the stock and simmer gently for 15 minutes. Keep the saucepan covered so the liquid does not evaporate. Season lightly and allow to cool. Do not strain, for the grated orange rind should become quite soft.

Halve the 4 oranges, squeeze out the juice, add to the chicken and orange mixture together with the yoghurt. Serve very cold, garnished with the orange slices and lettuce.

VARIATION
Orange Tomato Soup: Sieve 3 large ripe tomatoes, add to the orange mixture above.

Fish

Fish has been appreciated as an important food throughout history. The range of fish available today makes it one of the most interesting and versatile of basic foods. The classic methods of cooking fish are by baking in the oven, by grilling (broiling), poaching, frying and steaming. All these methods are covered in the various recipes.

The first pages in this chapter deal with recipes for white fish. This important group of fish includes economical cod, coley, hake, fresh haddock, plaice and skate, and the more luxurious halibut, turbot and sole. Buy white fish carefully – the flesh should be firm, the scales and eyes bright and clear. Any odour of ammonia is a clear sign that the fish is stale. Recipes for using oily fish, smoked fish, shell and freshwater fish follow.

Fish is spoiled by overcooking, that is why most fish dishes should be eaten as soon as they are cooked. Freezing and reheating cooked fish is not to be recommended. Freshly caught fish however freezes well; store white fish in the freezer for up to 6 months.

Recipes using smoked fish are on page 43; oily and freshwater fish on pages 40 and 47; shellfish on pages 44 and 47.

WHITE FISH

To Bake Fish

Baking is an excellent method of cooking fish, for it enables the cook to add a variety of ingredients to give flavour and interest to the fish. On the other hand it is possible, and very successful, to bake fish with a topping of butter or margarine only. If you want the fish to brown on top, keep the cooking container uncovered.

One way of baking fish is illustrated by the recipe that follows. In this, the fish and other ingredients are enclosed in foil. This means that no liquid evaporates during cooking. It is a particularly good way of cooking sole, which can dry easily.

On page 36, fish is baked with an interesting stuffing.

Do not bake fish too slowly, use a moderate to moderately hot oven, approximately, 190°C/375°F Gas Mark 5, or even a little hotter for thin fillets of fish (or as stated in the recipe). Thin fillets of fish take approximately 12 minutes if just topped with a little butter or margarine, thicker fillets about 20 minutes, thick cutlets or whole fish up to about 25 minutes.

Allow about 5 minutes extra cooking time if the container is covered and longer also if a substantial amount of extra ingredients are added to the fish. Never overcook the fish otherwise it becomes dry and tasteless.

CREAM BAKED SOLE

Cooking Time: 30 minutes   Serves 4   ❋❋

This method of cooking sole can be used for other fish, see under Variations. By wrapping the fish while baking in the oven, all the flavour is retained and the fish keeps beautifully moist.

	Metric/Imperial	American
sole	4	4
butter	75 g/3 oz	6 tbsp
grated lemon rind	2 teasp	2 teasp
chopped parsley	2 tbsp	3 tbsp
chopped chives	2 tbsp	3 tbsp
double (heavy) cream	4 tbsp	5 tbsp
salt and pepper	to taste	to taste
To garnish: tomato roses, see page 33	4	4

Skin the fish as the line drawings on page 36. Cut 4 squares of foil, these must be sufficiently large to envelop each sole. Spread the centre of each square of foil with half the butter; sprinkle with half the lemon rind and half the chopped herbs. Place a sole on the butter in the middle of the foil square.

Melt the remaining butter, blend with the cream and the rest of the lemon rind and herbs. Season very lightly. Put the foil and fish on to baking trays. Spoon the cream mixture over the fish, then fold the foil carefully over the fish, so it is covered completely.

Bake in the centre of a moderately hot oven, 190 to 200°C/375 to 400°F Gas Mark 5 to 6, for approximately 30 minutes. Open each foil parcel carefully, tip the fish and the sauce on to heated plates or dishes. Garnish with tomato roses, made as page 33.

VARIATIONS

Cutlets of cod, hake, turbot and fresh salmon are delicious cooked this way. The baking time will vary slightly due to the thickness of the fish. Thin fillets take about 20 to 25 minutes; thick cutlets of fish about 35 minutes.

A TOMATO ROSE

A tomato rose is an excellent garnish for many savoury dishes. It is especially good for fish dishes that may need colour. Although it is a somewhat extravagant way of removing the skin from a tomato, it can be a wise choice if the dish in question needs skinned tomatoes. The object is to cut away the skin in such a way that it can be twirled into a rose shape.

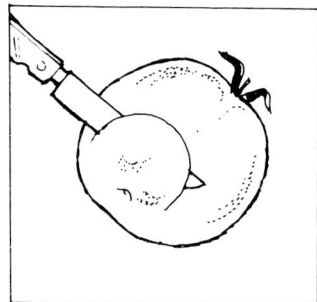

You need a very sharp knife and small firm tomatoes. Cut as near to the pulp as possible, but leave sufficient so the skin does not break.

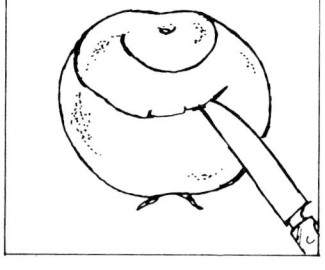

Make a cut on the base of the tomato (the end opposite the stalk) and then cut a small round (do not sever this from the rest of the tomato).

Insert the tip of the knife under the skin and gradually cut a continuous strip from the tomato.

Use the base of the tomato skin as the bottom of the 'rose' and turn the skin to give the appearance of an open flower.

TO GRILL FISH

Grilling (broiling) is a simple way of cooking fish and one that retains the maximum flavour of the food. It is also a good way of reducing the amount of fat used, for less fat is needed than when frying fish. At the same time, the fish needs to be brushed with fat of some kind, so that it does not dry. The recipe on this page for Cod Mornay illustrates how the fish is grilled, then an interesting topping is added and browned under the grill (broiler).

Sole is frequently grilled and one way to keep this dry fish moist is to marinate it in seasoned milk for about 30 minutes before cooking. The fish should then be well drained and brushed with plenty of melted butter before and during cooking. Thin portions of fish, like fillets, take approximately 5 minutes cooking time; thicker fish cutlets (often called steaks) or small whole fish about 10 minutes. The grill should be well heated before the cooking begins.

COD MORNAY

Cooking Time: 12–15 minutes   Serves 4   ✳

	Metric/Imperial	American
cod cutlets	4	4
butter	50 g/2 oz	¼ cup
grated lemon rind	1 teasp	1 teasp
salt and pepper	to taste	to taste
cream cheese	100 g/4 oz	½ cup
Cheddar cheese, grated	50 g/2 oz	½ cup
double (heavy) cream	2 tbsp	3 tbsp
To garnish: lemon slices	2 or 4	2 or 4
watercress	few sprigs	few sprigs

Place the cod in the grill (broiler) pan. Melt the butter, blend with the lemon rind and a little salt and pepper. Brush half the butter over the fish. Grill (broil) under a high heat for 2 to 3 minutes. Turn the fish over, brush with the remaining melted butter and cook quickly on the second side for 2 to 3 minutes. Lower the heat and continue cooking until the fish is just tender.

Meanwhile, blend together the cream cheese and grated cheese, the cream and a very little seasoning. Spread over the top of each piece of cod. Return to the grill for a further 2 to 3 minutes. Garnish with whole lemon slices or with halved slices made into butterfly shapes, and watercress.

VARIATIONS
Any other portions of white fish may be cooked in the same way.
● *Paprika Cod:* Omit the cheese. Blend the melted butter with 1 teaspoon sweet paprika, the lemon rind and seasoning. Top the cooked fish with thinly sliced tomatoes, return to the grill for 1 to 2 minutes to soften the tomatoes. Spoon cold yoghurt over each portion and garnish with paprika.

TO CRIMP FISH

Crimping is a rather old-fashioned way of preparing fish. It means making cuts in the flesh of fish at regular intervals, as shown in the drawing right. This adds an interesting look to the fish.

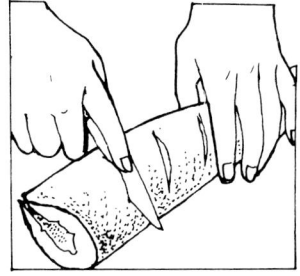

Crimping enables the butter or other fat to penetrate into the fish as it is grilled (broiled) or baked. This is not a good way of dealing with fish that is to be fried, for it makes the portions more fragile and inclined to break.

Crimping also helps to tenderize the fish flesh and keep it moist.

TO POACH FISH

The term poaching means cooking in liquid. Often the term 'boiling' used to be given to describe this method of cooking fish. It is a mistake to allow the liquid in which the fish is cooked to boil rapidly, for this causes the outside of the fish to break before the middle is properly cooked. It also can spoil the flavour, as well as the texture, of the fish. Fish can be poached in water, in milk, as in the recipe that follows, or in a mixture of fish stock and wine as on page 36.

The fish can be placed into cold liquid and this brought to simmering point, time the cooking from then. Allow 5 to 6 minutes for thin fillets; 10 to 12 minutes for thick steaks or small whole fish; about 7 minutes per 450 g/1 lb for larger whole fish. If the fish is placed into liquid that has been heated, you may need to increase these times by 1 or 2 minutes.

Plaice and Mushroom Ramekins

PLAICE AND MUSHROOM RAMEKINS

Cooking Time: 35–40 minutes   Serves 4   ❊

	Metric/Imperial	American
old potatoes, peeled	450 g/1 lb	1 lb
salt and pepper	to taste	to taste
butter or margarine	75 g/3 oz	6 tbsp
egg yolk, optional	1	1
mushrooms, sliced or left whole if small	100 g/4 oz	¼ lb
medium plaice (flounder or dab) fillets	4	4
milk, see method	300 ml/½ pint	1¼ cups
flour	25 g/1 oz	¼ cup
soft breadcrumbs	50 g/2 oz	1 cup

Cook the potatoes in salted water until just soft. Strain and sieve (if you intend to pipe a potato border) or mash. Add 25 g/1 oz (2 tbsp) of the butter or margarine and the egg yolk; do not add any milk for it causes the piped potatoes to lose their shape. Season the potatoes well. Heat another 25 g/1 oz (2 tbsp) butter or margarine in a saucepan and fry the mushrooms.

Meanwhile, put the fish with the milk and a little seasoning into a frying pan (skillet). Bring the milk just to simmering point and poach the fish until soft. Lift out the fish, halve if necessary and place in heated individual ovenproof ramekin dishes, add the mushrooms. Keep hot.

Heat the remaining butter or margarine in a saucepan, stir in the flour and cook for 2 to 3 minutes. Blend in the milk used to cook the fish, stir as the sauce comes to the boil and thickens; it should just coat the back of a wooden spoon, if too thick add a little more milk. Season to taste. Spoon over the fish and mushrooms. Top with the breadcrumbs. Pipe or spoon a border of the potato mixture around the edge of each dish. Place towards the top of a moderately hot oven, 200°C/400°F Gas Mark 6, for 10 to 15 minutes or until the potatoes and breadcrumbs are crisp and brown. Garnish with lemon slices and parsley.

TO FRY FISH AND CHIPS

To Fry Fish: The fish can be kept whole or divided into fillets or steaks. Coat in seasoned flour, then beaten egg and fine crisp breadcrumbs, or in batter; as in the recipe on the page right. Fry in shallow fat or oil until tender or as in the recipe on the right.

To Fry Potatoes Well: Prepare the potatoes, cut into fingers or slices, keep in cold water until ready to cook, then dry well. For the first frying heat the fat or oil to 170° C/340°F or until a cube of day-old bread turns golden in 1 minute. Dry the potatoes well and fry steadily until soft, but still white in colour. Remove from the pan; then reheat the fat or oil to 190°C/375°F (at this temperature bread turns golden within 30 seconds). Fry the potatoes for 1 to 2 minutes or until crisp and golden. Remove from the pan, drain on absorbent paper (kitchen towels) and serve.

FISH AND CHIPS

Cooking Time: 3–6 minutes   Serves 4   ❊

	Metric/Imperial	American
portions of cod, hake, plaice (flounder or dab) or sole or other fish	4	4
flour	25 g/1 oz	¼ cup
salt and pepper	to taste	to taste
For the batter coating: flour*	100 g/4 oz	1 cup
egg	1	1
milk	150 ml/¼ pint	⅔ cup
water, see method	2–3 tbsp	3–4 tbsp
To fry: deep oil or fat		
To garnish: lemon slices or wedges	4–8	4–8
parsley sprigs		

* use plain (all-purpose) flour, or self-raising flour if you prefer a light 'puffy' batter

Wash, then dry the fish well. Mix the 25 g/1 oz (¼ cup) flour with a little salt and pepper. Lightly coat the fish with the seasoned flour; this helps the batter adhere to the fish.

Blend all the ingredients for the batter in a large mixing bowl – use the greater amount of water for thin fillets of fish, such as plaice or sole, where a lighter coating is required. Heat the oil or fat to 180°C/350°F. A cube of day-old bread should take 1 minute to turn golden coloured. The frying basket must be heated in the oil or fat to prevent the batter sticking.

Above: Fish and Chips. Below: Whiting in Lemon Butter

Put the fish into the batter, turn with two forks or spoons. Lift the fish above the bowl and allow any surplus batter to drop back into the bowl.

Lower the fish into the hot oil or fat and fry steadily for 3 to 6 minutes, depending upon the thickness of the fish. If frying thicker portions of fish (i.e. cod steaks), then lower the heat very slightly after the initial browning of the batter.

Lift the fish from the oil or fat, hold the frying basket over the fryer or saucepan for a few seconds to allow any surplus oil or fat to drop back, then drain on absorbent paper (kitchen towels). Garnish. Serve with potato chips, opposite, and Tartare Sauce, page 120.

WHITING IN LEMON BUTTER

Cooking Time: 6 minutes   Serves 4   ❊

	Metric/Imperial	American
large fillets of whiting *or*	4	4
small fillets of whiting	8	8
butter	50–100 g/2–4 oz	¼–½ cup
lemon juice	2 tbsp	3 tbsp
chopped parsley	2 tbsp	3 tbsp
salt and pepper	to taste	to taste
To garnish: lemon wedges	4–8	4–8

Dry the whiting fillets well. Heat the butter in a large frying pan (skillet); use the larger amount if you like a buttery sauce. Fry the fish until nearly tender, then add the lemon juice, parsley and seasoning and complete the cooking. Garnish with the lemon wedges.

VARIATION
This method of cooking is suitable for most fish.

POACHED SOLE WITH ORANGE

Cooking Time: 30 minutes   Serves 4   ✳✳

It is interesting to note that oranges were served with fish in the past, almost as often as lemons. This is probably because imports of the citrus fruits were uncertain, so the cook learned to use what was available. While the dish can be prepared with lemons, oranges will please people who like a less 'biting' taste.

	Metric/Imperial	American
small sole	4	4
water	450 ml/¾ pint	scant 2 cups
bay leaf	1	1
salt and pepper	to taste	to taste
white wine	150 ml/¼ pint	⅔ cup
orange juice	2 tbsp	3 tbsp
grated orange rind	2 teasp	2 teasp
butter	50 g/2 oz	¼ cup
To garnish: orange slices	4–8	4–8
For the sauce: arrowroot or cornflour (cornstarch), see method	1–2 teasp	1–2 teasp
butter, see method	25–50 g/1–2 oz	2–4 tbsp

Ask the fishmonger to skin the fish, remove the heads and tails (or do this yourself, as line drawings on this page). Put the skins, heads and tails into a saucepan with the water, bay leaf and a little seasoning. Simmer gently for 15 minutes. Strain the liquid and if necessary reboil until reduced to 300 ml/½ pint (1¼ cups).

Put this fish stock, the wine, orange juice and whole fish into a large saucepan or a deep frying pan (skillet). Season lightly, then bring the liquid to the boil, reduce the heat and simmer for 8 to 10 minutes; spoon the liquid over the fish once or twice during the cooking period. Do not overcook the fish as it is grilled (broiled) after poaching.

Lift the fish from the liquid. Blend the orange rind and butter. Spread over the fish. Place under the grill (broiler) which should have been preheated at a high temperature. Cook for 4 to 5 minutes only. Put the fish on to a heated dish and garnish with the orange slices.

A sauce is not essential with this dish, but if you like to use the liquid, measure this and to each 150 ml/¼ pint (⅔ cup), allow 1 teaspoon arrowroot or cornflour (cornstarch) and 25 g/1 oz (2 tbsp) butter. Blend the thickening with the liquid, tip into the pan, add the butter and stir until thickened. Serve with the fish.

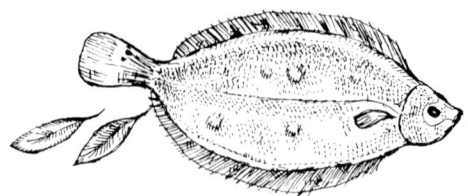

BAKED COD STEAKS AND BACON

Cooking Time: 20–25 minutes   Serves 4   ✳

	Metric/Imperial	American
cod steaks, 225g/8 oz (½ lb) each	4	4
salt and pepper	to taste	to taste
lemon juice	1 tbsp	1 tbsp
streaky bacon rashers (slices)	4	4
butter	40 g/1½ oz	3 tbsp
For the stuffing: soft breadcrumbs	100 g/4 oz	2 cups
salt and pepper	to taste	to taste
shredded suet	50 g/2 oz	½ cup
grated lemon rind	1 teasp	1 teasp
lemon juice	1 tbsp	1 tbsp
chopped parsley	1 tbsp	1 tbsp
egg	1	1
To garnish: small tomatoes	4–8	4–8

Wash and dry the fish well, season lightly on both sides and sprinkle with the lemon juice. De-rind the bacon rashers, make sure the rashers are sufficiently long to go around the fish; if not stretch them as page 45.

Blend all the ingredients together for the stuffing, divide into 4 portions. Press the stuffing on top of the steaks of cod in a neat shape. Put the bacon around the fish, secure with wooden cocktail sticks (toothpicks). Use half the butter to grease the bottom of an ovenproof dish and lift the fish carefully into the dish. Melt the remaining butter. Brush each piece of fish and stuffing with melted butter, do not cover the dish. Bake towards the top of a moderately hot oven, 190 to 200°C/375 to 400°F Gas Mark 5 to 6, for approximately 20 to 25 minutes or until the fish is tender. Do not overcook. Bake the tomatoes for about 10 minutes. Garnish the fish with the baked tomatoes.

TO SKIN FISH

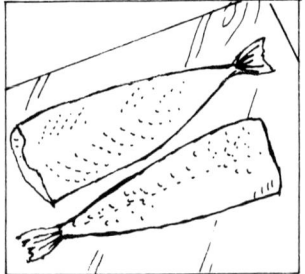
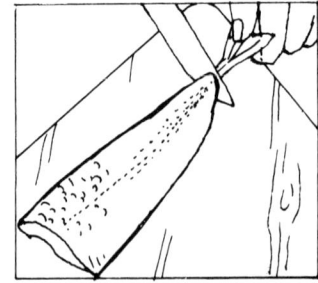

Flat fish can be skinned when whole or when divided into fillets. Rounded fish should be made into fillets first, as page 37.

Place the fish or first fillet on to a board, then make a cut just above the tail or tip of the fillet.

STEAMED FISH

In this method the fish is cooked over steam, instead of in liquid or fat. Steaming is considered to make fish particularly easy to digest. It also keeps the fish very firm, which is excellent if serving cold as in the following recipe. The cooking time is slightly longer than when poaching fish, see page 34.

HAKE WITH WALNUT SAUCE

Cooking Time: 12–15 minutes Serves 4 ❋❋

	Metric/Imperial	American
hake cutlets	4	4
salt and pepper	to taste	to taste
oil	2 teasp	2 teasp
pickled walnuts, finely chopped	8	8
double (heavy) cream	150 ml/¼ pint	⅔ cup
yoghurt	150 ml/¼ pint	⅔ cup
lemon juice	1 tbsp	1 tbsp
hard-boiled (hard-cooked) eggs, chopped	2	2
lettuce	1	1

Place the hake on a large ovenproof dish or plate. Add a little seasoning and the oil. Cover the dish or plate with a saucepan lid or piece of foil, brushed with a little oil. Stand this over a saucepan of boiling water and allow to boil steadily for 12 to 15 minutes or until the fish is cooked but unbroken. Allow the fish to cool.

Mix together the walnuts and cream, stir briskly so the cream thickens slightly. Blend in the yoghurt, lemon juice and one of the chopped eggs. Season the mixture.

Arrange the lettuce on a serving dish, top with the fish. Coat with the walnut mixture and top with the remaining chopped egg.

VARIATION
Halibut or turbot are equally good in this dish.

 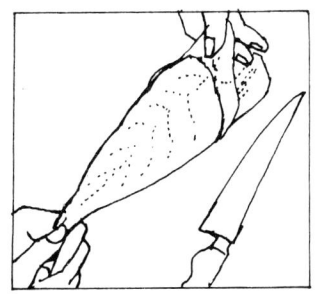

Sprinkle a little salt on the board, dip the blade of a sharp and pliable knife in this, and then gently cut the flesh away from the bottom skin, do this slowly and carefully.

Turn the fish over so the skin of the second side is touching the board and repeat the process above. The skins can be used to make good fish stock, see Sole with Orange.

TO FILLET ROUND FISH

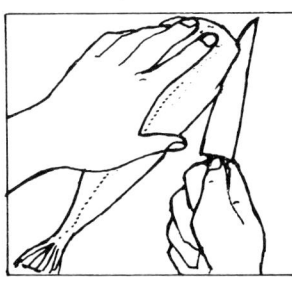 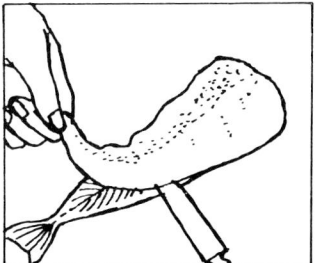

The fish can first be boned and then filleted as under the stages on page 41 or filleted as follows. Cut off the head, then slit along the backbone from the head to the tail.

Insert the tip of a knife into the back of the fish, gently cut the flesh away from the backbone, giving one fillet.

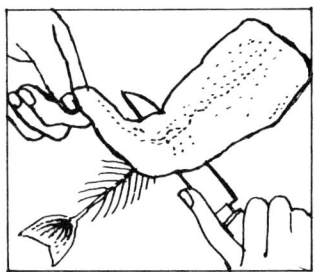

Turn the fish over and repeat this procedure on the second side of the fish.

HADDOCK BAKE

Cooking Time: 1 hour Serves 4 ❋

	Metric/Imperial	American
whole fresh haddock	450 g/1 lb	1 lb
eggs	3	3
milk	450 ml/¾ pint	scant 2 cups
salt and pepper	to taste	to taste
chopped parsley	1 tbsp	1 tbsp
grated nutmeg	to taste	to taste

Cut the head and tail from the haddock, then fillet the fish, as shown on this page. Skin the fillets, see left, and put the fish into an oblong casserole or deep ovenproof dish. Beat the eggs in a bowl. Warm the milk and pour over the eggs, then add a little salt, pepper and the parsley. Pour over the fish, top with a little grated nutmeg.

Stand the casserole or dish in a 'bain-marie' (tin of cold water), this prevents the egg custard curdling. Bake in the centre of a cool oven, 150°C/300°F Gas Mark 2, for 1 hour or until the custard is just set. This makes a good supper dish if served with crisp toast.

VARIATIONS
Use other fine textured fish, such as dab, flounder, pike, plaice or sole, instead of the fresh haddock.
● Add 50 g/2 oz (½ cup) grated cheese to the eggs and milk.

Above: Mackerel and Gooseberry Sauce. Right: Wheaty Plaice

HALIBUT IN CIDER

Cooking Time: 14–18 minutes   Serves 4   ✲✲

	Metric/Imperial	American
halibut steaks	4	4
milk	2 tbsp	3 tbsp
flour	25 g/1 oz	¼ cup
salt and pepper	to taste	to taste
butter	50 g/2 oz	¼ cup
dry cider	225 ml/8 fl oz	1 cup
mushrooms, sliced	100 g/4 oz	¼ lb
gherkins (sweet dill pickle), sliced	2–3 tbsp	3–4 tbsp
lemon	1	1

Dip the fish in the milk. Blend the flour with a generous amount of salt and pepper and coat the fish. Heat the butter in a large frying pan (skillet) and fry the fish briskly on one side for 3 to 4 minutes. Turn and cook for the same time on the second side. Lower the heat and fry for a further 3 to 4 minutes or until the fish is cooked. Lift out of the pan on to a heated dish and keep hot.

Pour the cider into the frying pan, stir well to absorb any butter left on the base of the pan. Add the mushrooms and gherkins (sweet dill pickle) and simmer gently for 5 to 6 minutes. Halve the lemon, remove the fruit pulp, add this to the cider mixture and season lightly. Spoon over the fish and serve.

STUFFED FLAT FISH

Flat fish, such as sole, plaice, flounder or large dabs, can be stuffed as in the following recipe. Slit the fish down the backbone for a length of 5 to 7.5 cm/2 to 3 inches; do this on the top side of the fish. Insert the tip of the knife to one side of the cut and loosen the fish away from the bone to make a pocket. Repeat this on the second side of the cut.

If using a stuffing that requires cooking, press this into the pockets before coating the fish. In the recipe that follows, the stuffing is inserted into the fish after frying.

MACKEREL AND GOOSEBERRY SAUCE

**Cooking Time:
15 minutes
Serves 4** ❋

The ideal herb to use with mackerel, as with many other fish, is fennel. This herb grows well in temperate regions. The leaves are used in this recipe. The white base is delicious as a cooked vegetable to accompany fish, or other foods, or it can be served raw in a salad.

WHEATY PLAICE

Cooking Time: 8–10 minutes   Serves 4   ❋❋

This title is given to the fish because it is coated with a crushed wheat breakfast cereal or fine brown breadcrumbs crisped slowly in the oven.

	Metric/Imperial	American
medium plaice	4	4
salt and pepper	to taste	to taste
flour	25 g/1 oz	¼ cup
egg(s)	1–2	1–2
wheat breakfast cereal, crushed, or crisp wheatmeal or wholemeal breadcrumbs	50–75 g/2–3 oz	½–¾ cup
To fry: deep oil or fat		
For the stuffing: butter	50 g/2 oz	¼ cup
small button mushrooms, sliced	100 g/4 oz	¼ lb
pickled cucumbers, coarsely diced	8 tbsp	9 tbsp
To garnish: lemon wedges	8	8
fennel heads, sliced	2	2

Make the pockets in the fish as described above. Mix the seasoning with the flour and use to coat the fish. Beat the egg(s) and brush over the fish, then coat in the crushed cereal or crisp breadcrumbs.

Deep fry the fish as on page 35. Drain on absorbent paper (kitchen towels).

While the fish is cooking, heat the butter and fry the mushrooms for 5 minutes. Add the pickled cucumbers. Carefully insert into the pockets of the fish and use any extra as a topping on the fish. Garnish with lemon wedges and sliced fennel.

	Metric/Imperial	American
mackerel	4	4
fennel	sprig	sprig
butter	75 g/3 oz	6 tbsp
salt and pepper	to taste	to taste
For the sauce: gooseberries	450 g/1 lb	1 lb
sugar	50 g/2 oz	¼ cup
water	150 ml/¼ pint	⅔ cup
butter	25 g/1 oz	2 tbsp
chopped parsley, optional	2–3 teasp	2–3 teasp
To garnish: chopped fennel or parsley		

Wash the mackerel, remove the heads, split and take out the bones, as shown on page 40. Chop the fennel leaves. Sprinkle the open fish with half fennel, spread with half butter and season well. Melt the remaining butter. Fold the fish back into shape, brush with the melted butter and sprinkle with the rest of the fennel. Grill (broil) steadily for 10 to 15 minutes, depending upon the size of the fish.

There is no need to 'top and tail' (clean) the gooseberries if sieving the sauce, but this must be done if you intend to put the cooked fruit into a liquidizer (blender) or beat it to make a purée. Simmer the gooseberries with the sugar and water until just soft. Either beat until smooth or sieve or liquidize and reheat with the butter. The chopped parsley is a pleasant addition to the sauce, but is not necessary. Dish up the fish, garnish with the fennel or parsley and serve with the gooseberry sauce.

VARIATIONS

The addition of fennel is pleasant but can be omitted. The mackerel can be cooked without boning. Simply brush with lightly seasoned melted butter and grill (broil).

● When gooseberries are out of season, use cooking (baking) apples instead.

OILY FISH

Some of the most interesting fish come under this heading. Oily fish include inexpensive but delicious, sprats, herrings, mackerel and whitebait, and luxury fresh salmon and salmon trout. Sardines are, of course, oily fish too, but fresh sardines are considerably dearer than sprats. These tiny fish make an excellent snack or savoury dish; they can be barbecued, fried or baked. A recipe is on page 182.

Recipes for other oily fish follow. Salmon is now bred in fish farms, so that it extends the season. Farmed salmon is cheaper than wild salmon.

If freezing oily fish, use within 4 months.

COSSETED HERRINGS

Cooking Time: 40 minutes   Serves 4 ✻✻✻

This recipe could be described as stuffed herrings, but many years ago it was given to me by the title above. I think the dish justifies the name, for the term 'cosset' means, among other things, 'to pamper'.

	Metric/Imperial	American
medium herrings, preferably with hard roes	8	8
For the filling: butter	50 g/2 oz	¼ cup
medium onion, finely chopped	1	1
button mushrooms, sliced	75 g/3 oz	scant cup
large oysters, sliced	8	8
grated lemon rind	1 teasp	1 teasp
lemon juice	1 tbsp	1 tbsp
salt and pepper	to taste	to taste
To poach the fish: water	300 ml/½ pint	1¼ cups
lemon juice	squeeze	squeeze
To garnish: slices of bread	2–3	2–3
butter	50 g/2 oz	¼ cup
button mushrooms	75 g/3 oz	scant cup
lemon slices	8	8

Split the herrings along the stomach, remove the intestines, discard these, except for the roes. Hard roes are better in this dish, but either soft or hard roes are good; each will impart a different taste to the stuffing. Chop the roes neatly. Bone the herrings as shown on page 41.

Heat the butter and fry the onion for 5 minutes. Add the mushrooms and sliced oysters. Fry for a further 2 minutes then blend with the roes, lemon rind and juice, salt and pepper to taste.

Press the stuffing into each herring. In the past the fish would have been 'sewn up' with fine thread and poached in a large fish kettle, this can still be done if there is a saucepan sufficiently large. However, the easiest method is to lay the herrings in a shallow tin or dish, add about 300 ml/½ pint (1¼ cups) well-seasoned water with a squeeze of lemon juice. Cover the dish with foil and cook in the centre of a moderate oven, 180°C/350°F Gas Mark 4, for approximately 30 minutes. Do not hurry the cooking as the stuffing is fairly solid.

While the fish is cooking, prepare the garnish. Cut the bread into small rounds. Heat the butter and fry the bread croûtes until golden brown on both sides, then fry the mushrooms. Lift the fish on to a heated dish with the croûtes, mushrooms and lemon slices.

VARIATIONS
Use about 24 mussels or 4 thinly sliced scallops in place of the oysters.

HERRINGS IN OATMEAL

Cooking Time: 10 minutes   Serves 4 ✻

This very simple dish has the reputation of being one of Edward VII's favourite breakfast dishes.

The oatmeal makes a firm crisp coating in contrast to the delicate texture of the fish.

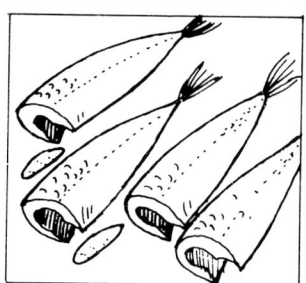

Bone 4 large herrings as described on page 41; discard the intestines but save the roes and fry these with the fish.

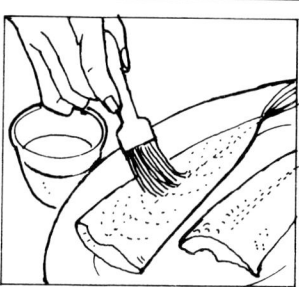

Divide each fish into 2 fillets; brush with a very little milk.

Blend 40 g/1½ oz (⅓ cup) fine or medium oatmeal with seasoning. Put on to a flat dish.

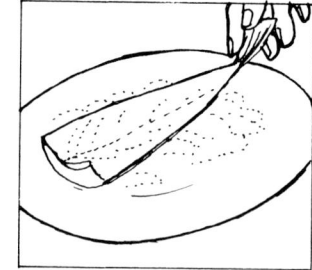

Press the herring fillets into the oatmeal until evenly coated. Coat the roes too.

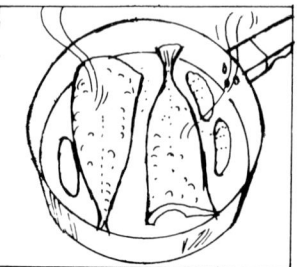

Heat 50 g/2 oz (¼ cup) butter in a large frying pan (skillet) and fry the herrings and roes for 6–8 minutes.

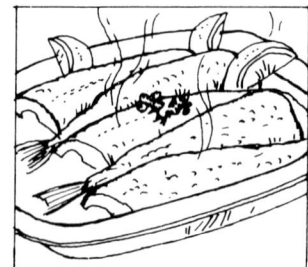

Drain on absorbent paper (kitchen towels). Serve garnished with wedges of lemon.

TO BONE HERRINGS

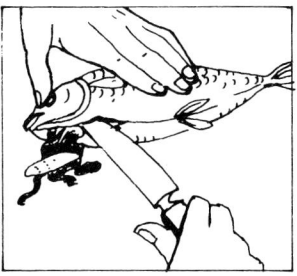

Slit the fish along the stomach and carefully remove the intestines. Put the hard or soft roes on one side to cook.

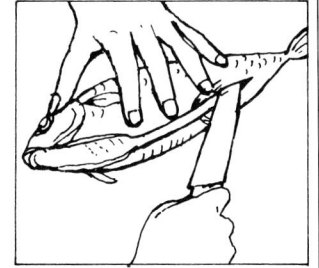

Insert the knife again and extend the cut, then open the fish out flat.

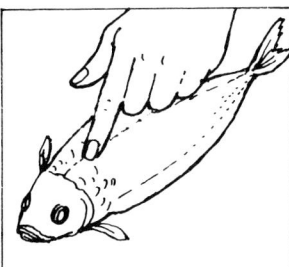

Turn it so the cut side is touching the chopping board and run your forefinger down the centre of the fish, pressing hard.

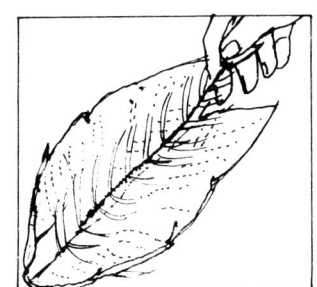

Turn the fish over and you will be able to lift out the backbone and most of the little bones adhering to this.

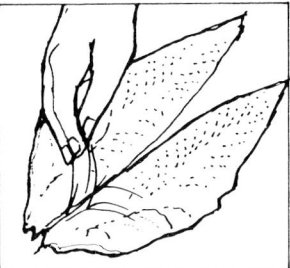

Take out bones with fingers or tweezers.

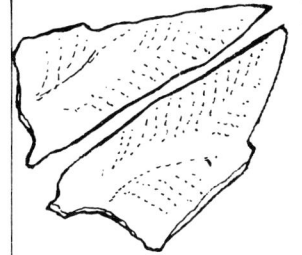

Cut the whole boned fish into two fillets, if desired.

RED HERRINGS

Cooking Time: 8 minutes   Serves 4   ❋

Normally the term 'red herring' means 'laying a false trail', but there is a very old recipe with the same name in which fresh herrings are marinated in beer then fried. Although this does not produce very red looking fish, it does produce herrings that have an excellent flavour.

	Metric/Imperial	American
large herrings	4	4
beer, light or dark according to personal taste	300 ml/½ pint	1¼ cups
salt and pepper	to taste	to taste
butter	25 g/1 oz	2 tbsp

Split then bone the fish: discard the intestines but save the roes. Put the flattened herrings with the cut side uppermost into a casserole, add the roes. Heat the beer with a little salt and pepper; pour over the fish. Leave for 1 hour. Lift the fish out of the beer and allow to drain.

Melt the butter, brush over the fish and cook under the grill (broiler) for about 5 to 6 minutes. Serve with creamed potatoes and a green vegetable.

COOKING SALMON

Salmon has often been described as the 'King of fish' and it has a flavour that is quite unique. Fine salmon is caught in many different countries and this fish can be cooked in a variety of methods. As it is a suitable fish for special celebrations, there are suggestions for serving hot or cold on pages 193.

Salmon can be poached, fried or grilled (broiled), or cooked in less usual ways as the recipes on this and the next page.

SALMON PATTIES

Illustrated in colour on page 42

Cooking Time: 5–6 minutes   Serves 6–8   ❋❋

	Metric/Imperial	American
Puff Pastry, as page 154 made with	225 g /8 oz flour etc	2 cups flour etc
For the filling: cooked salmon	350 g/12 oz	1½ cups
finely grated lemon rind	1 teasp	1 teasp
lemon juice	2 tbsp	3 tbsp
double (heavy) cream, whipped	3 tbsp	4 tbsp
salt and pepper	to taste	to taste
To fry: deep oil or fat		
To garnish: lemon slices	16	16
parsley	small sprigs	small sprigs

Roll out the pastry until about 3 mm/⅛ inch in thickness and cut into 16 rounds about 13 cm/5 inches in diameter. Blend the salmon with the rest of the ingredients to make a fairly soft mixture – the cream should be whipped so the mixture is not oversoft. Put a spoonful of the mixture on half of each pastry round. Moisten the edges of the pastry with water. Fold the pastry to make a patty shape, seal the edges well.

Put the patties into a cool place for about 1 hour before cooking so the pastry becomes quite firm. Heat the oil or fat to 180°C/350°F (until a cube of bread turns golden brown within 45 seconds). Put in the patties, reduce the heat at once, so the pastry does not overbrown before being cooked. Fry steadily for 5 to 6 minutes. Lift out and drain on absorbent paper (kitchen towels). Serve hot with lemon slices and parsley.

VARIATION
To make about 40 smaller patties, cut the pastry into 7.5 cm/3 inch rounds, as in the picture.

SALMON IN WINE SAUCE

Cooking Time: 30–35 minutes   Serves 4   ✳✳✳

	Metric/Imperial	American
salmon cutlets, approximately 2 cm/¾ inch thick	4	4
For baking salmon: white wine	225 ml/8 fl oz	1 cup
salt and pepper	to taste	to taste
butter	25 g/1 oz	2 tbsp
For the sauce: butter	25 g/1 oz	2 tbsp
flour	25 g/1 oz	¼ cup
milk	225 ml/8 fl oz	1 cup
egg yolks	2	2
single (light) cream	4 tbsp	5 tbsp
To garnish: hard-boiled (hard-cooked) egg, chopped	1	1
canned anchovy fillets, chopped	4	4
lemon slices	4	4
parsley	sprigs	sprigs

Place the salmon cutlets (often referred to as 'steaks') into a shallow ovenproof casserole, add the wine and a little salt and pepper. Spread greaseproof (waxed) paper or foil with the 25 g/1 oz (2 tbsp) butter, cover the casserole with this (buttered side inwards). Bake in the centre of a moderate to moderately hot oven, 180 to 190°C/350 to 375°F Gas Mark 4 to 5, for approximately 25 to 30 minutes or until the salmon is just cooked – do not overcook.

Meanwhile heat the butter for the sauce in a pan, stir in the flour and cook for 2 to 3 minutes. Blend in the milk, stir as the sauce comes to the boil and thickens. Remove from the heat. Strain 150 ml/¼ pint (²/₃ cup) liquid from the dish in which the salmon was cooked into the hot, but not boiling, sauce; keep the salmon covered and hot while completing the sauce. Whisk the egg yolks and cream together in a bowl, then whisk in a little of the sauce. Return to the pan and cook slowly for 4 to 5 minutes or until the sauce thickens again; it should just coat a wooden spoon and not be too thick. Season to taste.

Lift the salmon carefully, so it drains and keeps a good shape, on to a heated serving dish. Put a little sauce in the centre only of each cutlet (so the pink fish still shows round the edge). Mix the hard-boiled (hard-cooked) egg and anchovy fillets. Spoon over the sauce. Arrange the lemon slices and parsley round the dish. The rest of the sauce may be poured around, but not over, the fish or served separately.

VARIATION
Use salmon trout or cutlets of halibut or turbot instead of salmon.

Above: Salmon Patties – recipe page 41. Below: Creamed Haddock

Salmon in Wine Sauce

SMOKED FISH

Some of the most popular smoked fish, such as eel, mackerel, salmon, sprats and trout, are served without cooking as an hors d'oeuvre or light main course.

There are other excellent smoked fish produced from fresh herrings, these are bloaters, buckling and kippers. These fish can be grilled, fried or poached in water and served as a breakfast dish.

Smoked haddock makes another excellent breakfast or main dish, as the recipes given below will show.

Due to the different texture of smoked fish, it is better to freeze this for up to 3 or 4 months only.

FINNAE HADDIE

Cooking Time:
10 minutes
Serves 4 ✳

Although haddocks are smoked in many countries, the name 'Finnan' is so often used to describe the smoked fish. This is because the small village near Aberdeen where fresh haddock has been caught, split and smoked for generations, is pronounced 'Finnae', although it is in fact spelt 'Findon': and so this word has come into the gastronomic vocabulary.

	Metric/Imperial	American
smoked or fresh haddock	1	1
milk	450 ml/¾ pint	scant 2 cups
bay leaf	1	1
pepper	to taste	to taste
butter	50 g/2 oz	¼ cup

Remove the tail and fins, cut the fish into 4 portions. Put the milk into a shallow saucepan or frying pan (skillet), add the fish, bay leaf and a little pepper (salt should not be necessary). Bring *just* to boiling point, then lower the heat and simmer until the fish is cooked but unbroken. Serve topped with the butter.

VARIATIONS
Cook the fish in water, rather than milk; omit the bay leaf.
● The cooked haddock can be topped with poached eggs, as in the recipe on this page.

CREAMED HADDOCK

Cooking Time: 15 minutes   Serves 4   ✳

	Metric/Imperial	American
ingredients as Finnae Haddie		
flour	25 g/1 oz	¼ cup
single (light) cream or extra milk	150 ml/¼ pint	⅔ cup
salt	to taste	to taste
chopped parsley	1 tbsp	1 tbsp
cooked sweetcorn	3–4 tbsp	4–5 tbsp
eggs	4	4

Cook the smoked haddock in milk as in the recipe on this page. Do not top the cooked fish with the butter, instead heat this in a saucepan while the fish is cooking. Stir in the flour and cook for 2 minutes, then blend in the cream or the extra milk.

Lift the fish from the milk, remove any bones and coarsely flake the fish. Strain the milk into the cream mixture, stir as the sauce comes to the boil and thickens. Taste and add salt if desired. Put the fish, parsley and sweetcorn into the sauce, heat for 2 to 3 minutes. Spoon into a heated serving dish. Meanwhile, poach the eggs.

Top the creamed mixture with the eggs and serve.

SHELLFISH

There is a wide variety of shellfish ranging from inexpensive cockles and mussels to the lobster, which nowadays is expensive.

Cockles should be well-washed in cold water, as they tend to be very gritty and sandy. Serve cold with salad, or add to stuffings and sauces to serve with other fish, or in a fish pie as on page 205.

Mussels are used in the very delicious stew on this page. Crab, which many people prefer to lobster, can be served hot or cold.

It is inadvisable to freeze shellfish yourself. If using commercially frozen shellfish, allow it to defrost slowly. Never overcook any shellfish for this makes it extremely tough.

MUSSEL STEW

Illustrated in colour on page 210

Cooking Time: 15–20 minutes   Serves 4   ❊❊

This very homely stew of mussels, one of the really economical shellfish, is an ideal way of serving the fish. The dish is given a touch of luxury by the cream topping.

	Metric/Imperial	American
mussels	2.4 litres/4 pints	5 pints
parsley	small bunch	small bunch
water	1.5 litres/2½ pints	generous 6 cups
butter	50 g/2 oz	¼ cup
medium onions, finely chopped	2–3	2–3
salt and pepper	to taste	to taste
To garnish: chopped parsley	1 tbsp	1 tbsp
double (heavy) cream	150 ml/¼ pint	⅔ cup

Scrub the mussels well, discard any that do not close when the shells are tapped firmly, for this indicates they could be dead. Put into a large saucepan with the bunch of parsley, cover with the water, then cook steadily until the shells all open. Again, discard any that have not opened.

Strain off the liquid and reserve, put the mussels on one side. Heat the butter in the pan, fry the onions until transparent – take care they do not brown. Add the mussel liquid, salt and pepper to taste and simmer in an open pan until the liquid is reduced to about 900 ml/1½ pints (3¾ cups).

Meanwhile, remove the mussels from the shells completely or remove one half of the shell; this is entirely a matter of personal taste. Put the mussels into the liquid and heat gently – do not overcook, otherwise they could become tough. Spoon into heated soup plates and top with the chopped parsley and cream.

VARIATION
This is a very basic dish; it is almost like a soup. To make a more sustaining stew, peel and dice 2 potatoes, fry with the onions. Skin 4 large tomatoes, cut into wedges; chop 3 to 4 celery stalks. Add the celery with the mussel liquid and the tomatoes with the mussels.

DEVILLED CRAB

Cooking Time: 20 minutes   Serves 4   ❊❊

	Metric/Imperial	American
small crabs	4	4
soft breadcrumbs	75 g/3 oz	1½ cups
cayenne pepper	pinch	pinch
curry powder	½-1 teasp	½-1 teasp
Worcestershire sauce	1–2 teasp	1–2 teasp
salt	to taste	to taste
butter	75 g/3 oz	6 tbsp
oil	few drops	few drops
To garnish: lemon slices	4	4
parsley	sprigs	sprigs
small crab claws		

TO PREPARE A CRAB

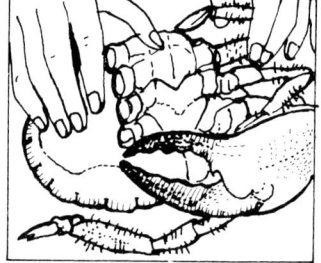

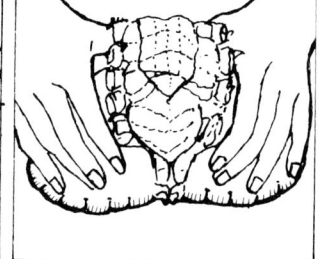

Pull off all the claws and wipe the shell. Turn the crab on its back.

Remove the body of the crab.

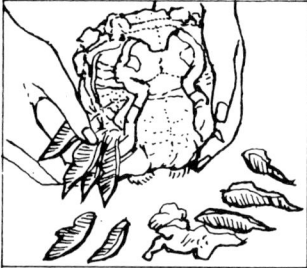

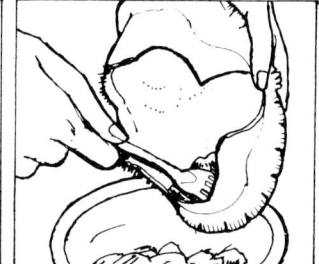

Take out and discard the stomach bag and any grey fingers.

Remove the meat from the body of the crab.

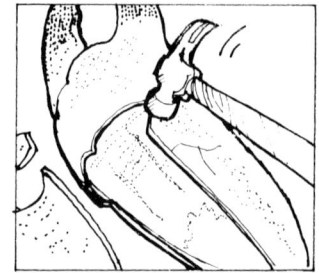

Crack the large claws and remove the flesh. The crabmeat is then ready to use in various dishes.

Remove all the flesh from the body and large claws of the crabs, as shown on page 44. Save the small claws for garnish. Flake the crabmeat, blend the light and dark flesh together with 25 g/1 oz (½ cup) of the breadcrumbs, the cayenne pepper, curry powder and Worcestershire sauce. Add a little salt.

Heat the butter in a frying pan (skillet) or in a dish in a microwave cooker. Add the remaining breadcrumbs and turn in the butter until well coated; do not allow to brown.

Clean the crab shells, polish with the oil. Fill with the flavoured crabmeat and top with the buttered crumbs. Place on a dish or baking tray and cook towards the top of a moderately hot oven, 200°C/400°F Gas Mark 6, for approximately 15 minutes. Garnish each crab with the lemon slices and parsley. Arrange on heated plates with the small crab claws.

VARIATIONS
Brown under a grill (broiler) with the heat set to moderate for about 5 to 6 minutes.
● *Creamy Devilled Crab:* Blend 2 to 3 tablespoons double cream (3 to 4 tbsp heavy cream) with the crab mixture.

SCALLOPED CRABS

Cooking Time: 15 minutes   Serves 4–6   ✳✳

When making this dish, save the small crab claws for a colourful garnish.

	Metric/Imperial	American
medium crabs	2	2
canned anchovy fillets, chopped	2 tbsp	3 tbsp
white or brown malt vinegar	2 teasp	2 teasp
butter	75 g/3 oz	6 tbsp
soft white breadcrumbs	75 g/3 oz	1½ cups
cayenne pepper	½–1 teasp	½–1 teasp
olive oil	few drops	few drops
To garnish: canned anchovy fillets	4–6	4–6
lemon wedges	8	8
parsley sprigs	few	few
small crab claws		

Prepare the crab, as the method given on this page. Blend the light and dark meat of the crab together in a bowl. Add the chopped anchovy fillets and vinegar.

Heat the butter in a frying pan (skillet) and toss the crumbs in this until just golden. Blend approximately one-third of the crumbs with the crab. Season with cayenne pepper, add this gradually since it is very hot. Clean the crab shells, polish with the oil. Press the crab meat mixture back into the shells. Sprinkle with the remainder of the buttered crumbs. Heat in a hot oven, 220°C/425°F Gas Mark 7, for 10 to 12 minutes or under the grill (broiler).

If there is too much mixture for the crab shells, put the surplus into scallop shells and arrange around the crab. Top the filled crabs with a lattice of anchovy fillets. Garnish the serving dish with wedges of lemon, sprigs of parsley and small crab claws.

GRILLED SCALLOPS
Illustrated in colour on page 206
Cooking Time: 8–10 minutes   Serves 4   ✳

Scallops are some of the most delicious shellfish. There are many ways of cooking them and this combination of fish and bacon is particularly simple and delicious.

When scallops (called Coquilles St Jacques by the French) are fresh, the flesh should be firm and the roes bright orange. Do not overcook scallops, this makes them tough and leathery instead of tender and succulent.

If scallops are large, buy 8 instead of 16 small ones in this recipe. Halve the large fish, cut them in such a way that each half has part of the roe.

Cut 16 small scallops from their shells. Put into a dish, add any liquid from the shells to the fish.

Moisten the fish with 2 tablespoons (3 tbsp) lemon juice and ½ tablespoon oil. Season with a little freshly milled black pepper. Leave for 30 minutes.

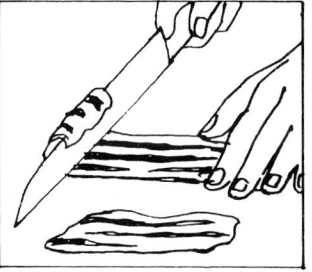
De-rind 8 long streaky bacon rashers (slices). Cut each rasher in half. *Stretch the bacon:* to do this, stroke with the back of a knife, this makes the bacon pieces longer and roll more easily.

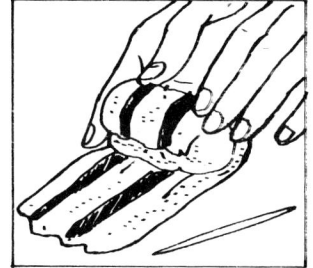
Roll the bacon around the scallops. Secure with wooden cocktail sticks (toothpicks).

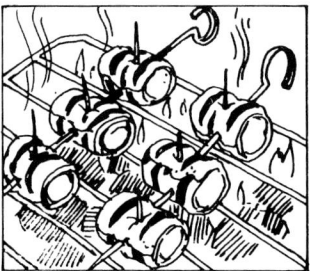
Put the fish and bacon on to long metal skewers.

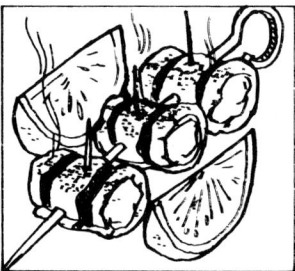
Grill (broil) or cook over a barbecue fire until the bacon is crisp and the scallops opaque and tender. Serve with lemon wedges.

ISLE OF MAN PLATTER

Cooking Time: 6 minutes   Serves 4 *

	Metric/Imperial	American
mussels, prepared as page 44	12–16	12–16
medium sole or plaice (flounder or dab) fillets	4	4
small oysters	8	8
small scallops	8	8
large cooked prawns (large shrimp)	8	8
small cooked lobster	1	1
flour	25 g/1 oz	¼ cup
salt	to taste	to taste
For the batter: self-raising flour	100 g/4 oz	1 cup
eggs	2	2
milk	150 ml/¼ pint	⅔ cup
water	2 tbsp	3 tbsp
To fry: deep oil or fat		
To garnish: parsley	few large sprigs	few large sprigs
lemon wedges	4–8	4–8

Above: Isle of Man Platter. Above right: Dressed Crab. Below right: Trout with Almonds

Prepare the mussels as page 44; remove from their shells. Skin the fillets of fish, as shown on page 36. Remove the oysters and scallops from their shells, halve large scallops. Peel the prawns (shell the shrimp). Remove the lobster meat from the body and large claws, cut this into neat pieces. Toss all the fish in the 25 g/1 oz (¼ cup) flour, seasoned with salt and pepper.

Sift the flour and a pinch of salt. Separate the eggs. Beat the yolks into the flour together with the milk and water. Beat the whites until stiff and fold into the batter just before coating the fish.

Heat the oil or fat to 185°C/365°F (or until a cube of day-old bread turns golden in just half a minute). Coat in batter and fry the white fish, scallops and oysters for 3 minutes. Add the coated mussels, lobster and prawns (shrimp) and continue to fry for another 3 minutes or until the batter is crisp and brown and the fish cooked or very hot (in the case of the mussels and prawns). Lift from the oil or fat, drain on absorbent paper (kitchen towels). Fry the parsley sprigs for 2 to 3 seconds only; this makes sure they keep green and yet become crisp. Arrange the fish on a heated dish, top with the fried parsley. Garnish with the lemon wedges.

VARIATION
Use 4 larger scallops and cut into halves.

DRESSED CRAB

No Cooking   Serves 4   ⁂

There are various ways of serving the crabmeat to produce this simple but excellent dish. The simplest method is to take all the flesh from the crab, as described on page 44, and then to return the crabmeat to the polished shell, arranging the light white meat to one side of the shell and the dark meat to the other side. The following method is however a more interesting way of serving the crabmeat.

	Metric/Imperial	American
large crabs	2	2
soft breadcrumbs	40 g/1½ oz	¾ cup
double (heavy) cream	2 tbsp	3 tbsp
lemon juice	1½ tbsp	2 tbsp
anchovy essence (extract)	few drops	few drops
olive oil	few drops	few drops
To garnish: parsley	small sprigs	small sprigs
hard-boiled (hard-cooked) egg(s), optional	1–2	1–2

TROUT WITH ALMONDS

Cooking Time: 10–15 minutes   Serves 4   ⁂

This recipe, which is very popular today, is probably one of the oldest methods of cooking this particular fish. Almond trees have flourished in Britain, as in so many other countries, for centuries; trout have been in the streams, lakes and rivers for as long, and the habit of combining nuts with fish (and meat) is an old one.

	Metric/Imperial	American
large fresh trout	4	4
butter	75 g/3 oz	6 tbsp
salt and pepper	to taste	to taste
almonds, blanched and cut into strips	50 g/2 oz	½ cup
lemon juice	2 teasp	2 teasp
chopped herbs, optional, see method	1–2 teasp	1–2 teasp
To garnish: parsley or fennel	sprigs	sprigs
black olives	4	4

Remove all the crabmeat from the bodies of the crabs and the large claws, as shown on page 44. Put the white flesh in one bowl and the dark meat in a second bowl.

Blend half the breadcrumbs with the light crabmeat and the remainder with the dark crabmeat. Mix the cream with the white crabmeat together with half the lemon juice. Blend the remaining lemon juice and anchovy essence (extract) with the dark crabmeat.

Clean the body shell of the crabs, trim the edges with kitchen scissors to give a neater appearance, polish with the oil. Fill half the shell with the white crabmeat and the other half with the dark crabmeat. Garnish with a line of small sprigs of parsley or parsley and the chopped hard-boiled (hard-cooked) egg(s). Serve with salad.

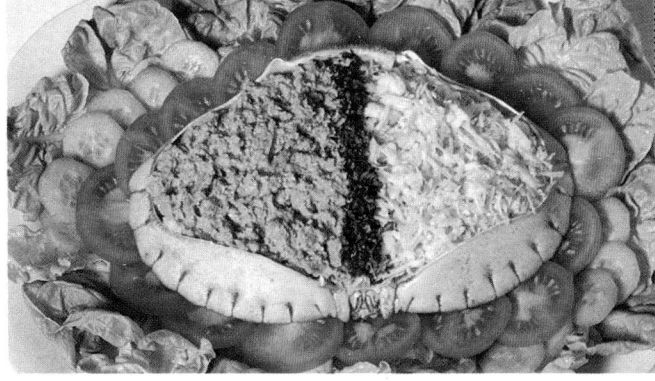

FRESHWATER FISH

Trout is the most plentiful of freshwater fish, for not only is it found in natural surroundings but trout farms flourish and first rate trout are available.

Eel is certainly less popular than trout. This is a pity, for carefully cooked eel is quite delicious, see pages 17 and 48.

Carp, perch and smelt are all rather scarce freshwater fish. This group of fish are, like white fish, suitable for freezing for up to 6 months.

Slit the fish, remove the intestines, but do not cut away the heads, and clean well. Heat the butter in a large frying pan (skillet), season the fish and fry steadily on both sides until tender, but unbroken. Lift on to a heated dish. Fry the almonds in the butter remaining in the pan until both the nuts and the butter are golden brown. Add the lemon juice, blend with the hot butter and nuts. In old recipes for this dish, chopped fennel, parsley and thyme were also added towards the end of the cooking time. Spoon the nuts and butter over the fish. Garnish with the parsley and olives and serve with lemon wedges.

JELLIED EELS

Cooking Time: 45 minutes-1 hour   Serves 4   ✳

This particular delicacy is considered very much a 'cockney' (Londoner's) dish. Jellied eels are sold at the famous Derby racecourse and other sporting activities.

	Metric/Imperial	American
fresh eel(s)	900 g/2 lb	2 lb
water	900 ml/1½ pints	3¾ cups
salt and pepper	to taste	to taste
lemon juice	squeeze	squeeze
bay leaf	1	1
allspice	¼ teasp	¼ teasp
gelatine, optional	7 g/¼ oz	1 envelope

Ask the fishmonger to skin the eel (or eels). Cut the fish into 3.5 to 5 cm/1½ to 2 inch lengths. Put the fish into a saucepan with the water, salt and pepper to taste. Add the lemon juice, bay leaf and allspice. Cover the pan and simmer gently until tender. If the eels are fairly small, this will take 45 minutes but allow 1 hour if the eels are thicker.

When the fish is cooked, spoon into small individual dishes. If time permits, boil the liquid in the saucepan until reduced to 300 to 450 ml/½ to ¾ pint (1¼ to a scant 2 cups); the amount depends on the depth of the fish to be covered. At the end of this time, the liquid will form a jelly when cold. If however time is short, or the weather unduly hot, measure out the correct amount of liquid as above. Heat and add the gelatine, stir until dissolved. Strain the liquid over the eels. Allow to cool. Serve with a spoon.

USING VARIOUS FISH

There are many basic recipes in which a variety of fish can be used according to the time of the year and amount of money you wish to spend. Two examples are given on this and the next page, they are a Soufflé and Pancakes. A Fish Pie, which can be luxurious or economical, according to your wish, is another readily adaptable dish; the recipe is on page 205.

SOUFFLÉS

Although the word 'soufflé' is French and soufflés originated in France, a range of dishes based upon the original concept of a light mixture have been made in various forms in other countries for some decades.

A fish soufflé is excellent and it can be varied in flavour according to the type of fish you want to use. Flaked cooked shellfish makes a luxurious soufflé which is ideal for the first course of a meal.

White or freshwater fish can be used. If you choose white or freshwater fish with a fine texture, such as flounder, dab, pike, plaice, sole or whiting, then use uncooked rather than cooked fish. Either mince (grind) this or put it into a food processor to give an uncooked, rather than a cooked, purée. Never overprocess the fish, this makes it sticky and less pleasant in texture. The raw fish should be blended with the very hot sauce and cooked in this for 2 to 3 minutes before adding the egg yolks and then the egg whites.

Smoked haddock has been given as the flavouring in this basic soufflé. This particular fish should be precooked before flaking and adding to other ingredients. The generous amount of butter or margarine and liquid in this recipe helps to keep the soufflé moist.

SMOKED HADDOCK SOUFFLÉ

Cooking Time: 40 minutes   Serves 4   ✳✳

Heat 50 g/2 oz (¼ cup) butter or margarine in a large saucepan, stir in 40 g/1½ oz (scant ⅓ cup) flour and cook for 2–3 minutes. Gradually blend in 225 ml/8 fl oz (1 cup) milk or use milk blended with a little single or double (light or heavy) cream. Stir as the sauce boils and thickens.

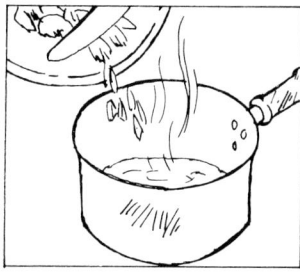

Remove the pan from the heat and add 175 g/6 oz (generous ¾ cup) finely flaked cooked smoked haddock. Mix well with the sauce.

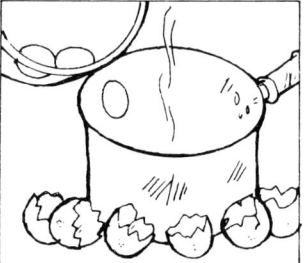

Separate 3 eggs, add the yolks to the fish mixture.

Whisk the whites of 4 eggs until just stiff – they should stand in peaks but not be as firm as when making a meringue.

Fold the egg whites into the fish mixture. Taste and add salt and pepper to taste.

Spoon into a 15–18 cm/6–7 inch buttered soufflé dish. Bake in the centre of the oven, 190°C/375°F Gas Mark 5, for 30 minutes until well risen. Serve at once.

SEAFOOD PANCAKES

Cooking Time: 25 minutes   Serves 4–6   ❖❖

	Metric/Imperial	American
Pancakes, as page 130 made with	100 g/ 4 oz flour etc	1 cup flour etc
For the filling: plaice, sole or whiting fillets, see this page and page 37	4–6	4–6
butter	50 g/2 oz	¼ cup
scallops, sliced	3–4	3–4
peeled prawns (shelled shrimp)	12	12
For the sauce: butter	50 g/2 oz	¼ cup
flour	50 g/2 oz	½ cup
milk	450 ml/¾ pint	scant 2 cups
single (light) cream	150 ml/¼ pint	⅔ cup
salt and pepper	to taste	to taste
To garnish: lemon wedges	4–6	4–6

Cook the pancakes as page 130 and keep hot.

Fillet the fish as the instructions on this page, then cut each fillet into several small pieces. Heat the butter in a large frying pan (skillet) and cook the fish and scallops for 5 to 6 minutes. Add the prawns (shrimp) but do not heat again.

Meanwhile, heat the remaining butter in a saucepan, stir in the flour and cook gently for 2 to 3 minutes. Blend in the milk and cream, stir or whisk as the sauce comes to the boil and thickens. Season lightly. Pour nearly half the sauce over the fish in the frying pan, heat gently for several minutes.

Fill each pancake with the fish mixture. Roll and place in a heated serving dish. Top with the remaining sauce and serve at once. Garnish with lemon wedges.

VARIATIONS

Seafood Pancakes au Gratin: Add 50 g/2 oz (½ cup) grated cheese to the sauce for coating the pancakes. Pour over the filled pancakes, top with a layer of crisp breadcrumbs and grated cheese. Heat for a short time under the grill (broiler) or in the oven until the cheese topping melts.

Note: If heating under a grill (broiler), use a flameproof dish.

● The fish can be skinned before cooking, see page 36.

FISH ROES

The roes of fish can provide interesting snacks or main dishes. Herring roes are particularly good in flavour. Soft roes (from the male herring) can be steamed with a little butter and/or milk and served on toast. Soft roes can, however, also be made into an excellent Fish Pie, see page 205. Hard roes (from the female fish) are better if coated with a little seasoned flour and fried until crisp and brown. These can be served with, rather than on, toast, or as a breakfast dish with fried or grilled (broiled) bacon and tomatoes.

The roe of cod is particularly nutritious. Whilst smoked cod's roe has become a popular delicacy, the fresh cod's roe has been a favourite for many generations. If sold uncooked, it is translucent in appearance. The roe should be steamed for approximately 15 minutes until it turns opaque, white and firm. It can then be sliced and fried in a little butter or bacon fat, and served with fried cooked bacon as a supper or breakfast dish.

TO FILLET FLAT FISH

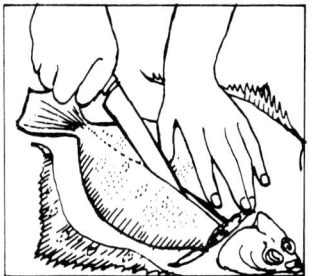 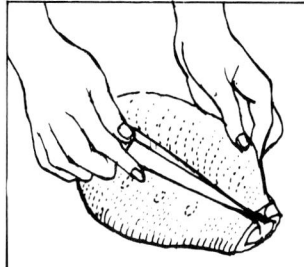

Cut away the fins and the head of the fish. Make a deep cut from head to tail down the centre of the fish.

Insert the tip of the knife at the top of the cut and gently ease the fish away from the bone with short sharp strokes. Hold the fillet back with your fingers as you work.

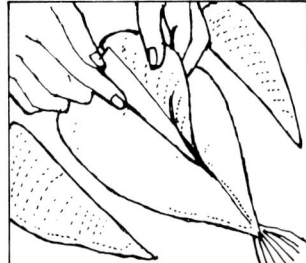

Having cut away one fillet from the top side, repeat this procedure with the second fillet. Turn the fish over and repeat the process, so giving 4 fillets.

Meat

The following pages give a wide range of meat dishes. The chapter begins with information on how to achieve perfect roast joints, together with suggestions for adding a new look to these. This is followed by recipes based upon frying and grilling (broiling) meats, then ways to use minced (ground) uncooked and cooked meat.

Recipes for interesting casseroles and stews, which make the best use of economical ingredients, begin on page 67, with both traditional and new and unusual pies and puddings on pages 73 to 77.

Every country varies in the way it cuts the carcass of an animal, so both American and British names are used for the various joints and portions of meat where different terms are used.

TO ROAST MEAT

Modern joints generally are excellent in quality, so the simple cookery process used in roasting is an ideal way to retain the natural flavour of the meat. There may however be one criticism of our modern roast joints and that is that both the flavour of the meat and the traditional accompaniments are inclined to be monotonous; we know exactly how the meal will taste.

If we go back to the days when meat was neither as fresh nor as tender as it is today, we find that clever and imaginative cooks used all kinds of different flavours to enhance the taste of their roast meat. Some of these culinary practices are recalled on the following pages.

The method of cooking used in those days was a turning spit over a great fire; we can copy that technique if we wish by using a modern rotisserie or turning spit. The suggestions that follow are, however, equally as successful when the meat is roasted (purists call it 'baked') in the oven.

How to Roast Meat

Meats may be roasted quickly at the setting given under FAST ROASTING on pages 50, 52, 53 and 54; this is suitable for prime cuts. Less tender cuts of meat that have been frozen and then defrosted, are better cooked at the temperature given under SLOWER ROASTING on the same pages. If cooking meat from the frozen state, always use the SLOWER ROASTING temperature.

Meat can be roasted in an open roasting tin (pan) or on a turning spit, called today a rotisserie. The cooking times in each case are similar. If meat is placed into a modern plastic roasting bag, the cooking time is not increased.

When the meat is cooked in a covered roasting tin or enclosed in foil, the total cooking time should either be increased by 15 minutes or a slightly higher setting used, i.e. 10°C or 25°F, or 1 Mark higher with a gas cooker.

Meat can be roasted very satisfactorily in a microwave cooker. Follow the manufacturers' instructions as to the setting and timing to use.

It is better to allow meat to defrost first before roasting it, unless you use a meat thermometer, in which case you can cook joints from the frozen state, as the

thermometer will show the degree of cooking. Without a thermometer, it is less satisfactory. The temperatures a meat thermometer should register are given on page 56.

Always use the correct meat thermometer for a microwave cooker.

When roasting a joint that has been stuffed, it is important to weigh the meat after stuffing to calculate the correct cooking time. The weight of stuffing does not increase the total cooking time when using a microwave cooker.

Do not use too much fat (shortening) or dripping when roasting meat, for this is inclined to harden the outside of the meat and add extra calories, which most people try to avoid. One advantage of using a roasting bag or a covered roasting tin or wrapping the meat in foil is that the meat is kept moist with little, if any, extra fat. Obviously if potatoes are being roasted round the joint, extra fat must be used. It is only possible to roast potatoes well if the higher setting, given under FAST ROASTING is used.

Simmer any bones from the meat in water to cover to make good stock for gravy.

TO ROAST BEEF

Choose beef with a reasonable amount of marbling, i.e. a little fat distributed in the lean meat. Good beef is firm in texture. The lean should be reddish in colour, but this will vary according to the time the meat was cut; it should never be dull and brown. The fat should be firm and cream in colour. Allow per person before cooking: 175 to 225 g/6 to 8 oz (½ lb) if boned and 350 g/12 oz (¾ lb) on the bone.

Prime cuts for roasting: Baron (a huge joint only used for ceremonial banquets), fillet, rib, sirloin. American names are similar.

More economical cuts for roasting: Good quality aitch-bone and fresh brisket, topside. American cuts do not always include aitch-bone and topside is called top round.

FAST ROASTING: Allow 15 to 20 minutes per 450 g/1 lb and 15 to 20 minutes over to give 'rare' or medium cooked beef at 200 to 220°C/400 to 425°F, Gas Mark 6

Roast Beef and Yorkshire Pudding – recipe page 52

to 7. Well-cooked beef (not usually popular) needs 25 minutes per 450 g/1 lb and 25 minutes over. After one hour's cooking, the temperature can be reduced slightly to 190 to 200°C/375 to 400°F, Gas Mark 5 to 6.
SLOWER ROASTING: Allow 25 to 30 minutes per 450 g/1 lb and 25 to 30 minutes over at 160 to 180°C/325 to 350°F, Gas Mark 3 to 4. Well-cooked beef needs 35 minutes per 450 g/1 lb and 35 minutes over.

If there is a certain amount of fat on the meat, as in a sirloin or rib of beef, then extra fat is not necessary. If lean, such as topside (top round) then use a very little fat. Sirloin and rib can be boned and rolled to make it easier to carve the meat. It is not usual to stuff beef, but a recipe for Stuffed Topside is on this page.

Serve roast beef with Yorkshire Pudding and Horseradish Sauce or Cream, see pages 52, 102 and 103, and a thin gravy.

CRUSTED RIB OF BEEF

Cooking Time: see method   Serves 4–5   ❊❊

	Metric/Imperial	American
rib joint of beef on the bone	1.3–1.8 kg/3–4 lb	3–4 lb
red wine	150 ml/¼ pint	⅔ cup
For the coating: butter	50 g/2 oz	¼ cup
flour	50 g/2 oz	½ cup
soft breadcrumbs	25 g/1 oz	½ cup
mustard powder	2 teasp	2 teasp
salt	pinch	pinch
cayenne pepper	pinch	pinch

Place the joint into the roasting tin. Pour the red wine over the meat. Roast for 30 minutes if following the

STUFFED TOPSIDE

Cooking Time: as above plus 15 minutes   Serves 5–6   ❊❊

	Metric/Imperial	American
topside (top round) of beef	1.1–1.35 kg/ 2½-3 lb	2½-3 lb
For the stuffing: streaky bacon rashers (slices)	3	3
beef dripping or margarine	50 g/2 oz	¼ cup
medium onions, chopped	2	2
soft breadcrumbs	75 g/3 oz	1½ cups
chopped parsley	2 tbsp	3 tbsp
grated horseradish or mustard powder	1 teasp	1 teasp
egg	1	1
salt and pepper	to taste	to taste

Cut the joint vertically so giving two complete sections. De-rind and chop the bacon. Put the bacon rinds and half the dripping or margarine into a saucepan and fry the onions until nearly soft. Add the chopped bacon and cook for 2 to 3 minutes. Remove the bacon rinds, then add all the remaining stuffing ingredients and mix well. Sandwich the two halves of the meat together with the stuffing. Weigh the joint and calculate the roasting time as above. Spread remaining fat on top of the joint.

Cut a band of foil and wrap around the joint, then tie this with fine string. Put into the roasting tin or roasting bag or wrap in foil. Cook the joint as the timing above and the advice given on page 50, left.

When the joint is carved, every person has slices of meat and stuffing. Topside (top round) is inclined to be a less succulent beef joint than many other cuts, this method of cooking keeps the meat moist.

VARIATION
Sausage and Onion Stuffing: Blend 3 medium chopped and lightly fried onions with 225 to 350 g/8 to 12 oz (½ to ¾ lb) pork sausagemeat, put in the meat as above.

timing for FAST ROASTING or 40 minutes if following the timing for SLOWER ROASTING. Spoon the wine over the beef once during this period.

Cream the butter and add the ingredients for the coating. Spread this over the top of the joint, press firmly against the flesh. Continue roasting as the timing on page 50, left. *Note:* If cooking a larger joint, increase the amount of coating.

Stuffed Topside

TRADITIONAL ROAST BEEF

The photograph on page 51 shows a traditional meal of roast rib of beef with Yorkshire Pudding.

In order to make a good pudding, the oven must be very hot. This means that whether you are following the FAST ROASTING or SLOWER ROASTING method, the oven temperature must be raised to a much higher setting.

If using FAST ROASTING, the higher setting for a relatively short time will not spoil the meat. However, if roasting the meat on the slower setting, it is a good idea to time the cooking so that you can remove the meat from the oven for the time needed to heat the fat for the Yorkshire pudding, and for the first 10 to 15 minutes cooking period. After this time, when the oven setting is lowered, the meat can be replaced in the oven.

TRADITIONAL YORKSHIRE PUDDING

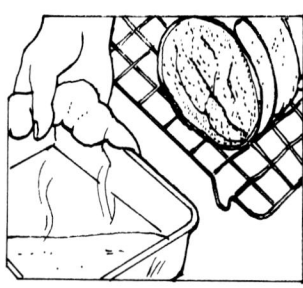 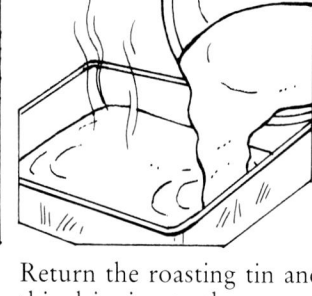

Set the oven to hot, 220°C/425°F Gas Mark 7. Take the roasting tin from the oven about 40 minutes before the end of the cooking time and remove the meat. Pour out all the dripping except approximately 2 tablespoons (3 tbsp).

Return the roasting tin and this dripping to the oven to get very hot. Pour the Yorkshire pudding batter into the tin.

 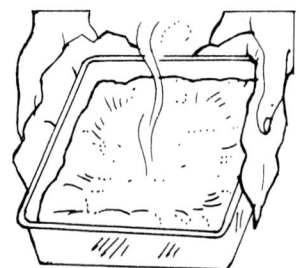

Place in the centre of the oven. Put the joint of beef on a rack or shelf above the pudding, so the drippings from the meat fall into the pudding as it cooks.

Bake the pudding until firm. This version does not rise as the pudding shown on page 51, but the flavour is delicious.

YORKSHIRE PUDDING

Cooking Time: see method   Serves 4–5   ❖❖

	Metric/Imperial	American
fat (shortening)	25 g/1 oz	2 tbsp
strong (hard wheat) or plain (all-purpose) flour	110 g/4 oz	1 cup
salt	pinch	pinch
egg	1	1
milk	300 ml/½ pint	1¼ cups

Set the oven to very hot, 230°C/450°F Gas Mark 8. Place the fat into the Yorkshire pudding tin or in individual tins and heat for 5 to 8 minutes. The fat and the tin(s) must be very hot.

Blend the ingredients together for the batter, as the method for Pancakes on page 130. Spoon or pour into the hot fat. Cook towards the top of the very hot oven. A large pudding takes approximately 30 minutes cooking time, but the heat should be reduced after approximately 10 to 15 minutes when the batter has risen well and is starting to brown. Reduce the setting to moderately hot, 190 to 200°C/375 to 400°F Gas Mark 5 to 6.

If cooking small individual puddings, the heat can be reduced after 8 to 10 minutes.

Serve the puddings as soon as cooked.

Note: It is believed by many people that a Yorkshire pudding rises better if the batter is made well in advance and kept in a cool place. Tests have proved that this is far less important than using the right kind of flour; making a batter of the correct consistency and cooking in a very hot oven.

VARIATIONS
Use exactly the same proportions as above, but cook the pudding in the 'old fashioned' way, shown in the line drawings.
● Use 2 eggs and deduct 2 tablespoons (3 tbsp) liquid from the 300 ml/½ pint (1¼ cups).

TO ROAST BACON
Bacon should look pleasantly moist, with clear reddish lean meat and firm white fat. Mildly cured bacon joints, which are considerably more popular these days than a few years ago, can be roasted quite satisfactorily without pre-boiling. Often in Britain these joints are known as 'green bacon' or 'sweet-cure bacon'.

More strongly flavoured bacon is better partially cooked in liquid, then roasted for a short time in the oven.

Very mild bacon does not need soaking before roasting. If in doubt as to how salt in flavour the meat will be, or when you know it has been well-smoked, it is essential to soak the joint in cold water to cover for several hours at least, for roasting retains more of the salt taste than when the bacon is cooked in liquid. Allow per person before cooking: approximately 225 g/8 oz (½ lb), for salted meats tend to shrink more than fresh meats in cooking.

Prime joints for cooking as above: Various cuts of gammon, back bacon joints. American joints are various cuts of smoked ham and Canadian style bacon.

Less expensive joints for cooking as above: Collar,

forehock and joints of streaky bacon. American joints are smoked picnic shoulder and smoked shoulder butt.

If roasting the bacon from the raw state, follow the timing for pork, below.

Recipes for partially-roast and roast bacon are on page 194.

TO ROAST VEAL

The lean of veal should be a very pale pink and the fat (of which there is little) firm and white. Allow per person before cooking: 175 to 225 g/6 to 8 oz (½ lb) if boned and 350 g/12 oz (¾ lb) on the bone.

Prime cuts for roasting: Fillet, leg, loin with chump end of loin, shoulder. American names similar but there are many different cuts from the leg and shoulder, including arm roast and blade roast.

More economical cuts for roasting: Breast and neck. American cuts, breast similar, although neck rarely considered a roasting joint.

FAST ROASTING: Follow the timing under roast pork above.

SLOWER ROASTING: Follow the timing under roast pork above.

Veal is an exceptionally lean meat and one that is inclined to dry in cooking. To prevent this, introduce extra fat in the form of very fat streaky bacon or belly of pork (fresh pork sides) and lard the meat, as the line drawings given on this page. It is also very wise to cook veal in a plastic roasting bag or a covered roasting tin or wrapped in foil.

Veal is generally stuffed, see the recipes on page 106 for Parsley and Thyme Stuffing or Veal Forcemeat, or the other stuffings on pages 105 and 106. It can be served with bacon rolls, sausages and a thickened gravy. Bread Sauce or Cranberry Sauce, pages 102 and 100, as served with chicken or turkey, are excellent accompaniments.

TO LARD VEAL

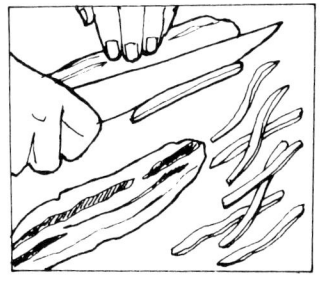

To 'lard' a joint of veal of approximately 1.3 to 1.8 kg/3 to 4 lb in weight, you need approximately 225 to 350 g/8 to 12 oz (½ to ¾ lb) fat belly of pork (fresh pork sides) or fat streaky bacon. Cut the meat into very narrow strips that will fit into the eye of a larding needle.

Note: A very lean joint of beef, such as topside (top round) or a joint of rump or fillet of beef, could be treated in the same way.

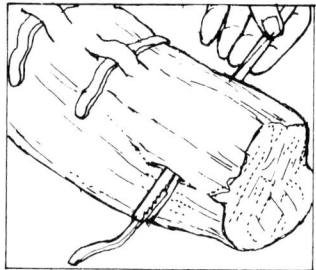
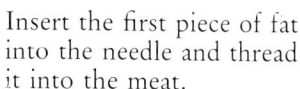
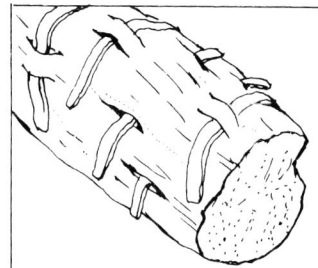

Insert the first piece of fat into the needle and thread it into the meat.

Continue like this at regular intervals so that the joint will be kept moist in cooking.

TO ROAST PORK

Pork should have firm very pale pink lean and firm white fat. Allow per person before cooking: 175 to 225 g/6 to 8 oz (½ lb) if boned and 350 g/12 oz (¾ lb) on the bone.

Prime cuts for roasting: Leg or part of the leg, loin and spare rib. American names, fresh ham (not leg), spare ribs are often called barbecue ribs.

More economical cuts for roasting: Blade, hand and spring. American cuts, Boston butt, fresh picnic roast. It is essential that pork is adequately cooked, so do not reduce the following cooking times.

FAST ROASTING: Allow 25 mintues per 450 g/1 lb and 25 minutes over at 200 to 220°C/400 to 425°F, Gas Mark 6 to 7. After one hour's cooking the heat can be reduced slightly to 190 to 200°C/375 to 400°F, Gas Mark 5 to 6.

SLOWER ROASTING: Allow 40 minutes per 450 g/1 lb and 40 minutes over at 160 to 180°C/325 to 350°F, Gas Mark 3 to 4.

As the fat of pork needs to become crisp, it is not advisable to cover the meat during roasting. It is a good idea to stand pork on a rack in the roasting tin.

There is no need to add extra fat when roasting pork, but in order to achieve good 'crackling' (crispness of the fat), the rind should be cut away and the fat 'chined', i.e. cut deeply at regular intervals and to a good depth. Brush the fat with a little melted lard or with oil before cooking. A light sprinkling of salt also encourages crisping, but this may not be popular with everyone.

If pork has been frozen then defrosted, wipe the fat very well with absorbent paper (kitchen towels). Roast for 20 to 30 minutes, then remove from the oven and blot dry again. Brush the fat with the melted lard or oil and sprinkle with salt. In this way, any surplus moisture from the defrosted meat runs out and encourages good crackling, often a problem with frozen pork.

A stuffing is generally considered an asset with roast pork. The most usual stuffing being Sage and Onion, but there are two suggestions for newer ideas on pages 55, 62, 105 and 106. Loin of pork can be boned and rolled or turned into a crown, as shown under lamb on page 55.

Serve roast pork with Sage and Onion Stuffing or any of the stuffings on pages 105 and 106, and Apple Sauce or Cranberry and Apple Sauce or Orange Sauce, as the recipes on pages 98, 99, 100 and 101, and with a thickened gravy.

TO ROAST LAMB

Choose lamb that is pale pink with firm transparent fat. Mutton is becoming increasingly difficult to obtain; it is darker in colour than lamb, stronger in flavour and takes a little longer to cook. Allow per person before cooking: 175 to 225 g/6 to 8 oz (½ lb) if boned and 350 g/12 oz (¾ lb) on the bone.

Prime cuts for roasting: Best end of neck, leg (in Scotland known as gigot), loin, saddle (a double loin) and shoulder. American names similar, but there are many different cuts from both the leg and shoulder.

More economical cuts for roasting: Breast. American name similar.

FAST ROASTING: Allow 20 minutes per 450 g/1 lb and 20 minutes over (if you like lamb pink, reduce this timing very slightly) at 200 to 220°C/400 to 425°F, Gas Mark 6 to 7. After one hour's cooking, the temperature can be reduced slightly to 190 to 200°C/375 to 400°F, Gas Mark 5 to 6.

SLOWER ROASTING: Allow 35 minutes per 450 g/1 lb and 35 minutes over at 160 to 180°C/325 to 350°F, Gas Mark 3 to 4. It is less easy to have pink (undercooked) lamb at this setting.

Extra fat is rarely necessary when roasting lamb, unless it is exceptionally lean. It is usual to stuff boned breast of lamb, for a stuffing helps to counteract the fairly high fat content of this joint. The leg, shoulder and loin of lamb can be boned and stuffed. A crown is one of the most impressive joints, see page 56 and page 55 for Walnut and Raisin Crown.

There are a variety of stuffings, many of which are suitable for lamb, in the chapter that begins on page 98.

Serve roast lamb with Mint Sauce, recipe on page 107, or the less usual Cucumber Sauce on page 101. Serve roast mutton with redcurrant jelly or Onion Sauce, as page 102. These meats are served with a thin gravy except when stuffed where a thicker gravy is a better accompaniment.

Lamb in Honey and Orange

Piquant Pork

LAMB IN HONEY AND CIDER

Cooking Time: as left   Serves 6   **

	Metric/Imperial	American
leg or shoulder of lamb, as left		
dry or sweet cider, depending on personal taste	300 ml/½ pint	1¼ cups
thin honey	2–3 tbsp	3–4 tbsp

Roast the lamb as in the method left. Remove the roasting tin from the oven 30 minutes before the end of the cooking time if using the higher setting, i.e. FAST ROASTING, or 40 minutes if using the lower setting, i.e. SLOWER ROASTING.

Lift the meat out of the tin, pour away the dripping from the tin. Return the meat to the tin. Make neat cuts in the skin of the lamb. Spoon the cider over the meat then spread with the honey.

Return the meat to the oven and continue to cook. Baste twice with the cider in the tin. Add all or part of the cider and honey to the gravy to serve with the meat.

VARIATION

Lamb in Honey and Orange: Omit the cider in the recipe above. Remove the peel from 2 oranges and cut into matchstick pieces. Simmer in water until tender. Heat 4 tablespoons (5 tbsp) orange juice with the honey and a few sprigs of fresh thyme. Brush over the joint before and during roasting, and just before serving. Garnish the joint with the well-drained orange rind.

PIQUANT PORK

Cooking Time: see page 53   Serves 6–8   ❊❊

	Metric/Imperial	American
joint of pork, see page 53	1.3 kg/3 lb	3 lb
For the sauce: orange marmalade	3 tbsp	4 tbsp
orange juice	3 tbsp	4 tbsp
Worcestershire sauce	1 teasp	1 teasp
garlic cloves, crushed	1–2	1–2
To garnish: orange slices	6–8	6–8
watercress	few sprigs	few sprigs

Roast the pork as the timing on page 53. Bring the meat out of the oven 20 minutes before the end of the cooking time if following the timing for FAST ROASTING or 30 minutes for SLOWER ROASTING. Lift the meat from the tin and pour out all the dripping.

Heat the marmalade with the orange juice, Worcestershire sauce and garlic. Return the meat to the tin and spoon the sauce over all sides of the meat. Return to the oven and complete the cooking. Baste once with the marmalade mixture. Lift the pork on to a heated meat dish and garnish with the orange slices and the watercress. Add 2 to 3 tablespoons of the sweet mixture left in the roasting tin to the gravy served with the meat.

WALNUT AND RAISIN CROWN

Cooking Time: as page 54   Serves 6–7   ❊❊

	Metric/Imperial	American
crown of lamb, see page 56 consisting of	12–14 chops	12–14 chops
For the stuffing: seedless raisins	100 g/4 oz	¾ cup
grated lemon rind	1 teasp	1 teasp
lemon juice	1 tbsp	1 tbsp
grated orange rind	2 teasp	2 teasp
orange juice	2 tbsp	3 tbsp
walnut halves, chopped	100 g/4 oz	1 cup
celery stalks, finely chopped	3	3
soft breadcrumbs	100 g/4 oz	2 cups
butter or margarine	50 g/2 oz	¼ cup
salt and pepper	to taste	to taste
egg	1	1
To garnish: orange(s)	1–2	1–2
seedless raisins	2 teasp	2 teasp
walnut halves	8–10	8–10

Walnut and Raisin Crown

Prepare the meat as page 56. Put the raisins into a bowl, add the fruit rinds and juice. Allow to stand for 30 minutes. Blend in the nuts, celery and breadcrumbs. Melt the butter or margarine, add to the other ingredients with seasoning and the egg. Stir briskly to bind, then spoon into the centre of the crown. Protect the top of the stuffing with foil or the fat removed from the ends of the bones. Put foil round the bones, so they do not burn in cooking. Roast as the instructions on page 54, left. Remove the covering over the stuffing for the last 30 to 45 minutes cooking time, so the stuffing becomes a pleasing golden colour.

When cooked, lift carefully on to a heated meat dish. Remove the foil from the bones and top with cutlet frills.

Cut away the peel from the orange(s) and cut out the segments. Arrange on top of the stuffing then put the raisins and walnuts between the orange segments.

Flavour the accompanying gravy with a little lemon and orange juice.

VARIATIONS
This stuffing blends well with a crown of pork, or replace the chopped celery with 3 peeled and diced dessert apples – these keep a better shape in cooking than cooking (baking) apples.
● *Spring Crown of Lamb:* When vegetables are young and tender, omit the stuffing. Cook the crown and fill with young vegetables.

CROWN ROAST

Lamb or pork can be formed into a circle known as a 'crown'. Choose lean loin chops or best end of neck of lamb. A minimum of 12 chops and preferably more, are required to make a good round. A butcher will prepare this, if given sufficient notice, but it is not difficult to do it at home. The photograph on page 55 shows a cooked Crown of Lamb.

TO PREPARE A CROWN ROAST

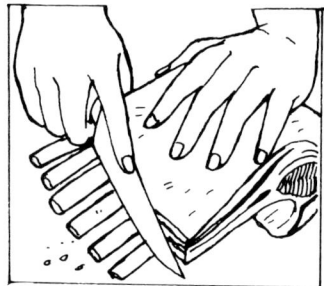

Trim the fat from the ends of the bones from the loin joint of 2 joints of best end of neck of lamb.

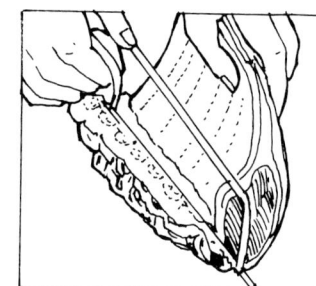

Chine (Cut) between the chops at the other end of the joint(s) so the meat can be made into the round (called a crown).

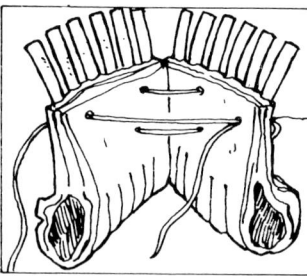

The sides of the loin of pork or lamb should be joined. Use a trussing needle and fine string. If using 2 joints of best end of neck of lamb, you will need 2 joins.

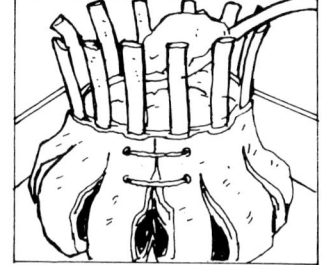

Put into the roasting tin, add the stuffing to the centre cavity, cover this with foil or the fat removed from the ends of the chops.

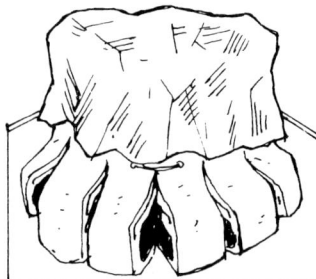

Protect the ends of the bones with foil. Roast as the timing on page 53 and 54, calculating the weight of the meat plus the stuffing.
Put the meat on to the serving plates. Spoon out portions of stuffing.

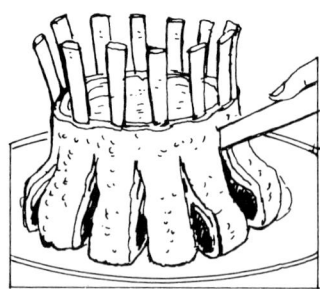

To Serve a Crown Roast: Slice the meat downwards give each person 2–3 cutlets.

ROAST VEAL IN CREAM

Cooking Time: as page 53   Serves 6   ❋❋

	Metric/Imperial	American
fillet of veal, larded as page 53	1.3 kg/3 lb	3 lb
For the coating: finely grated lemon rind	2 teasp	2 teasp
paprika	1 teasp	1 teasp
flour	1 tbsp	1 tbsp
double (heavy) cream	150 ml/¼ pint	⅔ cup
salt and pepper	to taste	to taste

Roast the veal as the timing on page 53. Bring the meat out of the oven 20 minutes before the end of the cooking time if following timing for FAST ROASTING or 30 minutes for SLOWER ROASTING. If roasting in a roasting bag or in foil, carefully remove the hot meat from the bag or foil and place it into a roasting tin or casserole.

Pour out the dripping from the bag or foil or the roasting tin. Blend 1 tablespoon of this hot dripping with the ingredients for the coating. Spoon this over the veal and complete the cooking in an uncovered container. Spoon the cream mixture over the veal once again before the end of the cooking period. Strain any liquid from the roasting tin into the gravy served with the veal.

This dish is delicious with new potatoes, young peas and baby carrots.

Roasting with a Meat Thermometer
Insert the thermometer into the centre of the joint; take care to avoid any bones. Cook the meat until the following temperatures are reached:

Beef: very rare to rare 60 to 66°C/140 to 150°F
        medium 71°C/160°F
        well-cooked (which many people consider is spoiled beef) up to 76°/170°F
Lamb: slightly undercooked (pink) 76°/170°F
        well-cooked 82°C/180°F
Bacon, pork and veal: must always be well-cooked and the thermometer should register 88°C/190°F.

TO FRY AND GRILL MEAT
Frying and grilling (broiling) are speedy cooking processes and it is important to choose prime cuts of meat. Tougher meat will not be tenderized in the short time, this needs longer slower heating.

Frozen meat can be fried or grilled without defrosting, providing it does not need coating or marinating.

BEEF FOR FRYING AND GRILLING
There is a wide choice of steaks.
Entrecôte steak: A cut from between the ribs.
Fillet steak: The most tender of all steaks. The narrow end of the fillet is used for tournedos (neat rounds of steak) or for filet mignon or medallion steaks.

Châteaubriand, the large steak that can weigh up to 550 g/1¼ lb and when sliced serves 2 to 3 people, is cut from the thickened end of the fillet.
Minute steak: Very thin slices from the rump or occasionally from the sirloin. As the name indicates, this steak is cooked within 1 to 2 minutes.

Porterhouse steak: A thick steak rather like sirloin, but including some fillet.

Rump steak: A firmer meat than fillet, but excellent flavour; the point of rump being the best part.

Sirloin steak: Slices of sirloin which gives a good blending of lean and fat.

T-bone steak: The end of the sirloin near the bone giving a T-shape, flavour as sirloin steak.

TO FRY STEAKS: Add any flavouring required to the meat, such as seasoning or crushed peppercorns or spread the meat with a little made English mustard.

Heat approximately 75 g/3 oz (6 tbsp) butter in a large frying pan (skillet). (Instead of butter, you could use 2 to 3 tablespoons (3 to 4 tbsp) best quality oil.) Put in 4 steaks and fry rapidly on either side, then lower the heat and cook to personal taste. To cook a steak of approximately 2.5 cm/1 inch in thickness, allow a total cooking time of:

  6 minutes for rare (underdone) steaks
  8 minutes for medium-cooked steaks
  10 minutes for well-cooked steaks.

Steak should be served as soon as it is cooked. If frying mushrooms or other vegetables, cook these with the steaks. In the case of onions, fry them in a separate pan or begin cooking before adding the steaks, see the photograph on page 58.

TO GRILL STEAKS: Add any flavouring required, see under 'To fry steaks', or marinate the meat.

An easy marinade for 4 steaks is made by blending 4 tablespoons (5 tbsp) red wine, 2 tablespoons (3 tbsp) olive oil, 1 crushed garlic clove, 1 teaspoon chopped tarragon and a little salt and pepper. Leave the steaks in the marinade for 30 minutes, drain and grill (broil) as below.

Always preheat the grill (broiler) before cooking the meat. A charcoal grill should be glowing red. Brush the steaks with melted butter, use approximately 40 g/1½ oz (3 tbsp) for 4 steaks. Grill rapidly for 2 minutes, turn and brush with more butter and continue cooking to personal taste. The cooking times are similar to those for frying meat.

Grilled steak can be served with Herb Butter or Lemon Butter, both recipes on page 177, or topped with Béarnaise Sauce, page 171. Grilled tomatoes and/or mushrooms are a usual addition to the meat.

Fried potatoes and cooked vegetables or a green salad are excellent accompaniments to fried or grilled steak.

BEEF COLLOPS

Illustrated in colour on page 214

Cooking Time: 10–15 minutes   Serves 4   ❖❖

	Metric/Imperial	American
fillet of rump steak, thinly sliced	550 g/1¼ lb	1¼ lb
Madeira or red wine	4 tbsp	5 tbsp
medium onions, finely chopped	3	3
butter	25 g/1 oz	2 tbsp
oil	2 tbsp	3 tbsp
pickled walnuts, sliced	4	4
liquor from jar of walnuts, see method		
salt and pepper	to taste	to taste

Cut the thin pieces of steak into small neat pieces, as described on page 63. Pour the wine into a dish, add the steak and 1 tablespoon of the chopped onion. Allow the meat to marinate for 1 hour. Remove from the wine and drain well. Retain any wine left.

Heat the butter in a large frying pan (skillet) and fry the rest of the chopped onions until golden in colour and tender; remove on to a heated dish. Add the oil to the pan and fry the steaks to personal taste. i.e. for 5 to 10 minutes. Place the meat on top of the onions. Pour the remaining wine into the pan, add the pickled walnuts, liquor from the jar and salt and pepper to taste. Heat for a minute, spoon over the steaks and serve.

TOURNEDOS

There are innumerable toppings for tournedos (fillet steak tied to make rounds). The tournedos are generally served on rounds of fried bread. Here are 4 interesting ways to serve grilled or fried tournedos.

TOURNEDOS BÉARNAISE	TOURNEDOS WITH OYSTERS	TOURNEDOS ROSSINI	TOURNEDOS AFRICAINE

Top the tournedos with Béarnaise Sauce, as page 171.

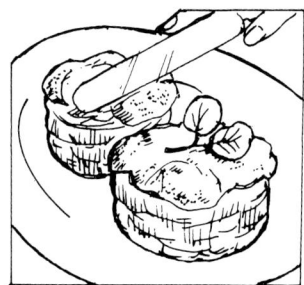

Top each tournedos with fried oysters (mussels could be substituted).

Top each tournedos with liver pâté.

Top the tournedos with Horseradish Cream, page 103, and fried banana halves.

MIXED GRILL

Cook a good variety of ingredients to make an interesting mixed grill (broil). Include lamb chops or cutlets and/or steak, lambs' kidneys, bacon rashers (slices) and sausages. If you are fond of liver, add slices of calves' or lambs' liver. Keep these slices particularly well basted with melted butter or oil during the grilling (broiling) period. Other ingredients that frequently form part of the grill are grilled mushrooms and tomatoes and fried eggs.

Arrange the ingredients in the order of cooking, and calculate carefully the cooking time of each meat or other food. Start grilling the chops, or whatever meat takes the longest time, then add the other ingredients gradually. In this way all the ingredients are cooked and ready to serve together. If your grill (broiler) will not accommodate all the food, cook those meats that can be kept for a short standing time. Place them on a very hot dish and keep hot while ingredients such as liver and bacon, which spoil with standing, are cooked.

Always brush the food with melted butter or oil before and during cooking. This is particularly important when cooking liver, as mentioned above, but also for kidneys, steak and mushrooms.

Serve a mixed grill with a garnish of watercress. The lean meats, such as steak and/or liver, can be topped with Herb Butter, see page 177. Fried potatoes and a green vegetable or a green salad are pleasant accompaniments.

SAVOURY STEAKS

Cooking Time: 15 minutes   Serves 4   ❋❋

	Metric/Imperial	American
fillet or rump steaks	4	4
small button mushrooms	100 g/4 oz	¼ lb
butter	100 g/4 oz	½ cup
medium onions, sliced and separated into rings	2–3	2–3
beef stock	300 ml/½ pint	1¼ cups
chopped parsley	2 teasp	2 teasp
chopped thyme	½ teasp	½ teasp
chopped sage	¼ teasp	¼ teasp
capers	2 teasp	2 teasp
salt and pepper	to taste	to taste
eggs	4	4
To garnish: watercress	few sprigs	few sprigs

Tie fillet steaks into neat rounds; make rump steaks into the neatest shapes possible. Remove the stalks from the mushrooms, chop the stalks finely. Heat the butter in a large frying pan (skillet) and fry the onions, mushrooms and mushroom stalks for 4 minutes. Add the steaks and fry for 2 minutes on either side. Add the stock, herbs and capers with a little seasoning and simmer for 10 minutes. Lift the steaks on to a heated serving dish; keep hot.

Break the eggs into the liquid remaining in the pan

BACON IN WHISKEY AND CREAM

Cooking Time: 20–25 minutes Serves 4 ❖❖❖

As one might imagine, whiskey is used in Irish cooking to give flavour in casserole dishes. The bacon must be lean otherwise the dish is over-rich. If preferred, slices of uncooked ham may be substituted for the bacon.

	Metric/Imperial	American
For the potato garnish: potatoes, weight when peeled	450 g/1 lb	1 lb
salt and pepper	to taste	to taste
butter	25 g/1 oz	2 tbsp
egg yolk	1	1
For the bacon mixture: lean gammon (ham) slices	4	4
flour	25 g/1 oz	¼ cup
medium cooking (baking) apples, peeled, cored and thinly sliced	2	2
brown sugar	1 tbsp	1 tbsp
butter	50 g/2 oz	¼ cup
brown stock	150 ml/¼ pint	⅔ cup
Irish whiskey	150 ml/¼ pint	⅔ cup
double (heavy) cream	4 tbsp	5 tbsp
egg white	1	1

Cook the potatoes in salted water until tender. Strain, mash and season well, then beat in the butter and yolk.

Cut the rind from each gammon (ham) slice, then coat in the flour and pepper. Coat the apples in the brown sugar. Heat the butter in a large frying pan (skillet) and cook the gammon steadily for 5 to 6 minutes on either side until tender. Do not let the outside become hard. Lift out on to a heated dish. Add the stock and whiskey to the pan and heat together for a few minutes. Put in the sliced apples and simmer gently for 5 minutes. Add the cream to the dish, stir well – do not boil. Return the pieces of gammon to the sauce.

Pipe the potatoes in a border around the edge of a flameproof meat dish, brush with the unbeaten egg white and brown under the grill (broiler). Arrange the bacon and apple rings in the centre of the potato border and coat with sauce.

Above: Mixed Grill. Below left: Fried Steak with Onions – see page 57. Below right: Bacon in Whiskey and Cream

and poach until set. Place the eggs on top of the steaks. Spoon the sauce and mushrooms around. Garnish with watercress.

SHERRIED PORK

Cooking Time: 30 minutes   Serves 4 ❉

	Metric/Imperial	American
pork chops	4	4
sweet sherry	150 ml/¼ pint	⅔ cup
medium onion, finely chopped	1	1
garlic clove, crushed	1	1
flour	25 g/1 oz	¼ cup
very finely chopped sage	1 teasp	1 teasp
very finely chopped tarragon	1 teasp	1 teasp
salt and pepper	to taste	to taste
oil, optional, see method	1 tbsp	1 tbsp

Cut away all the surplus fat from the pork chops, retain this fat. Place the sherry, onion and garlic into a shallow dish. Add the chops, leave to marinate for 30 minutes minutes. Turn them over and leave for another 30 minutes.

Lift the chops out of the remaining sherry, drain well, but do not dry on absorbent paper (kitchen towels). Mix the flour with the chopped herbs and a little salt and pepper and coat the chops. Retain the sherry marinade.

Heat the pork fat (cut away from the chops) in a large frying pan (skillet). If insufficient fat runs out, add and heat the oil. Put in the chops and cook until brown on either side. Place them into an ovenproof dish. Strain the remaining sherry over the chops.

Bake just above the centre of a moderately hot oven, 190 to 200°C/375 to 400°F Gas Mark 5 to 6, for 15 to 20 minutes or until tender. Serve with Apple or Cranberry Sauce, recipe pages 98 and 100.

VARIATIONS
Devonshire Pork: Substitute sweet cider or sweetened apple juice for the sherry.
● *Jamaican Pork:* Substitute sweetened pineapple juice for the sherry. You can add a few drops of rum for extra flavour.

LAMB FOR FRYING AND GRILLING
Choose lamb chops from the best end of neck, from the loin, or chump chops from the end of the loin. Mutton is generally rather too tough to fry or grill (broil).

Slices from the top of the leg, called the fillet part of the leg, can be fried as escalopes.

Cutlets are made by cutting away any excess fat from the ends of the bones of the chops, generally those from the best end of the neck.

If you want to get rid of the bones, turn the meat into noisettes as the line drawings, right.
TO FRY LAMB: Add any flavouring required; two recipes are on the next pages.

Finely chopped rosemary or tarragon leaves can be pressed into the meat before cooking, or halve garlic cloves and rub the cut end over the meat.

Although lamb chops have a good proportion of fat, cutlets and escalopes of lamb are very lean so approximately 50 g/2 oz (¼ cup) of butter should be

TO BONE AND ROLL LAMB CHOPS

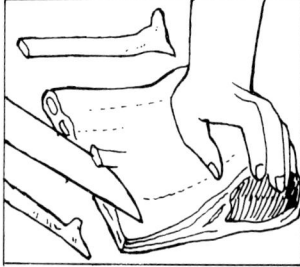
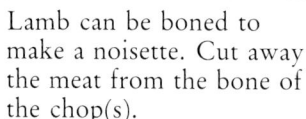

Lamb can be boned to make a noisette. Cut away the meat from the bone of the chop(s).

Cut off any *surplus* fat, leaving the lean meat with a very little fat to keep it moist.

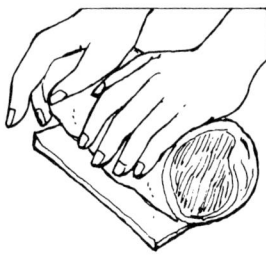

Roll the meat into a neat round and secure with fine string or a wooden cocktail stick (toothpick).

If making a number of noisettes, bone and roll the whole joint of best end of neck or loin. Cut noisettes of required thickness.

allowed for 6 to 8 cutlets or 4 escalopes of lamb. The butter should be heated in the frying pan (skillet) before adding the meat. The average cooking time for tender lamb chops of about 2 to 2.5 cm/¾ to 1 inch in thickness will be approximately 10 to 12 minutes. Cook the meat rapidly on either side then lower the heat and cook more slowly.
TO GRILL LAMB: Add any flavouring required, see under 'To fry lamb'. Preheat the grill (broiler). Always brush lean lamb with a little melted butter or oil before cooking and after turning the meat over. Cook quickly on both sides, then lower the heat and continue cooking. Allow the same time as when frying.

Serve fried or grilled lamb with Herb Butter, page 177, or Paloise Sauce or a Cucumber Sauce, pages 173 and 101, and with mixed vegetables.

Gingered Lamb Chops

Cooking Time: 45 minutes   Serves 4   ❊

	Metric/Imperial	American
small lamb chops	8	8
flour	1 tbsp	1 tbsp
eggs	2	2
milk	300 ml/½ pint	1¼ cups
salt and pepper	to taste	to taste
ground ginger	1 teasp	1 teasp

Ask the butcher to bone the chops and turn them into rounds; these are called noisettes. If he cannot, follow the stages given on page 60.

Place the lamb chops in a shallow casserole or ovenproof serving dish. Cook towards the top of a moderately hot oven, 200°C/400°F Gas Mark 6, for 15 minutes. At the end of this time, most of the fat should have run from the lamb and the meat should be a pleasant colour.

Lift the noisettes out of the dish, pour out any fat then return the meat to the dish. Beat the flour and eggs. Warm the milk, whisk on to the eggs, add a little seasoning and the ginger. Pour this custard over the meat.

Lower the heat to very moderate, 160°C/325°F Gas Mark 3. Cook the dish in the centre of the oven for 30 minutes, by which time the meat should be tender and the egg custard lightly set.

PORK FOR FRYING AND GRILLING
Choose chops from the loin, spare ribs, chump chops or slices from the fillet end of the fillet (tenderloin).

Good pork from the fillet can be surprisingly lean and it should be kept well moistened with butter or oil in cooking.

The pork can be coated with a little seasoned flour, beaten egg and breadcrumbs before frying.

TO FRY PORK: Cut the fat of chops at regular 1.5cm/½ inch intervals to encourage it to become crisp. Grease the frying pan (skillet) with a little oil or butter if the chops have a fair amount of fat. When cooking very lean chops or cutlets, heat approximately 40 g/1½ oz (3 tbsp) butter or oil for 4 chops, then put in the meat. The cooking time for chops of about 2 cm/¾ inch in thickness will be approximately 15 to 18 minutes.

To fry thin slices of pork fillet, allow approximately 50 g/2 oz (¼ cup) butter for 4 escalopes and 12 to 15 minutes cooking time.

TO GRILL PORK: Add any flavouring required; this is not essential as pork has a very definite taste, but a light sprinkling of apple or orange juice is very pleasant. Preheat the grill (broiler). Brush the lean part of the meat with a very little melted butter or oil. Chopped fresh sage or tarragon can be added to the butter or oil. Cook the pork rapidly for 3 to 4 minutes, turn the meat over and brush the lean with a little more butter or oil and continue cooking. Allow the same cooking time as for frying.

Serve fried or grilled pork with cooked apple, pineapple slices or heated prunes and mixed vegetables or a salad.

BACON FOR FRYING AND GRILLING
While thin bacon rashers (slices) are a favourite breakfast or supper dish or an accompaniment to eggs, sausages and other foods, it is usual to choose thicker bacon slices as a main dish meal.

Choose gammon (ham) slices or thick back bacon rashers (Canadian bacon slices).

Always slit the fat, as suggested under pork, so this will become crisp.

TO FRY BACON: Gammon is very lean and a little butter will be necessary when frying this. Allow 40 to 50 g/1½ to 2 oz (3 to 4 tbsp) butter for 4 gammon slices. Melt the butter, but do not allow it to become too hot, then cook the gammon. The cooking time for slices of between 1.5 to 2 cm/½ to ¾ inch in thickness will be approximately 12 minutes. Bacon chops, the name given to thick back bacon rashers, have a good proportion of fat so place these into a cold frying pan (skillet) and cook steadily until tender. The timing will be as above.

TO GRILL BACON: Do not preheat the grill (broiler). Heat this as the gammon or bacon is placed under it. Brush gammon very well with melted butter before and during cooking. The timing is similar to that for frying.

Serve fried or grilled bacon with fried or grilled tomatoes and mushrooms, with fried or grilled apple, or pineapple slices or other hot fruit. Serve with fried potatoes and mixed vegetables or salad.

VEAL FOR FRYING AND GRILLING
Choose chops from the loin or make these into cutlets. The most popular cuts of veal for frying are slices from the leg, called escalopes (cutlets) or fillets of veal. These slices can be cooked without a coating as in Collops, page 63, or coated as in the recipe for Veal with Croûtons, page 62.

TO FRY VEAL: Allow approximately 75 to 100 g/3 to 4 oz (scant ⅓ to ½ cup) butter when cooking veal or use a mixture of butter and oil. The total cooking time for veal is similar to that of pork, i.e. approximately 15 to 18 minutes for chops and 12 to 15 minutes for fillets of veal, according to the thickness of the meat. The veal, or the butter in which it is fried, can be flavoured with a little lemon juice or with chopped rosemary or other fresh herbs.

TO GRILL VEAL: The secret of good grilled (broiled) veal is to brush the meat with plenty of melted butter, or butter and oil, before cooking and during the cooking process.

The meat can be flavoured, as suggested under 'To fry veal'. The cooking time for grilling veal is similar to frying veal.

Serve fried or grilled veal with lemon slices or with a Béarnaise Sauce or Tangy Lemon Sauce as pages 171 and 100.

VEAL WITH CROÛTONS

Cooking Time: 25 minutes   Serves 4   ❀❀

This dish gives an interesting contrast in textures. The outside of the veal is crisp, the veal soft and moist and the filling crisp again.

	Metric/Imperial	American
For the stuffing: slices of bread	2	2
butter	50 g/2 oz	¼ cup
medium onion, finely chopped	1	1
mushrooms, finely chopped	100 g/4 oz	¼ lb
chopped parsley	1 tbsp	1 tbsp
salt and pepper	to taste	to taste
veal escalopes (cut from the leg)	4	4
To coat: flour	25 g/1 oz	¼ cup
egg	1	1
crisp breadcrumbs	50 g/2 oz	½ cup
To fry: oil	2 tbsp	3 tbsp
butter	25 g/1 oz	2 tbsp
To garnish: lemon slices	4	4
watercress		

Cut the crusts off the bread, then cut the slices into very small dice. Heat half the butter for the stuffing in a frying pan (skillet) and fry the bread dice until crisp and golden brown. Remove from the pan. Heat the remaining butter for the stuffing and fry the onion and mushrooms for a few minutes. Add the parsley, seasoning and the fried bread croûtons.

Flatten the slices of veal to make them as large and thin as possible; do this by hitting with a rolling pin over waxed paper. Place the stuffing on half of each veal slice, then fold the remaining veal over the filling to cover.

Mix a little salt and pepper with the flour, coat the veal in the seasoned flour. Beat the egg and brush over both sides of the veal, then coat in the crisp breadcrumbs. Do this very carefully so the filling does not fall out.

Heat the oil and butter in a large frying pan and fry the veal quickly on one side until crisp and brown. Very carefully turn the veal slices and brown on the second side. Lower the heat and cook more slowly until tender. The total frying time is approximately 12 minutes. Drain on absorbent paper (kitchen towels). Garnish with lemon slices and watercress.

Above: Spiced Lamb Cutlets. Right: Veal with Croûtons

COLLOPS

Cooking Time: 40 minutes Serves 4 ❊❊

The word 'collops', so familiar to Scottish cooks, is probably an adaptation of the French escallops and is often used to describe small pieces of meat. It is also used for one of the most popular and economical of Scottish meat dishes, a savoury stew made with minced beef called Mince Collops. Here, however, is a rather more luxurious and older version of collops which has a marked resemblance to the Viennese 'schnitzel'.

	Metric/Imperial	American
veal or lamb or venison fillets or thin slices of fillet or rump steak	4	4
salt and pepper	to taste	to taste
grated nutmeg	to taste	to taste
chopped fresh herbs	1 teasp	1 teasp
grated lemon rind	1 teasp	1 teasp
lemon juice	1 tbsp	1 tbsp
small globe artichokes	4–8	4–8
For the forcemeat: soft breadcrumbs	100 g/4 oz	2 cups
shredded suet	50 g/2 oz	½ cup
mustard pickle, finely chopped	1 tbsp	1 tbsp
capers	2 teasp	2 teasp
small onion, finely grated	1	1
egg	1	1
To fry and for the sauce: butter	100 g/4 oz	½ cup
small button mushrooms	100 g/4 oz	¼ lb
red or white wine	150 ml/¼ pint	²/₃ cup

Form the meat into neat rounds; if the slices are rather large, cut into smaller pieces so each person has 2 to 3 smaller collops. Season the meat lightly and flavour each side with the nutmeg, herbs, lemon rind and juice. Allow to stand for at least 30 minutes.

Meanwhile, prepare and cook the globe artichokes in boiling salted water, as described on page 108. Remove the leaves and choke from the cooked artichokes. Put the artichoke bottoms on one side to heat again.

While the artichokes are cooking, mix together all the ingredients for the forcemeat. Form into 4 to 8 small rounds. Heat 25 g/1 oz (2 tbsp) of the butter in a large frying pan (skillet) and fry the forcemeat patties for 10 minutes. Lift out of the pan and place on a large heated dish; cover with foil and keep hot.

Heat the remaining butter in the frying pan, put in the meat with the mushrooms and fry for 5 minutes. Turn and cook on the second side for a further 5 minutes or until tender. Add the artichoke bottoms just before the meat is cooked.

Arrange the meat collops on the dish with the forcemeat patties, add the mushrooms and artichokes. Pour the wine into the frying pan, stir well to absorb all the meat juices. Heat for 1 to 2 minutes then spoon over the meat.

SPICED LAMB CUTLETS

Cooking Time: 10 minutes Serves 2–3 ❊❊

	Metric/Imperial	American
lamb cutlets	6	6
For the marinade: garlic cloves, crushed	2	2
chopped mint	1 teasp	1 teasp
allspice	1 teasp	1 teasp
ground cinnamon	½ teasp	½ teasp
oil	2 tbsp	3 tbsp
white wine vinegar	2 tbsp	3 tbsp
brown sugar	2 teasp	2 teasp
salt and pepper	to taste	to taste
To garnish: tomato wedges	6–8	6–8
watercress		

Defrost the cutlets if they have been frozen and dry well with absorbent paper (kitchen towels). Mix all the ingredients together for the marinade, pour into a long shallow dish. Add the cutlets and allow to stand in the mixture for 1 hour; turn over at the end of 30 minutes.

Lift the meat from the marinade, hold over the container for a minute so any excess liquid drops off the meat. Grill (broil) the cutlets as described on page 60. Add the tomato wedges to the grill for the last 2 to 3 minutes of the cooking time, if liked. Put cutlet frills on to the ends of the cutlets. Place on a heated dish, garnish with the tomato and watercress. Serve with fried potatoes.

TO USE MINCED MEAT

Minced (ground) meat can be made into a variety of interesting dishes. Always use minced uncooked or cooked meat quickly, for the cut surfaces cause rapid deterioration.

When heating cooked minced meat, take care the mixture containing the meat is heated thoroughly, but do not overcook the meat for it loses both texture and taste.

Some dishes made with minced meat are fried, as the Patties and Rissoles on the opposite page. Make sure these are cooked rapidly to give a crisp coating on the outside and keep the centres pleasantly moist.

GLAZED MEAT ROLL

Cooking Time: 1¼ hours   Serves 4–6 ❖

	Metric/Imperial	American
carrots, sliced	450 g/1 lb	1 lb
salt and pepper	to taste	to taste
butter or margarine	50 g/2 oz	¼ cup
medium onions, finely chopped	2	2
chopped parsley	2 tbsp	3 tbsp
chopped thyme	1 teasp	1 teasp
uncooked topside of beef (top round), minced (ground)	350 g/12 oz	¾ lb
belly of pork (fresh pork sides) or streaky bacon rashers (slices), minced (ground)	100 g/4 oz	¼ lb
soft breadcrumbs	50 g/2 oz	1 cup
egg	1	1
milk	2 tbsp	3 tbsp
To glaze: tomato ketchup (catsup)	3 tbsp	4 tbsp
brown sugar	2 teasp	2 teasp
made English or French mustard	1 teasp	1 teasp

Cook the carrots in boiling salted water until tender. Strain and mash. Heat the butter or margarine in a frying pan (skillet) and fry the onions until soft. Add half the onions with half the parsley and thyme and seasoning to the mashed carrots.

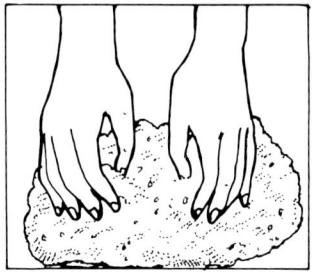

Blend the remaining onion and herbs with the minced meats. Add the breadcrumbs, egg, milk and seasoning. Knead well.

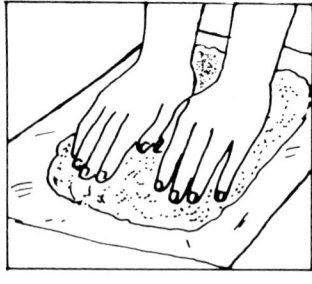

Place a sheet of waxed or greaseproof paper on to a board. Press the meat mixture over the paper.

Cover with a second sheet of waxed or greaseproof paper and roll out to a neat oblong.

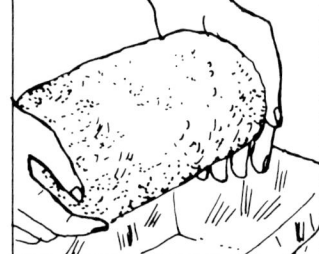

Top with the carrot mixture, then roll like a Swiss roll. Place into a tin or dish lined with greased foil.

Blend the ingredients for the glaze together, brush over the roll. Bake in the centre of a moderate oven, 180°C/350°F Gas Mark 4, for 50 minutes.

RISSOLES

These savoury cakes, which can be made with most cooked meats, poultry or game, are very similar to the French 'Croquettes'. If well made, the outside should be golden brown and crisp, and the centre moist and full of flavour. The secret is to make the mixture soft, but to chill it well before handling and coating.

The ingredients added to the meat and sauce should be chosen to enhance the flavour of the meat. The shape of the rissoles can vary; the mixture should be formed into round cakes or cutlet shapes, if using shallow fat. If deep frying, choose these shapes and make them a little thicker, or shape into a thick finger, like true Croquettes.

Rissoles can be prepared then frozen. Fry them without defrosting. Use within 3 months.

Heat the dripping or fat (shortening) in a saucepan and fry the onions and tomatoes gently until soft and any excess moisture has evaporated. Stir in the flour and cook for 2 to 3 minutes. Blend in the stock, stir as the mixture comes to the boil and forms a very thick sauce. Add the meat, salt, pepper and mustard and breadcrumbs. The mixture will be very soft at this stage, so allow to cool and become firmer. Form into 8 rissoles; if still slightly soft for coating, chill once more. Coat the shapes with the flour. Beat the egg and brush over the rissoles, then thickly coat in the crisp breadcrumbs.

Heat the oil in a large frying pan (skillet) and fry the rissoles quickly on one side for 2 minutes or until crisp and brown. Turn and cook for the same time on the second side. If the rissoles are not sufficiently hot, lower the heat and cook for a further 1 to 2 minutes. Drain on absorbent paper (kitchen towels). Serve hot as a light dish with salad or with vegetables and a piquant sauce such as Devilled Sauce on page 103.

BEEF RISSOLES

Cooking Time: 20–25 minutes   Serves 4   ❖

	Metric/Imperial	American
beef dripping or fat (shortening)	50 g/2 oz	¼ cup
medium onions, finely chopped	2	2
medium tomatoes, skinned and chopped	2	2
flour	25 g/1 oz	¼ cup
beef stock	150 ml/¼ pint	⅔ cup
cooked beef, minced (ground)	350 g/12 oz	¾ lb
salt and pepper	to taste	to taste
mustard powder	pinch	pinch
soft breadcrumbs	50 g/2 oz	1 cup
To coat: flour	25 g/1 oz	¼ cup
egg	1	1
crisp breadcrumbs	50–75 g/2–3 oz	½–¾ cup
To fry: oil	2 tbsp	3 tbsp

CURRIED LAMB PATTIES

Cooking Time: 20 minutes   Serves 4   ❖

These patties are very like a piquant hamburger. They can be served on toasted rolls as an easy snack or with cooked rice and Curry Sauce, as page 173, for a main meal. Allow the mixture to become quite cold before forming into the patties.

VARIATIONS
Ham and Tongue Rissoles: Mince 225 g/8 oz (½ lb) cooked lean ham and 100 g/4 oz (¼ lb) cooked tongue and use in place of the beef in the recipe, left. Heat the fat and fry the onions as left, but omit the tomatoes. Follow the basic recipe but use milk instead of stock.

● *Veal and Chicken Rissoles:* Mince 225 g/8 oz (½ lb) cooked veal and 225 g/8 oz (½ lb) cooked chicken. Heat 25 g/1 oz (2 tbsp) butter or margarine in a pan, stir in 25 g/1 oz (¼ cup) flour and cook for 2 to 3 minutes. Blend in 4 tablespoons (5 tbsp) chicken stock and 4 tablespoons (5 tbsp) single (light) cream. Stir as the liquid comes to the boil and thickens. Season well, add the meats, ½ teaspoon finely chopped tarragon and 1 egg. In this recipe, breadcrumbs are omitted although they could be added to make a more economical mixture if desired. It is particularly important to chill the mixture well before shaping and coating.

Cut away the rind from 2 bacon rashers (slices). Mince (grind) the bacon with 450 g/1 lb lean uncooked lamb from the leg or shoulder.

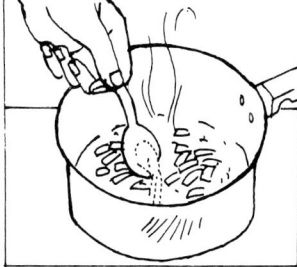

Peel and chop 2 medium onions. Heat the bacon rinds with 25 g/1 oz (2 tbsp) butter or margarine and fry the onions until soft. Add 1 tablespoon curry powder and cook for a further 2 minutes. Remove rinds.

Add the bacon and lamb, 2 tablespoons (3 tbsp) raisins and 25 g/1 oz (½ cup) soft breadcrumbs. Season well. Chill the mixture. Form into 8 small round cakes. Heat 2 tablespoons (3 tbsp) oil in a large frying pan (skillet).

Fry the patties quickly for 2 minutes on both sides, then lower the heat and cook for 5 to 6 minutes.

STEAK TARTARE

No Cooking   Serves 4   ✳✳✳

One of the most famous of all dishes made with minced steak is Steak Tartare. The origin of this dish may go back to the days of the 19th Century, when apparently most steaks were cooked very lightly and were only a short step from raw meat. The high quality beef steaks available today makes this a very successful dish. The meat must be freshly minced (ground) and served almost immediately.

If rump steak is very tender, it can be used for this dish, but fillet steak is a better choice. It would be a good choice to use the narrow end of the fillet, called filet mignon, for medallions or for small tournedos, if you have bought a large portion of this cut of meat and plan to make Beef Wellington as page 181 with the wider end of the fillet.

The presentation of this dish is important, generally the meat is formed into neat patties with the additional ingredients arranged around these. Every diner can then decide just how much onion or gherkin (sweet dill pickle) or other ingredients they like, and mix, or have the steak mixed for them with these extras.

	Metric/Imperial	American
fillet or rump steak, freshly minced (ground)	450–550 g/ 1–1¼ lb	1–1¼ lb
salt and pepper	to taste	to taste
medium onions, neatly and finely diced	2	2
capers	4 tbsp	5 tbsp
gherkins (sweet dill pickles), neatly and finely diced	4–5 tbsp	5–6 tbsp
finely chopped parsley	2–4 tbsp	3–5 tbsp
eggs, yolks only used	4	4
Optional extra ingredients: finely chopped chives	2–3 tbsp	3–4 tbsp
finely chopped thyme	1–2 teasp	1–2 teasp
made mustard	to taste	to taste
horseradish cream	to taste	to taste
cooked beetroot (beets), neatly diced	4–5 tbsp	5–6 tbsp
Worcestershire or Tabasco (hot pepper) sauce	few drops	few drops

Blend the steak with the other ingredients, except the yolks if preferred, see right. Form each portion into a neat patty. Place the egg yolk in the shell on top of the patty or mix this with the steak and other variations. Some of the less usual ingredients that can be incorporated into the steak are given in the ingredients and marked 'optional'.

PIQUANT BURGERS

Cooking Time: 10 minutes   Serves 4   ✳✳

These meat cakes have a combination of deliciously moist and crisp textures given by the choice of vegetables.

	Metric/Imperial	American
topside of beef (top round), minced (ground)	550 g/1¼ lb	1¼ lb
spring onions (scallions), finely chopped	3 tbsp	4 tbsp
small red pepper, de-seeded and finely chopped	1	1
tomato purée (paste)	1½ tbsp	2 tbsp
chopped mixed herbs	1 teasp	1 teasp
salt and pepper	to taste	to taste
To coat: flour	25 g/1 oz	¼ cup
To fry: fat (shortening)	50 g/2 oz	¼ cup

Blend all the ingredients together. Form into 8 small or 4 large round cakes. Coat in the flour. Chill for 1 hour.

Heat the fat (shortening) in a large frying pan (skillet) and fry the meat cakes quickly on both sides for 2 minutes. Lower the heat and cook for a further 1 minute for undercooked beef or up to 4 minutes for well-cooked beef.

Serve on toasted rolls with salad or with vegetables

STEWS AND CASSEROLES

There is a great variety in the kind of stews and casserole dishes that can be made. Whatever the basic foods used in these dishes, the most important cooking feature is to obtain a good blend of flavours. Taste the stew or casserole before serving and be prepared to add extra seasoning or additional herbs if necessary. The use of good dripping as the fat in a stew or casserole adds flavour, see page 72.

In most recipes, long slow cooking is important to tenderize the meat used.

SPRINGTIME STEW

Cooking Time: 1¾ hours   Serves 4   **

	Metric/Imperial	American
pearl barley	100 g/4 oz	generous ½ cup
oil	2 tbsp	3 tbsp
lamb cutlets	8	8
young carrots, whole or cut in halves or quarters	450 g/1 lb	1 lb
celery stalks, chopped	3	3
medium leeks, sliced	4	4
medium onions, sliced	4	4
flour	50 g/2 oz	½ cup
chicken stock	900 ml/1½ pints	3¾ cups
salt	to taste	to taste
peppercorns	6–8	6–8
bay leaves	2	2
bouquet garni	1	1

Put the pearl barley into a saucepan of cold water. Bring the water to the boil, strain the barley. This process, called 'blanching', whitens the barley.

Heat half the oil in a large saucepan. Fry the lamb until brown then place into a casserole. Add the remaining oil to the pan, heat this and fry all the vegetables for a few minutes. Spoon into the casserole.

Blend the flour and stock, pour into the saucepan. Stir well so the liquid absorbs any meat juices, then continue stirring until the sauce thickens slightly. Add the pearl barley and the remaining ingredients. Pour over the lamb and vegetables.

Cover the casserole and cook in the centre of a moderate oven, 180°C/350°F Gas Mark 4, for 1¼ hours. Remove the bay leaves and bouquet garni before serving.

Above left: Piquant Burgers. Above right: Steak Tartare. Right: Springtime Stew

IRISH STEW

Cooking Time: 1½ hours Serves 4–6 ❖❖

Originally this stew, which is virtually a complete meal in itself, was made with young goat's flesh rather than lamb or mutton.

	Metric/Imperial	American
best or middle neck of lamb chops	8–12	8–12
large onions, sliced	2	2
old potatoes	675 g/1½ lb	1½ lb
chicken stock	450 ml/¾ pint	scant 2 cups
bay leaf	1	1
chopped herbs	½ teasp	½ teasp
salt and pepper	to taste	to taste
To garnish: chopped parsley		

Put the meat and onions into a large saucepan. Peel and thinly slice approximately 225 g/8 oz (½ lb) of the potatoes. Add to the meat and onions with the stock, bay leaf and herbs. Season lightly. Cover the pan and cook gently for approximately 1 hour.

Peel the remaining potatoes, leave whole or slice thickly, add to the saucepan. Cook steadily for a further 20 to 30 minutes, add extra salt and pepper to taste. Lift the meat and vegetables from the pan on to a heated dish, top with the chopped parsley.

VARIATIONS
Use sliced old potatoes at the beginning of the cooking period and small new potatoes later.
● Add 450 g/1 lb peeled whole young carrots with the whole or thickly sliced potatoes.
● Add 3 to 4 skinned and halved lambs' kidneys with the whole or thickly sliced potatoes.

BOILED BEEF

Cooking Time: 2 hours 40 minutes Serves 6–8 ❖❖

Boiled beef is one of the traditional family recipes in Britain and America. The term 'boiled' is wrong, for the liquid should just simmer. In Britain the beef is salted, generally by the butcher, whereas in America it is 'corned', see under New England Boiled Dinner in the variations of this recipe. When corned beef originated in Anglo-Saxon times, the salt was so coarse that it looked like corn – hence the name.

	Metric/Imperial	American
salted brisket	1.8 kg/4 lb	4 lb
freshly ground black pepper	to taste	to taste
small carrots	450 g/1 lb	1 lb
small onions	450 g/1 lb	1 lb

Soak the beef in cold water to cover for 12 hours, then pour away this water. Place the meat in a saucepan with fresh water to cover, or see under Variations. Add the pepper and 2 of the carrots and 2 of the onions. Bring the liquid to the boil, remove any grey scum from the top, cover the pan and allow the meat to simmer gently. Good quality brisket takes 40 minutes per 450 g/1 lb but it is wise to be a little generous in timing. Add the remaining vegetables towards the end of the cooking time so they are firm.

Serve the meat hot or cold with the vegetables and Horseradish Sauce or Horseradish Cream, see pages 102 and 103.

VARIATIONS
Cook salted silverside (a better quality cut) instead of brisket. Silverside is a British cut of meat; in America one would ask for 'eye of round'.
● Fresh beef can be cooked in the same way but in this case you need to add salt and a large bunch of mixed herbs to give flavour to the meat. About 6 cloves could be added or 2 to 3 whole garlic cloves.
● Make Dumplings, as the recipe on page 204, and add to the liquid about 20 minutes before the end of the cooking time.
● Use ale or beer instead of water as the beef cooking liquid.
● *New England Boiled Dinner:* Buy fresh brisket or plate. Plate is an American cut and fresh silverside could be bought instead. Put a 1.8 kg/4 lb joint of beef into a large heat-resistant container. Bring 4.6 litres/8 pints (1 gallon plus 1 quart) water to the boil. Add 675 g/1½ lb salt and 225 to 300 g/8 to 10 oz (1 to 1¼ cups) sugar. Pour over the meat while boiling. Place a plate over the meat to push it under the solution. Leave for 48 hours. Remove from the solution, rinse under cold water but do not soak. Cook as above but add as large a selection of vegetables to the liquid as possible.
● *Boiled Bacon:* Bacon joints can be cooked in the same way as the beef. The various joints are described under Roast Bacon on page 52. Soak smoked bacon for several hours in cold water to cover; unsmoked green or sweet-cure bacon does not require soaking. Put the bacon into the pan, cover with cold water or ale or cider or ginger ale (an excellent flavouring). Continue as the recipe above, but allow the same timing as for Bacon in Cider in the recipe on page 69 if cooking gammon (ham) or a prime back bacon (Canadian bacon) joint. Allow 40 to 45 minutes per 450 g/1 lb for the less expensive joints.

TO COAT A BACON JOINT

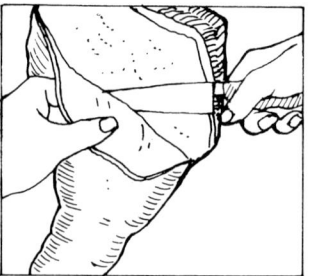

Cut away the rind of the joint.

Press fine crisp breadcrumbs against the fat. A little brown sugar could be mixed with the breadcrumbs before coating.

The vegetables can be cooked with the joint as described left. Serve hot bacon with a Mustard or Parsley Sauce, see page 102, and cold bacon with a relish or pickle (see the selection on page 191) or with Cumberland Sauce, page 100.

The bacon joint can be partially cooked in liquid, then glazed and roasted in the oven. There are various suggestions for glazes on page 194.

BACON IN CIDER

Cooking Time: 1¾ hours   Serves 6–8   ✷✷

Cider is a perfect partner for bacon. Choose either a dry or a sweet cider, according to the flavour preferred.

	Metric/Imperial	American
gammon (smoked ham) joint	1.8 kg/4 lb	4 lb
cider, see method	600–900 ml/ 1–1½ pints	2½-3¾ cups
cloves	3–4	3–4
small onions	12	12
bouquet garni	1	1
pepper	to taste	to taste
To coat: crisp breadcrumbs	40–50 g/1½-2 oz	⅓-½ cup

If the bacon is well salted, soak overnight in cold water to cover. Next day remove from the water. Put the bacon into a saucepan with the cider; the amount depends upon the shape of the piece of bacon and the size of the saucepan, but the liquid must cover the bacon. Bring the liquid just to the boil, remove any 'scum' that might come to the top. Simmer for 40 minutes. Add the cloves, onion, bouquet garni and a good shake of pepper. Continue to cook for a further hour or until tender but unbroken. Lift the bacon joint out of the pan, remove the skin, sprinkle with the crumbs.

The cider can be served as an unthickened sauce, but it will have given a more interesting flavour to the bacon, even if not used.

TO MAKE OLIVES

Take the large slices of meat, place the stuffing on them and shape as below.

Gather up the corners of the meat around the stuffing and tie with fine string or cotton.

Or, roll the meat around the stuffing and tie with fine string or cotton.

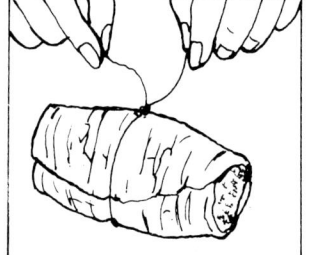

MAKING MEAT OLIVES

Olives have long been a favourite way of casseroling meat with a savoury filling; in fact, the method has been used for several centuries. The most usual olives are made with thinly sliced beef filled with a savoury mixture, such as Parsley and Thyme Stuffing, given on page 106.

The following recipes – one with beef and pork and the second with veal – provide an unusual touch to the old favourite.

The name 'olives' originated from the fact that the meat and filling used to be formed into a round ball, like an olive. Nowadays, it is generally shaped into a neat roll which is easier to prepare.

BEEF AND PORK OLIVES

Cooking Time: 1¾ hours   Serves 4   ✷✷

	Metric/Imperial	American
For the stuffing: butter or beef dripping	25 g/1 oz	2 tbsp
medium onions, finely chopped	2	2
soft breadcrumbs	50 g/2 oz	1 cup
large cooking (baking) apple, peeled and diced	1	1
chopped sage	½ teasp	½ teasp
salt and pepper	to taste	to taste
thin slices of topside of beef (top round)	4	4
thin slices of pork fillet	4	4
medium onions, sliced	2	2
medium carrots, sliced	4	4
celery stalks, chopped	2–3	2–3
For the sauce: butter or beef dripping	50 g/2 oz	¼ cup
flour	25 g/1 oz	¼ cup
beef stock	450 ml/¾ pint	scant 2 cups

Heat the 25 g/1 oz (2 tbsp) butter or dripping in a frying pan (skillet) and fry the chopped onions for 5 minutes only. Add the breadcrumbs, apple, sage and a very little salt and pepper.

Lay the slices of beef on a board, top with the pork slices then with the stuffing. Roll the meats together to form neat rolls and tie these with fine cotton.

Heat the 50 g/2 oz (¼ cup) butter or dripping in the frying pan or a large saucepan and fry the olives for 5 to 6 minutes until golden. Place in a deep casserole. Add all the vegetables to the olives. Stir the flour into the fat remaining in the pan, then blend in the stock. Stir as the liquid comes to the boil and thickens; season to taste. Pour the sauce over the olives and vegetables.

Cover the casserole and cook in the centre of a very moderate oven, 160°C/325°F Gas Mark 3, for 1½ hours. Cut off the cotton and place the olives and vegetables on a heated dish. Boil the sauce rapidly until a little thicker, serve with the olives.

VEAL OLIVES

Cooking Time: 35–40 minutes   Serves 4   ❊❊

Veal olives are excellent with either Cranberry Sauce or a thick blueberry purée, see pages 100 and 98.

	Metric/Imperial	American
slices of veal fillet, cut from the top of the leg as for escalopes	4	4
bacon rashers (slices)	5–6	5–6
soft breadcrumbs	75 g/3 oz	1½ cups
grated lemon rind	1 teasp	1 teasp
lemon juice	1 tbsp	1 tbsp
canned anchovy fillets, drained and chopped	6–8	6–8
egg	1	1
salt and pepper	to taste	to taste
To coat: flour	15 g/½ oz	2 tbsp
egg, beaten	1	1
soft breadcrumbs	75 g/3 oz	1½ cups
To fry: butter	50 g/2 oz	¼ cup
For the sauce: butter	50 g/2 oz	¼ cup
button mushrooms, sliced	100 g/4 oz	¼ lb
flour	25 g/1 oz	¼ cup
white stock	450 ml/¾ pint	scant 2 cups
double (heavy) cream	2 tbsp	3 tbsp
To garnish: lemon slices	4	4

Beat the meat with a rolling pin until very thin. De-rind and chop the bacon. Blend the chopped bacon, breadcrumbs, lemon rind, juice, the anchovies and egg. Add a little seasoning if desired; the anchovies provide a salty taste. Spread the stuffing over the slices of veal, roll firmly. Tie with fine string or secure with small wooden cocktail sticks (toothpicks). Mix the flour with salt and pepper, dust the veal with this. Do not exceed this small amount for it does not give a real coating, just dries the meat. Brush the rolls in the beaten egg. Coat with the crumbs, press these firmly against the meat rolls.

Put the bacon rinds into a frying pan (skillet) and heat to extract the fat. Add and heat the butter, put in the veal rolls; turn carefully in the fat until golden brown. Lift from the pan, place into an ovenproof casserole. Pour any butter and bacon fat from the pan into the dish. Cover and cook towards the top of a moderately hot oven, 190 to 200°C/375 to 400°F Gas Mark 5 to 6, for 25 minutes or until the meat is tender.

Meanwhile, heat the butter for the sauce in a pan and fry the sliced mushrooms. Stir in the flour and cook for several minutes. Gradually blend in the stock and bring to the boil, stirring. Cook until the mushrooms are tender and the sauce thickened. Just before serving, remove the pan from the heat and, when the sauce is no longer boiling, whisk in the cream. Season well. Arrange the veal olives on a heated dish, remove the string or cocktail sticks and pour the sauce round. Garnish with lemon slices.

VARIATION
A little sherry or Madeira could replace some of the stock.

SWEET AND SOUR PORK

Cooking Time: 1¼ hours   Serves 4–6   ❊❊

	Metric/Imperial	American
pork fillet, cut from leg	450 g/1 lb	1 lb
belly of pork (fresh pork sides)	350 g/12 oz	¾ lb
carrots, cut into narrow strips	225 g/8 oz	½ lb
green pepper, de-seeded and diced	1	1
very small shallots or onions	12	12
cornflour (cornstarch)	1 tbsp	1 tbsp
canned pineapple juice	300 ml/½ pint	1¼ cups
vinegar	2 tbsp	3 tbsp
honey	2 tbsp	3 tbsp
soy sauce	½-1 tbsp	½-1 tbsp
salt and pepper	to taste	to taste

Cut the pork fillet and belly meat into neat strips about 1.5 cm/½ inch in width and thickness, and 5 cm/2 inches in length; keep the two kinds of pork apart. Fry the belly of pork for a few minutes in a frying pan (skillet) until the natural fat from the meat runs out. Add the lean pork fillet and fry for a further 5 minutes. Spoon the meat into a casserole. Add the carrots, pepper and whole shallots or onions.

Blend the cornflour (cornstarch) with the pineapple juice and pour into a saucepan. Stir over a low heat until thickened, then add the vinegar, honey, soy sauce and a little salt and pepper. Pour over the meat and vegetables. Cover the casserole and cook in the centre of a very moderate oven, 160°C/325°F Gas Mark 3, for 1 hour. Serve with cooked rice.

Above: Beef and Beer Casserole. Below left: Veal Olives

BEEF AND BEER CASSEROLE

Cooking Time: 2½-2¾ hours   Serves 4–6   ❊❊

	Metric/Imperial	American
stewing beef	675 g/1½ lb	1½ lb
small turnips	2–3	2–3
medium carrots	6–8	6–8
medium swede (rutabaga)	1	1
small onions	8–12	8–12
flour	50 g/2 oz	½ cup
salt and pepper	to taste	to taste
beef dripping or fat (shortening)	75 g/3 oz	6 tbsp
beer	450 ml/¾ pint	scant 2 cups
beef stock	300 ml/½ pint	1¼ cups
chopped parsley	2 tbsp	3 tbsp
tomato purée (paste)	2 tbsp	3 tbsp
brown sugar	2 teasp	2 teasp

Cut the beef into neat fingers. Peel the root vegetables and cut into pieces about the same size as the beef, or keep them a little larger. The onions should be kept whole.

Mix the flour with the seasoning and coat the beef – use all the flour. Heat half the dripping or fat (shortening) in a large saucepan and toss the beef in this for 10 minutes or until golden in colour. Place into a large ovenproof casserole. Add the remainder of the dripping or fat to the pan and toss the onions in this for 5 minutes, then mix with the beef.

Pour the beer and stock into the saucepan, stir well to absorb all the dripping or fat, flour and meat juices that may be left. Bring to the boil. Add the root vegetables, the parsley, tomato purée (paste), brown sugar and seasoning to taste. Simmer for 5 minutes, then pour over the beef. Cover the casserole and cook in the centre of a slow oven, 150°C/300°F Gas Mark 2, for 2 to 2¼ hours.

Serve with a crisp Coleslaw as page 119. Cooked noodles or other pasta blend well with the casserole.

VARIATIONS

Fry the meat in the saucepan, remove on to a plate then fry the onions. Add the beer and stock, stir well then put in the root vegetables, parsley, tomato purée, sugar and seasoning. Finally return the beef to the pan. Cover the saucepan and simmer gently as the timing above. The liquid in a stew tends to evaporate more than when the food is cooked in a covered casserole, so it is advisable to be a little more generous with this and to check during the cooking period.
● Use all beef stock in place of beer and stock.
● *Oxtail Casserole:* Use 2 jointed oxtail in place of the beef and cook for about 3 hours. Since oxtail has a high percentage of fat, use only 50 g/2 oz (¼ cup) dripping or fat. Some of the root vegetables can be omitted. Cook this casserole 24 hours before required. Cool, skim off surplus fat. Reheat when needed.

LANCASHIRE HOT POT

Cooking Time: 2 hours   Serves 4–6   ❊❊

This dish originated in Lancashire. It was named after the original attractive deep brown pottery casserole in which the food was cooked. In the olden days, bakers put these hotpots into the bakery ovens for families who had insufficient cooking facilities. By cooking the meat between the layers of vegetables, all the good flavour is retained. Use the minimum of liquid in cooking.

	Metric/Imperial	American
middle neck lamb chops	8–12	8–12
lambs' kidneys	2–3	2–3
salt and pepper	to taste	to taste
potatoes, thickly sliced	675 g/1½ lb	1½ lb
onions, thinly sliced	350–450 g/12 oz-1 lb	¾-1 lb
lamb or chicken stock	225 ml/8 fl oz	1 cup
margarine or dripping	25 g/1 oz	2 tbsp

Divide the meat into neat portions, if necessary. Skin and slice the kidneys, sprinkle with a little salt and pepper. Put a layer of potatoes, then onions and then meat into a deep casserole. Season each layer, continue filling the casserole in this way. End with a layer of potatoes and arrange these carefully so they overlap in a neat pattern. Pour the liquid into the casserole. Melt the margarine or dripping and brush over the potatoes.

Bake in the centre of a slow to very moderate oven, 150 to 160°C/300 to 325°F Gas Mark 2 to 3, for about 2 hours. Do not cover the casserole for the first 30 minutes. This allows the fat to melt and the potatoes become firm, so they do not stick to the casserole lid. Remove the lid for the last 30 minutes.

VARIATIONS
Beef Hotpot: Use 450 to 550 g/1 to 1¼ lb diced stewing beef instead of the lamb, and beer in place of the stock.

● *Irish Hotpot:* Use 450 to 550 g/1 to 1¼ lb diced lean pork instead of lamb. Add 2 large peeled and thinly sliced cooking (baking) apples to the onions. Use beer instead of stock.

TO CLARIFY DRIPPING

Put the dripping into a saucepan; cover with cold water. Heat gently until the dripping has melted. Strain through muslin (cheesecloth) into a container; allow to cool.

Remove the solid fat from the water.

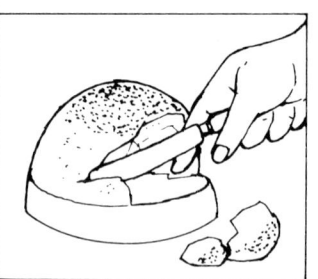

Turn upside down and scrape the sediment from the bottom. Store in the refrigerator for 1 week or up to 1 month in the freezer.

Ask any authority on Welsh food what is one of the more important traditional dishes of Wales and they will give you this recipe. It is called Ffest Y Cybrdd.

I do not think there was any particular miser in mind when it was given the name, it was just a practical everyday dish. The idea was for the miser to eat the potatoes on one day (knowing these would have absorbed the good flavour of bacon and onions) and to save the bacon for another meal. This really is the Welsh version of a traditional 'hotpot' and if you use really good thick slices of bacon, it makes a very excellent dish. Many recipes use onions but I prefer a mixture of onions and leeks.

Before ovens became part of standard kitchen equipment, this was cooked in a tightly covered saucepan, but it is much easier and looks more attractive if cooked in a casserole. Like most 'hotpots', it is improved if served with pickled red cabbage and/or pickled walnuts. Crab-apple jelly also blends well with the dish.

THE MISER'S FEAST

Cooking Time: 2 hours   Serves 4–6   ❊

	Metric/Imperial	American
old or new potatoes, weight before peeling or scraping	900 g/2 lb	2 lb
onions, thinly sliced	350 g/12 oz	¾ lb
leeks, sliced	225 g/8 oz	½ lb
butter or margarine	40 g/1½ oz	3 tbsp
salt and pepper	to taste	to taste
thick back rashers (Canadian bacon) or gammon (smoked ham) slices	450 g/1 lb	1 lb

Peel or scrape the potatoes and cut them into fairly thin slices. Put the vegetables into water until ready to use. Do not dry them, since the small amount of liquid that adheres to them is needed. Put a layer of potatoes and onions and leeks into a lightly greased casserole (use just under half the butter or margarine). Add a very little salt (unless using a modern mild-cured bacon when rather more salt could be used) and a generous sprinkling of pepper. Put half the bacon rashers on top of the vegetables then add another layer of seasoned potatoes and the rest of the onions and leeks, then the remainder of the bacon. Top with a final layer of sliced potatoes. Cover the casserole tightly (if the lid does not fit well, put foil under this to retain as much moisture as possible). Cook in the centre of a slow to very moderate oven, 150 to 160°C/300 to 325°F Gas Mark 2 to 3, for approximately 1½ hours.

Melt the remaining butter or margarine, remove the casserole lid and brush the potatoes with this fat. Raise the oven temperature slightly to encourage the potatoes to brown and cook for a further 30 to 35 minutes without covering the casserole.

SUET CRUST PUDDINGS

Suet crust pastry is essentially an English pastry, for there is little reference to the recipe in old cookery books from other parts of Britain. The pastry should be 'featherlight' in texture; this is achieved by making it relatively moist and by speedy cooking in the initial stages. Suet crust pastry is used for both savoury and sweet puddings; an example of the latter is on page 123. Undoubtedly the most famous of all the puddings made with this pastry is a Beefsteak and Kidney Pudding (abbreviated nowadays to Steak and Kidney). It became popular during the 19th Century and was a feature of the eating houses of London. You will still find it on the menus of hotels and restaurants, and the enthusiasm of the diners indicates it still is a favourite dish.

The puddings can be prepared and frozen, or cooked then cooled and frozen. Use within 3 months.

Blend the flour with salt and pepper to taste and coat the meat. Put the meat into the lined basin. Add the stock or water; this should come three-quarters of the way up the basin. Roll out the remaining pastry into a round to fit the top of the basin. Moisten the edges of the pastry, put the pastry round in position. Cover with lightly greased greaseproof (waxed) paper and foil. Put a pleat in the coverings so there is room for the pudding to rise, see page 125.

Steam over boiling water for 4 to 4½ hours. The water should boil rapidly for the first 2 hours so that the pastry will be light; after this time the heat can be reduced. Top up with boiling water when necessary.

Remove the basin from the steamer, dry the basin and serve the pudding with a slightly thickened gravy. In the days when pudding basins were less attractive than they are today, this pudding was served with a table napkin wrapped around the basin.

VARIATIONS

Steak and Game Pudding: Use approximately 350 g/12 oz (¾ lb) diced beefsteak and the flesh from a grouse, pheasant or 2 to 3 partridges or other game bird. Serve with Game Sauce, page 88.

● *Steak, Kidney and Oyster Pudding:* Add about 12 oysters to the meat mixture. Alternatively remove the pudding from the heat about 25 minutes before serving, remove the covers and carefully cut a large slice from the top pastry. Add the oysters and replace the lid. Cover the pudding again and continue to cook. The latter method is more trouble but the flavour and texture of the oysters is much better.

● *Steak and Mushroom Pudding:* Add approximately 225 g/8 oz (½ lb) small mushrooms to the steak. Omit the kidney.

STEAK AND KIDNEY PUDDING

Illustrated in colour on page 207
Cooking Time: 4–4½ hours   Serves 6 ✳✳

	Metric/Imperial	American
Suet Crust Pastry, as page 123 made with	300 g/10 oz flour etc	2½ cups flour etc
For the filling: stewing beef	675 g/1½ lb	1½ lb
ox kidney (beef kidney)	100–225 g/4–8 oz	¼–½ lb
flour	2 tbsp	3 tbsp
salt and pepper	to taste	to taste
beef stock or water	3–4 tbsp	4–5 tbsp

Sift the flour and salt for the pastry. Add the suet and enough water to give a soft rolling consistency.

Prepare the meat. In these busy days, the steak and kidney are generally cut into 2.5 cm/1 inch dice then mixed together, but the traditional method was to cut the steak into long narrow strips and the kidney into small dice. A piece of kidney was then put on to each strip of stewing steak and this was rolled around the kidney, so ensuring everyone had a good portion of the kidney.

Roll out the pastry and line a lightly greased 1.5 litre/2½ pint pudding basin (6½ cup pudding mold) with three-quarters of the pastry as shown on this page.

TO LINE A BASIN WITH SUET CRUST

Roll out the pastry into a large round. Cut out a quarter of the round.

Insert the three-quarters of the pastry into the basin, press the joins together. This method means there are no pleats of double-thickness pastry.

Use the remaining portion and any trimmings to make the top pastry 'lid'.

SAVOURY PIES

Many countries of the world have traditional dishes in which meat is enclosed in pastry. One of the most famous is the Steak and Kidney Pie on this page. Rather similar pies have been known since the Middle Ages, when they were called 'boxes' or 'coffers' because the food was completely encased in pastry.

Modern tastes on the whole prefer to have the meat mixture in a pie dish with just a pastry covering, but you can make a pie with pastry below and above the filling using shortcrust pastry made with 350 g/12 oz (3 cups) flour etc., as page 175.

STEAK AND KIDNEY PIE

Cooking Time: 2¾ hours   Serves 4–6   ❋❋

	Metric/Imperial	American
stewing beef	675 g/1½ lb	1½ lb
lambs' kidneys or ox (beef) kidney	225 g/8 oz	½ lb
salt and pepper	to taste	to taste
flour	25 g/1 oz	¼ cup
butter or dripping	50 g/2 oz	¼ cup
beef stock	600 ml/1 pint	2½ cups
small button mushrooms	100–225 g/4–8 oz	¼-½ lb
Flaky Pastry, as page 154 made with	225 g/8 oz flour etc	2 cups flour etc
To glaze: egg	1	1

LAMB AND CHUTNEY TURNOVERS

Cooking Time: 30 minutes Serves 4–5   ❋

	Metric/Imperial	American
Puff Pastry, as page 154 made with	175 g/6 oz flour etc	1½ cups flour etc
For the filling: butter or margarine	40 g/1½ oz	3 tbsp
flour	40 g/1½ oz	6 tbsp
milk	300 ml/½ pint	1¼ cups
cooked lamb, finely diced	350 g/12 oz	¾ lb
Apple and Mint Chutney, as page 192	3 tbsp	4 tbsp
salt and pepper	to taste	to taste
To glaze: egg	1	1
water	½ tbsp	½ tbsp
To garnish: tomato wedges	8–10	8–10
mint	few sprigs	few sprigs

Make the pastry and allow it to stand in the refrigerator until ready to use. Heat the butter or margarine in a saucepan, stir in the flour and cook gently for 2 to 3 minutes.

Add the milk, stir as it boils and thickens. Add the diced meat. Cool. Stir in the chutney and seasoning.

Roll out the pastry until very thin and cut into 8 to 10 x 10 cm/4 inch squares. Divide the mixture between the pastry squares, keep this well to the centre of the pastry. Damp the edges, then fold the pastry to make neat triangles. Seal and flake the edges of the pastry, see the line drawings on page 129, stage 6. Make a slit on top of each turnover for the steam to escape. Beat the egg with the water and brush over the pastry. Place on a slightly damp baking tray.

Bake just above the centre of a very hot oven, 230°C/450°F Gas Mark 8, for 10 to 15 minutes, then reduce the heat to 190 to 200°C/375 to 400°F Gas Mark 5 to 6, for 5 to 10 minutes. Garnish.

Cut the meat into 4 cm/1½ inch cubes. Skin the kidneys and cut into small dice, discard any excess fat. Mix the salt and pepper with the flour and coat the meats – use all the flour.

Heat the butter or dripping in a saucepan and fry the meat gently until just golden. Gradually blend in the stock, stir as the mixture comes to the boil and thickens. Cover the pan, lower the heat and simmer for 1½ hours or until the meat is almost tender. Do not overcook as the meat is cooked again in the pie. Stir the mushrooms into the hot mixture, then spoon into a 1.2 litre/2 pint (5 cup) pie dish. Use a perforated spoon so only enough liquid to keep the meat moist is used. The extra liquid can be served as a gravy. Cover the pie filling with greaseproof (waxed) paper so the meat does not dry. Allow to become cold.

Roll out the pastry and cover the pie. Use any trimmings to make pastry leaves and a tassel or rose, as page 76. Make a slit on top of the pastry to allow excess steam to escape. Beat the egg and brush over the pastry. Bake in the centre of a very hot oven, 230°C/450°F Gas Mark 8, for 15 minutes or until the pastry rises well; then reduce the heat to moderate, 180°C/350°F Gas Mark 4, and cook for a further 20 to 25 minutes until the pastry is crisp and golden brown and the filling hot.

VARIATION
Steak and Kidney Pie de Luxe: Buy rump steak instead of stewing steak. Use only 450 ml/¾ pint (scant 2 cups) stock; add 150 ml/¼ pint (⅔ cup) red wine or port wine to cook the meat. Chop 2 onions and fry with the meats. Add the mushrooms as in the basic recipe and about 12 oysters to the cooked meat mixture.

Mutton Pies

MUTTON PIES

Cooking Time: 40 minutes   (5 minutes for pastry)   Serves 4   ✳✳

The sheep that graze on the Welsh hillsides produce some of the finest mutton and lamb in Britain.

The crust used should be hot water crust pastry; the pastry used for many British raised pies. Shortcrust pastry (basic pie dough) could be substituted.

	Metric/Imperial	American
For the filling:		
mutton, from leg, shoulder or loin, weight without bones	450 g/1 lb	1 lb
currants	175 g/6 oz	1 cup
brown sugar	50–75 g/2–3 oz	⅓–½ cup
salt and pepper	to taste	to taste
For the Hot Water Crust Pastry:		
plain (all-purpose) flour	350 g/12 oz	3 cups
salt	good pinch	good pinch
lard or fat (shortening)	150 g/5 oz	⅝ cup
water	150 ml/¼ pint	⅔ cup
To glaze:		
egg	1	1

Cut the mutton into small neat pieces or mince (grind) rather coarsely. Wash and dry the currants; even if pre-washed and clean, it is advisable to pour boiling water over these to make them plump. (If preferred seedless raisins or a mixture of currants and raisins could be used.) Mix the fruit and sugar together. Season the meat well with salt and pepper.

Sift the flour and salt into a mixing bowl. Heat the lard or fat (shortening) with the water until melted; do not allow the mixture to boil for any length of time as some of the water would evaporate and make the pastry too dry. Pour the melted lard and water on to the flour. Knead lightly. Roll out while still warm until a generous 5 mm/¼ inch in thickness. Cut out 4 large or 8 smaller rounds and put these into lightly greased deep patty tins. Cut out 4 or 8 rounds as 'lids', put these on a plate in a warm place until ready to use.

Put a layer of meat at the bottom of each pastry case then a layer of currants, then a final layer of meat. Press down lightly, for the pies should be fairly full. Brush the edges of the pastry with water, put on the 'lids'. Make a hole in the centre of each small pie and decorate with pastry roses and leaves. Beat the egg and glaze the pastry. Bake in the centre of a hot oven, 220°C/425°F Gas Mark 7, for approximately 35 minutes. Reduce the heat to moderately hot, 190°C/375°F Gas Mark 5, after 20 minutes if the pastry seems to be too brown. Eat hot with leeks or cold with salad.

Above left: Steak and Kidney Pie. Below left: Lamb and Chutney Turnovers

CORNISH PASTY

**Cooking Time:
45–65 minutes
Serves 4** *

A Cornish pasty has been made for generations. It is one of the best known British dishes, although most people, away from Cornwall, imagine that the filling for the pasty must be beef, potatoes and onions. In Cornwall, you will find both sweet and savoury pasties – fillings of fruit (fresh or dried) and jam; vegetables and herbs; fish, poultry, rabbit, lamb or a mixture of ingredients that blend well.

The pasty probably originated as a practical means of packing food for the tin-miners of Cornwall; often their pasties would have one end filled with savoury ingredients and the other end filled with something sweet. A shortcrust pastry (basic pie dough) is used when making this dish for home consumption but a more economical pastry, as given in this recipe that will not break so easily, is better when making the pasty for a picnic.

	Metric/Imperial	American
For the pastry: flour, preferably plain (all-purpose)	350 g/12 oz	3 cups
salt	pinch	pinch
butter or lard	100–150 g/4–5 oz	½-⅝ cup
water	to bind	to bind
For the filling: rump steak	350 g/12 oz	¾ lb
medium potatoes, diced	2	2
medium onions, diced	2	2
salt and pepper	to taste	to taste
stock or water*	1 tbsp	1 tbsp
chopped herbs, optional		
To glaze: egg	1	1
water	1 tbsp	1 tbsp

* omit if carrying the pasty for a picnic

Sift the flour and salt into a mixing bowl. Rub in the butter or lard until the mixture is like fine breadcrumbs. Bind with water. Roll out and cut into 4 rounds about the size of a tea plate or make into 1 large round for a 'family-sized' pasty – this is very usual in Cornwall.

Cut the meat into pieces about 1.5 cm/½ inch square. Mix the meat with the vegetables, season well and blend with the stock or water. Chopped herbs could be added. Place the filling in the centre of the pastry rounds or round. Damp the edges with water and fold the pastry to form an upright patty, flute the edges. Mix the egg and water, brush over the pastry. Lift the pasties or pasty carefully on to a lightly greased baking tray.

Cook in the centre of a hot oven, 220°C/425°F Gas Mark 7, for 20 minutes to give a crisp pastry; then reduce the heat to very moderate, 160°C/325°F Gas Mark 3, and cook for a further 25 to 30 minutes for small pasties or for 45 minutes for a large one. Serve hot or cold.

VARIATIONS
Add a small amount of diced turnip or swede (rutabaga) to the other ingredients.
● Use diced uncooked lean lamb with potatoes, onions, chopped mint and parsley.
● Use diced lean pork with the vegetables and a peeled diced cooking (baking) apple.

PASTRY GARNISHES

Savoury pies are garnished with pastry leaves, roses and tassels.

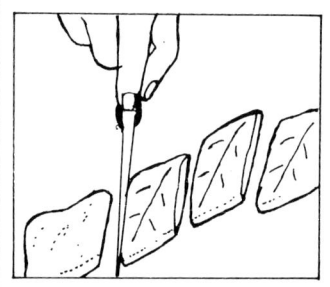

For leaves: Cut a strip of pastry. Cut diamond shapes from this, to form the leaves.

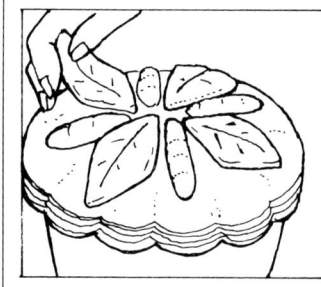

Mark the veins in the leaves. Moisten the pastry put on the pie; twist some leaves for an effective result.

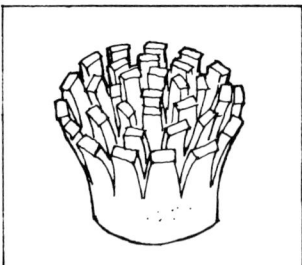

For a tassel: Cut a long narrow strip of pastry. Make cuts close together and half the pastry width.

Turn the strip so the cut part becomes the top of the tassel. Open out the cuts slightly.

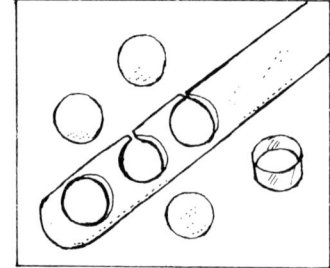

For a rose: Cut a long strip of pastry. Form into a round.

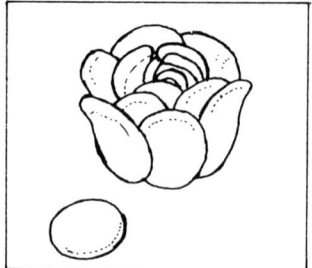

Depress this at intervals to form the 'petals' of an opened rose.

VARIETY MEATS

These meats, also called offal, provide the basis for some of the most appetizing and interesting of all dishes.

Liver is highly esteemed for its food value, but the relatively definite taste is disliked by some people. The recipes that follow on this page may well make the liver more appealing.

Tripe is another kind of offal that is not a general favourite, but the mould given on page 178 adds a completely new look and flavour to this economical meat.

One of the traditional favourites in parts of Britain, that still is enjoyed today, is the combination of Faggots and Pease Pudding. Some butchers still sell these readymade; however, both dishes are quite simple to make at home, see page 80.

LIVER AND MUSHROOM BAKE

Cooking Time: 40 minutes   Serves 4   ❈❈

	Metric/Imperial	American
butter, margarine or dripping	50 g/2 oz	¼ cup
medium onions, finely chopped	2	2
tomatoes, skinned and sliced	450 g/1 lb	1 lb
mushrooms, sliced	225 g/8 oz	½ lb
chopped parsley	2 tbsp	3 tbsp
salt and pepper	to taste	to taste
lambs' liver, thinly sliced	350 g/12 oz	¾ lb
bacon rashers (slices), de-rinded and chopped	2–3	2–3
For the topping: butter or margarine	50 g/2 oz	¼ cup
soft breadcrumbs	100 g/4 oz	2 cups
To garnish: medium tomatoes, sliced	2	2
parsley	few sprigs	few sprigs

Heat the butter, margarine or dripping in a saucepan and fry the onions for 5 minutes. Blend the sliced tomatoes, mushrooms, parsley and seasoning with the onions and any fat remaining in the pan.

Put half the mushroom mixture into a 1.2 litre/2 pint (5 cup) ovenproof dish. Top with the liver and bacon, then with the remaining mushroom mixture.

Melt the butter or margarine for the topping, blend with the breadcrumbs. Sprinkle over the mushroom mixture, smooth flat on top. Bake in the centre of a moderate oven, 180°C/350°F Gas Mark 4, for 35 minutes. Garnish with the tomato slices and parsley.

AVOCADOS AND LIVER

Cooking Time: 8–10 minutes   Serves 4   ❈

This recipe gives a new look to fried liver. It is a thoroughly up-to-date way of serving this nutritious meat. The combination of flavours is delicious and unusual. Lambs' liver has a very definite flavour which some people find rather too strong: marinate the liver in a little milk for an hour, drain the meat and dry it well and the flavour becomes much more delicate. Never overcook liver or keep it waiting before serving – this makes it tough.

	Metric/Imperial	American
ripe avocados	2–3	2–3
lemon juice	2 tbsp	3 tbsp
salt and pepper	to taste	to taste
calves' or lambs' liver, thinly sliced	550 g/1¼ lb	1¼ lb
flour	2 tbsp	3 tbsp
butter	75 g/3 oz	6 tbsp
To garnish: lemon slices	4	4
watercress	few sprigs	few sprigs

Skin and halve the avocados, remove the stones. Slice the flesh, sprinkle with the lemon juice and a little salt and pepper.

Dip the liver in the flour; do not exceed the amount given, for a thicker coating tends to harden the outside of the liver.

Heat the butter in a large frying pan (skillet) and fry the liver for about 2 minutes on both sides if you like it lightly cooked. Add the avocado slices after the liver has been cooking for 1 minute.

Arrange the liver and avocados on a heated dish, garnish with the lemon slices and watercress. Serve as soon as possible after cooking.

VARIATION

Oranges and Liver: Omit the avocados. Blend 2 teaspoons finely grated orange rind with the lemon and sprinkle the liver with this. Fry the liver as above, add 5 tablespoons (½ cup) orange juice blended with 2 teaspoons brown sugar when the liver is nearly cooked. Serve with the small amount of orange juice. Garnish with watercress.

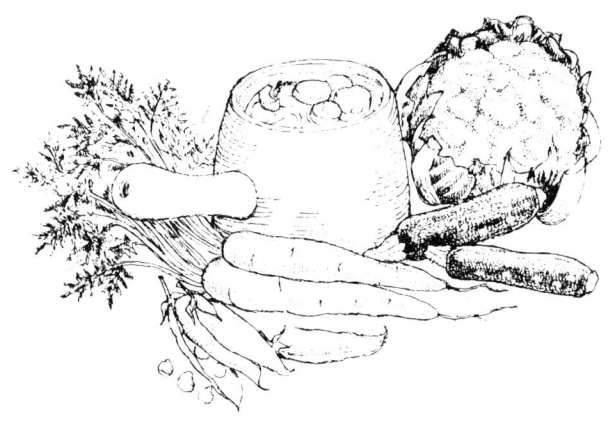

COOKING TONGUE

Home-cooked tongue makes the basis of a variety of delicious meals. An average ox (beef) tongue weighs between 1.5 and 1.8 kg/3½ and 4 lb, which may appear an excessive amount for a small family but the cooked tongue freezes well for up to 3 months.

Calf's tongue is generally about 675 g/1½ lb in weight and lambs' tongues, 100 g/4 oz (¼ lb) each. Ox tongue can be obtained as fresh meat or ready-salted (this gives the pleasing colour to the meat). Calf's and lambs' tongues are rarely salted.

A salted tongue should be soaked in cold water to cover for 12 hours, then drained before cooking. Season with pepper only as in the recipe for Jellied Tongue. Fresh tongues do not need soaking.

TONGUE EN CRÔUTE

Cooking Time: 35–40 minutes   Serves 4–6   ✻✻

	Metric/Imperial	American
cooked fresh or salted ox (beef) or calf's tongue	550–675 g/ 1¼–1½ lb	1¼–1½ lb
streaky bacon rashers (slices)	225 g/8 oz	½ lb
Puff Pastry, as page 154 made with	225 g/8 oz flour etc	2 cups flour etc
mixed chopped herbs (chives, parsley, thyme)	2–3 teasp	2–3 teasp
To glaze: egg	1	1
water	1 tbsp	1 tbsp

JELLIED TONGUE

Cooking Time: 4 hours   Serves 8   ✻✻

	Metric/Imperial	American
salted ox (beef) tongue, soaked for 12 hours	1.8 kg/4 lb	4 lb
small onions	3–4	3–4
small carrots	3–4	3–4
bay leaves	2	2
bouquet garni	1	1
freshly milled black pepper or peppercorns	to taste 6–8	to taste 6–8
gelatine (gelatin)	7 g/¼ oz	1 envelope

Lift the tongue from the cold water in which it has been soaking. Put into a large saucepan with fresh water to cover. Add all the ingredients except the gelatine. Bring the water to the boil, remove any scum from the top of the liquid. Cover the saucepan and simmer until tender. This takes about 4 hours or even a little longer.

A pressure cooker, however, shortens the cooking time appreciably. A tongue of the size given would take approximately 15 minutes per 450 g/1 lb on the HIGH/15 lb setting.

Allow the tongue to cool sufficiently to handle, then remove the skin and any small bones. Roll the hot tongue to fit a tin (without a loose base) or round mould. Boil the stock with the vegetables until reduced to 300 ml/½ pint (1¼ cups), then add the gelatine. Strain over

Choose the thicker end of the tongue if possible. De-rind the bacon and wrap the rashers (slices) round the tongue.

Roll out the pastry until very thin and an oblong sufficiently large to completely cover the tongue. Put any trimmings on one side to make the leaves. Sprinkle the herbs over the pastry. Place the tongue in the centre of the pastry. Moisten the pastry edges, then fold into a neat roll. Seal the joins carefully.

Place on a baking tray with most of the joins underneath. Beat the egg and water, brush over the pastry. Cut out pastry leaves, place on the pastry roll and glaze with the egg mixture. Bake in the centre of a very hot oven, 230°C/450°F Gas Mark 8, for 10 to 15 minutes or until the pastry has risen well, then reduce the heat to moderate, 180°C/350°F Gas Mark 4, for a further 20 to 25 minutes. Serve hot or cold, cut into neat slices.

Jellied Tongue

the tongue and allow to set. Serve cold with salad or slice the tongue and heat as in the recipes on page 80.

VARIATIONS
If using fresh tongue cook as before, but add salt to taste. A small cooked beetroot (beet) added to the other vegetables improves the colour of the tongue.
● Cook a calf's tongue for about 3 hours, or 15 minutes per 450 g/1 lb on HIGH/15 lb setting in a pressure cooker.
● Cook lambs' tongues for 1½ to 2 hours, or about 25 minutes on HIGH/15 lb setting in a pressure cooker.

KIDNEYS IN TARRAGON

Cooking Time: 25–30 minutes   Serves 4   ✳

	Metric/Imperial	American
lambs' kidneys	450 g/1 lb	1 lb
small onions, sliced	2–3	2–3
small button mushrooms	100 g/4 oz	¼ lb
streaky bacon rashers (slices)	6	6
butter	100 g/4 oz	½ cup
chicken stock	150 ml/¼ pint	⅔ cup
dry sherry	2 tbsp	3 tbsp
chopped tarragon	2 teasp	2 teasp
salt and pepper	to taste	to taste
soured cream	150 ml/¼ pint	⅔ cup
To garnish: slices of bread	2–3	2–3
canned red pepper(s), cut into strips	1–2	1–2
tarragon sprigs	2	2

Remove the outer membrane (skin), then halve each kidney and take out the white core and fat. Separate the onions into rings. Take the stalks from the mushrooms, chop these but leave the mushroom caps whole. De-rind the bacon; finely chop 3 rashers. Cut each of the remaining rashers into 4 portions, roll these to make small bacon rolls and place on 2 metal skewers.

Heat half the butter and the bacon rinds in a frying pan (skillet) and fry the kidneys and onions until tender. Lift out of the pan; discard the bacon rinds. Add 25 g/1 oz (2 tbsp) butter to the pan and fry the chopped mushroom stalks, whole mushrooms and bacon. When tender, replace the kidneys and onion rings. Add the stock, sherry, chopped tarragon and seasoning. Simmer for about 5 minutes to heat all the ingredients and allow the liquid to reduce by about half. Stir the soured cream into the mixture just before serving; heat gently for 2 to 3 minutes.

While the kidneys are cooking, cut the bread into small crescent shapes. Heat the remaining butter in a second frying pan and fry the shaped croûtons until crisp. Grill (broil) the bacon rolls.

Serve the kidneys in a heated shallow dish. Garnish around the edge with the croûtons and bacon rolls. Top with narrow strips of red pepper and sprigs of tarragon.

Kidneys in Tarragon

GOLDEN SWEETBREADS

Cooking Time: 45 minutes   Serves 4–6   ✳✳

This method of serving the sweetbreads gives them an appetizingly golden look.

	Metric/Imperial	American
calves' (veal) or lambs' sweetbreads	675 g/1½ lb	1½ lb
white or brown malt vinegar	1 tbsp	1 tbsp
butter	40 g/1½ oz	3 tbsp
medium onions, chopped	2	2
medium carrots, chopped	4	4
chicken stock	600 ml/1 pint	2½ cups
salt and pepper	to taste	to taste
chopped parsley	2 teasp	2 teasp
chopped chives	1 tbsp	1 tbsp
chopped thyme	½ teasp	½ teasp
double (heavy) cream	3 tbsp	4 tbsp
To garnish: canned red pepper, cut into strips	1–2	1–2
lemon slices	4–6	4–6

Soak the sweetbreads for 2 to 3 hours in cold water to cover; change the water a few times and add the vinegar to the last amount of water.

Drain the sweetbreads. Put into a saucepan with fresh cold water and bring to the boil; drain the sweetbreads. This process, known as 'blanching', whitens and gives the sweetbreads a better flavour. Allow the meat to cool sufficiently to handle. Remove the skin and any gristle. If time permits, place the sweetbreads on a board, cover with a second board and a light weight and leave for 1 to 2 hours to flatten. (This stage is not essential.)

Meanwhile, heat the butter in a saucepan, toss the onions and carrots in this. Add the chicken stock and seasoning, simmer for 20 minutes. Sieve the liquid and vegetables or put into a blender to make a smooth, thin purée. Return to the saucepan, add the sweetbreads and the herbs and simmer steadily for 20 minutes. Take the pan off the heat so the liquid cools very slightly, whisk in the cream; adjust the seasoning if necessary. Garnish with strips of red pepper and lemon slices.

FAGGOTS

Cooking Time: 1¾ hours   Serves 4   ✳✳

A combination of two dishes that have been popular for generations are Faggots with Pease Pudding. Faggots are sometimes called Savoury Ducks, as the flavour is not unlike that of a duck. They can be purchased ready cooked in a a few traditional pork butchers, but are quite easy to prepare at home. They are made with liver, heart and pork. The recipe for Pease Pudding is on this page.

	Metric/Imperial	American
large onion, sliced	1	1
liver, preferably pigs, sliced	350 g/12 oz	¾ lb
heart, preferably pigs, sliced	100 g/4 oz	¼ lb
belly of pork, sliced (fresh pork sides)	100 g/4 oz	¼ lb
water, see method		
salt and pepper	to taste	to taste
ground ginger	good pinch	good pinch
chopped sage	½ teasp	½ teasp
chopped thyme	¼ teasp	¼ teasp
soft breadcrumbs	50 g/2 oz	1 cup
egg	1	1

TONGUE IN MADEIRA SAUCE

Cooking Time: 10 minutes plus time to make the sauce   Serves 4   ✳

The delicate bite and slight sweetness of the Madeira Sauce, recipe for which is on page 104, blends well with cooked tongue. This recipe, and the variations below, are excellent ways to heat tongue bought from a delicatessen.

	Metric/Imperial	American
Madeira Sauce, see page 104		
cooked tongue, sliced	450 g/1 lb	1 lb

Pour the sauce into a frying pan (skillet) or large saucepan (this allows all the slices of tongue to be heated quickly and easily). Add the tongue and heat. Serve with young carrots and peas, which blend well with this sauce.

VARIATIONS
Tongue with Almonds and Raisins: Make the Madeira Sauce; add 3 tablespoons (4 tbsp) raisins to the sauce and allow to stand for 5 minutes. Heat the tongue as above and top with 2 tablespoons (3 tbsp) blanched almonds.
● *Tongue with Onion Rings:* Slice 3 to 4 large onions, separate into rings. Fry in hot butter or dripping until crisp and golden. Heat the tongue as above and top with the hot onion rings.

Put the onion, liver, heart and pork into a saucepan. Cover with cold water and a little salt and pepper. Simmer gently for approximately 45 minutes until the meat is tender. Lift from the liquid, put through a mincer (grinder) or chop in a food processor. Mix with the ginger, herbs, breadcrumbs and egg. If the mixture is a little dry, then blend with some of the stock made by simmering the onion and meats. Season again well. Spread into a well-greased baking dish about 18 to 20 cm/7 to 8 inches square. Mark the mixture into squares and cover with well-greased foil.

Bake in the centre of a moderately hot oven, 190 to 200°C/375 to 400°F Gas Mark 5 to 6, for approximately 1 hour. Serve hot with gravy and Pease Pudding, below.

VARIATIONS
Use oatmeal in place of the breadcrumbs.
● The traditional faggot mixture was formed into small balls and wrapped in a pig's caul, instead of baked in a tin as the recipe above.

PEASE PUDDING

Cooking Time: 3½ hours   Serves 8–10   ✳✳

In the old days, before the development of heat-resisting basins and bowls, the pease pudding mixture was tied in a cloth. Nowadays, it is cooked in a container. The savoury mixture is an excellent accompaniment to bacon or ham as well as faggots.

It would be an excellent choice to serve with barbecued meat, see page 184. As the cooking time is long, it is worth making a large amount. Any leftover freezes well for up to 3 months.

	Metric/Imperial	American
dried split peas	450 g/ 1 lb	i lb
medium onions, coarsely chopped	2	2
bouquet garni	1	1
chopped mint	1 teasp	1 teasp
salt and pepper	to taste	to taste
butter or margarine	50 g/2 oz	¼ cup
eggs	2	2

Put the peas into a container, cover with water and soak for 12 hours. Strain, then place into a saucepan with the onions, herbs and a little seasoning. Cover with fresh cold water. Simmer gently for 2½ hours, check once or twice and add extra water if the peas are becoming dry. Allow any excess liquid to evaporate towards the end of the cooking time so leaving a moist, but not wet, mixture.

Sieve the pea pulp or put it into a food processor or blender to make a smooth purée (do not remove the herbs). Beat in the butter or margarine and the eggs, with a generous amount of seasoning. Place into one or two greased containers, cover with well greased greaseproof (waxed) paper and foil. Steam for 1 hour. Turn out and serve hot.

Poultry
──and Game──

Modern methods of rearing poultry mean that chickens, ducks and turkeys are readily available, for nowadays there is an excellent choice of both fresh or frozen birds. The birds are young and tender and therefore suitable for most methods of cooking, although roasting is still one of the favourite ways of serving poultry, see the next page. As fresh or frozen chicken and turkey portions are sold, as well as whole birds, it is very easy to prepare a dish like Chicken Medallions or Stuffed Turkey as the recipes on this page and on page 84.

Guinea fowl and geese are less readily available but these make a delicious change from the more usual poultry. Guinea fowl can be cooked like chicken or as game birds, see page 86. Goose is cooked and served like duck; this bird makes an excellent alternative to turkey for a special occasion, although it is less economical for goose has a high percentage of bone compared to the quantity of flesh.

Game birds and venison may be comparatively rare in cities and towns, but good poulterers and supermarkets should have reasonable supplies of the more usual game, such as pigeons, pheasants, rabbit and hare. In country areas, you may be able to buy grouse, partridge, wild duck and other game birds and venison. Some game birds and rabbit, like most poultry, can be obtained ready frozen.

It is absolutely essential to allow frozen poultry and game birds to thaw out completely before cooking. It is a health hazard to cook birds that are partially defrosted. Chicken portions can be cooked from the frozen state, unless they need to be marinated or coated.
Allow adequate time for birds to defrost; a comparatively small bird takes at least 12 hours at room temperature, or almost twice this time in a refrigerator. A microwave cooker hastens this process, follow the manufacturers' advice about the timing and setting to use when defrosting.

CHICKEN MEDALLIONS

Cooking Time: 20–25 minutes   Serves 4   ⁕

	Metric/Imperial	American
large slices of bread	2	2
butter	75 g/3 oz	6 tbsp
flour	1 tbsp	1 tbsp
chicken breasts	4	4
liver pâté slices	4	4
double (heavy) cream	150 ml/¼ pint	²/₃ cup
dry sherry	2 tbsp	3 tbsp
salt and pepper	to taste	to taste
chopped chives	1 tbsp	1 tbsp

Cut away the crusts from the bread and divide each slice in half. Heat 25 g/1 oz (2 tbsp) butter in a large frying pan (skillet) and lightly fry the bread until golden brown on both sides. Keep hot.

Heat the remaining butter in the pan. Sprinkle the flour over the chicken breasts and fry for 15 minutes or until tender. Spread the pâté on to the fried bread. Top with the chicken breasts. Heat the cream and sherry in the frying pan, do not allow to boil; stir well to absorb all the meat juices. Add a little seasoning and the chives. Spoon over the chicken breasts and serve at once.

VARIATION
Chicken Breasts with Stilton Cheese: Put thin slices of Stilton cheese on the fried bread in place of the liver pâté. Add port wine to the cream instead of sherry.

TO MAKE GOOD STOCK
Many dishes depend upon first class stock. This is particularly true of dishes based upon poultry and game. A good stock makes an equally good gravy or sauce to serve with the food, and it is an essential ingredient in the majority of casserole dishes.
CHICKEN STOCK: Simmer the giblets of the bird in water to cover for about 30 to 45 minutes. Add a bouquet garni, a very little salt and pepper for extra flavour.

A better stock is made by simmering the whole carcass of the bird in water to cover for 1½ to 2 hours.

The carcass and/or giblets of other kinds of poultry and game birds can be used in the same way. Chicken and turkey produce a white and delicately flavoured stock, game birds a more robust flavour.

VARIATIONS
Beef Stock: This is the ideal stock for many meat dishes. It is often known as a brown stock. Simmer the bones of beef in water to cover for 1½ to 2 hours. Marrow bones give the best flavoured stock.
● Veal bones make an excellent white stock which can be used in poultry dishes instead of chicken stock.
● Fish stock is made by simmering the skin and bones and the fish head, when available, in water to cover with a little seasoning and a bay leaf to flavour.

TO ROAST POULTRY

All poultry cannot be treated in the same way when it is roasted; chicken and turkey need to be kept moist, for these birds dry very easily, whereas duck and goose have an appreciable amount of fat and should be cooked in such a way that the excess fat runs out of the flesh, leaving birds with crisp skin and tender flesh.

It is important, therefore, to cover chicken and turkey with some kind of fat during roasting, see right.

When roasting duck or goose, lift the bird on to a rack and place this in the roasting tin so the fat runs away. It must, however, be stressed that modern methods of rearing ducks produce birds with a much smaller proportion of fat than in the past. Recipes using guinea fowl are on pages 84 and 96.

Poultry, like meat, can be roasted fairly quickly or more slowly. If cooking birds that have not been frozen, you can choose either method, but poultry that has been defrosted after freezing should be cooked by the temperatures given under SLOWER ROASTING. Allow frozen poultry to defrost before roasting.

Always weigh the poultry after putting in the stuffing. If you have purchased a very large turkey and your kitchen scales are not able to weigh it, ask the butcher to give you the oven-ready weight, then weigh the stuffing before putting this into the bird.

Roasting times and temperatures are similar for all poultry and most game birds too.
FAST ROASTING: Set the oven to 200 to 220°C/400 to 425°F, Gas Mark 6 to 7. Allow 15 minutes per 450 g/1 lb and 15 minutes over for birds up to 5.4 kg/12 lb in oven-ready weight (or weight with stuffing). When the weight exceeds 5.4 kg/12 lb, add an extra 12 minutes for every additional 450 g/1 lb up to 9 kg/20 lb.

If a large turkey exceeds 9 kg/20 lb then add an extra 9 to 10 minutes for every additional 450 g/1 lb. The slight difference in timing is because very large birds can be surprisingly tender. See the advice under roasting the various birds as to how to tell when the bird is cooked. The oven temperature can be reduced slightly to 190 to 200°C/375 to 400°F, Gas Mark 5 to 6 after 1 hour.
SLOWER ROASTING: Set the oven to 160 to 180°C/325 to 350°F, Gas Mark 3 to 4. Allow 22 to 25 minutes per 450 g/1 lb and 22 to 25 minutes over for birds up to 5.4 kg/12 lb in oven-ready weight (or weight with stuffing). The slight difference in timing is because frozen birds vary a great deal in quality, so check carefully towards the end of the cooking time.

When the weight exceeds 5.4 kg/12 lb, add an extra 20 minutes for every additional 450 g/1 lb up to 9 kg/20 lb. If a large turkey exceeds 9 kg/20 lb then add an extra 15 to 18 minutes for every additional 450 g/1 lb.

Chicken, guinea fowl or turkey can be placed into a plastic roasting bag to keep the flesh moist or cooked in a covered roasting tin or enclosed in foil. It is still advisable to cover the bird with some form of fat, but less can be used than when cooking in roasting tin.

The total cooking time should be increased by 15 minutes if using a covered roasting tin or foil, or the oven setting raised by 10°C/25°F or by 1 Mark higher with a gas cooker. The poultry browns well in a plastic roasting bag or covered tin, but it is important to open the foil for the last 20 to 30 minutes, or even a little longer when cooking a turkey, to encourage browning.

Duck or goose should be roasted in an open tin so that the excess fat runs away and the bird browns.

Timing for roasting is given above but birds vary slightly in quality and tenderness, so it is advisable to check before serving poultry. Insert the tip of a sharp knife into the flesh where the leg joins the body. If a little reddish juice runs out, the bird is not cooked.

TO ROAST CHICKEN

The chickens available for roasting range from small spring chickens (broilers), which the French call poussin, and which give a generous meal for one person, to large chickens and capons which can be carved, like a turkey, to serve 6 to 8 people.

It is very important to keep the chicken moist in roasting, so cover the bird with butter or bacon rashers.

If one stuffing only is used, this should be placed in the neck end and the flap of skin should be pulled over this stuffing so it keeps in position during cooking. If a

TO ROAST GOOSE

The points about roasting duck are just as important when cooking goose, but as this is a considerably larger bird it is advisable to prick the flesh 2 or 3 times during roasting.

In view of the high percentage of bone, allow a minimum of 450 g/1 lb per person when purchasing goose.

TO ROAST GUINEA FOWL

While guinea fowl can be stuffed and roasted in the same way as chicken, this bird can take the place of pheasant and be served with the same traditional accompaniments as game.

There is, however, a special recipe on page 96 which makes the very best use of this delicately flavoured bird.

Above left: Tangy Chicken – recipe page 84. Below left: Roast Turkey. Left: Roast Pheasant

second stuffing is used, put into the body cavity.

The usual stuffings for a chicken are Parsley and Thyme (often called Veal Stuffing) or a Liver Forcemeat. Modern cooks often prefer the more flavoursome Sage and Onion Stuffing. The recipes are on pages 105 and 106. Sweet stuffings and dressings blend well with the delicate flavour of chicken and there are a selection of recipes on pages 55, 90, 91 and 105.

Serve roast chicken with bacon rolls, sausages and Bread Sauce or Cranberry Sauce (like turkey) or a Creamy Tangy Sauce, recipes are on pages 102 and 100, and a thickened gravy or a Wine Sauce, see page 100.

TO ROAST TURKEY

When buying turkey, look for a bird with a solid breast, plump firm legs and a soft pliable wishbone. Allow at least 350 g/12 oz (¾ lb) of meat per person to compensate for the high amount of bones.

The fat content of turkey is even less than that of chicken so every effort must be made to keep it moist. The bird should be covered with butter or fat bacon before roasting. The very best way to keep turkey moist though, is to cover it with softened butter then place the bird in the roasting tin with the breast downwards. Roast the bird like this for the first half of the total cooking time, then turn it with the breast upwards so it will

brown and look appetizing.

The traditional stuffings for turkey are Chestnut, Parsley and Thyme or a Liver Forcemeat, these are on pages 105 and 106, together with recipes for less usual mixtures. Both Bread Sauce and Cranberry Sauce are the usual accompaniments to roast turkey together with bacon rolls, sausages and a thickened gravy. Try a Port Wine Sauce or Cream and Sherry Sauce, as the recipes on pages 103 and 104, to make a pleasant change.

TO ROAST DUCK

The duck should be a good cream colour with the minimum of fat. A small duckling is divided in half to serve 2 people and a large bird will serve up to 4 people.

Do not add extra fat to fresh duckling, but a defrosted frozen bird should be dried well with absorbent paper (kitchen towels) then brushed with a very little melted fat (shortening) or oil to encourage the skin to crisp and brown. The most effective way to ensure that roast duckling is never over-fat is to lightly prick the skin half way during the cooking process. When this is done, the fat runs out.

The traditional British accompaniments to roast duck are Apple Sauce, Sage and Onion Stuffing, Orange Sauce and a well flavoured gravy made from the giblet stock, pages 98, 106, 99, 104.

A NEW LOOK TO ROAST POULTRY

On the previous pages are the traditional ways of serving roast poultry. It is possible to vary the flavour of every kind of bird with a few simple ingredients:

Tangy Chicken: The roast chicken shown in the photograph on page 82 has a delicious lemon flavour. Instead of stuffing, fill the bird with 50 g/2 oz (¼ cup) butter blended with ½ tablespoon lemon juice. Before roasting, brush the chicken with 25 g/1 oz (2 tbsp) melted butter mixed with another ½ tablespoon lemon juice.

Honey Duckling: Roast the duckling(s) as usual but brush with a little thin honey about 20 minutes before the end of the cooking time.

Savoury Turkey: De-rind and finely chop 5 bacon rashers (slices). Heat the bacon rinds and 25 g/1 oz (2 tbsp) butter in a frying pan (skillet); remove the bacon rinds. Fry 2 medium finely chopped onions and the chopped bacon. Blend with 350 g/12 oz (¾ lb) pork sausagemeat, 50 g/2 oz sultanas (⅓ cup golden raisins), 50 g/2 oz (½ cup) chopped walnuts, 1 tablespoon chopped parsley and 1 egg. Loosen the skin over the breast of a turkey, leaving a pocket between the flesh and the skin. Spread the sausagement mixture evenly and neatly over the turkey breast. Press the turkey skin over the mixture and roast in the usual way. The mixture of ingredients flavours the breast during cooking.

This mixture can be used as a stuffing inside the bird, if preferred.

Goose with Prunes and Apples: Soak 225 g/8 oz (1½ cups) prunes; drain and remove the stones. Peel and core 4 small cooking (baking) apples, sprinkle with 1 teaspoon finely chopped sage. Put the prunes and apples inside the goose and roast.

Crusted Guinea Fowl: Cream 50 g/2 oz (¼ cup) butter with 100 g/4 oz (2 cups) soft breadcrumbs, a little seasoning and the yolk of 1 egg. Spread half the mixture over the body of the guinea fowl before cooking. Roast for half the total cooking time. Remove from the oven and spread with the remaining breadcrumb mixture. Complete the cooking.

This crumb coating was a favourite way of coating and roasting a chicken in the last century. It is even more successful as a coating on the ultra-lean guinea fowl and gives the bird a very appetizing appearance.

STUFFED TURKEY LEGS

Cooking Time: see method Serves 6 ❋❋

	Metric/Imperial	American
turkey legs, about 675 g/1½ lb each	2	2
For the stuffing: large tomatoes, skinned and chopped	4	4
sausagemeat	350 g/12 oz	¾ lb
chopped parsley	2 tbsp	3 tbsp
chopped chives	2 tbsp	3 tbsp
chopped sage	1 teasp	1 teasp
To coat: butter or margarine, softened	40 g/1½ oz	3 tbsp

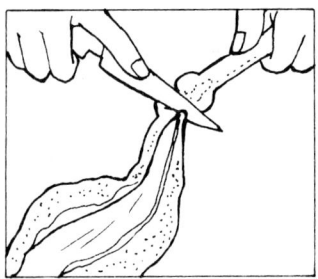

Slit the first leg lengthways with a sharp knife, then cut around the bone to loosen it from the flesh.

To serve, carve the legs in slices.

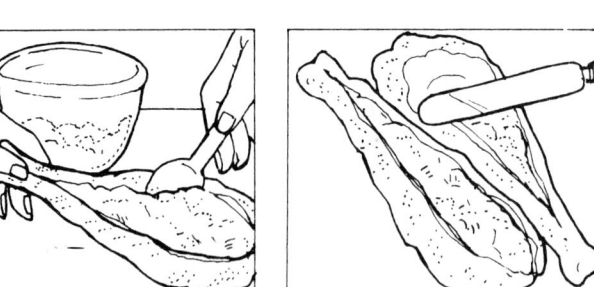

Remove the bone. Repeat with the second leg. The bones can be simmered in water to cover with seasoning and a bouquet garni to make stock for gravy, see page 81.

Blend together the ingredients for the stuffing and insert into the turkey legs.

Spread the butter or margarine over the turkey legs.

Weigh and roast in an open tin, or wrapped as described on page 82.

TO FRY OR GRILL CHICKEN

Young tender small chickens can be split and cooked under the grill (broiler) as in the Spatchcock of Chicken on this page. The Chicken Medallions on page 81 give an equally simple way of cooking chicken breasts by frying them.

One of the easiest and quickest ways to cook chicken joints is to coat them in a little seasoned flour and then in a batter or in beaten egg and crisp breadcrumbs, then fry the joints in deep or shallow fat. Follow the same recipes as given for coating and frying fish on page 34. Allow 10 to 15 minutes cooking time.

The recipe below for Herbed Chicken incorporates more flavour into the chicken flesh.

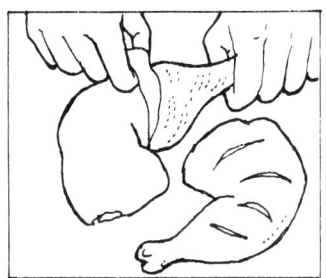

Remove the skin from 4 chicken leg joints and make about 4 *shallow* cuts in the flesh of each leg (this allows the marinade to penetrate the flesh).

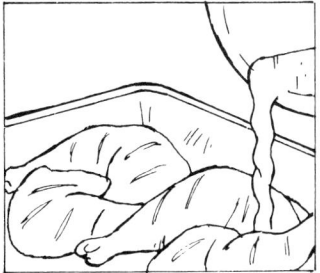

Blend 2 tablespoons (3 tbsp) oil, 2 tablespoons (3 tbsp) lemon juice, 1 crushed garlic clove, 2 teaspoons chopped rosemary, 2 teaspoons chopped chervil or parsley, a little salt and pepper.

SPATCHCOCK OF CHICKEN

Cooking Time: 15 minutes   Serves 4   ❋

This is an ideal method of cooking really young spring chicken (broilers), for the flavour is enhanced by the use of lemon and herbs. Today, the habit of splitting the chicken is vanishing as the young chickens are frequently cooked on a spit. Rosemary is a herb that blends well with chicken as it does with lamb.

	Metric/Imperial	American
small spring chickens (broilers)	4	4
butter	75 g/3 oz	6 tbsp
grated lemon rind	2 teasp	2 teasp
lemon juice	1 tbsp	1 tbsp
chopped parsley	1 teasp	1 teasp
chopped lemon thyme	½ teasp	½ teasp
chopped rosemary	½ teasp	½ teasp
salt and pepper	to taste	to taste

Split each chicken down the back so it can be flattened, do not remove any bones. Melt the butter, blend with the finely grated lemon rind, lemon juice and herbs, then season lightly. Put the chickens on the grid (rack) of the grill (broiler) pan, cut side uppermost, brush with a little of the butter mixture. Cook under a hot grill for 6 to 7 minutes. Turn the chicken carefully and spoon the rest of the butter mixture over the birds. Continue cooking until tender, crisp and golden. Serve with a green salad and game chips.

VARIATION
The birds can be cooked over a barbecue fire.

HERBED CHICKEN

Cooking Time: 15 minutes   Serves 4   ❋

As a change from herbs, add 1 to 2 teaspoons curry powder to the oil mixture.

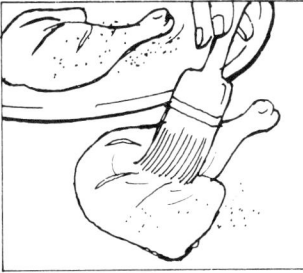

Pour into a shallow dish and marinate the chicken in this for 1 hour. Remove the joints, roll in seasoned flour then brush with beaten egg.

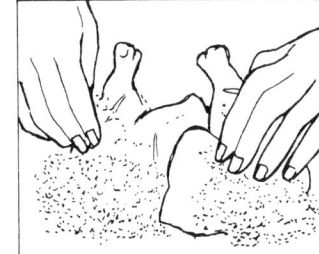

Coat in crisp breadcrumbs. Press these firmly against the legs, shake off any surplus crumbs. Chill for a short time before frying.

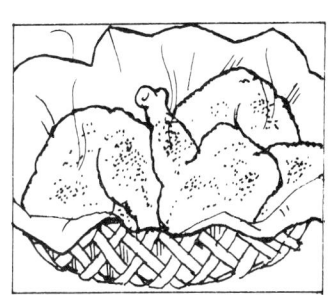

Drain on absorbent paper (kitchen towels) and serve with salad or hot vegetables.

Fry in hot oil or fat for 15 minutes or until crisp and brown.

TO ROAST GAME

Game birds are roasted like chicken and turkey. The cooking times on page 82 apply to the larger birds such as pheasants and grouse and the Scottish wild turkey, known as capercailzie and now becoming very scarce.

Wild ducks, such as teal, widgeon and mallard, do not have the crisp skins of the specially reared cultivated ducks. They can be wrapped or cooked in a covered roasting tin. These birds can be served with the same accompaniments as duck, see page 83.

When buying a pair of pheasants or similar sized birds (called a 'brace'), you usually have a hen and a cock bird. The cock bird is generally a little larger and slightly less tender than the hen, so allow an extra 10 minutes cooking time.

Most game birds are drawn like a chicken, but it is usual to cook plover and woodcock without drawing (i.e. removing the intestines). Naturally, this is purely a matter of personal taste.

Small game birds are often roasted with a slice of toast under them. This means that the delicious drippings drop down during cooking and impregnate the toast, which is then served with the bird. These small birds include young pigeons (squabs), partridge and woodcock. Allow about 30 to 35 minutes cooking time on the temperature given for FAST ROASTING or nearly twice that time on SLOWER ROASTING if the birds have been defrosted after freezing.

Game birds are generally served with Game Chips and Fried Crumbs, both recipes are on this page, and Bread Sauce or Redcurrant or Rowan Jelly, for which recipes are on pages 102 and 188. The giblets can be simmered to make a good gravy, but the Game or Venison Sauce on page 88 makes an excellent accompaniment.

All game birds need a plentiful amount of fat to keep them moist. Capercailzie can sometimes taste of resin, due to the fact it often lives upon pine shoots. Soak this in milk before cooking.

All game must be hung for several days, but if you like the flavour stronger then simply hang for a little longer.

Hare, rabbit and venison can all be roasted, provided the flesh really is young and tender. The best cuts of venison for roasting are the leg (known as the haunch) and the back (called the saddle).

Although venison has a very definite taste, a little like strong lamb, it is like veal in that it is a lean meat and larding, as page 53, improves the flavour and keeps it moist in cooking. Venison can be served with the same accompaniments as game birds, or as veal or pork. Another way of dealing with this game meat is to marinate it before roasting, as the recipe on page 88.

Less tender venison, like older hare and game birds, can be used in casserole dishes.

ROAST PHEASANTS

Cooking Time: see method   Serves 4–6   ❋❋

The photograph on page 83 shows 2 pheasants roasted in the classic manner, i.e. as the timing under poultry on page 82. To keep the pheasants moist, put approximately 25 g/1 oz (2 tbsp) butter inside each bird before cooking and cover the breast with fat bacon rashers (slices) or softened butter.

The pheasants are also served in the classic manner, i.e. with their tail feathers pushed into rounds of bread on the serving dish, and garnished with watercress. The dishes around contain the traditional accompaniments, i.e. Fried Crumbs and Game Chips, recipes on this page, Bread Sauce as page 102 topped with a little paprika for colour, gravy made from giblet stock, as page 82. The choice of vegetables is an ideal one for game, i.e. Brussels sprouts mixed with cooked chestnuts, see page 195.

ROAST PIGEONS

Cooking Time: 1 hour   Serves 4   ❋

Plump pigeons (squabs) are excellent when roasted. Simmer the giblets in seasoned water to make the gravy. Mash the tender liver with 25 g/1 oz (2 tbsp) butter, put on one side. Put 15 g/½ oz (1 tbsp) butter inside each of the 4 pigeons. Cover the birds with fat bacon rashers (slices). Roast just above the centre of a moderate to moderately hot oven, 180 to 190°C/350 to 375°F Gas Mark 4 to 5 for 1 hour.

Just before the end of the cooking time, spoon some of the fat from the roasting tin into a frying pan (skillet) and fry 4 slices of bread. Serve the birds on the bread, which should first be spread with the liver mixture, made as above. Garnish with Game Chips and serve redcurrant jelly or Cranberry Sauce, see pages 188 and 100.

FRIED CRUMBS

Cooking Time: 10–15 minutes   Serves 4–6   ❋

	Metric/Imperial	American
coarse breadcrumbs*	100 g/4 oz	2 cups
butter	50 g/2 oz	¼ cup

* see method

While fine breadcrumbs are generally mentioned, rather coarse breadcrumbs become more crisp and are nicer. Heat the butter in a frying pan (skillet), turn the breadcrumbs until coated with butter. Either fry steadily, turning all the time, or spread the butter-coated crumbs on to a flat baking tray or ovenproof plate and crisp for about 10 minutes in the oven while roasting the game.

GAME CHIPS

Cooking Time: 3 minutes   Serves 4–6   ❋

	Metric/Imperial	American
potatoes, peeled	225 g/8 oz	½ lb
To fry: deep oil or fat		

Cut the potatoes into wafer thin slices; this can be done with the old-fashioned kitchen utensil called a mandolin or with a very sharp knife, or the slicing attachment on a food processor or electric mixer. Dry the slices very well. Heat the oil or fat to 190°C/375°F and fry the potato slices for about 3 minutes or until golden brown and crisp. Frying twice, as the method for other fried potatoes, is quite unnecessary with these ultra thin slices.

Drain on absorbent paper (kitchen towels) and serve.

Roast Pigeons

ROAST VENISON

Cooking Time: see method   Serves 8 ✳✳✳

Mix together 150 ml/¼ pint (²/₃ cup) red wine vinegar, 150 ml/¼ pint (²/₃ cup) red wine, 2 teaspoons brown sugar, 1 teaspoon made mustard, 1–2 crushed garlic cloves, 150 ml/¼ pint (²/₃ cup) olive oil and 2 medium sliced onions.

Crush about 8 peppercorns and 1–2 bay leaves (or chop these in small pieces). Add to the ingredients, left, then pour into a large container.

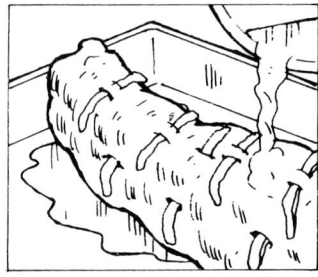 

Place a larded venison joint, about 1.8 kg/4 lb, into the container. Marinate for about 2 days, turn frequently. Lift from the marinade. Roast as pork or veal on page 53.

The marinade can be strained and some (or all of it) added to the sauce or gravy to serve with the game or meat.

GAME OR VENISON SAUCE

Cooking Time: 15–20 minutes   Serves 4 ✳✳✳

	Metric/Imperial	American
butter or game dripping	50 g/2 oz	¼ cup
small onion, chopped	1	1
large tomato, skinned and chopped	1	1
large mushrooms, chopped	2	2
flour	25 g/1 oz	¼ cup
brown stock	300 ml/½ pint	1¼ cups
salt and pepper	to taste	to taste
dry sherry	2 tbsp	3 tbsp
red or Madeira wine	150 ml/¼ pint	²/₃ cup
sugar	1 tbsp	1 tbsp
redcurrant jelly	4 tbsp	5 tbsp
brown malt or red wine vinegar	1 tbsp	1 tbsp

Heat the butter in a saucepan and fry the onion, tomato and mushrooms for 5 minutes. Add the flour and cook gently for 2 to 3 minutes. Gradually add the brown stock. Bring the sauce to the boil and cook until thickened. Season well and sieve the sauce or put into a liquidizer (blender) (this may not remove the seeds of the tomato, so the sauce should be sieved if you wish a perfectly smooth mixture). Return the sauce to the pan, add the wines, half the sugar, the redcurrant jelly and all the vinegar. Heat steadily until the redcurrant jelly has melted. Taste and add the rest of the sugar as desired. Serve hot.

SALMIS OF GROUSE

Cooking Time: 40 minutes   Serves 4–6 ✳✳✳

The origin of the word 'Salmis' is believed to date back to the 14th Century. Originally, this meant that game or poultry was roasted, then reheated in a wine sauce. Nowadays, a rich casserole dish is often called a 'Salmis'.

  The cooking time above refers only to the reheating of the roasted grouse. Timing for roasting game birds is on page 82.

	Metric/Imperial	American
young grouse, roasted	2	2
dripping from roasting the birds, see page 82, or butter	75 g/3 oz	6 tbsp
medium onion *or* shallots, chopped	1 / 2	1 / 2
mushrooms	100 g/4 oz	¼ lb
medium carrots, sliced	3	3
flour	50 g/2 oz	½ cup
stock from simmering giblets of grouse	600 ml/1 pint	2½ cups
sweet sherry or sweet Madeira wine	150 ml/¼ pint	²/₃ cup
chopped chervil or parsley	2 teasp	2 teasp
bay leaf	1	1
ground mace	½ teasp	½ teasp
salt and pepper	to taste	to taste
cooked ham, cut in one slice and neatly diced	100 g/4 oz	¼ lb
glacé (candied) cherries	2–3 tbsp	3–4 tbsp
To garnish: fried croûtons, see page 21		
glacé cherries	1–2 tbsp	1–3 tbsp

Skin and joint the grouse. Heat the dripping from roasting the grouse, or the butter, in a saucepan. Fry the onion or shallots, mushrooms and carrot for 5 minutes. Stir in the flour and cook gently for 2 to 3 minutes. Gradually blend in the stock and sherry or Madeira wine, stir as the sauce comes to the boil and thickens. Add the herbs, ground mace and seasoning, simmer for 10 minutes. Rub the sauce through a sieve or put into a liquidizer (blender) to make a smooth mixture; if using a liquidizer, remove the bay leaf.

Pour the sauce into a large saucepan, add the jointed grouse, diced ham and cherries. Heat gently for 20 minutes. Serve garnished with the fried croûtons and extra cherries.

VARIATIONS
Make the sauce as above. Put the jointed grouse, ham and cherries into a casserole, top with the sauce. Cover the casserole and heat in the centre of a moderate to moderately hot oven, 180 to 190°C/350 to 375°F Gas Mark 4 to 5, for 45 minutes.

● *Salmis of Duck or Goose:* This dish enables you to cut away any excess fat as well as the skin of a duck or goose. Use 1 large roasted duck or 2 smaller duckling instead of the grouse, or part of a cooked goose. Make the sauce as above. Add the jointed duck(s) or goose with the ham and 350 g/12 oz (¾ lb) cooked and skinned chestnuts; heat as above.

RABBIT IN MUSTARD SAUCE

Cooking Time: 2½ hours   Serves 4   ❋❋

	Metric/Imperial	American
rabbit with liver, jointed	1	1
water	900 ml/1½ pints	3¾ cups
bay leaves	2	2
parsley	small bunch	small bunch
white wine vinegar	2 tbsp	3 tbsp
flour	40 g/1½ oz	6 tbsp
salt and pepper	to taste	to taste
mustard powder	½-1 tbsp	½-1 tbsp
fat (shortening)	50 g/2 oz	¼ cup
medium onions, sliced	2–3	2–3
ground cloves	pinch	pinch
white wine	150 ml/¼ pint	⅔ cup
made mustard, optional	to taste	to taste
sugar, optional	1–2 teasp	1–2 teasp

Remove the liver from the rabbit. Cover with 900 ml/1½ pints (3¾ cups) water, add the herbs and simmer for 45 minutes. Meanwhile, wash the rabbit in cold water, soak for 1 hour in cold water and 1 tablespoon of the vinegar. Drain and dry well. Mix the flour, salt, pepper and mustard powder, and coat the rabbit joints.

Heat the fat (shortening) in a large saucepan and fry the joints for 10 minutes; add the onions for the last 2 to 3 minutes. Pour in 600 ml/1 pint (2½ cups) of the strained liver stock and the remaining vinegar. Add the ground cloves and white wine.

Cover the pan very tightly and simmer for 1½ hours. Taste the liquid, add a little made mustard and the sugar if desired, together with extra seasoning. Serve with mixed vegetables.

PHEASANTS WITH CREAM CHEESE AND GRAPES

Cooking Time: see method   Serves 4–6   ❋❋❋

	Metric/Imperial	American
pheasants with giblets	2	2
cream cheese	225 g/8 oz	½ lb
salt and pepper	to taste	to taste
lemon juice	1 tbsp	1 tbsp
grapes	350–450 g/12 oz-1 lb	¾-1 lb
butter	50 g/2 oz	¼ cup
flour	40 g/1½ oz	6 tbsp
pheasant stock, see method	450 ml/¾ pint	scant 2 cups
red wine	150 ml/¼ pint	⅔ cup

Put the giblets of the pheasants in a pan with water to cover. Simmer for 45 minutes to 1 hour until reduced to 450 ml/¾ pint (scant 2 cups).

Blend the cream cheese with a very little seasoning and the lemon juice. Skin and de-seed the grapes, see the line drawings on this page. Put half the grapes on one side for the sauce.

Put the cream cheese and the remaining grapes into the bodies of the pheasants. Place a piece of foil into the body cavities to keep the filling inside the pheasants during cooking. Spread the butter over the breasts of the birds.

Roast as the timing on page 82 choosing FAST ROASTING for fresh birds or SLOWER ROASTING for defrosted frozen birds. Lift the cooked pheasants on to a heated dish. Spoon 3 tablespoons (4 tbsp) of the dripping from the roasting tin through a strainer into a saucepan, stir in the flour and cook for 2 to 3 minutes. Blend in the stock and wine, stir as the sauce comes to the boil and thickens. Boil briskly for 5 minutes, then add the grapes and seasoning.

Joint the pheasants. Serve with the cheese and grape stuffing and the sauce.

TO SKIN AND DE-SEED GRAPES

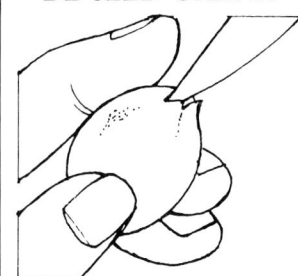

Insert the tip of a small sharp knife under the skin at the stalk end of the grape.

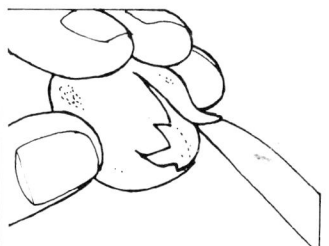

Pull away the skin.

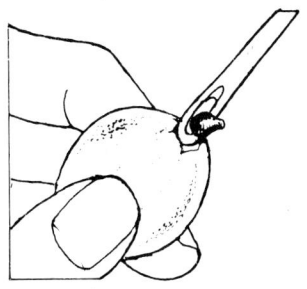

Insert the tip of the knife or eye of a large needle into the grape and pull out the pips (seeds) without spoiling the shape of the fruit.

Pot Roast of Chicken

POT ROAST OF CHICKEN

Weigh the roasting chicken to ascertain the cooking time, see below. Heat 50 g/2 oz (¼ cup) butter or dripping in a large saucepan or deep casserole. Turn the chicken in this until golden in colour. Remove from the pan or casserole. Put at least 450 g/1 lb prepared mixed root vegetables into the container. A little diced bacon can be added for flavour or a few diced Frankfurter sausages as shown in the photograph, with 2 teaspoons chopped herbs, such as parsley and rosemary. Half cover the vegetables with well-seasoned water or a mixture of water and wine. Place the chicken on top of the vegetable mixture. Cover the pan or casserole very tightly; if the lid is a bad fit, place a piece of foil under this, for the small quantity of liquid evaporates rapidly with an ill-fitting lid.

If cooking in a saucepan: Calculate the weight of the chicken and allow 25 minutes per 450 g/1 lb from the time the liquid in the saucepan begins to simmer gently. Check once or twice during cooking to make certain there is still sufficient liquid. To achieve the effect of roasting, the liquid should never more than half cover the vegetables.

If cooking in a casserole in the oven: Heat the bed of vegetables and liquid in the covered container in a moderate oven, 180°C/350°F Gas Mark 4, for about 20 minutes. Place the chicken on top of the hot vegetables and allow 22 to 25 minutes per 450 g/1 lb.

Lift the chicken from the saucepan or casserole and carve or joint. Serve with the well-strained vegetables. Garnish with chopped herbs. The liquid from the saucepan or casserole makes an excellent gravy.

STEWS AND CASSEROLES

The recipes that follow give a variety of interesting stews and casseroles based on poultry and game. The photograph on this page shows a Pot Roast of Chicken. This can be called a 'stew or casserole' for the food is cooked in a covered container with a little liquid, but the final result is very like a traditional roast chicken.

ALMOND CHICKEN

Cooking Time: 2¼ hours   Serves 6   ***

This combination of almond and lemon flavours is perfect with chicken. Nuts, almonds in particular, have been used with chicken for many centuries.

	Metric/Imperial	American
For the stuffing: soft breadcrumbs	100 g/4 oz	2 cups
almonds, blanched and flaked	100 g/4 oz	1 cup
grated lemon rind	1 teasp	1 teasp
lemon juice	2 tbsp	3 tbsp
chopped parsley	2 tbsp	3 tbsp
chopped lemon thyme	1 teasp	1 teasp
butter or margarine, melted	50 g/2 oz	¼ cup
salt and pepper	to taste	to taste
egg	1	1
chicken with giblets (except liver)	1.8 kg/4 lb	4lb
medium onion, sliced	1	1
water	600 ml/1 pint	2½ cups
parsley	sprig	sprig
lemon thyme	sprig	sprig
For the sauce: butter or margarine	25 g/1 oz	2 tbsp
flour	25 g/1 oz	¼ cup
chicken stock, see method	600 ml/1 pint	2½ cups
ground almonds	50 g/2 oz	½ cup
lemon juice	1 tbsp	1 tbsp
egg yolks	2	2
almonds, blanched and flaked	25 g/1 oz	¼ cup

Mix together all the ingredients for the stuffing. Put into the neck end of the chicken and sew or skewer the skin over the stuffing to enclose it completely.

Put the chicken giblets, except the liver, which tends to give too strong a flavour to the stock, into a very deep casserole. Add the onion, water, herbs and a little seasoning. Place the chicken in the casserole. Cover with a very well fitting lid.

Cook in the centre of a very moderate oven, 160°C/325°F Gas Mark 3, for 2 hours. Lift the chicken on to a heated dish and keep hot.

Heat the butter or margarine in a saucepan, stir in the flour and cook for 2 to 3 minutes. Strain the stock from the casserole into the pan (it should still be about 600 ml/1 pint (2½ cups). If some of the stock has evaporated, add a little water to give the right amount. Whisk or stir as the sauce comes to the boil and thickens very slightly. Whisk in the ground almonds. Blend the lemon juice and egg yolks in a bowl. Whisk on a little of the hot sauce, then add to the pan and simmer gently for 10 minutes; do not allow to boil. Season to taste.

To serve this dish, first spoon the stuffing on to a dish. Carve the chicken and place over the stuffing. Coat with about a quarter of the sauce and the almonds. Serve the rest of the sauce separately.

Serve with cooked rice and broccoli or another green vegetable.

VARIATIONS

Hindle Wakes: This unusual name is the title of an old traditional chicken recipe. The stuffing used is similar to that of the recipe above but with 225 g/8 oz (1⅓ cups) prunes, which should be soaked and chopped but not precooked. If using tenderized prunes, simply weigh or measure and chop. The chicken and sauce are served cold. In this recipe, the ground almonds in the sauce can be omitted; they were not used in the old recipes for this dish.

● If a sufficiently large casserole is unavailable, cook in a large saucepan but fill up with more water during the cooking period.

● An older boiling fowl can be used, in which case extend the cooking time to 3 to 3½ hours and reduce the oven temperature to 150°C/300°F, Gas Mark 2.

COUNTRY RAGOÛT

Cooking Time: 1¼ hours   Serves 4   ❊❊

	Metric/Imperial	American
chicken joints	4	4
flour	25 g/1 oz	¼ cup
salt and pepper	to taste	to taste
butter or chicken dripping	50 g/2 oz	¼ cup
onion, diced	1	1
chicken stock	450 ml/¾ pint	scant 2 cups
large mushrooms	225 g/8 oz	½ lb
medium tomatoes, skinned	8	8
To garnish: almonds, blanched and flaked, optional	1 tbsp	1 tbsp
chopped parsley	1 tbsp	1 tbsp

Dry the chicken joints. Blend the flour and seasoning together and coat the chicken – use all the flour. Heat the butter or dripping in a large saucepan and brown the chicken very well. Add the onion and stock. Cover the pan and bring the liquid to boiling point. Lower the heat to simmering and cook for 45 minutes. Add the mushrooms and tomatoes. Simmer for another 15 minutes. Serve the chicken and fairly thin sauce with cooked rice and peas.

Top with the almonds and parsley.

Creamed Chicken and Olives

CREAMED CHICKEN AND OLIVES

Cooking Time: 1¼ hours   Serves 4   ❊❊

	Metric/Imperial	American
thick streaky bacon rashers (slices)	4	4
butter	25 g/1 oz	2 tbsp
chicken joints	4	4
medium onions, finely chopped	2	2
flour	25 g/1 oz	¼ cup
chicken stock	300 ml/½ pint	1¼ cups
single (light) cream or milk	150 ml/¼ pint	⅔ cup
grated lemon rind	1 teasp	1 teasp
salt and pepper	to taste	to taste
medium potatoes, diced	2–3	2–3
green olives, stoned (pitted)	2–3 tbsp	3–4 tbsp
To garnish: lemon slices	4	4

De-rind and dice the bacon rashers (slices). Heat the bacon rinds and butter in a large saucepan, put in the chicken and heat for 3 to 4 minutes. Remove the chicken and bacon rinds from the pan, add the diced bacon and onions, fry gently for 3 minutes. Blend in the flour, chicken stock and cream or milk. Stir as the sauce comes to the boil and thickens, then replace the chicken joints with the lemon rind and seasoning to taste. Cover the pan and simmer gently for 45 minutes. Add the potatoes and olives. Simmer for a further 15 minutes.

Garnish with the lemon slices. Serve with cooked rice or creamed potatoes.

JUGGED HARE

Cooking Time: 4½ hours   Serves 6–8   ❈❈

	Metric/Imperial	American
hare with liver and blood, jointed	1	1
water	1 litre/1¾ pints	3¾ cups
salt and pepper	to taste	to taste
vinegar	2 tbsp	3 tbsp
fat (shortening)	50 g/2 oz	¼ cup
medium onions, sliced	2–3	2–3
medium carrots, sliced	2–3	2–3
flour	50 g/2 oz	½ cup
port wine	150 ml/¼ pint	⅔ cup
redcurrant jelly	3 tbsp	4 tbsp

Put the liver of the hare and the water into a saucepan, add a very little seasoning. Cover the pan and simmer for 30 to 40 minutes. Meanwhile, put the hare in cold water to cover with the vinegar and soak for 30 to 45 minutes.

Heat the fat in a large pan and fry the onions and carrots for about 5 minutes. Stir in the flour and cook gently for 3 to 4 minutes. Lift the liver from the stock. Measure the stock and blend 750 ml/1¼ pints (generous 3 cups) with the ingredients in the pan, stir as the sauce comes to the boil and thickens. Sieve the liver, mash, rub through a sieve or put into a liquidizer (blender) to give a smooth texture. Add to the sauce together with the blood of the hare, port wine and redcurrant jelly. Simmer the sauce for 5 minutes, then sieve or liquidize. Add seasoning to taste.

Lift the hare from the water and vinegar, dry very well, put into a casserole. Pour over the sauce. Cover the casserole and cook in a slow oven, 150°C/300°F Gas Mark 2, for approximately 3 hours.

Serve garnished with croûtons of fried bread, see page 21, and Forcemeat Balls, made as below. Redcurrant jelly is the usual accompaniment for Jugged Hare, recipe page 188.

FORCEMEAT BALLS

Cooking Time: 25–30 minutes   Serves 6–8   ❈

	Metric/Imperial	American
soft fine breadcrumbs	100 g/4 oz	2 cups
chopped parsley	1–2 tbsp	1–3 tbsp
chopped mixed herbs (sage, thyme, rosemary)	1–1½ teasp	1–1½ teasp
finely grated lemon rind	1 teasp	1 teasp
lemon juice	2 teasp	2 teasp
butter, melted	50 g/2 oz	¼ cup
salt and pepper	to taste	to taste
small egg	1	1

Blend all the ingredients together. Press into 12 to 16 small balls. Place on to a well-greased baking tray. Bake just above the centre of a slow oven, 150°C/300°F Gas Mark 2, for 25 to 30 minutes until firm. Arrange around the edge of the dish of hare.

CIVET OF VENISON

Cooking Time: 2 hours   Serves 6   ❈❈❈

	Metric/Imperial	American
venison, weight without bone	900 g/2 lb	2 lb
oil	1 tbsp	1 tbsp
brandy or red wine vinegar	2 tbsp	3 tbsp
salt and pepper	to taste	to taste
fat belly of pork (fresh pork sides)	225 g/8 oz	½ lb
butter	50 g/2 oz	¼ cup
small pickling onions or shallots	18–24	18–24
button mushrooms	100–225 g/4–8 oz	¼–½ lb
flour	25 g/1 oz	¼ cup
beef stock	300 ml/½ pint	1¼ cups
red wine	150 ml/¼ pint	⅔ cup
double (heavy) cream	4 tbsp	5 tbsp
To garnish: fried croûtons, see page 21		

Cut the venison into 2.5 cm/1 inch slices, then into fingers of about 5 cm/2 inches in length and 2.5 cm/1 inch in width. Mix together the oil, brandy or vinegar and a little seasoning. Pour into a shallow dish, add the venison and leave to marinate for 1 hour, turn once during this time.

Cut the belly of pork (fresh pork sides) into thin slices, then into narrow fingers. Heat this with the butter in a large frying pan (skillet) and fry the onions until golden. Put the onions into a casserole with the mushrooms. Add the venison to the frying pan and turn in the fat for 5 minutes, add to the onions together with the belly of pork (lift this out of the pan with a perforated spoon to leave as much fat behind as possible). Stir the flour into the fat, then blend in the stock and red wine. Stir as the sauce comes to the boil and thickens slightly, season to taste. Pour over the ingredients in the casserole.

Cover and cook in the centre of a very moderate oven, 160°C/325°F Gas Mark 3, for 1¾ hours. Lift the lid off the casserole about 10 minutes before serving, stir in the cream, cover the casserole and complete the cooking process. Top with the croûtons just before serving.

TO FREEZE GAME
Game must be adequately hung before freezing. Game birds can be frozen for up to 9 months, so can venison, rabbit and hare.

It is wise to divide venison, hare and rabbit into joints before freezing.

Pheasants with Apples

Cooking Time: 1½ hours   Serves 4–6   ❊❊❊

	Metric/Imperial	American
young pheasants	2	2
pheasant stock	300 ml/½ pint	1¼ cups
flour	25 g/1 oz	¼ cup
salt and pepper	to taste	to taste
butter	100 g/4 oz	½ cup
cooking (baking) apples	675 g/1½ lb	1½ lb
double (heavy) cream	150 ml/¼ pint	⅔ cup
sugar, see method		

Remove the giblets from the pheasants, put into a saucepan, add water to cover and simmer for 30 minutes. Strain the stock and boil briskly until 300 ml/½ pint (1¼ cups) remain.

Meanwhile, blend the flour, salt and pepper and coat the pheasants. Heat half the butter in a large casserole in a hot oven, 220°C/425°F Gas Mark 7. Turn the pheasants in the butter, then return to the oven for 10 minutes until starting to brown. Lift the birds out of the casserole. Divide the remaining butter into 2 pieces and put a piece into each pheasant.

Peel and slice the apples, put about half in the casserole, top with the pheasants. Place the remaining apple slices around the birds. Cover the casserole. Reduce the heat to moderate, 180°C/350°F Gas Mark 4, and cook for 30 minutes. Pour the cream and 4 tablespoons (5 tbsp) stock over the birds. Return to the oven and cook for a further 40 minutes.

Lift the pheasants and about half the apple slices on to a heated dish. Spoon the remaining apples out of the casserole with most of the fat and creamy liquid. Rub through a sieve or put into a liquidizer (blender) to give a smooth pulp. Add some of the extra pheasant stock, any extra seasoning required and a little sugar if the sauce seems a little sour. Heat and serve with the sliced pheasants and apple slices.

PIES AND PUDDINGS

The following recipes show some of the dishes in which poultry and game can be used.

Pigeon and Mushroom Pie

Cooking Time: 2½ hours   Serves 6   ❊❊

	Metric/Imperial	American
For the filling:		
large plump pigeons (squabs)		
or	3	3
small plump pigeons (squabs)	6	6
red wine	4 tbsp	5 tbsp
grated lemon rind	1 teasp	1 teasp
lemon juice	2 tbsp	3 tbsp
salt and pepper	to taste	to taste
medium onions, chopped	2	2
chopped parsley	1 tbsp	1 tbsp
ground mace	pinch	pinch
medium carrots, sliced	2	2
celery stalks, chopped	2	2
water	450 ml/¾ pint	2 cups
bouquet garni	1	1
rump steak	100 g/4 oz	¼ lb
mushrooms	100 g/4 oz	¼ lb
flour	25 g/1 oz	¼ cup
butter	50 g/2 oz	¼ cup
Forcemeat Balls, as page 92		
Puff Pastry, as page 154 made with	175 g/6 oz flour etc	1½ cups flour etc
egg	1	1

If the livers have been supplied with the pigeons, put these on one side. Cut the flesh away from the pigeons, do this slowly and carefully with a sharp knife, so none of the flesh is wasted. Mix the red wine, lemon rind and juice, salt and pepper and 1 chopped onion with the parsley and mace. Put on to a large flat dish and lay the pigeon flesh in the marinade; leave overnight, turning once.

Meanwhile put the pigeon bones, the remaining onion, carrots and celery into a saucepan. Add the water, bouquet garni and a little seasoning. Cover the pan and simmer steadily for 1 hour. Strain and if more than 225 ml/8 fl oz (1 cup) stock remains, boil for a short time in an open pan so the excess liquid evaporates. Allow to cool.

Cut the steak into neat fingers. Wash and dry the mushrooms (if perfect, they should not be skinned for the skin provides additional flavour). Toss the pigeons livers, steak and mushrooms in the flour, then fry in the butter for 5 minutes. Make the Forcemeat Balls as under Jugged Hare on page 92. Put the pigeons with the marinade, the steak, livers, mushrooms and forcemeat balls in a 2 litre/3½ pint (8¼ cup) pie dish. Mix the ingredients together so that when the pie is served, each person will have a selection of all the foods. Add the cold stock. Cover the filling with the Puff Pastry made as page 154. Beat the egg, brush over the pastry, chill for a short time if possible.

Bake the pie in the centre of a hot to very hot oven, 220 to 230°C/425 to 450°F Gas Mark 7 to 8, for 20 minutes This enables the pastry to rise well, then reduce the heat to very moderate, 160°C/325°F Gas Mark 3, and cook for a further 1 hour. Cover the pastry with greaseproof (waxed) paper if necessary during baking to prevent it becoming too brown. Many old recipe books mention that pastry should be covered with slightly damp paper, which prevents it becoming too hard, but that was before the days when the oven heat could be adjusted so readily. Serve the pie hot with a selection of vegetables.

LATTICED CHICKEN

Cooking Time: see method   Serves 4–6   ❖❖

This dish is based upon a 'boiled' (stewed) chicken. The term 'boiling' is really incorrect as the liquid in which the bird is cooked should just simmer gently. If it does boil, you break the tender breast meat before the legs are cooked.

	Metric/Imperial	American
boiling (stewing) fowl	1.3 kg/3 lb	3 lb
medium potatoes	3–4	3–4
rosemary	sprig	sprig
medium carrots	8–12	8–12
medium onions	8–12	8–12
medium turnips, quartered	2–3	2–3
salt and pepper	to taste	to taste
bouquet garni	1	1
To garnish: large slices of bread	3	3
egg	1	1
parsley	sprig	sprig

To tenderize an older fowl, put the peeled whole potatoes into the body; add the rosemary for flavour. Place the chicken, remaining vegetables, a little seasoning and the bouquet garni into a large saucepan. To give a stronger

Latticed Chicken

flavoured stock you can add the giblets, but omit these if you require a light coloured and delicate flavoured stock.

Cover the chicken and vegetables with cold water, bring this just to boiling point. Remove any grey bubbles from the surface, lower the heat, cover the pan and simmer steadily. If the boiling fowl is relatively young, allow 40 minutes per 450 g/1 lb cooking time (i.e. a total cooking time of 2 hours). If, however, the bird is very elderly, allow 1 hour per 450 g/1 lb cooking time.

Lift the cooked chicken out of the liquid, drain well. Place into a large roasting tin. Cut away the crusts from the bread, then cut the slices into narrow strips. Arrange these in a lattice design over the bird, as shown in the photograph. Beat the egg and brush over the bread. Brown in a hot oven, 220°C/425°F Gas Mark 7, for 8 to 10 minutes, or under the grill (broiler) for 5 to 6 minutes. Top with parsley.

Serve the chicken with the vegetables and a Parsley Sauce or Onion Sauce, see page 102.

VARIATION
If a young chicken is used, allow 20 minutes simmering per 450 g/1 lb.

KENTISH CHICKEN PUDDING

Cooking Time: 4–4½ hours   Serves 6   ❖❖

	Metric/Imperial	American
Suet Crust Pastry, as page 123 made with	300 g/10 oz flour etc	2½ cups flour etc
chicken with giblets	2 kg/4½ lb	4½ lb
water	450 ml/¾ pint	scant 2 cups
salt and pepper	to taste	to taste
medium onions, sliced	3	3
medium carrots, sliced	4–6	4–6
flour	15 g/½ oz	2 tbsp
stock, see method		

Make the Suet Crust Pastry as the recipe on page 123. Meanwhile, put the chicken giblets into a saucepan with the water and a little seasoning. Simmer for a minimum of 30 minutes to give a good stock. If wished, the diced meat from the giblets may be added to the chicken in the pudding after partially cooking; some people like to omit the liver as it gives a rather strong taste to the filling.

Remove all the meat from the chicken bones (these can be used to make a good stock for other dishes). Discard the skin, if wished. Mix the onion, carrots, flour and salt and pepper to taste with the chicken meat.

Line a 1.5 litre/2½ pint (6¼ cup) basin with part of the Suet Crust Pastry, see page 73. Fill this with the chicken and vegetable mixture. Add enough stock to come half way up the basin; save any stock left to add to the pudding when it is cooked and cut. Roll out the remaining pastry and form into a 'lid' over the filling. Cover with greased greaseproof (waxed) paper or foil. Steam for 3½ to 4 hours.

When the first slice is cut and the first portion of pudding removed, fill up with the hot chicken stock.

CHICKEN CHARTER PIE

Cooking Time: 2 hours 10 minutes   Serves 4–6 **

This is a traditional recipe from South Western England, where cream has always been an important part of family catering.

	Metric/Imperial	American
chicken fat or butter	75 g/3 oz	6 tbsp
chicken, jointed	1.3 kg/3 lb	3 lb
small onion	1	1
For the sauce: flour	25 g/1 oz	¼ cup
milk	150 ml/¼ pint	⅔ cup
double (heavy) cream	300 ml/½ pint	1¼ cups
salt and pepper	to taste	to taste
chopped parsley	2 tbsp	3 tbsp
For the pastry: Shortcrust Pastry (basic pie dough), as page 175 made with	225 g/8 oz flour etc	2 cups flour etc
To glaze: egg	1	1
To garnish: parsley	sprig	sprig

Heat 50 g/2 oz (¼ cup) of the chicken fat or butter in a large frying pan (skillet) and fry the chicken and onion until just golden in colour. Put into a pie dish of approximately 1.8 litre/3 pint (7½ cup) capacity. Melt the remaining 25 g/1 oz (2 tbsp) chicken fat or butter in the frying pan, add the flour and stir over a gentle heat to absorb any chicken juices. Blend in all the milk and half the cream. Stir briskly until a thickened sauce, then add the seasoning and parsley. Spoon over the chicken and onion in the pie dish.

Roll out the pastry, cover the pie, decorate with pastry leaves (see page 76) and flute the edge of the pastry. Make a definite hole in the centre of the pastry and put a small piece of foil in this, so that the hole does not close in cooking.

Beat the egg, brush over the pastry. Bake in the centre of a moderately hot oven, 200°C/400°F Gas Mark 6, for 20 minutes then reduce the heat to very moderate to moderate, 160 to 180°C/325 to 350°F Gas Mark 3 to 4, and bake for a further 1½ hours. Cover the pastry with foil or greaseproof (waxed) or other suitable paper towards the end of the cooking time so the pastry does not become too dark.

Remove the foil from the centre hole and pour the remaining cream into the hole just before serving. Top with parsley.

It was traditional to serve this pie with the Devilled Biscuits, right, but many people will find the pie sufficiently sustaining without them.

VARIATIONS
Fry a few sliced mushrooms and/or diced bacon and add to the chicken. The amount of onion could be increased.

DEVILLED BISCUITS

Cooking Time: few minutes   Makes 12   *

	Metric/Imperial	American
cream crackers or plain large biscuits (cookies)	12	12
butter	100 g/4 oz	½ cup
mustard powder	2 teasp	2 teasp
smooth chutney	2 tbsp	3 tbsp
brown sugar	1 tbsp	1 tbsp
flour	25 g/1 oz	¼ cup
Worcestershire sauce	1–2 tbsp	1–3 tbsp

Place the biscuits on a flat baking tray. Cream the butter and gradually blend in all the other ingredients. Spread over the biscuits. Heat for a few minutes in the oven or under the grill (broiler) until the topping begins to melt.

These are excellent with egg dishes as well as the Charter Pie.

Chicken Charter Pie

COLD POULTRY AND GAME

The Chicken Galantine looks most impressive, and is easily prepared. A small turkey could be used instead of the large chicken.

The method of marinating and coating guinea fowl moistens this rather dry-fleshed bird and makes it deliciously succulent.

Both the Game Pâté and the Game Terrine are equally good as an hors d'oeuvre or main dish.

CHICKEN GALANTINE

Cooking Time: 2½ hours   Serves 6–8   ✷✷

	Metric/Imperial	American
large chicken, weight when trussed	2.5–3 kg/5–6 lb	5–6 lb
water	1.5 litres/2½ pints	6¼ cups
veal knuckle or pig's trotter	1	1
bouquet garni	1	1
salt and pepper	to taste	to taste
lean veal fillet, from top of leg, minced (ground)	350 g/12 oz	¾ lb
lean cooked ham, minced (ground)	225 g/8 oz	½ lb
soft breadcrumbs	100 g/4 oz	2 cups
cooked tongue, sliced	225 g/8 oz	½ lb
hard-boiled (hard-cooked) eggs	3	3
To garnish: truffle, optional	1	1
pistachio nuts, skinned, optional	12	12

To make this galantine the chicken must be boned. Although this sounds difficult, it is not so, but it does need a sharp knife and patience to remove the flesh from the bones, otherwise some of the flesh is wasted. Loosen the skin at the neck of the bird, most people find it easier to use their fingertips rather than a knife. Continue loosening the skin on the breast away from the flesh, do not tear the skin. Cut the wishbone away from the flesh and remove. Turn the bird so the breast is on the table and use the point of the knife to cut out the shoulder joints, then to cut away the shoulder bones and remove.

Put the tip of the knife into the skin by the wings and neatly cut away the bones from the wings, the tips are better removed completely.

Lift the skin away from the thighs of both legs. Cut the thigh joints away from the body, then gradually cut the flesh away from both thigh bones and drumsticks. Having removed the wishbone, shoulder bones, wings and legs, you have now to work carefully to remove the complete breastbone and backbone and finally cut off the parson's nose. Do not remove the skin from the flesh.

Put the chicken bones into a saucepan with the water, knuckle of veal or pig's trotter (this ensures the jelly will set well), bouquet garni, salt and pepper to taste. Cover the pan and simmer for 1 hour.

Meanwhile, blend the veal and ham with the breadcrumbs, season to taste. Spread the boned chicken out flat, cover the flesh with half the forcemeat and then with the sliced tongue and shelled hard-boiled (hard-cooked) eggs. Cover the eggs with the remainder of the veal and ham forcemeat. Roll the chicken with its filling very firmly. Tuck in the pieces of skin to form a neat roll.

In the old days the prepared chicken was wrapped in a pudding cloth, but nowadays it is easier to wrap this in greased foil. Tie the foil roll securely and place into a saucepan with water to cover. Cover and simmer for 1½ hours.

Remove the roll from the liquid, take off the damp foil, cover the chicken with dry foil and leave until cold. If necessary, mould the soft hot flesh into a very neat roll before re-wrapping.

While the chicken is cooling, allow the bone stock to boil in a covered pan until 300 to 450 ml/½ to ¾ pint (1¼ to scant 2 cups) is left. Strain, allow to cool and stiffen very slightly to make a jelly.

When the chicken is cold, lift away the skin if desired. Dip a pastry brush in the jelly and brush over the chicken, place pieces of truffle and blanched pistachio nuts in position. Allow this layer to set, then brush the remaining jelly over the chicken roll once more. Serve cold with salad.

PIQUANT GUINEA FOWL

No Cooking
Serves 4   ✷✷

Skin and bone 4 portions of cooked guinea fowl. Blend 3 tablespoons (4 tbsp) white wine, 1 tablespoon olive oil, 1 crushed garlic clove, a pinch of curry powder and seasoning.

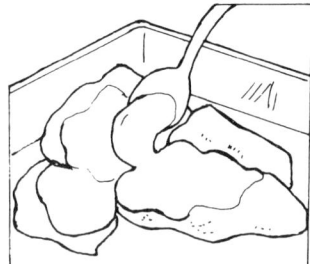

Pour the ingredients into a dish, marinate the guinea fowl for 3 hours. Spoon the marinade over the fowl once or twice. Drain then coat with Salad Sauce, as page 120.

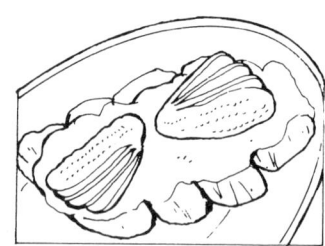

Garnish with pieces of gherkin (sweet dill pickle) and tomato. Serve with salad.

GAME PÂTÉ

Cooking Time: 2¾ hours   Serves 6–10   ❋❋❋

This should be made with the flesh of really young grouse or other game birds. The mixture of game, bacon and savoury liver stuffing is baked in a pastry case which keeps the filling beautifully moist. Although given the name of 'pâté', this is based upon traditional game pies. It is equally suitable as a main dish for 6 people or a first course for almost twice that number of people. Cumberland Sauce, as page 100, is an excellent accompaniment.

	Metric/Imperial	American
young grouse	2	2
calves' liver	225 g/8 oz	½ lb
mushrooms, finely chopped	175 g/6 oz	1½ cups
chopped chives	1 teasp	1 teasp
chopped parsley	1 tbsp	1 tbsp
chopped thyme	1 teasp	1 teasp
chopped sage	½ teasp	½ teasp
brandy	2 tbsp	3 tbsp
salt and pepper	to taste	to taste
bacon rashers (slices), de-rinded	225 g/8 oz	½ lb
water	300 ml/½ pint	1¼ cups
game stock, see method		
Shortcrust Pastry (basic pie dough), as page 175 made with	300–350 g/10 -12 oz flour etc*	2½-3 cups flour*
egg	1	1
water	1 tbsp	1 tbsp

*amount depends on the quantity of pastry decoration

Take the livers from both birds, add to the calves' liver. Put through a mincer (grinder) or chop in a food processor. Blend with the mushrooms, herbs, brandy, salt and pepper to taste.

Cut the flesh away from the birds, make sure the breast meat and as much of the meat from the legs as possible is cut in neat slices. Cut away any remaining small pieces of game flesh, mince (grind) or chop these in the processor and blend with the liver mixture. Cut the bacon rashers (slices) into 1.5 cm/½ inch strips.

Put the grouse bones and bacon rinds with the water and a little salt and pepper into a saucepan. Cover the pan and simmer for 45 minutes. Remove the lid and allow the stock to boil rapidly until reduced in volume and concentrated. Measure out 4 tablespoons (5 tbsp).

Prepare the pastry, roll out to about 5 mm/¼ inch in thickness; use just under two-thirds to line the base and sides of a 900 g/2 lb loaf tin (pan). Arrange a layer of sliced grouse in the pastry case, top with some of the bacon pieces, then a little liver mixture. Continue like this until all the filling is used. Moisten with the 4 tablespoons (5 tbsp) stock.

Re-roll the remaining pastry, cut to an oblong to make a 'lid' for the pâté. Moisten the edges of the pastry; seal firmly. Cut leaf shapes from any pastry trimmings left over. Beat the egg with the water; brush over the pastry and the 'leaves'. Press the 'leaves' on top of the pastry covering.

Bake in the centre of a moderately hot oven, 200°C/400°F Gas Mark 6, for 30 minutes then reduce the heat slightly to moderate, 160 to 180°C/325 to 350°F Gas Mark 3 to 4, for a further 1¼ hours. Allow the pâté to cool in the tin.

Serve the pâté, cut in neat slices, with lettuce or mixed salad. Piquant Redcurrant Jelly or Cranberry Sauce, as pages 188 and 100, are excellent accompaniments to this pâté.

This dish can be stored in the refrigerator for 2 days or up to 6 weeks in the freezer.

GAME TERRINE

Cooking Time: 3 hours   Serves 8–10   ❋❋❋

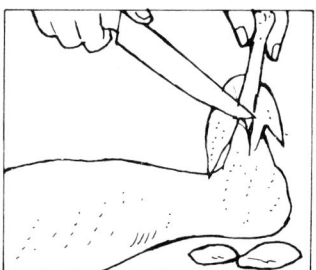

Remove the flesh from 2 uncooked pheasants or pigeons (squabs) or a small young hare.

Mince (grind) with 225 g/8 oz (½ lb) veal, 225 g/8 oz (½ lb) pork, the liver of the pheasants or the liver of the hare. If preferred, leave about ¼ of the game flesh neatly diced.

Blend the minced ingredients with 150 ml/¼ pint (⅔ cup) sherry, a pinch of ground ginger, a pinch of ground cinnamon, 2 eggs and seasoning.

Line the bottom and sides of a 1.4 kg/3 lb loaf tin (pan) with de-rinded streaky bacon rashers (slices). Put in the pâté mixture.

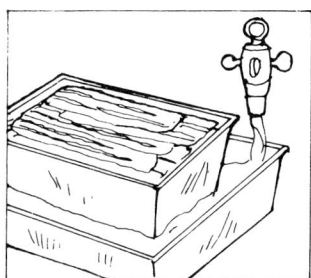

Top with more bacon rashers. Stand the loaf tin in a tin of cold water and cook in the centre of a very slow oven, 140°C/275°F Gas Mark 1, for 3 hours.

Put a weight on top as the terrine cools. Garnish with sage leaves and juniper berries or black (ripe) olives.

Sauces and Stuffings

There is a saying, attributed to an 18th Century writer, which says:

"In England there are sixty different religions, but only one sauce."

The author does not elaborate upon this statement, so no one is quite certain either about the exact religions or the sauce. Undoubtedly many of the sauces we enjoy today came originally from continental countries, but there are many delicious and traditional British sauces dating back to centuries past which still form an essential part of our cuisine. Some of these sauces have travelled to America and other countries, and are well-loved and appreciated.

TYPES OF SAUCE

The filled spoons illustrate some sauces. The first spoon contains a slightly unusual version of Cumberland Sauce, made by incorporating a little tomato purée (paste), the recipe is on page 100. This emphasizes the intriguing mixture of refreshing fruit and savoury flavours typical of fruit sauces to serve with meat, poultry and game. Next to that is a salad dressing; there are a selection on pages 120 and 121.

The third spoon holds a Mushroom Sauce, there are two ways of making this, the sauce illustrated is based upon White Sauce, page 102. The other darker and more strongly flavoured Mushroom Sauce, made with vegetables only, is on page 101.

The fourth spoon is filled with Apple Sauce, the fifth Bread Sauce, both traditional and simple sauces given on this page and page 102. These are followed by Parsley Sauce, one of the most popular of all of the creamy sauces, see page 102. The last spoon contains a Tomato Sauce. Although there is doubt as to whether tomatoes should be placed among fruits or vegetables, most people would regard them as a vegetable, the recipe is on page 101. Gravies and wine sauces appear on page 104.

FRUIT SAUCES

Fruit forms the basis of many excellent sauces that can be served with fish, meat, poultry and game.

Selection of sauces, see above

APPLE SAUCE

Cooking Time: 10 minutes　Serves 4–6 ❊

	Metric/Imperial	American
cooking (baking) apples, weight when peeled, cored and sliced	450 g/1 lb	1 lb
water	2–3 tbsp	3–4 tbsp
sugar	1–3 tbsp	1–4 tbsp
butter	15–25 g/½–1 oz	1–2 tbsp

Put the apples and water in a saucepan and simmer until nearly soft. Remove from the heat. Cover the pan and leave the steam to complete the cooking. Beat well with a wooden spoon, add sugar to taste and the butter. Good apples, carefully cooked, do not need putting through a sieve or into a liquidizer (blender). Serve hot or cold.

VARIATION
Apple and Orange Sauce: Use orange juice instead of water and add 1 to 2 teaspoons finely grated orange rind.

This sauce and Apple Sauce is equally as good with pork, duck or goose.

BLUEBERRY SAUCE

Cooking Time: 3–6 minutes　Serves 4 ❊

Blueberries make a delicious sauce to serve with meat dishes or they can be used in pies and other desserts.

	Metric/Imperial	American
blueberries	450 g/1 lb	1 lb
sugar	75 g/3 oz	6 tbsp
lemon juice	2 tbsp	3 tbsp
red wine or port wine	2 tbsp	3 tbsp
currants, optional	2 tbsp	3 tbsp

Wash the blueberries and sprinkle with the sugar. Allow to stand for about 1 hour so the juice flows.

Strain off the blueberry juice, place in a pan, add the lemon juice, red wine or port wine and currants and cook for 3 minutes. Pour the hot liquid over the blueberries and allow to cool. If serving the sauce hot, add the fruit to the hot liquid in the pan and simmer for 2 to 3 minutes only. This makes certain the berries remain whole.

CHERRY SAUCE

Cooking Time: 10–15 minutes   Serves 4–6   ✳✳

In the old recipes for this sauce, all red wine was used as the liquid and a stick of cinnamon was infused in the mixture during the cooking period.

All versions of this sauce are excellent with duck, goose or pork and with game birds or roast venison. A cherry sauce is an excellent accompaniment to liver pâté.

	Metric/Imperial	American
black or red ripe cherries*	450 g/1 lb	1 lb
water	150 ml/¼ pint	⅔ cup
sugar, white or brown**	50 g/2 oz	¼ cup
arrowroot	1½ teasp	1½ teasp
red wine	4 tbsp	5 tbsp

*If using Morello (cooking) cherries, increase the sugar.
**Brown sugar gives a darker coloured sauce but a richer flavour.

Remove the cherry stones with a cherry stoner gadget or the bent end of a fine hairpin. Do this over a saucepan so no juice is wasted, see line drawing page 189.

Heat the water and sugar in a saucepan until the sugar has dissolved. Poach the cherries in the syrup until soft. Blend the arrowroot with the red wine, add to the fruit mixture and stir over a low heat until thickened and clear. Serve very hot or cold.

ORANGE SAUCE (1)

Cooking Time: 1 hour 25 minutes   Serves 4   ✳✳

Traditionally Seville oranges are used in this sauce for they give a somewhat 'bitter' taste that blends well with duck. When not available use sweet oranges, but add a little lemon juice to provide a less sweet flavour.

Orange Sauce blends perfectly with duck or goose but is pleasant with roasted pork too.

	Metric/Imperial	American
duckling giblets		
water	600 ml/1 pint	2½ cups
Seville oranges	2	2
salt and pepper	to taste	to taste
port wine	3 tbsp	4 tbsp
cornflour (cornstarch)	2 tbsp	3 tbsp
redcurrant jelly	2 tbsp	3 tbsp

Put the giblets and water into a saucepan. Cover the pan tightly and simmer for approximately 1 hour until tender. You should have about 450 ml/¾ pint (scant 2 cups) stock. Strain the liquid very carefully indeed, so there are no pieces of meat or fat left. Remove the peel from 1 orange, discard the white pith and cut the orange zest into matchstick pieces. Simmer in 300 ml/½ pint (1¼ cups) giblet stock until tender.

Meanwhile, remove and heat the peel from the second orange in the remainder of the stock for about 5 minutes, to extract the orange flavour from the peel. Strain the pieces of peel from the stock, lift out the shreds of peel from the first pan of stock but retain these. Squeeze out the juice from the 2 oranges. Put all the giblet stock into a saucepan with the orange juice, heat steadily with salt and pepper and port wine.

In the olden days this was served as a thin sauce, but nowadays most people prefer it to be thicker, so blend the cornflour (cornstarch) with a little of the liquid, add to the pan and cook until smooth and thickened, stir well during this time. Add the redcurrant jelly, which gives colour and flavour, then cook again until the sauce just coats the back of a wooden spoon. Put in the fine strips of orange peel, heat and serve.

VARIATION
Dark Orange Sauce: An intriguing flavour and deep rich colour is given to the sauce if 50 g/2 oz plain chocolate (2 squares of cooking chocolate) is added to the sauce instead of the redcurrant jelly.

Serve roast duck with Orange Sauce, Cherry Sauce or Apple Sauce

CRANBERRY SAUCE

Cooking Time: 12–15 minutes   Serves 6–8   ❊❊

Cranberries have been known as 'crane berries' and 'bounce berries' too, for they bounce quite vigorously when ripe. Although this is regarded, quite rightly, as an American inspired sauce, cranberries were known in Scotland many years ago. This sauce is now highly esteemed in many countries.

Cranberry Sauce is a splendid 'mixer' with most savoury dishes.

	Metric/Imperial	American
sugar	175 g/6 oz	¾ cup
port wine	3 tbsp	4 tbsp
water	4 tbsp	5 tbsp
cranberries	450 g/1 lb	1 lb

Put the sugar, port wine and water into a saucepan. Heat until the sugar has dissolved, stirring. Add the cranberries, cover the pan tightly and lower the heat. Cook for 10 to 12 minutes or until the berries cease 'popping'. Serve hot or cold.

VARIATIONS

Prepare the sauce as above; blend 1½ teaspoons arrowroot with an extra 3 tablespoons (4 tbsp) port wine. Blend with the cooked fruit mixture and stir over a low heat until thickened and smooth.
● *Cranberry and Orange Sauce:* Add 2 teaspoons grated orange rind to the cranberries and use orange juice in place of port wine and water.
● *Cranberry and Beer Sauce:* Use beer as the liquid in the basic sauce. This is a robust sauce that is excellent with cooked hare or venison.
● *Apple and Cranberry Sauce:* Use 225 g/8 oz (½ lb) cranberries and 225 g/8 oz (½ lb) peeled, sliced cooking (baking) apples in any of the recipes.

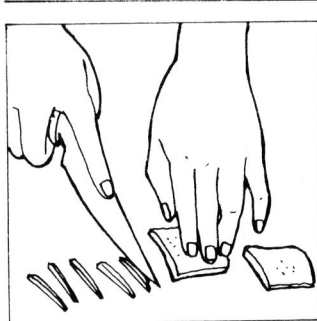

CUTTING FRUIT PEEL
Cut the fruit peel into narrow strips like this for Cumberland Sauce.

CUMBERLAND SAUCE

Cooking Time: 25 minutes   Serves 4–6   ❊❊

This is an old traditional sauce which has now become extremely popular again. All versions of Cumberland Sauce are excellent with cooked liver or liver pâté, cooked ham, venison and meats with a definite flavour.

	Metric/Imperial	American
medium oranges	2	2
medium lemon	1	1
water	225 ml/8 fl oz	1 cup
arrowroot	1 teasp	1 teasp
mustard powder	1 teasp	1 teasp
port wine	4 tbsp	5 tbsp
redcurrant jelly	4 tbsp	5 tbsp

Pare the rind from the oranges and lemon, cut away any bitter white pith, then cut the top coloured zest into matchstick pieces. Soak in the water for 15 minutes then simmer gently in a covered saucepan until the fruit rinds are tender. The liquid should be reduced to half.

Squeeze out the orange and lemon juice, blend with the arrowroot and mustard. Pour into the pan containing the peel, add the port wine and redcurrant jelly and stir over a low heat until thickened and clear. Serve cold.

VARIATIONS

Grate the orange and lemon rinds instead of cutting these into thin strips. Follow the sauce recipe from the second paragraph but reduce the water to 4 tablespoons (5 tbsp).
● *Oxford Sauce:* Another name for a similar piquant sauce. Add a good pinch of cayenne pepper, a few drops of Worcestershire sauce and 2 tablespoons (3 tbsp) quartered glacé (candied) cherries to the other ingredients in Cumberland Sauce.
● *Tomato Cumberland Sauce:* Stir 1 to 2 teaspoons fresh tomato or concentrated tomato purée (paste) into the other ingredients.

TANGY LEMON SAUCE

Cooking Time: 15 minutes   Serves 4–6   ❊❊

This sauce and the variations blend well with chicken and turkey.

	Metric/Imperial	American
grated lemon rind	½-1 teasp	½-1 teasp
chicken stock	300 ml/½ pint	1¼ cups
egg yolks	2	2
lemon juice	1½ tbsp	1¾ tbsp
salt and pepper	to taste	to taste

Put the lemon rind and stock into a saucepan, simmer for 5 minutes. Beat the egg yolks and lemon juice in a basin or bowl, whisk on a little of the hot chicken stock. Tip into the saucepan and whisk over a very low heat until a coating consistency. Season well.

VARIATIONS

Creamy Tangy Sauce: Use only 150 ml/¼ pint (⅔ cup) chicken stock and 150 ml/¼ pint single (⅔ cup light) cream. Whisk the cream with the egg yolks and lemon juice, proceed as above.
● *Wine Sauce:* Omit the lemon rind and juice and use only 225 ml/8 fl oz (1 cup) chicken stock and 4 tablespoons (5 tbsp) white wine.

ORANGE SAUCE (2)

Cooking Time: 15 minutes   Serves 4–6   ✳

This sauce can be served with savoury or sweet dishes. It has a pleasantly refreshing taste. To make it more savoury, use concentrated duckling stock (completely free from any fat) instead of water.

	Metric/Imperial	American
water	150 ml/¼ pint	⅔ cup
grated orange rind	1 tbsp	1 tbsp
arrowroot or cornflour (cornstarch)	15 g/½ oz	2 tbsp
orange juice	300 ml/½ pint	1¼ cups
sugar, brown or white	1 tbsp	1 tbsp
jelly type marmalade	3 tbsp	4 tbsp

Put the water and orange rind into a saucepan, cover the pan and simmer gently for 5 minutes. Blend the arrowroot or cornflour (cornstarch) with the orange juice, add to the pan together with the sugar and marmalade. Stir over a low heat until thickened and clear. Serve hot or cold.

VEGETABLE SAUCES
These sauces were extremely popular many years ago. With our modern desire to use as many fresh ingredients as possible and to include high fibre foods in our diet, they are well worth reviving. The sauces are simple and very delicious.

TOMATO SAUCE

Cooking Time: 20 minutes   Serves 4   ✳✳

This sauce is equally good hot or cold and excellent with most dishes.

	Metric/Imperial	American
bacon rashers (slices), de-rinded and chopped	2	2
medium onion, chopped	1	1
small dessert apple, peeled and chopped	1	1
tomatoes, skinned and chopped	450 g/1 lb	1 lb
water or chicken stock	150 ml/¼ pint	⅔ cup
salt and pepper	to taste	to taste
sugar	½-1 teasp	½-1 teasp

Put the bacon rinds and rashers into a saucepan, fry for 2 minutes. Add the onion and apple and cook for 5 minutes, stirring well. Remove the rinds. Add the tomatoes, water or stock, seasoning and sugar. Cover the pan and simmer for 15 minutes or until soft. Rub through a sieve or put into a liquidizer (blender) until smooth.

MUSHROOM SAUCE

Cooking Time: 30 minutes   Serves 4   ✳

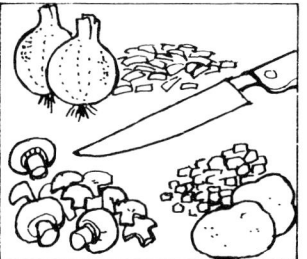

Wipe and chop 225 g/8 oz (½ lb) mushrooms. Peel and chop 2 medium onions and 2 potatoes.

Toss the vegetables in 25 g/1 oz (2 tbsp) melted butter.

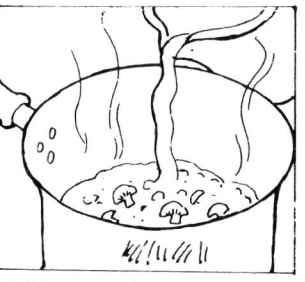

Add 300 ml/½ pint (1¼ cups) chicken or beef stock and a little seasoning. Simmer for 20 minutes.

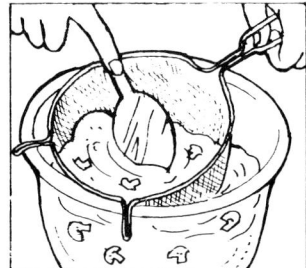

Rub through a sieve or put into a food processor or liquidizer (blender) until a smooth sauce. Reheat.

Note: A sprig of parsley and thyme and 1 garlic clove can be cooked with the other ingredients.

CUCUMBER SAUCE

Cooking Time: 15 minutes   Serves 4–6   ✳✳

Cucumber Sauce blends well with fish dishes, cooked lamb and some curries.

	Metric/Imperial	American
butter	50 g/2 oz	¼ cup
medium cucumber, peeled and sliced	1	1
water or chicken or fish stock	300 ml/½ pint	1¼ cups
salt and pepper	to taste	to taste
double (heavy) cream	4 tbsp	5 tbsp
lemon juice	1 tbsp	1 tbsp

Heat the butter in a saucepan, toss the cucumber slices in this for 5 minutes. Add the liquid (this should be selected according to the type of food with which the sauce is to be served), season well. Simmer for 10 minutes, then rub through a sieve or put into a liquidizer (blender) to give a smooth purée.

If serving hot, add the cream and lemon juice and reheat gently. If serving cold, allow the purée to become quite cold then whip the cream and blend with the purée and lemon juice.

CREAMY SAUCES

The following sauces are based on a good White Sauce. To improve the flavours of any of these sauces, use 1 or 2 tablespoons of single (light) or double (heavy) cream instead of the same amount of milk.

Sauces with a very definite flavour are on the next page.

WHITE SAUCE

Cooking Time: 10–12 minutes   Serves 4   ❋

This can be considered a basic sauce, for so many flavourings can be added. This sauce is made by the 'roux' method, the name given to the mixture of butter (or other fat) and flour.

The ingredients given below produce a sauce with a coating consistency. The photograph indicates quite clearly that this is sufficiently thick to coat a wooden spoon.

Always cook the sauce until the flavour of uncooked flour is lost. Under-cooking this type of sauce is a very general fault.

	Metric/Imperial	American
butter or margarine	25 g/1 oz	2 tbsp
flour	25 g/1 oz	¼ cup
milk	generous 300 ml/½ pint	generous 1¼ cups
salt and pepper	to taste	to taste

Heat the butter or margarine in a saucepan, remove from the heat and stir in the flour. Return to a low heat and stir for 2 to 3 minutes. Gradually blend in the milk, stirring all the time, and cook until thickened. Season to taste.

VARIATIONS

A quick way of making this sauce is to put all the ingredients into the saucepan and whisk briskly until the sauce thickens and the flour is cooked.
● Use 15 g/½ oz cornflour (2 tbsp cornstarch) instead of the flour.
● Use half milk and half vegetable stock if making this sauce to coat vegetables, or half milk and half fish or chicken stock if making the sauce to coat fish, chicken or meat dishes.
● Add 1 to 2 tablespoons (1 to 3 tbsp) cream to the sauce.
● *Béchamel Sauce:* This name is given to a White Sauce when the milk is first heated with a halved onion, part of a celery stalk, a bay leaf or bouquet garni. Allow the milk and other ingredients to stand in a warm place for at least 30 minutes to infuse. Strain the milk and use to make the sauce.
● *Brown Sauce:* Use brown stock instead of milk in the recipe above. Allow the 'roux' to brown slightly before incorporating the stock. If a halved onion and carrot, a bay leaf and/or a bouquet garni are infused in the stock for at least 30 minutes, it produces a much better flavoured sauce.
● *Caper Sauce:* Make the White Sauce; as this sauce is frequently served with lamb, use a little lamb stock instead of all milk. When the sauce has thickened, remove from the heat and add 1 to 2 teaspoons capers with 1 teaspoon vinegar from the jar. Heat gently without boiling.
● *Cheese Sauce:* Make the White Sauce, flavour with ½

to 1 teaspoon made mustard and approximately 100 g/4 oz (1 cup) grated cheese. This can be any good cooking cheese such as Cheddar. This sauce is served with many savoury dishes.
● *Fennel Sauce:* Make the White Sauce, add 1 to 2 tablespoons chopped fennel leaves and a squeeze of lemon juice. This sauce is excellent with fish.
● *Horseradish Sauce:* Make the White Sauce, remove from the heat, add 1 to 2 tablespoons freshly grated horseradish with 1 teaspoon made mustard and 2 tablespoons double (3 tbsp heavy) cream. A squeeze of lemon juice can be added. This is the classic sauce to serve with roast beef.
● *Onion Sauce:* Chop 2 medium onions neatly. Simmer in approximately 150 ml/¼ pint (⅔ cup) well-seasoned water for 10 minutes. Strain, measure the onion stock and then add enough milk, or milk and single (light) cream, to make a generous 300 ml/½ pint (1¼ cups) liquid. Make the White Sauce using this liquid, add the chopped onions and heat. This sauce is good with roast mutton.
● *Parsley Sauce:* Make the White Sauce, add 1 to 2 tablespoons chopped parsley. This sauce is served with many savoury dishes, particularly fish. A little cream and lemon juice can be added.

MUSTARD SAUCE

Cooking Time: as White Sauce   Serves 4   ❋

This sauce can be varied by the choice of mustard. Either blend ½ to 1 tablespoon mustard powder with the flour for the White Sauce, or make the sauce and blend prepared English or Dijon mustard into the sauce (the amount to personal taste). It is interesting to note that Dijon mustard has been used in Britain for many generations.

BREAD SAUCE

Cooking Time: 5 minutes   Serves 4–6   ❋❋

This is essentially a British sauce. The secrets of success are to prepare the sauce early in the day so the onion can infuse in the milk and give the sauce a good flavour; being slightly extravagant using cream, add this just before serving.

Bread Sauce is one of the classic accompaniments to roast chicken, turkey, veal and game birds.

	Metric/Imperial	American
milk	300 ml/½ pint	1¼ cups
butter	25 g/1 oz	2 tbsp
small onion	1	1
cloves, optional	3	3
soft breadcrumbs	50 g/2 oz	1 cup
salt and pepper	to taste	to taste
double (heavy) cream	2 tbsp	3 tbsp

Put the milk, butter and onion, stuck with cloves if using, into a saucepan. Heat the milk, add the breadcrumbs and a little seasoning. Cover the pan and leave in a warm place. Reheat the sauce with the cream just before the meal. Remove the onion and serve.

CREAM AND SHERRY SAUCE

Cooking Time: 10 minutes   Serves 4   ✳✳✳

These creamy sauces are excellent with roast turkey, chicken or veal. The sauce is simple and not too thick, and a perfect alternative to the more traditional gravy.

	Metric/Imperial	American
chicken stock	300 ml/½ pint	1¼ cups
cornflour (cornstarch)	1 tbsp	1 tbsp
dry sherry	3 tbsp	4 tbsp
double (heavy) cream	4 tbsp	5 tbsp
salt and pepper	to taste	to taste

Blend the chicken stock and cornflour (cornstarch). Pour into a saucepan, add the sherry and stir over a low heat until thickened. Remove from the heat, so the sauce is no longer boiling. Whisk in the cream. Return to a low heat and whisk until well heated. Season to taste.

VARIATION
Cream and Wine Sauce: Use a really good red wine, such as a claret, instead of sherry.

CREAMY DEVILLED SAUCE

Cooking Time: 20 minutes   Serves 4–6   ✳✳

This sauce is good with poultry and meat, and excellent served cold with cold poultry or meat.

	Metric/Imperial	American
butter or margarine	50 g/2 oz	¼ cup
medium onions, finely chopped	2	2
flour	25 g/1 oz	¼ cup
curry powder	1–2 teasp	1–2 teasp
milk or milk and single (light) cream	generous 300 ml/½ pint	generous 1¼ cups
Worcestershire sauce	1–2 teasp	1–2 teasp
salt and cayenne pepper	to taste	to taste

HORSERADISH CREAM

No Cooking   Serves 4–6   ✳✳

This is the classic accompaniment to roast beef. If serving the cream with smoked fish, be a little sparing with the horseradish to give a milder flavour.

	Metric/Imperial	American
double (heavy) cream	150 ml/¼ pint	⅔ cup
dry mustard powder	good pinch	good pinch
salt and pepper	to taste	to taste
sugar	good pinch	good pinch
fresh horseradish, peeled and grated	2 tbsp	3 tbsp
white malt or wine vinegar or lemon juice	¾ tbsp	¾ tbsp

Whip the cream until it just holds its shape then blend in the seasonings and horseradish. Gradually incorporate the vinegar or lemon juice.

Above left: White Sauce. Above: Caper Sauce

Heat the butter or margarine, fry the onions until soft. Blend in the flour and curry powder, then gradually add the milk, or milk and cream. Stir as the sauce comes to the boil and thickens. Add the Worcestershire sauce, salt and cayenne pepper to taste.

VARIATIONS
Devilled Sauce: Use chicken or beef or fish stock instead of milk or milk and cream.
● *Creamy Curried Sauce:* Use slightly more curry powder than in the recipe, left. Omit the Worcestershire sauce and cayenne pepper. Sieve the sauce or purée in a liquidizer (blender) when cooked.
    Other Curry Sauces are on page 173.

GOOD GRAVY

Cooking Time: 10 minutes Serves 4–6 *

Pour out all the dripping from the roasting tin (pan) except for 1½ tablespoons (scant 2 tbsp). Leave in all the tiny pieces of meat, stuffing, etc.

Blend in 2 *level* tablespoons (3 *level* tbsp) flour and a little gravy browning if desired (use a little more flour if you want a thick gravy). Cook gently over a low heat for 1 to 2 minutes.

Blend in 450 ml/¾ pint (scant 2 cups) stock or liquid from cooking vegetables. Stir as the liquid comes to the boil and thickens, season and flavour with a little mushroom ketchup or red wine if desired.

Pour through a strainer into a heated sauce boat and serve.

MADEIRA SAUCE

Cooking Time: 20 minutes Serves 4 ***

	Metric/Imperial	American
butter or margarine	25 g/1 oz	2 tbsp
flour	25 g/1 oz	¼ cup
ham or chicken or beef stock	150 ml/¼ pint	⅔ cup
Madeira wine, sweet or dry	generous 150 ml/¼ pint	generous ⅔ cup
salt and pepper	to taste	to taste

Heat the butter or margarine in a saucepan, stir in the flour and cook gently for 2 to 3 minutes. Gradually blend in the stock and Madeira wine, stir as the sauce comes to the boil and thickens. Add seasoning to taste.

PORT WINE GRAVY SAUCE (1)

Cooking Time: 15 minutes Serves 4–6 ***

This gravy sauce is simpler than the Game Sauce on page 88 but it is excellent with roasted game. Cover jointed cooked game birds with this sauce and reheat in a casserole or saucepan.

	Metric/Imperial	American
dripping from the roasting tin (pan) or butter	50 g/2 oz	¼ cup
flour	25 g/1 oz	¼ cup
brown stock, very carefully strained	300 ml/½ pint	1¼ cups
salt and pepper	to taste	to taste
brown sugar	pinch	pinch
port wine	4 tbsp	5 tbsp
sediment from the roasting tin (pan)	see method	see method

Heat the dripping from roasting the game in a saucepan; if there is no dripping use butter. Add the flour, cook gently for several minutes until the flour begins to turn golden brown; take great care it does not burn. Stir in the brown stock and bring to the boil, then cook until thickened, stirring all the time. Add the seasoning, sugar, port wine and any sediment from the roasting tin; do not add any extra dripping from the tin. Heat together, then strain before serving.

PORT WINE GRAVY SAUCE (2)

Cooking Time: 12–15 minutes Serves 4–6 ***

This simple gravy, or sauce, is excellent with venison or other roasted game. Port wine has been a favourite in Britain for generations, probably due to the very friendly relations that have existed between Portugal and Britain, and it is very usual to add a little port wine to game casseroles. The use of bread in thickening sauces is rare today, which is a pity, as it gives a very interesting texture and flavour.

	Metric/Imperial	American
sultanas (golden raisins) or seedless raisins	100 g/4 oz	¾ cup
port wine	150 ml/¼ pint	⅔ cup
juices and dripping from the roasting tin (pan)	see method	see method
brown stock	300 ml/½ pint	1¼ cups
fine breadcrumbs	25 g/1 oz	½ cup
salt and pepper	to taste	to taste

Put the sultanas (golden raisins) or raisins into a bowl. Warm the port wine, add to the dried fruit and allow to stand for approximately 15 minutes.

Pour away most of the fat from the roasting tin, but leave all the meat juices and 1 to 2 tablespoons fat. Put the dried fruit and port wine, the stock, breadcrumbs, meat juices and fat from the tin into a saucepan and heat together, beating until the breadcrumbs become smooth and thicken the sauce. Season well.

VARIATIONS
Use sherry instead of port wine in a gravy to serve with pork.

● *Sharp Port Wine Sauce:* Make a 'roux' of 25 g/1 oz (2 tbsp) butter and 25 g/1 oz (¼ cup) flour as in a Brown Sauce, see page 102. Blend in nearly 300 ml/½ pint (1¼ cups) game stock (made by simmering venison bones or giblets or the bones of game), then add the juice of 1 lemon, 3 tablespoons (4 tbsp) port wine and a generous amount of seasoning. Simmer for 15 minutes. This makes a rather 'biting' sauce and generally needs a good pinch of sugar or tablespoon of redcurrant jelly to overcome this.

STUFFINGS

An alternative word for stuffing is 'forcemeat', undoubtedly it was the Norman conquest of Britain in 1066 that introduced this word and interesting recipes to our menus, for the French word 'farcer' means 'to stuff'.

Stuffings can be made with a great variety of ingredients ranging from fruit, vegetables and cereals, with a wise selection of herbs to add a subtle flavour.

LIVER FORCEMEAT

Cooking Time: see method   Serves 4–6   ❖❖

This is a delicious stuffing and one that is rarely used today. The quantities here are based upon the liver of a good sized chicken or duck or 2 smaller duckling. If cooking a large turkey or goose, use double the ingredients given.

	Metric/Imperial	American
liver of chicken or duckling(s)	1–2	1–2
butter or chicken fat	50 g/2 oz	¼ cup
medium onions, finely chopped	2	2
breadcrumbs	100 g/4 oz	2 cups
chopped parsley	1 tbsp	1 tbsp
chopped thyme	½ teasp	½ teasp
chopped chives	1 tbsp	1 tbsp
almonds, blanched and chopped	50 g/2 oz	½ cup
milk or single (light) cream	2 tbsp	3 tbsp
salt and pepper	to taste	to taste

Finely dice the uncooked liver; do not mince (grind) this, for mincing squeezes out some of the juices. Heat the butter or chicken fat, toss the onions in this then blend with the liver and remaining ingredients, season well. Put into the body of a chicken or duck.

CELERY AND NUT STUFFING

Cooking Time: see method   Serves 6   ❖❖

	Metric/Imperial	American
small celery heart, finely chopped	1	1
large carrots, grated	2	2
chopped parsley	2 tbsp	3 tbsp
chopped walnuts or cashew nuts	100 g/4 oz	1 cup
butter or margarine, melted	50 g/2 oz	¼ cup
salt and pepper	to taste	to taste

Mix all the ingredients together. Put in the body of a chicken or 1 to 2 duckling.

CHESTNUT STUFFING

Cooking Time: see method   Serves 8–10   ❖❖

Chestnuts have been grown in Britain, as indeed in so many countries, for a very long time. This stuffing is mainly used for the Christmas turkey.

	Metric/Imperial	American
chestnuts	675 g/1½ lb	1½ lb
turkey stock or water	450 ml/¾ pint	scant 2 cups
salt and pepper	to taste	to taste
pork sausagemeat	450 g/1 lb	1 lb
walnuts, finely chopped	100 g/4 oz	1 cup

Wash the chestnuts, slit the skins and put into a saucepan of water. Boil steadily for 8 to 10 minutes, then remove the outer shells and brown skins while the nuts are hot.

Place the chestnuts into the turkey stock or water, season lightly then simmer for 20 minutes or until soft. Strain and either rub through a sieve or put into a food processor or liquidizer (blender) and make a smooth purée. Blend with the other ingredients, then put into the body or neck of the turkey.

VARIATIONS
Add 3 tablespoons (4 tbsp) chopped parsley, ½ teaspoon chopped thyme and ½ teaspoon chopped rosemary.
● Omit the sausagemeat; add 225 g/8 oz (½ lb) finely diced cooked ham, 100 g/4 oz (2 cups) soft breadcrumbs, 3 tablespoons (4 tbsp) chopped parsley, the finely chopped uncooked turkey liver and 2 eggs.

NETTLE STUFFING

Cooking Time: see method   Serves 4–6   ❖❖

This delicious stuffing was a favourite in the past in Ireland to serve with pork. It is particularly suitable if the pork is a little fat. If you can gather young nettle leaves it is well worth trying. Remember to wear gloves when picking and handling the nettles.

	Metric/Imperial	American
soft breadcrumbs	75 g/3 oz	1½ cups
young nettle leaves, finely chopped	300 ml/½ pint	1¼ cups
medium onion, chopped	1	1
butter or lard, melted	50 g/2 oz	¼ cup
chopped sage	1 teasp	1 teasp
egg	1	1
salt and pepper	to taste	to taste

Mix all the ingredients together and season well. Either put into the pork or place in an ovenproof dish, cover with buttered foil and bake for 45 minutes if using the temperature for FAST ROASTING or 1 hour 15 minutes if using the temperature for SLOWER ROASTING, see page 53.

VEAL FORCEMEAT

Cooking Time: see method   Serves 8–10 ❖❖

This is an excellent stuffing for turkey. Put into the neck end of the bird.

	Metric/Imperial	American
uncooked veal	350 g/12 oz	¾ lb
bacon rashers (slices), de-rinded	225 g/8 oz	½ lb
soft breadcrumbs	100 g/4 oz	2 cups
chopped savory or marjoram	2 teasp	2 teasp
chopped parsley	2 tbsp	3 tbsp
button mushrooms, sliced (optional)	100 g/4 oz	¼ lb
salt and pepper	to taste	to taste
eggs	2	2

Mince (grind) the veal and bacon together. Mix with the remaining ingredients.

SAGE AND ONION STUFFING

Cooking Time: see method   Serves 4–6 ❖❖

	Metric/Imperial	American
onions, chopped, see method	2	2
water	150 ml/¼ pint	⅔ cup
soft breadcrumbs	50 g/2 oz	1 cup
finely chopped sage	2 teasp	2 teasp
shredded suet	50 g/2 oz	scant ½ cup
egg *or*	1	1
onion stock	2 tbsp	3 tbsp
salt and pepper	to taste	to taste

For this stuffing the onions should be chopped fairly finely, but not too finely. Place into a pan with the water and heat, uncovered, for 5 to 10 minutes only until the onions are *slightly* but not entirely softened, and much of the liquid has evaporated during this brief cooking period. Many recipes give a longer time, but this destroys some of the flavour of the stuffing. Strain the onions, blend with the other ingredients, season well. The egg is not essential but it gives a firmer stuffing. A more crumbly texture is achieved by using the onion stock.

Put into the meat or poultry, or place into an ovenproof dish, cover with buttered foil and bake for 45 minutes if using the temperature for FAST ROASTING or 1 hour 15 minutes if using the temperature for SLOWER ROASTING, see pages 53 and 82.

Above: Parsley and Thyme Stuffing, Sage, Onion and Apple Stuffing, Veal Forcemeat, Sage and Onion Stuffing

PARSLEY AND THYME STUFFING

Cooking Time: see method   Serves 4–6 ❖❖

	Metric/Imperial	American
soft breadcrumbs	100 g/4 oz	2 cups
shredded suet	50 g/2 oz	scant ½ cup
chopped parsley	1–2 tbsp	1–3 tbsp
chopped thyme	1 teasp	1 teasp
grated lemon rind	1 teasp	1 teasp
lemon juice	2 teasp	2 teasp
egg	1	1
salt and pepper	to taste	to taste

Mix all the ingredients together. Put into the neck end of the chicken or turkey.

SAGE, ONION AND APPLE STUFFING

Cooking Time: see method   Serves 4–6 ❖❖

	Metric/Imperial	American
butter or margarine	50 g/2 oz	¼ cup
medium onions, finely chopped	2	2
mashed potatoes	225 g/8 oz	1 cup
chopped sage	2 teasp	2 teasp
salt and pepper	to taste	to taste
medium cooking (baking) apples, peeled, cored and diced	2	2

Heat the butter or margarine in a saucepan, toss the onions in this for 5 minutes. Blend with the mashed potatoes and sage, season very well. Add the apples. Cook as the Sage and Onion Stuffing on this page.

Vegetables and Salads

For centuries there has been an abundance of vegetables available to serve hot or cold in salads. There is a belief that salads are a modern dish, nothing could be further from the truth, for salads – or sallets as they once were called – have been enjoyed since the Tudor days.

Herbs were used extensively in salads together with fruits, such as diced melon, and such unexpected ingredients as nasturtium seeds, rose petals and marigold flowers.

An exotic salad, known as Salmagundy, was a delight to the eye as well as to the palate, for it consisted of a variety of salad vegetables plus flowers, see page 121. The following pages give suggestions for cooking vegetables in new and interesting · ways. Although many of the ideas are based upon old traditional recipes, they are brought up-to-date to give speedier cooking methods that retain the maximum flavour and nutritional value of the vegetables.

COOKING VEGETABLES

When boiling vegetables, put them into the minimum amount of salted water, cover the saucepan and bring the liquid back to boiling point as rapidly as possible. Obviously there must be sufficient liquid to prevent the pan boiling dry. In this way, both the maximum flavour and firm texture of the vegetables are retained. A small amount of liquid means only a little salt is required; a point that is considered important today when medical opinion is against using too much salt.

Green vegetables should be cooked as quickly as possible, but root vegetables, especially potatoes, should be cooked more steadily, so the outside does not become overcooked before the centre is tender.

Vegetables can be fried, see pages 108, 115 and 172, baked, as page 112, 113 and 114, and cooked under the grill (broiler).

Whichever method is used, make sure the vegetables are not overcooked.

USING HERBS

Herbs are an important ingredient in many vegetable and salad dishes as well as in soups, sauces and stews. If you infuse a good selection of herbs in vinegar, a salad dressing has a much more interesting flavour.

In the past, the herb garden was greatly prized for the herbs were used for medicinal and culinary purposes.

Good garden centres will sell herb plants and seeds; the majority of herbs are easily grown. If you do not have the fresh herb given in the recipe, use the dried variety but allow only half the quantity, i.e. 1 teaspoon of chopped fresh parsley means a maximum amount of ½ teaspoon of dried parsley. An excessive amount of any dried herb gives a strong and musty taste to a dish.

A *bouquet garni* is mentioned in several recipes, this means a small bunch of herbs, tied with cotton or in a piece of muslin. The herbs give flavour to the dish but are removed before serving. Choose thyme and parsley as the basic herbs, then add chives or sage or tarragon or rosemary (depending on the dish).

Green Herb Sauce: The sauce illustrated on this page can be varied according to the type of vegetable dish or salad with which it is to be served. Prepare the leaves from a bunch of watercress or about 100 g/4 oz (¼ lb) young spinach leaves; chop roughly and mix with a small amount of parsley, thyme, basil (especially if the dish contains tomatoes,) chives or other green herbs. Put into a food processor or a liquidizer (blender) with a little yoghurt and/or mayonnaise or cream, lemon juice and seasoning. Switch on for a few seconds only until finely chopped. Serve cold with hot fish dishes, with cooked root vegetables such as carrots or with fish salads.

Mint Sauce: This is made by blending finely chopped mint leaves with sugar and white or brown malt vinegar or wine vinegar or cider vinegar to taste. It can of course be prepared in a food processor or liquidizer, but be careful not to overchop the mint. If you do not like vinegar, then use lemon juice or orange juice which gives

Green Herb Sauce

a beautifully fresh flavour to the mixture. A little boiling water can be added to the chopped mint and sugar before adding the vinegar or fruit juice. This makes quite sure that the sugar is dissolved.

CREAMED PARSNIPS

Cooking Time: 45 minutes   Serves 4–6   ❖❖

	Metric/Imperial	American
parsnips, diced	675 g/1½ lb	1½ lb
salt and pepper	to taste	to taste
milk	600 ml/1 pint	2½ cups
butter	25–50 g/1–2 oz	2–4 tbsp
chopped parsley	1–2 tbsp	1–3 tbsp

Put the parsnips in a saucepan with the well-seasoned milk. Cover the pan and simmer steadily until nearly tender, then lift the lid so the excess liquid evaporates. Stir several times during this stage so the parsnips do not stick to the pan. Blend in the butter and parsley just before serving.

SPINACH FRITTERS

Cooking Time: 12 minutes   Serves 4–6   ❖❖

	Metric/Imperial	American
spinach, washed	450 g/1 lb	1 lb
salt and pepper	to taste	to taste
hard-boiled (hard-cooked) eggs, chopped	2	2
soft breadcrumbs	50 g/2 oz	1 cup
currants	2 tbsp	3 tbsp
ground cinnamon	½ teasp	½ teasp
For the coating batter: flour, plain (all-purpose) or self-raising	100 g/4 oz	1 cup
salt	pinch	pinch
egg	1	1
milk or milk and water	165 ml/¼ pint plus 1 tbsp	scant ¾ cup
oil	1 tbsp	1 tbsp
To fry: deep oil or fat		

Put the spinach into a saucepan with just the water adhering to the leaves. Heat gently, add a little seasoning and then cook until tender; very young spinach takes only 5 to 6 minutes for the vegetable must not be too soft for this dish.

Drain the spinach very well and press out all the surplus moisture, then chop finely. Mix with the eggs, breadcrumbs, currants and cinnamon. Taste and adjust the seasoning if necessary. Take small portions, roll into balls or neat shapes.

ARTICHOKES POLONAISE

Cooking Time: 20–30 minutes   Serves 4   ❖

Cut off the stems of 4 globe artichokes, remove any tough outer leaves. Trim the tips of the leaves with kitchen scissors.

Heat approximately 600 ml/1 pint (2½ cups) water in a large saucepan, add a pinch of salt and 2 teaspoons lemon juice. Put in the artichokes.

Cover the pan, cook for 20–30 minutes (depending on the size) until tender. To test, pull away one leaf, if soft at the base the artichokes are cooked.

While the artichokes are cooking, fry 25 g/1 oz (½ cup) soft breadcrumbs in 25 g/1 oz (2 tbsp) butter. Hard-boil (hard-cook) 1–2 eggs.

Remove the artichokes from the pan, drain well, remove the centre inedible 'chokes'.

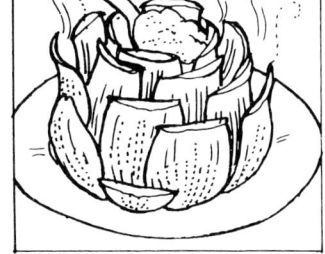

Fill the centres with the fried breadcrumbs, chopped hard-boiled egg(s) and chopped parsley. Serve with hot butter.

Mix all the ingredients for the batter together in a bowl. Coat the spinach balls in the batter and put into deep oil or fat heated to 190°C/375°F. Fry for 5 to 6 minutes or until crisp and brown. Reduce the heat after the first 2 minutes to prevent the batter coating becoming overbrown. Drain on absorbent paper (kitchen towels) and serve hot.

VARIATIONS
Omit the egg and milk from the batter and use 180 ml/¼ pint plus 2 tablespoons (¾ cup) ale.
● The batter given in the recipe can be used to coat any vegetable. It is advisable to coat raw vegetables with a little seasoned flour before dipping in the batter.

PAN HAGGERTY

Cooking Time: 30 minutes   Serves 4–6   ❖❖

This is a traditional Scottish recipe which once again emphasizes the link with French dishes, for the dish is very similar to Pommes Lyonnaise except the addition of cheese turns this into a complete meal. Pan Haggerty is also popular in the North of England.

	Metric/Imperial	American
butter	75 g/3 oz	6 tbsp
potatoes, weight when peeled, thinly sliced	450 g/1 lb	1 lb
onions, thinly sliced	450 g/1 lb	1 lb
Cheddar cheese, grated	175 g/6 oz	1½ cups
salt and pepper	to taste	to taste

Heat the butter in a large, deep frying pan (skillet). Put in a layer of potatoes, a layer of onions, then a layer of cheese. Continue like this until all the ingredients are used. Season each layer well. Cover the pan and cook steadily for 25 minutes. Place the pan under a preheated grill (broiler) for 5 minutes to crisp the top.

VARIATION
Arrange the ingredients in a casserole and cook in the centre of a moderate oven, 180 to 190°C/350 to 375°F Gas Mark 4 to 5, for 40 to 45 minutes. Keep the casserole covered until the last 10 minutes, then remove the lid.

MUSHROOM RAMEKINS

Cooking Time: 10 minutes   Serves 4   ❖

	Metric/Imperial	American
small button mushrooms	225 g/8 oz	½ lb
butter	50 g/2 oz	¼ cup
beef stock	2 tbsp	3 tbsp
eggs	4	4
double (heavy) cream	150 ml/¼ pint	⅔ cup
chopped chives	1 tbsp	1 tbsp
chopped parsley	1 tbsp	1 tbsp
chopped thyme	¼ teasp	¼ teasp
salt and cayenne pepper	to taste	to taste

Remove the mushroom stalks, chop finely. Wipe the mushroom caps, do not peel for there is a great deal of good flavour in the skins. Heat the butter in a large frying pan (skillet), fry the mushroom stalks and mushrooms for 4 minutes. Lift the mushrooms caps out of the pan, put into a container, cover and keep hot.

Add the stock to the pan, heat thoroughly. Blend the eggs, cream, herbs and seasoning. Pour over the mushroom stalks and small amount of liquid. Cook gently until very lightly set. Spoon into 4 heated individual dishes, top with the mushroom caps.

CUCUMBER AND ONION RAGOÛT

Cooking Time: 25 minutes Serves 4–6 ❖

Cucumbers were cooked very much more in the past than they are nowadays. Cooked cucumber is an excellent accompaniment to fish dishes or with roast lamb or roast chicken.

Do not overcook the cucumber; there is no need to peel the vegetable unless the skin is very tough as it is sometimes with late outdoor grown vegetables.

Slice 2 cucumbers. Peel and finely chop 2–3 medium onions.

Heat 50 g/2 oz (¼ cup) butter or margarine in a large frying pan (skillet), fry the cucumber slices and onions gently for 10 minutes.

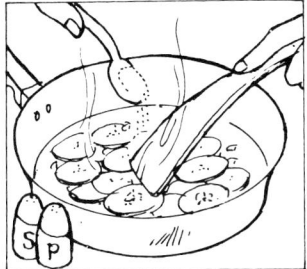

Shake 2 tbsp (3 tbsp) flour and a little salt and pepper over the vegetables, stir well to blend.

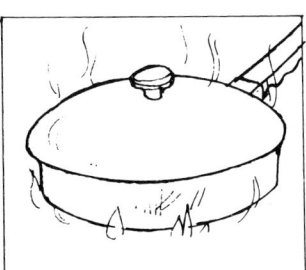

Pour 225 ml/8 fl oz (1 cup) white or red wine or chicken stock into the pan, cover and simmer for 8 minutes.

Lift the lid and continue cooking for 3–4 minutes so any excess liquid evaporates.

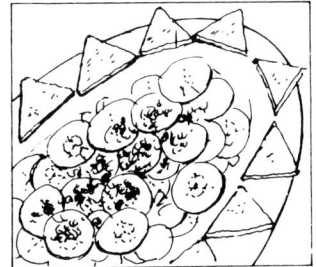

Top with chopped parsley and/or chopped chives and garnish with triangles of toast.

INTERESTING VEGETABLE MIXTURES

The secret of a good vegetable dish is that it should have 'eye-appeal' as well as an interesting flavour. The dishes on this page combine various kinds of vegetables. If the vegetables are not all available then mix fresh and frozen, or canned, vegetables to make the dishes on this and the next page.

CABBAGE AND BEAN MEDLEY

Cooking Time: 15 minutes   Serves 4–6   ❊❊

This dish is excellent with duck, pork and goose.

	Metric/Imperial	American
butter or margarine	25 g/1 oz	2 tbsp
large onion, cut into rings	1	1
water	300 ml/½ pint	1¼ cups
salt and pepper	to taste	to taste
broad beans (fava), removed from bean pods	225 g/8 oz	1½ cups
white cabbage heart, shredded	½	½
dessert apples, sliced	2	2
mustard seeds	½ teasp	½ teasp

Heat the butter or margarine in a large saucepan, toss the onion rings in this, do not allow to brown. Add the water, bring to the boil. Season lightly, add the beans, simmer steadily for 5 minutes. Add the shredded cabbage, apple slices and mustard seeds, cook for a further 5 minutes. Strain and serve.

GOLDEN CABBAGE

Cooking Time: 15 minutes   Serves 4–6   ❊❊

	Metric/Imperial	American
water or chicken stock	300 ml/½ pint	1¼ cups
salt and pepper	to taste	to taste
small carrots, halved lengthways	225 g/8 oz	½ lb
small red cabbage, shredded	½	½
butter or margarine	25 g/1 oz	2 tbsp
sultanas (golden raisins)	2 tbsp	3 tbsp
almonds, blanched	1 tbsp	1 tbsp
caraway seeds	½-1 teasp	½-1 teasp

Bring the water or stock to the boil in a saucepan, season lightly. Add the carrots and cook for 5 to 6 minutes. Add the cabbage and cook for 4 to 5 minutes or until just tender, then strain the vegetables.

Heat the butter or margarine in the saucepan, toss the cabbage, carrots and remaining ingredients in this over a low heat for 2 to 3 minutes.

Piquant Brussels Sprouts, Vegetable Hotpot, Golden Cabbage, Welsh Potatoes, Cabbage and Bean Medley

VEGETABLE HOTPOT

Cooking Time: 20–25 minutes   Serves 4–6   ❊❊

This makes an excellent dish with an omelette or a cheese sauce. It can be served with fish, meat or poultry.

	Metric/Imperial	American
water	600 ml/1 pint	2½ cups
salt and pepper	to taste	to taste
small cauliflower, divided into florets	½-1	½-1
medium onions, chopped	2	2
small leeks, sliced	2	2
medium turnip, diced	1	1
medium parsnip, diced	1	1
medium swede (rutabaga), diced	¼	¼
medium carrots, sliced	2–3	2–3
white or green cabbage, shredded	¼	¼
tomatoes, skinned	4–6	4–6
butter or margarine	25 g/1 oz	2 tbsp
To garnish: chopped parsley	2–3 tbsp	3–4 tbsp

Heat the oil in a large saucepan, fry the onions and garlic gently for 4 to 5 minutes. Add the water, bring to the boil, season lightly. Put in the swede (rutabaga) and cook for 15 minutes or until nearly soft. Add the sprouts and boil briskly until just soft. Strain and serve.

WELSH POTATOES

Cooking Time: 25–30 minutes   Serves 4–6 ❋❋

	Metric/Imperial	American
new potatoes, scraped	450 g/1 lb	1 lb
salt	to taste	to taste
leeks, sliced	2–3	2–3
butter or margarine	25 g/1 oz	2 tbsp
fennel seeds	to taste	to taste

Put the potatoes into a saucepan of boiling salted water. Cover the pan and cook steadily for 15 minutes if small, or 20 minutes if larger. Do not cook too quickly, remember 'a potato boiled is a potato spoiled'.

Add the leeks and cook for a further 10 minutes. Strain then return to the pan with the butter or margarine and fennel seeds, heat for 1 to 2 minutes.

Hot Green Salad – recipe page 112

Bring the water to the boil in a large saucepan, season well. It is important to prepare, i.e. chop, dice, etc., the vegetables so they take the same cooking time. Put all the vegetables, except the cabbage and tomatoes, into the boiling water. Cook steadily for 15 to 20 minutes until nearly soft. Add the cabbage and tomatoes and cook for a further 5 minutes.

Strain, return the vegetables to the pan with the butter or margarine and heat for 2 minutes. Spoon into a heated serving dish and top with the parsley.

PIQUANT BRUSSELS SPROUTS

Cooking Time: 30 minutes   Serves 4–6 ❋❋

This dish blends well with most meat or poultry.

	Metric/Imperial	American
oil	1 tbsp	1 tbsp
medium onions, finely chopped	2	2
garlic cloves, crushed	1–2	1–2
water	300 ml/½ pint	1¼ cups
salt and pepper	to taste	to taste
swede (rutabaga), diced	175 g/6 oz	1 cup
Brussels sprouts	350 g/12 oz	¾ lb

SIMPLE VEGETABLE DISHES

If vegetables are really fresh and young, they do not require elaborate cooking methods or accompaniments to make them truly appetizing. Some of the old traditional recipes for vegetable cookery combine unexpected ingredients, such as dried and fresh fruit, with the vegetables. Grapes, in particular, blend well with several vegetables, as in the recipe opposite.

All the vegetable dishes on this and the next page date back several centuries but they represent the very best ways of serving the particular vegetable.

HOT GREEN SALAD

Illustrated in colour on page 111

Cooking Time: 5 minutes   Serves 4–6   ✳

This salad makes a very pleasant change from the more familiar accompaniment to a meal. Prepare and marinate the vegetables before the meal and heat at the very last minute. This dish can be served with hot or cold meats.

	Metric/Imperial	American
spring onions (scallions)	12–18	12–18
medium cucumber, sliced	½	½
celery stalks, chopped	3–4	3–4
green beans, lightly cooked	225 g/8 oz	½ lb
grapefruit juice	4 tbsp	5 tbsp
olive oil	1 tbsp	1 tbsp
salt and pepper	to taste	to taste
lettuce	1	1
parsley sprigs	4	4

Put the spring onions (scallions), cucumber, celery and beans into a saucepan, add the grapefruit juice, olive oil and a little seasoning. Stir to blend and allow to stand for about 1 hour.

Shred the lettuce, put into a deep serving dish. Heat the vegetable mixture for 5 minutes only, stir well. Spoon on to the lettuce, top with the parsley.

CLAPSHOT

Cooking Time: few minutes plus time to cook vegetables   Serves 4–6   ✳

	Metric/Imperial	American
cooked potatoes, mashed	450 g/1 lb	1 lb
cooked turnips, mashed	450 g/1 lb	1 lb
chopped chives	3 tbsp	4 tbsp
butter or dripping	50 g/2 oz	¼ cup
salt and pepper	to taste	to taste

Blend the potatoes, turnips and half the chives together. Heat the butter or dripping in a large saucepan, add the vegetable mixture, heat well; add seasoning to taste. Top with the remaining chives.

ARTICHOKE PIE

Cooking Time: 25–30 minutes   Serves 4–6   ✳✳

	Metric/Imperial	American
Jerusalem artichokes, scraped	450 g/1 lb	1 lb
lemon juice	½ tbsp	½ tbsp
salt and pepper	to taste	to taste
For the sauce: butter	25 g/1 oz	2 tbsp
flour	25 g/1 oz	¼ cup
milk	300 ml/½ pint	1¼ cups
single cream	2 tbsp	3 tbsp
hard-boiled (hard-cooked) eggs	2	2
grapes, de-seeded	100 g/4 oz	1 cup
sultanas (golden raisins)	50 g/2 oz	⅓ cup
For the topping: butter	25 g/1 oz	2 tbsp
soft breadcrumbs	50 g/2 oz	1 cup

Put the artichokes and lemon juice into a saucepan of well-seasoned boiling water, cook for about 15 minutes or until just tender. The lemon juice helps to keep the artichokes white.

Meanwhile, heat the butter in another saucepan, stir in the flour and cook for 2 to 3 minutes. Blend in the milk and cream. Stir as the sauce thickens, season to taste. Halve the hard-boiled (hard-cooked) eggs, remove the yolks, put on one side. Chop the egg whites, add to the sauce with nearly all the grapes and all the sultanas (golden raisins). Heat for 2 to 3 minutes.

Drain the artichokes, add to the hot sauce mixture. Put into a heated flameproof dish. Melt the butter, blend with the breadcrumbs. Sprinkle on top of the dish. Place under a preheated grill (broiler) for 2 to 3 minutes to brown.

Chop the egg yolks, sprinkle over the topping and add the remaining grapes.

VARIATION
Cook cauliflower florets and use instead of the Jerusalem artichokes. The lemon juice can be omitted.

POTATO AND ONION BAKE

Cooking Time: 45 minutes   Serves 4–6   ✳✳

Cook 450 g/1 lb potatoes in salted water until soft. Drain. Rub through a sieve or mash for a very short time in a food processor.

Finely chop 225 g/8 oz (½ lb) onions. Heat 50 g/2 oz (¼ cup) butter in a frying pan (skillet), fry the onions very slowly until soft.

Add to the potatoes with 1 teaspoon finely chopped sage, 2 tablespoons (3 tbsp) chopped parsley and 2 eggs.

Grease an ovenproof casserole with a generous layer of butter. Put half the potato mixture into the dish. Cover with 25 g/1 oz (¼ cup) finely grated cheese, then add the remaining potato mixture.

Top the potato with 50 g/2 oz (½ cup) grated cheese.

Bake just above the centre of a moderately hot oven, 200°C/400°F Gas Mark 6, for 35 minutes.

SOUFFLÉ POTATOES AND TURNIPS

Cooking Time: 1 hour 20 minutes   Serves 4 ❊❊

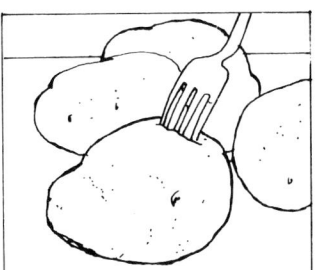

Scrub, prick and bake 4 large potatoes in a moderate oven, 180°C/350°F Gas Mark 4, for approximately 1 hour, or in a microwave cooker for the time given by the manufacturer.

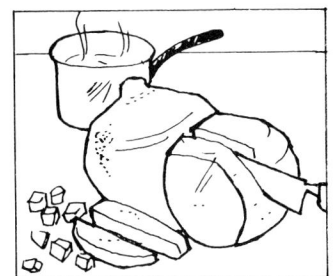

Meanwhile, peel, dice and cook 225 g/8 oz (½ lb) turnips in boiling salted water for about 10 minutes until tender. Drain.

Cut a slice from the top of each potato, scoop out the pulp into a bowl. Add the turnips, 50 g/2 oz (¼ cup) butter or margarine, 3 tablespoons (4 tbsp) single (light) cream or milk, a little grated nutmeg and seasoning to taste.

Separate 3 eggs, add the yolks to the potato and turnip mixture. Whisk the egg whites until stiff, blend with the vegetable purée.

Spoon the mixture into the potato cases. Bake in the centre of a moderately hot oven, 200°C/400°F Gas Mark 6, for 20 minutes or until well risen.

Serve the potatoes as soon as the filling is cooked.

CREAMED CARROTS

Cooking Time: 20 minutes   Serves 4–6 ❊❊

Serve with meat, fish or poultry.

	Metric/Imperial	American
chicken stock	450 ml/¾ pint	scant 2 cups
salt and pepper	to taste	to taste
medium onions, very finely chopped	2	2
young carrots, thinly sliced	675 g/1½ lb	1½ lb
double (heavy) cream	150 ml/¼ pint	⅔ cup
grated nutmeg	to taste	to taste
chopped parsley	3 tbsp	4 tbsp

Bring the chicken stock to the boil in a saucepan, season lightly. Add the onions and carrots and cook until tender; lift the lid towards the end of the cooking time so that as much liquid evaporates as possible.

Drain the vegetables, return to the pan with half the cream, the grated nutmeg and half the parsley. Heat for 2 to 3 minutes. Serve topped with the rest of the cream and parsley.

LEEK PIE

Illustrated in colour on page 218
Cooking Time: 55 minutes   Serves 4–6 ❊❊

	Metric/Imperial	American
bacon rashers (slices)	3–4	3–4
leeks	675 g/1½ lb	1½ lb
salt and pepper	to taste	to taste
milk	150 ml/¼ pint	⅔ cup
single cream	150 ml/¼ pint	⅔ cup
eggs	2	2
Shortcrust Pastry (basic pie dough), as page 175 made with	175 g/6 oz flour etc	1½ cups flour etc
To glaze: egg	1	1

Grill (broil) the bacon rashers, chop into small pieces. Cut the leeks into 2.5 cm/1 inch lengths. Cook in well-seasoned water for 8 to 10 minutes or until just soft.

Drain the leeks, put into a 1.2 litre/2 pint (5 cup) pie dish with the bacon. Beat the milk, cream and eggs together, season with a little pepper; salt should not be required with the bacon. Pour over the leeks.

Roll out the pastry and cover the filling; make a slit on top of the pastry so the steam can escape during cooking. Beat the egg and brush over the pastry to glaze.

Bake in the centre of a hot oven, 220°C/425°F Gas Mark 7, for 20 minutes, then reduce the heat to very moderate, 160°C/325°F Gas Mark 3, for a further 20 minutes. The reduction of heat is important, for this makes certain the savoury filling does not become overheated and curdle.

Lettuce Soufflé

Heat the butter in a large saucepan, stir in the flour and cook for 2 to 3 minutes. Blend in the milk, lemon rind and lettuce stock. Stir as the mixture comes to the boil and thickens. Add the cheese and lettuce, mix well.

Separate the eggs, fold the yolks into the lettuce mixture. Whisk the egg whites until just stiff, fold into the other ingredients, season well.

Coat a 15 to 18 cm/6 to 7 inch soufflé dish with the butter, the fine breadcrumbs and grated cheese. Spoon in the soufflé mixture. Bake in the centre of a moderate oven, 180 to 190°C/350 to 375°F Gas Mark 4 to 5, for 30 to 35 minutes. Serve at once.

VARIATIONS

Asparagus Soufflé: Use asparagus purée instead of the milk and put a layer of asparagus tips at the bottom of the soufflé dish.
● *Carrot Soufflé:* Use a cooked carrot purée or finely grated raw carrots instead of lettuce.
● *Spinach Soufflé:* Use cooked spinach in place of lettuce in the recipe above.
● *Tomato Soufflé:* Use fresh tomato purée instead of the milk and lettuce stock in the recipe above.

VEGETABLE SOUFFLÉS

A soufflé, based upon vegetables, makes an interesting light luncheon or supper dish or an excellent accompaniment to a main course. Asparagus, carrots, spinach and tomatoes can give flavouring to a soufflé as well as lettuce, which is used in the recipe below.

LETTUCE SOUFFLÉ

Cooking Time: 45 minutes   Serves 4   ❊❊

	Metric/Imperial	American
lettuce, firm Iceberg type ideal, shredded	225 g/8 oz	½ lb
water	150 ml/¼ pint	⅔ cup
salt and pepper	to taste	to taste
butter	50 g/2 oz	¼ cup
flour	25 g/1 oz	¼ cup
milk	150 ml/¼ pint	⅔ cup
grated lemon rind	½ teasp	½ teasp
lettuce stock, see method	2 tbsp	3 tbsp
Cheddar cheese, grated	100 g/4 oz	1 cup
eggs	4	4
To coat the dish: butter, softened	25 g/1 oz	2 tbsp
soft fine breadcrumbs	25 g/1 oz	½ cup
Cheddar cheese, finely grated	25 g/1 oz	¼ cup

Cook the lettuce in the boiling water with seasoning to taste for 7 to 8 minutes until just tender, drain. Boil any liquid left from cooking the lettuce until just 2 tablespoons (3 tbsp) liquid remain.

STUFFED VEGETABLES

A great variety of vegetables can be filled with savoury ingredients to turn them into a main dish. Recipes are given on this page and pages 115 and 118.

CHICKEN-STUFFED TOMATOES

Cooking Time: 25 minutes   Serves 4–8   ❊❊

This dish serves 8 as a light snack or 4 as a main meal.

	Metric/Imperial	American
large tomatoes	8	8
butter or margarine	50 g/2 oz	¼ cup
bacon rashers (slices), diced	3–4	3–4
mushrooms, coarsely chopped	100 g/4 oz	¼ lb
cooked chicken, diced	225 g/8 oz	½ lb
celery stalks with a few tender leaves, chopped	2	2
soft breadcrumbs	75 g/3 oz	1½ cups
chopped parsley	2 tbsp	3 tbsp
salt and pepper	to taste	to taste

Cut a slice from the top of each tomato, you will find they stand better if the stalk end is used as the base. The tomatoes can be cut in a 'Van Dyke' or zigzag pattern.

Carefully scoop out the pulp from the tomatoes and chop this finely. Heat the butter or margarine in a saucepan, fry the bacon and mushrooms for 2 to 3 minutes, then blend in all the other ingredients, including the tomato pulp. Season lightly and also season the tomato cases.

Fill the tomatoes with the chicken mixture, balance the tomato 'lids' on top of the filling. Put into an ovenproof dish. Bake just above the centre of a moderately hot oven, 200°C/400°F Gas Mark 6, for 15 to 20 minutes.

VARIATIONS

Add 1 to 2 finely chopped leeks and fry with the bacon and mushrooms.
● *Stuffed Onions:* Use 4 very large or 8 medium sized onions instead of the tomatoes. Cook the onions in boiling salted water for 15 to 20 minutes, or until it is possible to remove the centre of the onions. Carefully chop the centre pulp and mix with the filling suggested above (without the tomato pulp) or the filling given on page 118 under Vegetable Filled Aubergines. Place the onion shells in a greased dish.

Spoon the mixture back into the onions. Cover the dish and bake in the centre of a moderate oven, 180°C/350°F Gas Mark 4, for 45 minutes.

FRIED VEGETABLES

Frying has been a favourite way of cooking food for several centuries; it is an excellent method of tenderizing vegetables, for all the flavour of the food is retained. Fried vegetables always look inviting too.

Fried potatoes are probably the most popular of all vegetable dishes.

Aubergine Fritters

CUCUMBER FRITTERS

Cooking Time: 7 minutes   Serves 4–6   ✳

	Metric/Imperial	American
large cucumber	1	1
salt and pepper	to taste	to taste
flour	40 g/1½ oz	6 tbsp
To fry: oil	3 tbsp	4 tbsp
To garnish: lemons, sliced	2	2

Peel the cucumber if the skin is tough, but the vegetable looks more attractive if the skin is left on. Cut into 1.5 cm/½ inch slices. Sprinkle with a little salt and allow to stand on a flat dish for 1 hour. This draws out the excess liquid. Drain the cucumber slices and pat dry on absorbent paper (kitchen towels). Mix a good shake of pepper with the flour and coat the cucumber slices.

Heat the oil in a large frying pan (skillet), fry the cucumber slices about 5 minutes until brown on both sides and tender. Serve hot garnished with lemon slices.

VARIATIONS

Sliced courgettes (zucchini) and aubergines (eggplants) can be prepared and cooked in the same way as cucumber, instead of using a batter coating, see variation below.
● *Aubergine Fritters:* Slice 2 to 3 aubergines, coat with a little seasoned flour then with a fritter batter, made as the recipe on page 108. Deep fry for 5 to 6 minutes. Drain and serve with lemon wedges.

POTATO FRITTERS

Cooking Time: 15 minutes   Serves 4   ✳✳

	Metric/Imperial	American
potatoes	450 g/1 lb	1 lb
salt and pepper	to taste	to taste
flour	25 g/1 oz	¼ cup
eggs	2	2
soft very fine breadcrumbs	50 g/2 oz	1 cup
To fry: deep oil or fat		
To garnish: finely chopped parsley	2–3 tbsp	3–4 tbsp

Parboil the potatoes in a saucepan of salted water until they are nearly soft. Drain, cool then cut into 5 mm/¼ inch slices. Mix the flour with a little salt and pepper, coat the potato slices. Beat the eggs, dip the potato slices in the egg and then in the breadcrumbs.

Meanwhile, heat the pan of oil or fat until it reaches 190°C/375°F. Fry the potatoes for 4 to 5 minutes, drain on absorbent paper (kitchen towels). Garnish with the parsley.

VARIATIONS

Add 3 to 4 tablespoons (4 to 5 tbsp) very finely chopped cooked ham to the breadcrumbs.
● Add 50 g/2 oz (½ cup) very finely grated Cheddar or other good cooking cheese to the breadcrumbs.
● *Onion Fritters:* Coat uncooked onion rings as the method above or as one of the variations.

SALADS FOR ALL SEASONS

Every season of the year has vegetables and fruits that are at their best, when they are young, tender and full of flavour.

Make use of these ingredients in appetizing and health-giving salads. Suggested salads for the four seasons of the year are on this and the next page.

SUMMER SALAD BOWL
No Cooking   Serves 4–6   *

	Metric/Imperial	American
lettuce, shredded	1	1
young carrots, grated	2–3	2–3
strawberries	225 g/8 oz	½ lb
blackcurrants	100 g/4 oz	¼ lb
For the dressing: salad oil	2 tbsp	3 tbsp
lemon juice	1 tbsp	1 tbsp
orange juice	1 tbsp	1 tbsp
sugar	1 teasp	1 teasp
salt and pepper	to taste	to taste
cream cheese	225 g/8 oz	1 cup
almonds, blanched and chopped	2 tbsp	3 tbsp
To garnish: mint leaves	4–6	4–6

Place the lettuce and carrots on a flat dish. Top with the fruit. Mix the ingredients for the dressing together, spoon over the salad.

Blend the cream cheese and almonds, form into small balls. Arrange on the salad and garnish with mint leaves.

SPRINGTIME SALAD
No Cooking   Serves 4   *

WINTER SALAD
Cooking Time: 10 minutes   Serves 6–8   **

	Metric/Imperial	American
water	600 ml/1 pint	2½ cups
salt and pepper	to taste	to taste
small turnip, sliced	1	1
small swede (rutabaga), diced	½–1	½–1
small parsnip, diced or sliced	1	1
medium potatoes, sliced	2	2
small onion, cut into rings	1–2	1–2
marrow (large zucchini), diced	small portion	small portion
medium carrots, cut into strips	3–4	3–4
small green cabbage, shredded	½	½
medium leeks, sliced	2	2
For the dressing: salad oil	3 tbsp	4 tbsp
orange juice	1 tbsp	1 tbsp
lemon juice	1 tbsp	1 tbsp
grated lemon rind	½ teasp	½ teasp
grated orange rind	½ teasp	½ teasp
sugar	1 teasp	1 teasp
garlic clove, crushed	1	1
made mustard	1 teasp	1 teasp
celery salt	pinch	pinch

Bring the water to the boil in a saucepan, add a little seasoning. Put the turnip, swede (rutabaga), parsnip and potatoes into the water, boil for 10 minutes until the vegetables are soft. Add the onion rings and marrow (large zucchini) after 3 minutes cooking time. Drain the vegetables, cool and mix with the raw carrots, cabbage and leeks.

Blend the dressing ingredients, pour over salad.

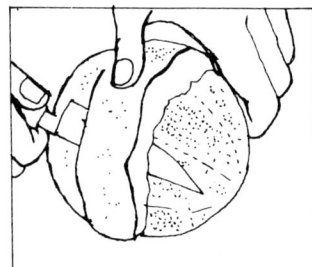

Cut away the skin from 2–3 oranges, so cutting away the white pith.

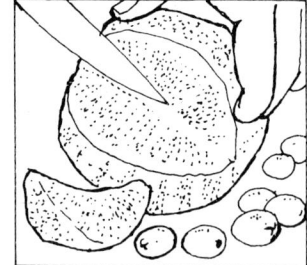

Cut out the segments of orange, leaving the skin between the segments.

Mix the orange segments with a small bunch of de-seeded grapes.

Halve 2 avocados, stone, skin and slice. Sprinkle with seasoned lemon juice. Blend with the orange and grape mixture.

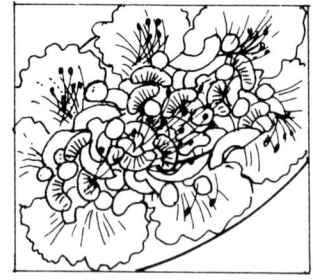

Serve on lettuce, garnish with watercress sprigs.

AUTUMN SALAD

No Cooking   *

Toss cooked runner (or other green beans) in well-seasoned oil and vinegar dressing, see page 121.

Peel and crush 1 to 2 garlic cloves (a little salt on the chopping board helps). Add to the beans and dressing.

Blend the beans with tomato wedges and diced cucumber.

Put on to a bed of lettuce. Garnish with diamond or heart-shaped croûtons just before serving.

To make shaped croûtons:
Cut out shapes with a biscuit (cookie) cutter. Fry in hot butter until crisp and brown on either side. Drain on absorbent paper (kitchen towels).

A NEW TOUCH TO SALADS

The salads on this page illustrate some of the ways in which familiar salad ingredients can be given a new look. Try making a cool jellied salad as in the first recipe, or give the ingredients the 'bite' of curry, as in the Cauliflower Salad and the Coleslaw.

LEMON VEGETABLE SALAD

Cooking Time: few minutes   Serves 4–6   **

This salad is excellent with cold meat or poultry.

	Metric/Imperial	American
water	150 ml/¼ pint	⅔ cup
lemon jelly (lemon flavoured gelatin)	1	1
white wine vinegar	300 ml/½ pint	1¼ cups
cucumber, peeled and sliced	¼	¼
cooked peas	100 g/4 oz	¾ cup
spring onions (scallions), chopped	2 tbsp	3 tbsp
small firm tomatoes, skinned and sliced	2	2
To garnish: lettuce, shredded	1	1
oranges	2	2
lemon, sliced	1	1
tomatoes, sliced	2	2

Heat the water to boiling point. Dissolve the lemon flavoured jelly in the water, add the vinegar and allow the jelly mixture to cool until slightly syrupy in texture.

Blend the cucumber slices, peas, onions and tomatoes with the jelly. Rinse out a 1 litre/1¾ pint (3¾ cup) mould in cold water or brush with 2 to 3 drops of olive oil. Spoon in the vegetable jelly mixture. Allow to set. Turn out, garnish with a border of shredded lettuce. Cut away the orange skin, then cut out the orange segments and arrange on the lettuce. Add the lemon and tomato slices.

CURRIED CAULIFLOWER SALAD

Cooking Time: 5 minutes   Serves 4–6   *

	Metric/Imperial	American
small cauliflower, divided into florets	1	1
salt and pepper	to taste	to taste
red pepper, de-seeded and diced	1	1
green pepper, de-seeded and diced	1	1
lettuce, shredded	1	1
For the dressing: salad oil	3 tbsp	4 tbsp
white wine vinegar	2 tbsp	3 tbsp
curry paste	1–2 teasp	1–2 teasp
mayonnaise	1 tbsp	1 tbsp

Cook the cauliflower in a saucepan of boiling well-seasoned water for 5 minutes only. Drain and put into a bowl. Line a salad bowl with the diced peppers and lettuce. Blend all the ingredients for the dressing together; this is easily and quickly done in a food processor or liquidizer (blender). Pour over the warm cauliflower. Allow to cool, then spoon into the salad bowl.

CURRIED COLESLAW

No Cooking   Serves 6–8   **

	Metric/Imperial	American
curry powder or curry paste	1–2 teasp	1–2 teasp
yoghurt	150 ml/¼ pint	⅔ cup
mayonnaise	2 tbsp	3 tbsp
lemon juice	1 tbsp	1 tbsp
salt and pepper	to taste	to taste
white cabbage, shredded	225 g/8 oz	½ lb
small onion, finely chopped	1	1
small leek, sliced	1	1
red pepper, de-seeded and diced	1	1
celery stalks, chopped	2–3	2–3
dessert apples, sliced	3–4	3–4

Blend the curry powder or paste with the yoghurt, mayonnaise and all the other ingredients. Chill well before serving.

VEGETABLES MAKE A MEAL

Well-cooked vegetables certainly help to ensure the success of a meal, but a varied selection of vegetables with some protein in the form of nuts or cheese or eggs provides as appetizing and nutritious a dish as if meat or fish were included.

NUT AND VEGETABLE HOTCHPOTCH

Cooking Time: 35 minutes   Serves 4–6   ✳✳✳

Although Brazils, almonds and ground almonds are used in this casserole, any nuts can be substituted.

The selection of vegetables can be varied according to the season. Vegetarians will omit the bacon, in which case increase the amount of nuts slightly.

	Metric/Imperial	American
oil	1 tbsp	1 tbsp
large onions, sliced	2	2
large leeks, sliced	2	2
bacon rashers (slices), de-rinded and diced	2–3	2–3
ground almonds	50 g/2 oz	½ cup
water	600 ml/1 pint	2½ cups
salt and pepper	to taste	to taste
carrots with turnips and parsnips, sliced	450–675 g/1–1½ lb	1–1½ lb
corn-on-the-cob, sliced	1–2	1–2
small cauliflower, divided into florets	1	1
courgettes (zucchini), sliced	225 g/8 oz	½ lb
small cabbage, shredded	¼-½	¼-½
double (heavy) cream	4 tbsp	5 tbsp
Brazil nuts	50 g/2 oz	½ cup
almonds, blanched	50 g/2 oz	½ cup
To garnish: fresh herbs	sprigs	sprigs
For the Garlic Sauce: soft breadcrumbs	50 g/2 oz	1 cup
garlic cloves, crushed	2–3	2–3
olive oil, amount depending on personal taste	150–300 ml/¼–½ pint	⅔-1¼ cups
white or red wine vinegar, amount depending on personal taste	1–2 tbsp	1–3 tbsp
salt and pepper	to taste	to taste

Heat the oil in a large saucepan, fry the onions, leeks and bacon until golden in colour. Add the ground almonds and water. Stir until the sauce thickens slightly, season lightly. Add the carrots, turnips, parsnips and cook for 5 minutes, then put in the sliced corn-on-the-cob. Cook steadily for 5 minutes then add the cauliflower florets, courgettes (zucchini) and cook for 5 minutes. Finally add the shredded cabbage.

Lift the lid and allow the excess liquid to boil away until only about 150 ml/¼ pint (⅔ cup) remains. Stir in the cream and nuts. Heat thoroughly, season to taste. Spoon into a heated serving dish, garnish with the herbs and serve.

This dish is excellent with a Garlic Sauce made by mixing all the ingredients together.

VARIATION

Add a selection of chopped herbs, i.e. parsley, tarragon, rosemary, sage and thyme, to the vegetables.

VEGETABLE FILLED AUBERGINES

Cooking Time: 45 minutes   Serves 2–4   ✳✳

	Metric/Imperial	American
large aubergines (egg plants)	2	2
salt and pepper	to taste	to taste
butter or margarine	50 g/2 oz	¼ cup
mushrooms, thickly sliced	100 g/4 oz	¼ lb
green beans, lightly cooked and diced	4–5 tbsp	5–6 tbsp
medium tomatoes, cut into wedges	4	4
peas, lightly cooked	100 g/4 oz	¾ cup
Cheddar cheese, grated	175 g/6 oz	1½ cups
For the topping: soft breadcrumbs	4 tbsp	5 tbsp
To garnish: few beans, peas, tomato wedges and pepper pieces, optional		

Score the outside of the aubergines (egg plants) skin and sprinkle lightly with salt, leave for 20 to 30 minutes. This 'draws out' the bitter flavour which many people dislike. Pour away the liquid, rinse the aubergines and dry well.

Halve the aubergines lengthways, scoop out the centre pulp and chop this. Heat the butter or margarine in a saucepan, cook the aubergine pulp until softened. Add the mushrooms and cook for a further 2 minutes then blend in most of the beans, tomatoes, peas and three-quarters of the cheese; season well. Spoon into the aubergine shells. Top with the breadcrumbs and remaining cheese.

Cover the dish. Bake in the centre of a moderately hot oven, 200°C/400°F Gas Mark 6, for 25 minutes. Remove the lid and cook for a further 10 minutes, so the topping can brown. Arrange the garnish around the edge of the aubergines and heat for a few minutes only.

SALADS MAKE A MEAL

A good salad can be an excellent accompaniment to hot or cold dishes, or provide a satisfying dish in itself.

The salads shown on this and the next page illustrate that point. The first salad consists of a wide variety of ingredients, i.e. crisp lettuce, watercress, tomatoes, raw cauliflower florets, grated carrots, radishes, cucumber slices and chicory (Belgian endive). The protein is provided by hard-boiled (hard-cooked) eggs.

The salad ingredients would be equally appetizing if served with a selection of cheeses or nuts to add important protein for a main meal dish.

The Chicken Salad Platter has fewer ingredients, but these are well chosen to complement the delicate flavour of cooked chicken. The chicken could be replaced by cooked beans and peas to provide vegetable protein for non-meat eaters.

In the Yoghurt Coleslaw, the dressing adds food value to the crisp, raw ingredients.

YOGHURT COLESLAW

No Cooking   Serves 4–6   ❖

	Metric/Imperial	American
white cabbage, shredded	½	½
small onion, finely sliced	1	1
medium leek, finely sliced	1	1
dessert apples, sliced	4	4
celery stalks, chopped	2–3	2–3
pepper, de-seeded and sliced	½	½
lemon juice	1 tbsp	1 tbsp
yoghurt	300 ml/½ pint	1¼ cups
olive oil	1 tbsp	1 tbsp
salt and pepper	to taste	to taste

Mix all the ingredients together. Allow to stand for 30 minutes, then serve. There is quite an appreciable amount of liquid with the dressing. If you like a firmer dressing, blend 50 g/2 oz (1 cup) soft wholemeal breadcrumbs with the yoghurt before using.

Above left: Nut and Vegetable Hotchpotch. Above: Vegetable Filled Aubergines. Left: Cold Salad Platter

CHICKEN SALAD PLATTER

No Cooking   Serves 4–6 ❊❊

	Metric/Imperial	American
button mushrooms, sliced	100 g/4 oz	¼ lb
cooked long grain rice	225 g/8 oz	1½ cups
cooked chicken, diced	350 g/12 oz	¾ lb
mayonnaise	150 ml/¼ pint	⅔ cup
lettuce, shredded	1	1
tomatoes, diced	225 g/8 oz	½ lb
grapes, de-seeded	100–225 g/4–8 oz	¼-½ lb
pineapple slices, diced (optional)	2–3	2–3
mustard and cress	to taste	to taste

Blend the raw mushrooms, rice, chicken and mayonnaise together. Arrange the lettuce on a flat dish, spoon the chicken mixture on to the lettuce. Arrange the tomatoes, grapes and pineapple on the lettuce. Top with mustard and cress.

INTERESTING SALAD DRESSINGS

Mayonnaise is the classic dressing associated with salad. It is, of course, a European sauce which now is made throughout the world.

The typical dressings associated with British cooking of the past were based upon hard-boiled (hard-cooked) eggs, oil and vinegar. The cold sauces were well-flavoured with a variety of chopped herbs.

SALAD SAUCE

No Cooking   Servings depend upon the dish ❊❊

The type of vinegar used in this sauce depends upon the dish with which the dressing is to be served. Housewives of the past made a great feature of flavouring vinegars with various herbs, and these are described on page 192. A wine vinegar gives a much more delicate flavour to the dressing than a malt vinegar. Cider vinegar could be used. This dressing is deliciously light and would please people who find mayonnaise rather rich.

	Metric/Imperial	American
hard-boiled (hard-cooked) eggs	2	2
mustard powder	1–2 teasp	1–2 teasp
olive or salad oil	2 tbsp	3 tbsp
vinegar, see method	2 tbsp	3 tbsp
salt and pepper	to taste	to taste
double (heavy) cream	5 tbsp	½ cup

Rub the eggs through a sieve, or put into a food processor or liquidizer (blender) until smooth. Do not over-process, otherwise they become sticky. Tip into a bowl and gradually blend in the other ingredients.

Use single (light) or whipping cream instead of double cream.
● *Potato Salad Sauce:* Use 4 tablespoons (5 tbsp) sieved cooked potatoes with the eggs.
● Halve a garlic clove and rub round the bowl in which the dressing is made.
● *Fennel Salad Sauce:* Although nowadays fennel is often considered as a delicious imported vegetable, it was grown in Britain a great deal in the past. The finely chopped leaves can be added to the sauce, or to a mayonnaise, together with a little of the chopped white root. This is a perfect dressing for cold fish.
● *Tartare Sauce 1:* Gherkins (sweet dill pickles), parsley and capers can be added to this sauce. Use the quantity given below.

MAYONNAISE

No Cooking   Servings depend upon the dish ❊❊

	Metric/Imperial	American
egg yolks	2	2
mustard powder or French mustard	to taste	to taste
salt and pepper	to taste	to taste
olive or salad oil	up to 300 ml/ ½ pint	up to 1¼ cups
lemon juice or white wine vinegar	to taste	to taste

Beat the yolks with the seasonings in an absolutely clean dry bowl. Gradually beat or whisk in the oil until the sauce thickens to the desired consistency. Add the lemon juice or vinegar to taste.

VARIATIONS
A teaspoon of sugar can be added.
● When the mayonnaise has thickened, gradually beat in 1 tablespoon very hot water; this lightens the dressing.
● *Green Mayonnaise:* While a selection of finely chopped herbs (chives, chervil, parsley, tarragon and/or fennel leaves or dill) are added to the mayonnaise, the basic colouring is made by sieving a little lightly cooked spinach or watercress leaves. Use approximately 2 tablespoons (3 tbsp) to the quantity of mayonnaise or Salad Sauce on this page.

This is a most attractive looking dressing.
● *Tartare Sauce 2:* Add 1 tablespoon chopped parsley, 2 tablespoons (3 tbsp) very finely diced gherkin (sweet dill pickles) and 2 teaspoons chopped capers to either the Mayonnaise or Salad Sauce on this page.
● *Tomato Dressing:* Add sieved fresh tomato purée or concentrated tomato purée (paste) to taste to the Mayonnaise or Salad Sauce on this page.
● There are many other flavourings that can be blended with the basic sauces, e.g. extra lemon juice, mushroom ketchup, Worcestershire sauce and a variety of different herbs.
Note: The oil and egg yolks should be at room temperature; if one of these ingredients is extra cold, the mayonnaise could curdle.

Mayonnaise the Modern Way

Whole eggs can be used if making the mayonnaise in a liquidizer (blender) or food processor; this gives a very light dressing. Check the manufacturer's instructions as to the *minimum* number of egg yolks or whole eggs that could be used to cover the blades or attachment recommended in a food processor.

Put in the egg yolks or eggs with seasonings, switch on for a few seconds to blend.

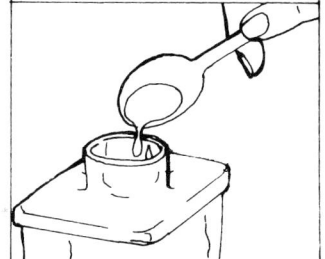

Gradually add the oil, do this drop by drop until about 2 tablespoons (3 tbsp) are incorporated, then pour it gradually on to the eggs. The machine should be running all the time, use the lowest speed.

When the mayonnaise has thickened, add the lemon juice or vinegar and other flavourings and the hot water (if using this).

Herbs or skinned tomatoes could be added to the mayonnaise; these will be finely chopped or blended with the other ingredients.

Oil and Vinegar Dressing

No Cooking   Servings depend upon the dish   ✼

This dressing, known as French Dressing or Vinaigrette Dressing, is used over many salads. Select the very best quality oil – corn oil gives a light dressing, olive oil a rich one.

	Metric/Imperial	American
olive or salad oil	4 tbsp	5 tbsp
little made English mustard or French mustard	½-1 teasp	½-1 teasp
salt and pepper	to taste	to taste
vinegar, preferably white or red wine vinegar	2 tbsp	2½ tbsp
sugar	to taste	to taste

Blend the oil with the seasonings. Gradually mix in the vinegar. Taste the dressing, adjust the seasoning and add the sugar.

VARIATIONS
The proportions above are the classic ones, i.e. twice as much oil as vinegar, but these should be adjusted to cover personal taste and the dish with which the dressing is to be served.
● Add chopped herbs to the dressing, the choice of herbs depends upon the dish, for example choose borage for tomato dishes; dill, fennel or tarragon for fish; chives, mint, parsley, rosemary, tarragon for meat and poultry dishes.
● Use flavoured vinegars, such as those on page 192.

Salmagundy

No Cooking   Serves   6–8   ❋❋❋

Select a very large flat, plain serving dish, so there is little pattern to interfere with the colours of the food and flowers. The recipe below can be varied in a great many different ways; have at least two protein foods, a good selection of salad ingredients and colourful fruit and flowers.

If the dish is too small for all the ingredients, fill several smaller plates or dishes and arrange in the centre of the table.

Slice about 450 g/1 lb tender chicken, arrange in the centre of the dish. Top with a good salad dressing and flower shapes in radishes and cucumber on top.

Arrange a ring of diced beetroot and diced dessert apple around the chicken, then halved hard-boiled (hard-cooked) eggs topped with anchovy fillets and capers.

Put the neat piles of diced cooked carrots, cooked peas, cooked green beans, shredded pickled red cabbage, pickled onions, sliced tomatoes, orange segments and lemon slices all around the dish with shredded lettuce, nasturtium leaves and flowers.

Arrange the colours so they blend well and complete the dish or dishes with more flowers. In the past, the most popular flowers were nasturtiums, marigolds and violets.

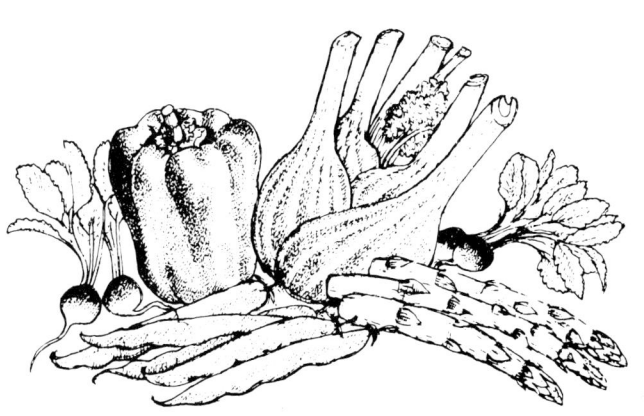

Puddings —and Desserts—

Many people living abroad have the impression that steamed puddings are the only dessert known to British cooks: that fact has never been correct. As far back as the Tudor days, in the 16th Century, light delicate creamy desserts were appreciated by the more wealthy families. Steamed puddings became popular among the less rich in the Victorian era, as they helped to make the family feel well fed; even in these households there were many other desserts, such as pies, tarts and milky puddings.

Nowadays, when most households have freezers, creamy cold or iced desserts are the most popular; but you need only to see the enthusiasm with which a good steamed pudding is greeted to realize that this tradition is well worth retaining.

SUET PUDDINGS

Suet was once the favourite fat for making savoury or sweet puddings. Nowadays, when butcher's suet is less easily obtained, most people choose packet shredded suet.

The suet pudding below is made light in texture by the mixture of flour and breadcrumbs. If you prefer not to use suet (an animal fat) then substitute melted margarine. Make certain the water boils rapidly for the first 1½ hours when cooking the pudding below, this makes certain the suet mixture is light.

SYRUP GOLDEN CAP PUDDING

Cooking Time: 2 hours   Serves 4–6   ❋❋

	Metric/Imperial	American
self-raising flour*	75 g/3 oz	¾ cup
soft fine breadcrumbs	75 g/3 oz	1½ cups
ground ginger, optional	1 teasp	1 teasp
shredded suet	75 g/3 oz	⅔ cup
caster sugar	75 g/3 oz	6 tbsp
golden (light corn) syrup	1 tbsp	1 tbsp
eggs	2	2
milk	to mix	to mix
For the topping: golden (light corn) syrup	3 tbsp	4 tbsp
For the sauce: grated lemon rind	1 teasp	1 teasp
lemon juice	2 tbsp	3 tbsp
golden (light corn) syrup	6 tbsp	generous ½ cup

*or plain (all-purpose) flour with ½ teaspoon baking powder

Mix the flour, breadcrumbs, ginger and suet together. Add the sugar, the 1 tablespoon syrup, then the eggs.

Blend thoroughly, then gradually add enough milk to make a sticky consistency. Put the 3 tablespoons golden (4 tbsp light corn) syrup into a greased 1.2 litre/2 pint (5 cup) pudding basin (ovenproof bowl), cover with the pudding mixture then with the greased greaseproof (waxed) paper or foil. Put into a steamer over rapidly boiling water and steam for 2 hours. Fill the saucepan with boiling water when necessary as rapid cooking is important for this pudding.

Turn out and serve with a sauce made by heating the lemon rind and juice with the syrup. Fresh cream can also be served with this pudding, or a custard sauce.
Spotted Dick: Omit the ginger and syrup in the pudding. Add 1 teaspoon mixed spice to the flour and blend about 175 g/6 oz (1 cup) mixed dried fruit to the other ingredients. Steam as above or bake as the timing on page 124.

Below Left: Spotted Dick. Above: Syrup Golden Cap Pudding. Below right: Fruit Pudding

VARIATIONS
Apple Dumplings: Peel and core 4 medium cooking (baking) apples. Roll out the pastry and cut into 4 large rounds or squares. Place an apple in the middle of each piece of pastry, moisten the edges of the pastry. Fill the centre of the apples with a small knob of butter and brown sugar, or with bramble jelly or with mincemeat. Wrap the pastry around the apples and seal the joins firmly. Enclose each dumpling in a large well greased square of foil, put into a steamer and steam for 1½ hours. Serve topped with sugar. There is another kind of apple dumpling on page 128.

● *Apple and Sultana filling:* Fill the pudding with sliced cooking (baking) apples and about 100 g/4 oz sultanas (²/₃ cup golden raisins). Use sweet cider as the liquid.

FRUIT PUDDINGS

Cooking Time: 2½ hours   Serves 4–6   ❉❉

This is one of the most delicious steamed puddings. It is made with suet crust pastry and fruits in season. Suet Crust Pastry is always made with half the quantity of suet to the flour used.

	Metric/Imperial	American
For the suet crust pastry: self-raising flour*	225 g/8 oz	2 cups
salt	pinch	pinch
shredded suet	110 g/4 oz	⁴/₅ cup
water	to bind	to bind
For the filling: fruit, weight when prepared	450–550 g/ 1–1¼ lb	1–1¼ lb
caster sugar	50–75 g/ 2–3 oz	¼-scant ¹/₃ cup
liquid, see method		
For the topping: caster or brown or Demerara sugar	to taste	to taste

*or plain (all-purpose) flour with 2 teaspoons baking powder

Sift the flour and salt, add the suet and enough water to make a soft rolling consistency. Use three-quarters to line a lightly greased 1.2 litre/2 pint (5 cup) ovenproof basin (bowl), see the line drawings on page 73. Fill with the prepared fruit, sugar and water to half cover the fruit, or as suggested above. Roll out the remaining pastry to form a 'lid'. Moisten the edges of the pastry with water, put on the pastry lid then cover with greased greaseproof (waxed) paper and foil. Steam for 2½ hours. The water should boil very rapidly for the first 1½ hours, after which it can simmer more gently.

Turn the pudding out of the basin, top with sugar and serve with cream or custard.

BAKED SUET PUDDINGS

It is possible to bake suet puddings, examples are given below.

Baked Spotted Dick: Omit the syrup, ginger and breadcrumbs from the Syrup Golden Cap Pudding, page 122. Use 175 g/6 oz (1½ cups) self-raising flour and 150 to 175 g/5 to 6 oz (1 cup) mixed dried fruit instead. Make the pudding, put into a well greased 18 cm/7 inch cake tin or ovenproof mould. Bake in the centre of a moderate oven, 180°C/350°F Gas Mark 4, for 1½ hours; reduce the heat very slightly after 1 hour if the pudding is becoming too brown. The sauce given under the Syrup Golden Cap Pudding is an excellent accompaniment.

This pudding also can be steamed like the Syrup Golden Cap Pudding.

CUMBERLAND PUDDING

Cooking Time: 2½ hours Serves 4–6 ❋❋

	Metric/Imperial	American
cooking (baking) apples, weight when peeled and cored	100 g/4 oz	¼ lb
currants	100 g/4 oz	⅔ cup
caster sugar	100 g/4 oz	½ cup
shredded suet	75 g/3 oz	generous ½ cup
self-raising flour*	100 g/4 oz	1 cup
soft breadcrumbs	75 g/3 oz	1½ cups
grated lemon rind	1 teasp	1 teasp
mixed crystallized (candied) peel, chopped	2 tbsp	3 tbsp
eggs	2	2

*or plain (all-purpose) flour with 1 teaspoon baking powder

Dice the apples neatly and mix with all the other ingredients. Put into a well greased 1.2 litre/2 pint (5 cup) ovenproof basin (bowl) and cover as the line drawings on this page. Steam over boiling water for 2½ hours. Serve with Lemon Sauce, on this page, or with cream.

LEMON SAUCE

Cooking Time: 15 minutes Serves 4–6 ❋❋

	Metric/Imperial	American
grated lemon rind	2 teasp	2 teasp
lemon juice	3 tbsp	4 tbsp
water	300 ml/½ pint	1¼ cups
arrowroot or cornflour (cornstarch)	2 teasp	2 teasp
sugar	75 g/3 oz	6 tbsp

Put the lemon rind and juice into a saucepan with half the water. Cover the pan and simmer for 10 minutes to soften the lemon rind. Blend the arrowroot or cornflour (cornstarch) with the remaining water. Add to the lemon liquid with the sugar; stir over a low heat until thickened and clear.

JAM ROLY POLY

Cooking Time: 50 minutes Serves 4–6 ❋❋

	Metric/Imperial	American
Suet Crust Pastry, as page 123 made with	225 g/8 oz flour etc	2 cups flour etc
jam	225 g/8 oz	½ lb

Make the Suet Crust Pastry as in the Fruit Pudding on page 123. Roll out to a neat oblong shape. Spread with jam, keep this well away from the edges of the pastry. Turn in the pastry at the ends to enclose the jam. Roll firmly and put on to a lightly greased baking tray.

Bake in the centre of a moderately hot oven, 200°C/400°F Gas Mark 6, for 25 minutes, then reduce the heat to moderate, 180°C/350°F Gas Mark 4, and bake for a further 25 minutes until the pastry is golden and firm. Golden syrup or mincemeat could be used as a filling.

The pudding can be steamed if preferred; wrap lightly in greased greaseproof (waxed) paper and then in a floured cloth or foil and steam for 2 hours. Unwrap, put on to a heated serving dish and top with sugar.

The pudding can be served with hot jam.

STEAMED PUDDINGS

To cover: Put the greased paper and/or greased foil over the top of the basin (bowl). Either tie in position or tuck in the edges very firmly.

To make it easy to remove from the steamer, make a long band of thick foil and place under the basin.

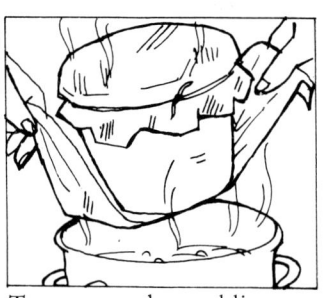

To remove the pudding from the steamer, lift out with the two ends of the foil.

CHRISTMAS PUDDING

**Cooking Time: 5–6 hours   plus reheating   each
pudding Serves 4–6   ✷✷**

*The most famous suet pudding of all is the traditional
Christmas Pudding, rich and dark with fruit. A Christmas
Pudding is one of the recipes that is known and enjoyed
in many parts of the world, but it certainly cannot be
said to be one of our oldest dishes. Before the 17th Century
we, in Britain, celebrated Christmas with a type of
porridge, not unlike that known in Nordic countries,
except that the British version contained dried fruit.*

*This was gradually replaced by the rich blending of
dried fruits and other good ingredients we know today.
Although Christmas Pudding is so often associated with
England, it was, and is, served during the festive season
by the other countries of Britain.*

*Although most Christmas Pudding recipes are similar,
it is virtually impossible to say that any one recipe is the
best; most households who have a family recipe will assure
you that theirs is the one they prefer.*

	Metric/Imperial	American
plain (all-purpose) flour	50 g/2 oz	½ cup
soft breadcrumbs	100 g/4 oz	2 cups
ground cinnamon	½ teasp	½ teasp
ground or grated nutmeg	½ teasp	½ teasp
ground allspice	½ teasp	½ teasp
dark moist brown sugar	100 g/4 oz	⅔ cup
shredded suet	100 g/4 oz	generous ¾ cup
glacé (candied) cherries, chopped	75 g/3 oz	½ cup
uncooked dried apricots, chopped	75 g/3 oz	½ cup
uncooked dried prunes, chopped	75 g/3 oz	½ cup
currants	175 g/6 oz	1 cup
sultanas (golden raisins)	175 g/6 oz	1 cup
raisins, de-seeded	350 g/12 oz	2 cups
almonds, blanched and finely chopped	100 g/4 oz	1 cup
medium carrot, grated	1	1
medium cooking (baking) apple, grated	1	1
mixed crystallized (candied) peel, chopped	100 g/4 oz	⅔ cup
grated lemon rind	1 teasp	1 teasp
grated orange rind	1 teasp	1 teasp
lemon juice	1 tbsp	1 tbsp
orange juice	1 tbsp	1 tbsp
black treacle (molasses)	1 tbsp	1 tbsp
beer or stout	150 ml/¼ pint	⅔ cup
brandy or sherry	1 tbsp	1 tbsp
eggs	2	2

Mix all the ingredients together and allow to stand in the
bowl overnight. Cover the bowl to keep the mixture
moist. Standing for some hours improves the flavour of
the pudding.

Grease two 1.5 litre/2½ pint (6¼ cup) ovenproof
basins (bowls) and spoon in the mixture. If you like a
pudding that slices perfectly, press the ingredients
together very firmly. For a lighter crumbly pudding,
pack the ingredients less tightly. Leave at least a 2.5 cm/1
inch space at the top of the basin because although a
Christmas Pudding does not rise like a light pudding, it
swells in cooking.

Cover the pudding with well greased greaseproof
(waxed) paper and foil. Put a central pleat in both covers
so the pudding will not split the covering, see the line
drawing on this page.

Steam each pudding over boiling water for 5 to 6 hours
or allow about 1 to 1½ hours in a pressure cooker;
follow the manufacturer's instructions as to the setting to
use. If you have no steamer, stand the basin on an
upturned saucer or tin in a saucepan of water, so the
water comes only half-way up the basin, see the line
drawing on this page. Keep the water boiling steadily and
always top up the pan with boiling water.

When the puddings are cooked, remove the damp
covers at once. When cold, cover with fresh dry
greaseproof (waxed) paper and foil. Store in a cool dry
place, away from the steam from cooking in the kitchen.

On Christmas Day, steam the pudding for 2 hours.
Serve with cream or custard sauce, or Brandy Butter or
Rum Butter, see page 197.
Note: This pudding keeps for months or several years if
stored carefully. It can be frozen but the flavour will
not mature as well.

VARIATIONS
If you do not want to use suet, substitute 100 g/4 oz (½
cup) melted butter or margarine. This makes a pudding
that is lighter in texture.
● *Golden Christmas Pudding:* To have a light coloured
pudding, replace the brown sugar with white sugar, the
currants and raisins with sultanas (golden raisins) and
more dried apricots. Use white wine or light sherry in
place of beer or stout.

COVERING PUDDINGS
Put a pleat in the covering
for a Christmas Pudding
or other steamed pudding
to allow space for the
mixture to swell or rise.

Note: There are plastic basins with lids for steaming
puddings; check carefully that the plastic is of the right
type.

If you have no steamer,
stand the pudding basin
(bowl) on an upturned
saucer or tin in a saucepan,
so lifting the basin away
from the base of the
saucepan.

SPONGE PUDDINGS

The advice given on page 162 in the cake section about creamed mixtures also applies when making a sponge pudding. The cooking time for steaming is given below but it is possible to cook light sponge puddings in a microwave cooker or a pressure cooker or an electric slow casserole (often called a 'crock pot'). Follow the manufacturer's advice as to the setting or pressure to use.

CHOCOLATE·VANILLA SPONGE

Cooking Time: 1¾ hours   Serves 4–6 ❊❊

	Metric/Imperial	American
butter or margarine	175 g/6 oz	¾ cup
vanilla essence (extract)	¼-½ teasp	¼-½ teasp
caster sugar	175 g/6 oz	¾ cup
large eggs	3	3
self-raising flour❊	175 g/6 oz	1½ cups
cocoa powder (unsweetened cocoa)	25 g/1 oz	¼ cup
milk, see method		
For the Chocolate Sauce: water	225 ml/8 fl oz	1 cup
caster sugar	50 g/2 oz	¼ cup
butter	50 g/2 oz	¼ cup
cocoa powder (unsweetened cocoa)	25 g/1 oz	¼ cup
chocolate powder	50 g/2 oz	½ cup
golden (light corn) syrup	1 tbsp	1 tbsp

❊or plain (all-purpose) flour with 1½ teaspoons baking powder

Cream the butter or margarine, vanilla essence and sugar until soft and light. Gradually beat in the eggs. Sift the flour and fold into the creamed mixture. Remove approximately half the sponge mixture and place into a second bowl. Sift the cocoa powder (unsweetened cocoa) into this and add a very little milk to make a dropping consistency.

Put spoonfuls of the vanilla and chocolate mixtures into a well greased 1.2 litre/2 pint (5 cup) ovenproof basin (bowl); swirl lightly but do not mix together, the two flavours should form a pattern; smooth flat on top. Cover the pudding with well greased greaseproof (waxed) paper and foil, see page 125. Steam for 1¾ hours, the water should boil rapidly for the first 1¼ hours.

To make the chocolate sauce, put all the ingredients into a saucepan and gently heat until a coating consistency. Turn the pudding out and serve with the chocolate sauce.

VARIATION

A plain sponge pudding is made by omitting the cocoa powder. Jam or lemon curd or golden (light corn) syrup can be put into the basin before adding the sponge mixture. Steam as above.

BAKED SPONGE PUDDING

Cooking Time: 1¼ hours   Serves 4–6 ❊❊

This method of baking a sponge mixture over fruit was undoubtedly the forerunner of the delicious American Upside Down Pudding.

	Metric/Imperial	American
For the sponge: butter or margarine	150 g/5 oz	⅝ cup
caster sugar	150 g/5 oz	⅝ cup
vanilla essence (extract)	few drops	few drops
small eggs	3	3
self-raising flour❊	175 g/6 oz	1½ cups
For the fruit layer: fruit, weight when prepared	450 g/1 lb	1 lb
caster sugar	to taste	to taste
water	2–3 tbsp	3–4 tbsp
For the topping: caster sugar	1 tbsp	1 tbsp

❊or plain (all-purpose) flour with 1½ teaspoons baking powder.

Note: The slightly stiffer consistency of the sponge is better as it is cooked over moist fruit.

Cream the butter or margarine with the sugar and vanilla essence (extract). Gradually beat in the eggs. Sift the flour and fold into the creamed mixture.

Place the prepared fruit in the bottom of a 1.2 to 1.5 litre/2 to 2½ pint (5 to 6¼ cup) pie dish, add sugar to taste and the small amount of water if the fruit is hard, cover the pie dish with foil. Precook sliced cooking (baking) apples or firm plums in the centre of a moderate oven, 180°C/350°F Gas Mark 4, for about 15 minutes. Soft or ripe stoned (pitted) fruit do not need precooking.

Top the partially cooked or raw fruit with the sponge and bake for approximately 1 hour or until firm. Top with the sugar and serve.

PUDDINGS WITH FRUIT

Many delicious puddings are based upon fruit. Here are two puddings; the first a pudding that has been traditional for many generations, the second is a fairly modern variation on a fruit pie.

SUMMER PUDDING

Cooking Time: 15 minutes   Serves 4 ❊❊

Do not be alarmed by the fact that fairly large quantities of bread are used in this pudding, for when the ingredients are put together, allowed to stand overnight (this is essential) then turned out, you have an attractively coloured and most refreshing summer dessert. This is always called a Summer Pudding, but it could be used throughout the year with fruits in season. This pudding is also known as a Sussex Pudding.

Redcurrant Cobbler – recipe page 128. Summer Pudding.

	Metric/Imperial	American
sliced white bread, weight with crusts	350 g/12 oz	¾ lb
raspberries	450 g/1 lb	1 lb
redcurrants	225 g/8 oz	½ lb
blackcurrants	225 g/8 oz	½ lb
water	2 tbsp	3 tbsp
sugar	100 g/4 oz	½ cup
To decorate, optional: double (heavy) cream	150 ml/¼ pint	²/₃ cup

Remove the crusts from the bread and cut into fairly thin slices. Put into a 1.2 litre/2 pint (5 cup) basin (bowl), arranging the bread so it fits perfectly, save enough for a lid.

Cook the raspberries and red and blackcurrants in a saucepan with the water and sugar until soft. If you dislike pips, rub the fruit through a hair or nylon sieve, in which case use slightly more raspberries.

Spoon the fruit into the bread-lined basin, cover with a layer of bread. Put greaseproof (waxed) paper then a flat saucer or plate and light weight on top. Leave overnight in a cool place.

Next day, turn out. Whip half the cream and pile or pipe this on top of the pudding. Serve the rest of the cream with the pudding.

CHERRY COBBLER

Cooking Time: 30–35 minutes Serves 4 ❄❄

	Metric/Imperial	American
For the fruit mixture: cherries	450–675 g/ 1–1½ lb	1–1½ lb
water	3 tbsp	4 tbsp
sugar	75 g/3 oz	6 tbsp
For the cobbler: self-raising flour*	175 g/6 oz	1½ cups
butter or margarine	40 g/1½ oz	3 tbsp
sugar	50 g/2 oz	¼ cup
milk	to bind	to bind
To glaze: milk	1 tbsp	1 tbsp
sugar	25 g/1 oz	2 tbsp

*or plain (all-purpose) flour with 1½ teaspoons baking powder

Put the cherries into the pie dish with the water and sugar. Put a piece of foil or greaseproof (waxed) paper over the fruit so it does not dry. Cook in the centre of a moderate oven, 180°C/350°F Gas Mark 4, for approximately 15 minutes.

Sift the flour into a bowl. Rub in the butter or margarine until the mixture looks like fine breadcrumbs. Add the sugar and enough milk to bind to a soft rolling consistency. Roll out until about 1.5 cm/½ inch thick. Cut into small rounds and brush these with the milk; sprinkle with the sugar. Place them on top of the hot half-cooked fruit. Raise the oven heat to hot, 220°C/425°F Gas Mark 7, put the cobbler in the centre of the oven and cook for approximately 15 to 20 minutes. Serve hot with cream.

VARIATION
Most other fruits can be used to make this simple pudding. If using soft fruit, such as redcurrants, shown in the photograph on page 127, just add sugar and precook for about 10 minutes.

BAKED APPLES

Choose best quality cooking apples for baking. Always slit the skin round the centre of the apples before they are baked; this prevents the pulp breaking through the skin. The apples can be cored and the centres filled with a knob of butter and a little brown sugar or golden (light corn) syrup or with dried fruit or mincemeat or with bramble (blackberry) jelly or apricot jam. They can be coated with pastry as the recipe on this page.

A medium sized cooking (baking) apple takes approximately 45 minutes to cook in the centre of a moderate oven, 180°C/350°F Gas Mark 4.

● *Snowball Apples:* When cooked, the apples can be covered with meringue as the photograph on page 134. Allow 1 egg white and 50 g/2 oz (¼ cup) caster sugar to each apple. Whisk the egg white(s) until stiff, gradually beat in half the sugar, then fold in the remainder. Skin the apple(s) if wished. Spoon the meringue over the apple(s). Bake in a slow to very moderate oven, 150 to

160°C/300 to 325°F Gas Mark 2 to 3, for 15 to 20 minutes. Decorate with angelica cut into leaf shapes, a tiny twig (non-edible) to look like the stalk and twists of orange or lemon rind. To make a more satisfying dessert, serve the apples on rounds of plain sponge cake.

APPLES IN A NIGHTGOWN

Cooking Time: 55 minutes Serves 4 ❄❄

This is the less usual name given to Apple Dumplings, when the apples are filled with marmalade or apricot jam and enclosed in puff pastry. When cooked, dredge the dumplings with caster sugar.

Make Puff Pastry as page 155 with 225 g/8 oz (2 cups) flour etc. Roll out until paper thin. Cut into 4 squares which should be sufficiently large to enclose the apples.

Peel and core 4 cooking (baking) apples. Place an apple in the centre of each piece of pastry.

Fill the centre of the apples with marmalade or jam.

Moisten the edges of the pastry, bring up around the apples, seal the edges.

If any pastry is left, decorate the dumplings with leaves of pastry. Brush with lightly whisked egg white.

Bake in the centre of a hot oven, 220°C/425°F Gas Mark 7, for 20 minutes, then reduce the heat to 180°C/350°F Gas Mark 4, for 35 minutes.

PEARS IN CIDER

Cooking Time: up to 1¾ hours Serves 4–8 ❄❄

Somerset is famous for its cider and this method of cooking pears is very similar to classic French dishes, and has been used for many years. The redcurrant or apple jelly helps to thicken and colour the syrup. The pears look more impressive if cooked whole and since they should be very tender, they are not difficult to serve. However, it does mean using rather a lot of cider and other ingredients in the sauce to make sure they are covered during cooking. If preferred the pears could be halved, in which case about half the ingredients for the sauce would be necessary. Any sauce left could be saved and served with baked apples.

	Metric/Imperial	American
sweet cider	1.2 litres/2 pints	5 cups
redcurrant or apple jelly	6 tbsp	½ cup
caster sugar	100 g/4 oz	½ cup
medium sized cooking (baking) pears	8	8
cloves, optional	8	8

Put the cider, jelly and sugar into a medium sized saucepan, stir until the jelly and sugar have dissolved. Peel the pears but try to retain the stalk. Remove the cores if it is possible to do this without damaging the fruit. Press one clove into the base of each pear, if using these.

Put the pears into the syrup in the pan, check to see they are completely covered, if not then make up a little more sauce. Cover the pan and simmer the cider mixture gently until the pears are tender. Really hard cooking (baking) pears sometimes need about 1½ hours; these are particularly good prepared in this method since the syrup soaks through the fruit and imparts an excellent flavour.

When the pears are soft, lift out of the cider mixture, put into a serving dish. Boil the cider mixture briskly in the uncovered pan until a thickened syrup. Cool slightly then pour around the pears. Chill well and serve with cream.

FRUIT PIES

Deep-dish pies filled with fruit have been a favourite pudding in Britain for many years. There is an abundance of seasonal fruits, which make it possible to produce a fruit pie at any time of the year.

Gooseberry pie is often given as the traditional pudding for Whitsun-tide but since this is a festival where the date changes yearly, there are many years where it is too early for gooseberries to be available.

TO MAKE A FRUIT PIE

In Britain, the term 'pie' is generally used when a deep pie dish is filled with fruit and covered with pastry. A dish where pastry is used below and above the filling is called a 'tart', and a pastry case with a filling is nowadays referred to as a 'flan'. Recipes for various tarts and flans are given on pages 132 to 135.

To make a pie to serve 4 people, you require at least 450 g/1 lb fruit (the weight of the prepared fruit) and pastry made with 150 to 175 g/5 to 6 oz (1¼ to 1½ cups) flour etc., see pages 175, 154 and 155.

Some of the interesting fillings for pies are:
Apple and Quince: A mixture of sliced cooking (baking) apples and quince makes an excellent filling.
Apple Cream Pie: A delectable dessert is made by making an apple pie, then lifting the lid (or a portion of the lid) about 10 minutes before the end of the cooking time and adding a generous amount of double (heavy) cream; return the pie to the oven to complete the cooking.
Ginger Rhubarb Pie: Add diced preserved or crystallized (candied) ginger to diced rhubarb in a pie. The amount of ginger is a matter of personal taste.
Surprise Cherry Pie: Stone approximately 675 g/1½ lb black or other dessert cherries. Heat 150 ml/¼ pint (⅔ cup) water with 50 g/2 oz (¼ cup) sugar or to taste. Add the cherries, poach gently for 10 minutes then cool slightly. Beat 3 egg yolks well, mix with the cherries and liquid. Add 50 g/2 oz (1 cup) fine plain cake or macaroon biscuit crumbs. Top with shortcrust pastry made with 175 g/6 oz (1½ cups) flour etc. and bake as the instructions right.

The pie can be topped with caster or sifted icing (confectioner's) sugar before serving. It is interesting that the fruit pies of today are decorated very simply with sugar, but in the past it was quite usual to cover the pie with icing.

A usual icing for a pie of the size given below was made by blending 100 g/4 oz sifted icing sugar (a scant cup of confectioner's sugar) with 1 lightly beaten egg and a squeeze of lemon juice. The pie was removed from the oven about 10 minutes before the end of the cooking time, the icing spread carefully over the pastry and the pie returned to the oven to complete the cooking period. The icing sets quickly in the heat of the oven.

To Bake a Fruit Pie

Place the pie in the centre of the oven. Use a moderately hot to hot oven, 200 to 220°C/400 to 425°F Gas Mark 6 to 7, for shortcrust pastry or a very slightly hotter temperature for flaky or puff pastry. Bake for 20 minutes or until the pastry becomes firm and well risen in the case of flaky and puff pastry; then reduce the heat to moderate, 180°C/350°F Gas Mark 4, and cook for another 15 to 20 minutes or until the fruit and the pastry are cooked.

PREPARING A FRUIT PIE

Prepare the fruit, put into a deep pie dish with a little water or other fruit juice and sugar or other sweetening, such as honey to taste. Always fill the pie dish well to support the pastry or use a pie support (an upturned heat-resistant egg cup could be used).

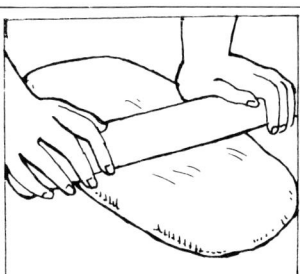

Roll out the pastry; this can be shortcrust pastry or flaky or rough puff pastry. A biscuit crust pastry is too brittle to be a good covering; puff pastry is used on savoury pies, but could be used.

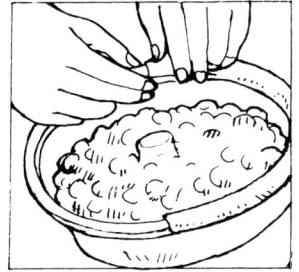

Cut narrow strips of pastry and put around the rim of the pie dish.

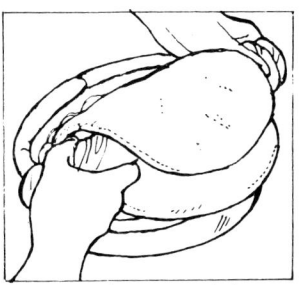

Support the rest of the pastry over the rolling pin; press the edges of the pastry lid to the pastry rim.

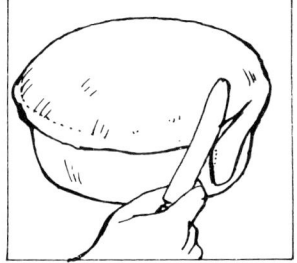

Trim away the surplus pastry. It is not usual to decorate sweet pies with pastry leaves.

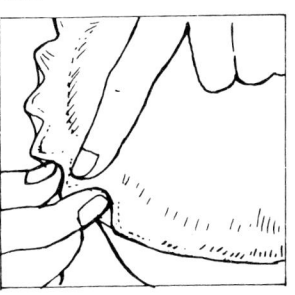

Flute the edges of the pastry with your forefinger and thumb.

If using flaky or rough puff or puff pastry, *flake* the edges with a knife. This produces layers in the pastry edge which encourages it to rise.

Put the flour and salt into a bowl. Add the egg and enough of the milk or milk and water to make a stiff batter; beat hard until smooth then gradually blend in the remaining liquid. Always whisk the batter just before cooking the pancakes, for the flour has a tendency to drop to the bottom of the mixture.

In order to cook a batch of pancakes quickly, it is wise to have two pans in use at the same time. If the pans are kept especially for pancakes, simply rub the pans with a little oil and then heat. If, however, the pans are used for all purposes, use about 1 teaspoon oil and heat this. After cooking the first pancake, only very little, if any, extra oil should be used.

Pour enough batter into the hot pan to give a wafer thin layer. Cook steadily for about 1½ minutes until golden on the bottom side. Turn or toss and cook for the same time on the second side. Slide the first pancake or pancakes out of the pan(s) and keep hot while cooking the remainder of the mixture.

To keep the pancakes hot: put on to a flat dish or large plate and place in the oven with the heat set low, or over a pan of boiling water. Do not cover the pancakes – this would make them soggy.

If keeping the pancakes hot for a considerable time, separate them with squares of greaseproof (waxed) paper or with absorbent paper (kitchen towels).

Pancakes freeze well for up to 3 months; they should be separated by greaseproof or waxed paper, oiled on both sides then packed in a plastic box. See below for mixture to freeze.

VARIATIONS
A better and more crisp batter is produced by adding 1 tablespoon olive or corn oil or good frying oil to the batter before

PANCAKES

Cooks in many countries of the world prepare and enjoy pancakes. In Britain, we have made pancakes for generations but if one compares a recipe of the 17th Century with a modern recipe, there is a great difference. The pancake batter of those early days consisted of a very rich mixture of cream and many eggs with the flour, whereas our modern batter is an economical one.

Pancakes are the important feature of Shrove Tuesday.

Above: Sweet Omelette. Above right: Apple Fritters.
Below right: Making Pancakes

BASIC PANCAKES

Cooking Time: about 3 minutes for each pancake   Makes 12–18 pancakes

	Metric/Imperial	American
plain (all-purpose) flour	110 g*/4 oz	1 cup
salt	pinch	pinch
egg	1	1
milk or milk and water	275 ml*/½ pint	1¼ cups
To cook: oil, see method	little	little

*use this metrication

frying. This is essential if the pancakes are to be frozen.
● Add 2 eggs to the batter and reduce the amount of liquid by 2 tablespoons (3 tbsp).
● A batter that has a little of the richness of the early mixtures is made by using the same amount of flour as in the basic recipe with a pinch of salt, 3 eggs and 225 ml/8 fl oz (1 cup) cream. This can be double (heavy) or whipping cream.

To Serve Sweet Pancakes
The most usual way to serve the pancakes is with sugar and lemon. Roll the pancakes, top with caster sugar and serve with thick wedges of lemon.

The pancakes can be served with spice, such as ground cinnamon, and sugar, or filled with cooked or dessert fruit, as shown in the photograph on this page, jam or other preserves or with mincemeat. Top or serve with cream.
Layered Pancakes:
Another interesting way to serve pancakes is to make layers of pancakes, jam or redcurrant jelly and fruit. The pyramid of pancakes can be topped with whipped cream and chopped nuts just before serving.

SWEET OMELETTES
An omelette is associated with classic French cuisine, but sweet omelettes have been made in Britain since the time of Elizabeth I. They were known as 'amulets'. A rich sweet omelette was a favourite dessert at Edwardian dinner parties. The following recipe is an excellent basic one.

SWEET OMELETTE

Cooking Time: 5–6 minutes   Serves 3–4   ❖❖

	Metric/Imperial	American
eggs	6	6
caster sugar	25 g/1 oz	2 tbsp
double (heavy) cream	2 tbsp	3 tbsp
brandy, optional	1 tbsp	1 tbsp
grated orange rind	1 teasp	1 teasp
butter	40 g/1½ oz	3 tbsp
For the topping: caster sugar	to taste	to taste

Separate the eggs. Mix the egg yolks with the sugar, cream, brandy and orange rind; beat well until light and fluffy.

Whisk the egg whites in a separate bowl, then fold into the egg yolk mixture. Heat the butter in a large omelette pan (approximately 20 cm/8 inches in diameter) or frying pan (skillet); at the same time preheat the grill (broiler). Pour the egg mixture into the omelette pan, allow to set lightly at the bottom, then place the pan under the grill with the heat set fairly low. (Make certain the handle of the pan is not exposed to the heat.) Cook until lightly set, then add the filling as the suggestions below.

Make a light cut in the centre of the very thick omelette, fold carefully and slide out of the pan on to a heated serving dish. Top with the sugar or as suggested below and serve.

To Serve Sweet Omelettes
The basic omelette can be varied in many ways. Add 1 or 2 finely diced macaroon biscuits to 2 tablespoons (3 tbsp) blanched and chopped almonds to the egg yolks.

Add 1 to 2 tablespoons (1½ to 3 tbsp) curaçao or other liqueur to the egg yolks.

Fill the omelette with fruit or any other ingredients suggested under pancakes on page 130.

FRUIT FRITTERS

Cooking Time: 4–6 minutes   Serves 4   ❖❖

The early batter coating for food was made with flour, egg and beer, not milk; it is given below.

	Metric/Imperial	American
plain (all-purpose) or self-raising flour*	100 g/4 oz	1 cup
salt	pinch	pinch
egg	1	1
light beer	225 ml/8 fl oz	1 cup
olive, corn or salad oil	2 tbsp	3 tbsp
To fry: deep oil or fat		
fruit, see this page		
To coat: flour, approximately	2 tbsp	3 tbsp

*use either flour depending on whether a thin or 'puffy' batter is preferred

Blend the flour with the salt, egg and a little of the beer. Beat well until a smooth mixture, then gradually add the remaining beer. Pour the oil into the batter just before coating the food and blend well. Heat the oil or fat to 175°C/345°F, or until a cube of day-old bread turns golden in just under a minute.

Coat the fruit with a very little flour, then dip in the batter. Hold over the bowl so any excess batter drops back. Fry for 4 to 6 minutes until crisp and golden. Drain on absorbent paper (kitchen towels) and serve.

VARIATION
Omit the beer and use milk or milk and water instead. The oil can be reduced to 1 tablespoon.

TARTS AND FLANS

The recipes on this and the next few pages are a selection of open tarts and flans. The Apricot Chiffon Pie is an up-to-date adaptation of an old recipe known as a Pudden Pye, it consists of a rich sweet pastry case filled with a light fruit filling; it is called a pie but is really a flan.

The Bakewell Pudding or Tart is an old established favourite, as is a Custard Tart.

TO MAKE A FLAN
Cooking Time: 20–25 minutes   Serves 4–6 ✳✳

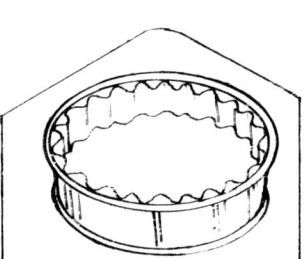 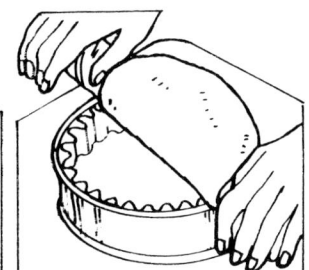

Place a flan ring on an upturned baking tray, this enables the pastry to be removed easily. A flan tin or dish can be used.

Make the pastry as right. Roll out, support it over the rolling pin and lower into the ring, tin or dish.

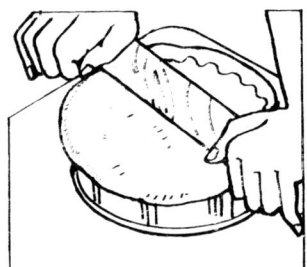 

Press the pastry down very firmly, then cut away the surplus or remove this by pressing the rolling pin over the edge.

Put lightly greased greaseproof (waxed) paper into the flan or use foil. Top with plastic baking beans, crusts of bread or pasta. Bake 'blind' (without a filling) in the centre of a moderate oven, 190°C/375°F Gas Mark 5, for 15 minutes.

Remove the paper or foil etc. and continue baking for a further 5–10 minutes. The flan ring could be removed at this stage too.

Handle the cooked pastry carefully while warm.

BISCUIT CRUST PASTRY

	Metric/Imperial	American
butter or margarine	100 g/4 oz	½ cup
caster sugar	50 g/2 oz	¼ cup
egg yolk	1	1
plain (all-purpose) flour	175 g/6 oz	1½ cups
salt	pinch	pinch
water	few drops	few drops

Cream the butter or margarine and sugar until soft, beat in the egg yolk. Sift the flour and salt, blend with the creamed mixture. Add just enough water to bind. Knead this pastry well. It may be very soft at this stage, so wrap in cling film (plastic wrap) and chill for 1 to 2 hours.

Roll out and line a flan ring or tin, as shown left. In view of the high sugar content, do not exceed the baking temperature given.

APRICOT CHIFFON PIE

Cooking Time: 55 minutes   Serves 6 ✳✳

	Metric/Imperial	American
flan case, baked as left		
For the filling: dried apricots, finely chopped	100 g/4 oz	¾ cup
water	450 ml/¾ pint	scant 2 cups
lemon juice	1 tbsp	1 tbsp
caster sugar	175 g/6 oz	¾ cup
cornflour (cornstarch)	2 teasp	2 teasp
eggs	2	2
gelatine	7 g/¼ oz	1 envelope

Soak the apricots in 300 ml/½ pint (1¼ cups) of the water for 3 hours. Pour into a saucepan, add the lemon juice and 100 g/4 oz (½ cup) sugar. Cover the pan and simmer gently for 40 minutes. Blend the cornflour (cornstarch) with half the remaining water, add to the ingredients in the pan. Stir over a low heat for 5 minutes or until thickened. Cool slightly.

Separate the eggs. Beat the yolks into the hot, but not boiling, apricot mixture then cook very slowly for 4 minutes. Pour the remaining water into a small heatproof basin (bowl), sprinkle the gelatine on top. Stand the basin over a pan of very hot water until the gelatine has dissolved. Blend the hot gelatine into the hot apricot mixture. Allow to cool and stiffen very slightly.

Whisk the egg whites until stiff, fold in the remaining sugar then gently blend with the cold apricot mixture. Spoon the partially set fluffy apricot mixture into the crisp cold pastry, leave until quite firm. Serve with cream.

BAKEWELL TART

Cooking Time: 40–50 minutes   Serves 4–6   ❖❖

Old recipes often refer to this dish as a Bakewell Pudding; it takes its name from a small town in Derbyshire. As so often happens with very old recipes that have been passed down by word of mouth, instructions for making this vary; in some recipes 2 to 3 tablespoons chopped crystallized (candied) peel are added to the filling; in others, the flour and crumbs are omitted and replaced by extra ground almonds. Shortcrust pastry can be replaced by puff or flaky pastry.

	Metric/Imperial	American
Shortcrust Pastry (basic pie dough), as page 175 made with	175 g/6 oz flour etc	1½ cups flour etc
For the filling: butter	75 g/3 oz	6 tbsp
caster sugar	75 g/3 oz	6 tbsp
egg	1	1
plain (all-purpose) flour	25 g/1 oz	¼ cup
ground almonds	75 g/3 oz	¾ cup
cake crumbs	40 g/1½ oz	½ cup
milk	2 tbsp	3 tbsp
raspberry jam	3 tbsp	scant ¼ cup
For the topping: icing (confectioner's) sugar, sifted	25 g/1 oz	¼ cup

Make the pastry. Roll thinly into a round large enough to line an 18 to 20 cm/7 to 8 inch flan ring on an upturned baking tray or flan dish.

Cream the butter and sugar together until very light. Beat in the egg, then fold in the sifted flour, ground almonds, cake crumbs. Add the milk. Spread the bottom of the flan case with raspberry jam. Place the filling on the top and spread over evenly with a knife. Bake in the centre of a moderately hot oven, 190 to 200°C/375 to 400°F Gas Mark 5 to 6, for 40 to 50 minutes. Cool slightly and dust lightly with the icing (confectioner's) sugar.

VARIATION
Bakewell Tart (2): Use flaky pastry made with 175 g/6 oz (1½ cups) flour etc, see page 154. Line a 23 cm/9 inch flan ring or dish with flaky pastry. Chill well. Spread with raspberry jam. Melt 100 g/4 oz (½ cup) butter, allow to cool. Beat 4 eggs and 100 g/4 oz (½ cup) caster sugar until thick and creamy, then gradually whisk in the butter and finally add 100 g/4 oz (1 cup) ground almonds. Pour into the pastry case. Bake in the centre of a hot oven, 220°C/425°F Gas Mark 7, for 15 minutes, then reduce the heat to very moderate, 160°C/325°F Gas Mark 3, for a further 30 minutes or until just set.

FRUIT TARTS
A double layer Fruit Tart is an excellent way of retaining the full flavour of the fruit filling, for this is cooked between layers of pastry with sugar to taste and no extra liquid.

Some people find difficulty in making the bottom pastry crisp well. A light dusting of cornflour (cornstarch) or semolina absorbs any fruit juice. Use Shortcrust Pastry made with 225 to 300 g/8 to 10 oz (2 to 2½ cups) flour, as page 175, to about 450 g/1 lb fruit and sugar to taste.

Interesting fillings are sliced apples, mixed with sultanas (golden raisins), raisins and grated lemon rind, or bilberries (blueberries), or gooseberries with raspberries; or apricots, plums or other halved stoned (pitted) fruit.

TO MAKE A FRUIT TART
Cooking Time: 40–45 minutes   Serves 4–6   ❖❖

Take approximately half the pastry, roll out and line a 20 to 23 cm/8 to 9 inch pie plate or shallow flan dish.

Sprinkle a scant tablespoon of cornflour (cornstarch) or fine semolina over the pastry. Top with the prepared fruit, mixed with the sugar.

Cover the filling with the remaining pastry, trim and flute the edges. Make a slit in the pastry to allow the steam to escape in cooking.

Stand the pie plate or flan dish on a baking tray (this helps to crisp the base of the tart). Bake in the centre of a moderately hot to hot oven, 200–220°C/400–425°F Gas Mark 6–7, for 15 minutes, then reduce the heat slightly and cook for a further 25 minutes.

Fruit Turnovers: The same ingredients used to make a large tart can be used for individual Fruit Turnovers. The amount of fruit used though will be approximately 350 g/12 oz (¾ lb).

Roll out the pastry. Cut into 4 large rounds. Put the prepared fruit and a little sugar in the centre of each round. Damp the edges of the pastry and fold over to make a half circle. Seal the edges firmly. Lift on to a lightly greased baking tray. Bake as for Fruit Tarts above, but allow only 25 to 30 minutes.

TREACLE CUSTARD PIE

Cooking Time: 45 minutes   Serves 4–6   ❖❖

	Metric/Imperial	American
flan case, made as page 132		
For the filling: golden (light corn) syrup	4 tbsp	5 tbsp
egg yolks	2	2
double (heavy) cream	2 tbsp	3 tbsp

Bake the flan case blind for 15 minutes only, see page 132. Warm the syrup slightly so it is liquid, then blend with the egg yolks and cream. Pour this mixture into the partially baked pastry, reduce the oven heat to very moderate, 160°C/325°F Gas Mark 3, and bake for a further 30 minutes or until the pastry is crisp and the filling firm.

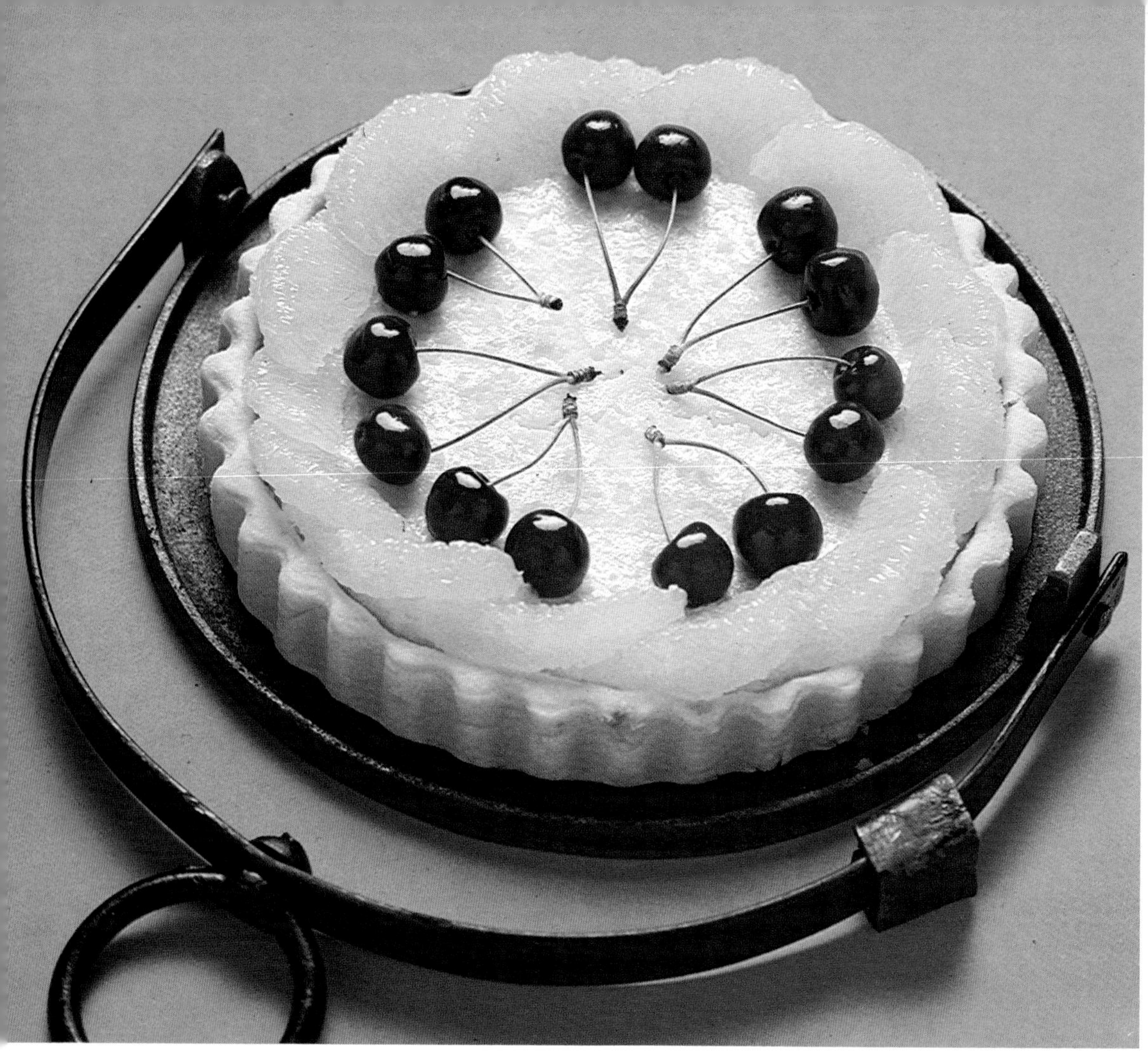

Above: Fruit Custard Tart. Below: Snowball Apple – recipe page 128

Meanwhile, beat the egg and egg yolks with the sugar. Heat the milk, do not allow it to boil; pour over the egg mixture. Strain the custard if necessary; but the method of blending eggs and sugar before adding the milk should make this process unnecessary. Carefully pour the hot custard into the hot pastry. Top with the nutmeg. Reduce the heat to 160°C/325°F Gas Mark 3, bake for 30 to 40 minutes until pastry is firm and custard set.

Method 2: Line the flan dish or tin as before, brush with unbeaten egg white; this forms a film over the pastry and prevents the liquid custard soaking into the pastry. Make the custard as before, but use cold milk. Pour the cold custard into the unbaked pastry case. Top with the nutmeg. Bake in the centre of a hot oven, 220°C/425°F Gas Mark 7, for 20 minutes, reduce the heat as above, continue cooking.

CUSTARD TART

Cooking Time: 50–60 minutes   Serves 4–6 ❊❊

A Custard Tart is as English as roast beef; every good cook in the north of England wants to make a perfect Custard Tart, with crisp pastry and a firm filling.

	Metric/Imperial	American
Shortcrust Pastry (basic pie dough) or Biscuit Crust Pastry, as pages 175 and 132 made with	175 g/6 oz flour etc	1½ cups flour etc
For the filling:		
egg	1	1
egg yolks	2	2
caster sugar	1–2 tbsp	1½–3 tbsp
milk	300 ml/½ pint	1¼ cups
To decorate: grated or ground nutmeg	to taste	to taste

Roll out the pastry and line an 18 to 20 cm/7 to 8 inch flan dish or tin. Press the pastry down firmly in the dish or tin. There are two methods of baking the pastry and filling.

Method 1: To obtain a really crisp pastry crust, bake 'blind' in the centre of a moderately hot oven, 200°C/400°F Gas Mark 6, for 15 to 20 minutes or until just firm.

VARIATIONS

Flavour the custard with 1 to 2 tablespoons coffee essence (extract) or with 25 g/1 oz cocoa powder (¼ cup unsweetened cocoa) or 50 g/2 oz (½ cup) chocolate powder. Omit the nutmeg.

● *Fruit Custard Tart:* Fresh or well-drained cooked or canned fruit makes an interesting topping to a custard tart. The photograph on this page shows the tart topped with fresh dessert cherries and segments of grapefruit.

Three Fruit Flan

FRUIT FLANS

Make and bake a flan case as the recipe on page 132. Allow this to cool.

Fill the flan with approximately 450 g/1 lb well-drained cooked or canned fruit or seasonal fresh fruit, such as strawberries or ripe stoned (pitted) cherries.

It is usual to glaze the fruit. If using cooked or canned fruit, follow the first recipe.

Glaze 1: Measure 150 ml/¼ pint (²/₃ cup) fruit syrup. Blend with 1 teaspoon cornflour (cornstarch) or arrowroot. Pour into a saucepan, add 1 tablespoon lemon juice if the syrup is rather sweet, or 1 tablespoon sugar if it is sour. Stir over a low heat until the syrup becomes clear and thickened. Add 2 tablespoons (3 tbsp) redcurrant jelly or sieved apricot jam, if liked.

Glaze 2: Heat 4 to 5 tablespoons (5 to 6 tbsp) redcurrant jelly or sieved apricot jam with 1 tablespoon lemon juice or water.

To coat the fruit: Allow the glaze to cool slightly then spread or brush over fruit. The three fruits (black and red cherries and mandarin oranges), shown in the photograph on this page, were coated with Glaze 1.

APPLE CHEESE CAKES

Cooking Time: 15–20 minutes   Makes 12   ❖

	Metric/Imperial	American
For the biscuit crust: plain (all-purpose) flour	175 g/6 oz	1½ cups
salt	pinch	pinch
butter	75 g/3 oz	6 tbsp
sugar	25 g/1 oz	2 tbsp
egg yolk	1	1
water	to bind	to bind
To glaze: egg white	1	1
For the filling: cooking (baking) apples (weight when peeled and cored), sliced	225 g/8 oz	½ lb
finely grated lemon rind	1 teasp	1 teasp
lemon juice	2 tbsp	3 tbsp
caster sugar	50 g/2 oz	¼ cup
ground cinnamon	pinch	pinch
butter	25 g/1 oz	2 tbsp
egg	1	1
fine soft breadcrumbs	25 g/1 oz	½ cup

This recipe is sometimes called Apple Chissicks in Yorkshire; undoubtedly these pastry cases, filled with an apple and lemon mixture, were a country-woman's way of providing an interesting tart filling at less expense than the true lemon curd.

Sift the flour and salt. Cream the butter and sugar until soft and light. Add the flour, egg yolk and enough water to make a firm rolling consistency. This particular pastry can be kneaded fairly firmly. Roll out the pastry and line 12 deep individual patty tins (patty shells). Prick the bottom of the pastry shapes, brush with the egg white. Bake 'blind' just above the centre of a moderately hot oven, 200°C/400°F Gas Mark 6, for 12 to 15 minutes until firm.

Meanwhile, put the apple slices, lemon rind, lemon juice and sugar into a saucepan, do not add extra water. Cook gently until the apples are soft. Beat with a wooden spoon to give a smooth pulp. Remove from the heat and add the cinnamon, butter, egg and breadcrumbs. Blend thoroughly and cook over a very low heat until thickened.

If serving hot, put the hot apple mixture into the hot pastry. Serve with cream or ice cream.

If serving cold, allow both the pastry and the filling to become cold, then spoon the apple mixture into the pastry cases.

DESSERTS BASED ON A CUSTARD

The English cooks were famous for their creamy egg custards. The thick custard sauce, made as in the trifle opposite, was frequently served in small glass cups. The cold custard was a favourite supper dish at formal balls during the 18th Century. A better egg custard is made if a higher proportion of egg yolks than egg whites are used.

The Floating Islands on the next page can be made with an egg custard, rather than cream.

The egg custards of the past were frequently flavoured with strips of orange rind, which were removed before serving.

IRISH COFFEE PUDDING

Illustrated in colour on page 210

Cooking Time: few minutes   Serves 6–8   ❊❊❊

This deliciously light cold dessert is really a version of Irish coffee. It tastes as good as it looks.

	Metric/Imperial	American
very strong coffee	225 ml/8 fl oz	1 cup
eggs	4	4
caster sugar	100 g/4 oz	½ cup
whiskey	3 tbsp	4 tbsp
gelatine	15 g/½ oz	2 envelopes
double (heavy) cream	300 ml/½ pint	1¼ cups
To decorate: walnuts, coarsely chopped	2 tbsp	3 tbsp
double (heavy) cream	to taste	to taste

Put the coffee into a heatproof bowl. Separate the eggs. Add the egg yolks and sugar to the coffee. Stand the bowl over a saucepan of hot, but not boiling, water and stir or whisk until the mixture is sufficiently thick to coat a wooden spoon.

Pour the whiskey into a small heatproof bowl. Sprinkle the gelatine on top. Stand the bowl over a pan of hot water until the gelatine has dissolved. Add to the warm coffee mixture, blend thoroughly. Allow to cool and stiffen very slightly. Whip the cream in a bowl until it just holds its shape. Whisk the egg whites in a second container until very stiff. Fold the cream and then the egg whites into the jellied mixture. Spoon into a large serving dish or individual sundae glasses and allow to set.

Sprinkle the nuts around the edge of the dish or glasses and spoon whipped cream in the centre of the mixture.

VARIATION
Grated chocolate can be used with, or instead of, the nuts.

SHERRY TRIFLE

Illustrated in colour on page 206

Cooking Time: 10–15 minutes   Serves 6–8   ❊❊

In the days before ice cream became so popular, a Sherry Trifle was considered the dessert for special occasions. The term 'trifle' can sometimes mean a really rather unexciting mixture of ingredients, but a well-made trifle is full of flavour and a delight to the eye as well as the palate.

	Metric/Imperial	American
For the custard: eggs	2	2
egg yolks	3	3
milk	300 ml/½ pint	1¼ cups
single (light) cream	450 ml/¾ pint	scant 2 cups
caster sugar	50 g/2 oz	¼ cup
vanilla pod (bean)	1	1
For the base: small sponge cakes	6–8	6–8
raspberry jam	4 tbsp	5 tbsp
sweet sherry	150 ml/¼ pint	⅔ cup
almonds, blanched and flaked	25 g/1 oz	¼ cup
ratafias, see page 151	about 18	about 18
To decorate: double (heavy) or whipping cream	300 ml/½ pint	1¼ cups
Maraschino or glacé (candied) cherries	about 8	about 8
angelica, cut into leaves	about 16	about 16
almonds, blanched	25 g/1 oz	¼ cup

Blend the eggs and egg yolks with the milk, cream and sugar. Pour into the top of a double saucepan, or into a heatproof bowl standing over a pan of water. Add the vanilla pod (bean). Allow the water to simmer gently and stir until the custard coats the back of a wooden spoon. Remove the vanilla pod.

Meanwhile, split the sponge cakes and sandwich together with the jam. Put into a glass serving dish and soak with the sherry. Add the flaked almonds and half the ratafias. Pour the warm custard over the sponge cakes. Place a plate over the bowl to prevent the formation of a skin as the custard cools.

Whip the cream until it just holds its shape; do not overwhip. Spread or pipe over the custard base, completely covering this. Decorate with the remaining ratafias, the Maraschino or glacé (candied) cherries, with leaves of angelica and the blanched almonds. Chill well before serving.

VARIATIONS
There are many variations on this typical British dessert. The recipe above is the one traditionally made in England, but the trifle can be made more interesting if a little fruit such as canned or fresh sliced peaches or pears are added to the sponges. Vanilla essence (extract) can be used instead of the vanilla pod.
● The sherry can be mixed with syrup from canned fruit

or with white wine; brandy can be used instead of sherry.
● In Scotland, the trifle is flavoured with whisky and white wine.
● Instead of cream topping, cover with the ingredients given for a Syllabub on page 140. Decorate with crystallized (candied) rose and violet petals and blanched flaked almonds.

FLOATING ISLANDS

Illustrated in colour on page 214
No Cooking   Serves 4–6   ✳✳✳

The name of Floating Islands is a reminder of the similarity in name between some French and Scottish dishes. The French dessert of this name consists of balls of meringue floating on a vanilla flavoured custard, the Scottish version is really rather more colourful and delicious.

Quince is a fruit that is seen less frequently, but was used a great deal in the past. One quince would be peeled, cut up and mixed with apples in a pie. It also produces the most delicious jellies or preserves. If quince jelly is unobtainable, use apple or redcurrant jelly.

	Metric/Imperial	American
egg whites	3	3
quince jelly	4 tbsp	5 tbsp
double (heavy) cream	300 ml/½ pint	1¼ cups
single (light) cream	150 ml/¼ pint	⅔ cup
white wine	2 tbsp	3 tbsp
very finely grated lemon rind	½-1 teasp	½-1 teasp
caster sugar	50 g/2 oz	¼ cup

Whisk the egg whites in a good sized bowl until they are very stiff indeed. Add the quince jelly – a smoother looking mixture is obtained if the jelly is first melted then allowed to cool, but not become set again. If added as a stiff jelly, there is a slightly 'mottled' effect. The mixture becomes rather like a marshmallow.

Beat the double (heavy) cream in a separate bowl or basin until it just begins to hold its shape, then gradually beat in the single (light) cream, then the wine, lemon rind and sugar. The cream should not be too solid; that is why it is better to use a mixture of double and single cream. Put the cream mixture into a very wide shallow glass dish or into individual sundae glasses. Pile the jelly meringue mixture on top. Chill well but serve fairly soon after making, although it is surprising how well the meringue mixture stays stiff.

VARIATION
There are 3 egg yolks leftover and, although it is not the traditional recipe, one could make an egg custard with the yolks and 600 ml/1 pint (2½ cups) milk and use as the base of the dessert instead of the cream mixture. The custard should be flavoured with wine and lemon, then sweetened.

QUEEN OF PUDDINGS

Cooking Time: 1¼-1½ hours   Serves 4   ✳✳

Many of the old British puddings used sponge cake or fine breadcrumbs and this meringue topped pudding is typical of a light family dessert. There are any number of variations on this basic theme, i.e. crumbs set in a flavoured custard, for in Staffordshire a similar pudding is made, but more butter is used and dried fruit added. Over the years, fresh lemon peel has been added to give flavour to the crumb mixture and the chopped mixed peel omitted. This recipe is one of the oldest I have found and certainly one of the most delicious.

	Metric/Imperial	American
raspberry jam	4 tbsp	5 tbsp
soft fine breadcrumbs	100 g/4 oz	2 cups
milk	600 ml/1 pint	2½ cups
eggs	3	3
caster sugar	100 g/4 oz	½ cup
grated lemon rind	1 teasp	1 teasp
crystallized (candied) lemon peel, chopped, optional	50 g/2 oz	¼ cup
To decorate: glacé (candied) cherries, halved	3–4	3–4
angelica, cut into leaves	small portion	small portion

Spread half the jam at the bottom of a 1.2 litre/2 pint (5 cup) pie dish. Put the breadcrumbs into a basin (bowl). Heat the milk. Separate the eggs. Beat the yolks with 25 g/1 oz (2 tbsp) of the sugar. Add the hot milk. Strain or pour over the breadcrumbs, add the lemon rind and crystallized (candied) peel. Allow to stand for 10 to 15 minutes, then carefully pour into the pie dish over the jam.

Bake in the centre of a slow to very moderate oven, 150 to 160°C/300 to 325°F Gas Mark 2 to 3, for 45 minutes to 1 hour or until just firm to the touch; do not overcook, otherwise the custard mixture could curdle. Spread the rest of the jam on top of the pudding. Whisk the egg whites until very stiff. Beat in half the sugar then fold in the remainder. Spoon over the pudding, decorate with the cherries and angelica. Return to the oven and bake for 25 to 30 minutes until the meringue is lightly browned.

Serve hot.

VARIATION
Use lemon curd instead of jam.

ICE CREAM

There is a belief that ice cream is a modern confection; certainly the popularity of ice cream has increased greatly during the last thirty or forty years, and modern freezers have made it easy to produce excellent ice cream and other frozen desserts at home.

Ices, of various kinds, have been known for centuries. It is reputed that in the Second Century B.C., Alexander the Great was given an iced dessert made by mixing crushed fruit, honey and snow. It was Marco Polo who brought the true ice cream recipe to Europe.

Ice cream has been produced in England since the time of the ill-fated Charles I in the 17th Century, but was enjoyed only by the wealthy. The gargantuan Victorian banquets frequently included ice cream and a sorbet which would be offered half way through the meal to refresh the appetite. Ice creams made with cream and fresh fruits are some of the most delectable of desserts. Sorbets and water ices, which can be served during the meal or as a dessert, are wonderfully refreshing.

RICH VANILLA ICE CREAM

No Cooking   Serves 6–8   ***

	Metric/Imperial	American
double (heavy) cream	300 ml/½ pint	1¼ cups
single (light) cream	300 ml/½ pint	1¼ cups
icing (confectioner's) sugar, sifted	75 g/3 oz	⅔ cup
vanilla essence (extract)	to taste	to taste

Whip the double (heavy) cream until it holds its shape, then gradually whisk in the single (light) cream. Fold in the sugar and vanilla essence (extract). Freeze until just firm. This ice cream needs to be brought out of the freezer 20 minutes before the meal and put into the refrigerator. It is an excellent basis for fruit ice cream.

VARIATIONS
Fluffy Vanilla Ice Cream: Whip the double cream with the vanilla essence until it holds its shape, then gradually whisk in 150 ml/¼ pint (⅔ cup) single cream. Whisk 3 egg whites until stiff, gradually whisk in 50 g/2 oz (scant ½ cup) sifted icing sugar. Fold into the cream and freeze.
● *Golden Vanilla Ice Cream:* Beat 3 eggs with the sugar and vanilla essence until thick and creamy. Whip the double cream until it holds its shape, then gradually whisk in 150 ml/¼ pint (⅔ cup) single cream. Fold in the fluffy egg mixture and freeze.

OLD FASHIONED CUSTARD ICE

Cooking Time: 15 minutes   Serves 6   **

This gives a lovely golden coloured ice cream. It is particularly good if you possess an electric ice cream maker that aerates the mixture, as happened when the old fashioned freezing buckets were used.

	Metric/Imperial	American
egg yolks	2	2
single (light) cream	300 ml/½ pint	1¼ cups
caster sugar	50 g/2 oz	¼ cup
vanilla pod (bean)	1	1
double (heavy) cream	300 ml/½ pint	1¼ cups

Blend the egg yolks, single (light) cream and sugar in a large heatproof bowl, add the vanilla pod (bean). Stand the bowl over a pan of hot, but not boiling, water and stir until the mixture coats the back of a wooden spoon. Allow to cool, cover the bowl so a skin does not form. Remove the vanilla pod.

Whip the double (heavy) cream and fold into the cold custard. Freeze the mixture.

VARIATIONS
Use vanilla essence (extract) instead of a vanilla pod.
● Use milk instead of single cream.

Flavourings for Ice Creams

The following flavourings can be added to any of the ice cream recipes opposite.

Blend approximately 100 to 175 g/4 to 6 oz (4 to 6 squares) melted and cooled chocolate with the other ingredients, or add 1½ to 2 tablespoons (2 to 3 tbsp) sweetened coffee essence (coffee extract), or blend in approximately 225 ml/8 fl oz (1 cup) fruit purée.

Be adventurous in your choice of fruit, the photograph on this page shows melon flavoured ice cream served in a hollowed out melon, decorated with glacé (candied) cherries.

water, cover the pan and simmer for 10 minutes. Strain the liquid, return to the pan. Discard the lemon rind.

Meanwhile, put the remaining cold water into a heatproof bowl, sprinkle the gelatine on top and allow to soften. Blend with the hot lemon liquid in the pan. Stir until the gelatine has dissolved, then add the sugar.

Allow the liquid to cool. Add the lemon juice, taste and add more sugar if desired, although a sorbet must not be too sweet.

Freeze lightly. Whisk the egg whites until stiff, fold into the lemon mixture and freeze until firm.

VARIATIONS
Whatever flavouring is used, ½ to 1 tablespoon lemon juice makes a more refreshing sorbet. Use orange or grapefruit or tangerine rinds and juice.
● Use only 300 ml/½ pint (1¼ cups) water, heat with the sugar until dissolved. Cool, then add the gelatine and 300 ml/½ pint (1¼ cups) smooth fruit purée. Choose refreshing fruits such as apples, raspberries, redcurrants or rhubarb.

Far left: Melon Ice Cream. Left: Caramel and Nut Ice Cream. Below: Raspberry Ice Cream

Caramel and Nut Ice Cream: This is based on the Old Fashioned Custard Ice on page 138. Put 75 g/3 oz (6 tbsp) caster sugar and 3 tablespoons (4 tbsp) water into a strong saucepan. Stir until the sugar has dissolved then allow to boil, without stirring, until a golden brown caramel. Cool in the pan. Add the 300 ml/½ pint (1¼ cups) single (light) cream and stir until the caramel and cream are blended. Make the custard as the recipe with the caramel-flavoured cream and proceed as before, but add 50 g/2 oz (½ cup) coarsely chopped nuts to the mixture before freezing. Decorate with whole nuts.
● *Brown Bread Ice Cream:* Crisp 100 g/4 oz (2 cups) fine brown or wheatmeal or wholemeal breadcrumbs, cool then blend with either of the basic ice creams on page left. A little brandy or rum could be added. Freeze until firm.

LEMON SORBET

Cooking Time: 10 minutes   Serves 4–6   ✷✷

Although most fruits can be used to make a good sorbet (sherbet), one based on lemon juice is the most refreshing.

The reason for the use of gelatine is to prevent the mixture becoming over-hard with ice crystals in freezing. Although home-made sorbets are at their best when served within 24 hours of freezing, you can store the mixture.

	Metric/Imperial	American
water	450 ml/¾ pint	scant 2 cups
large lemons	2	2
gelatine	1 teasp	1 teasp
sugar	50–75 g/2–3 oz	¼-scant ⅓ cup
lemon juice	6 tbsp	½ cup
egg whites	2–3	2–3

Place the water, except 2 tablespoons (3 tbsp), in a saucepan. Pare the rind from the lemons, add to the

LIGHT AND CREAMY

The recipes on this and the next page, together with those from page 136 onwards, disprove any idea that all British desserts are plain and rather solid in texture. These are all based on recipes that have been traditional for several centuries.

Cold creams, like creamy custards, have always been a feature of special occasion dishes.

Although a cold soufflé cannot claim to be of British origin, there are records which show it has been a favourite dessert for many generations. In the past, isinglass was used for setting the ingredients; nowadays, gelatine is chosen instead.

FLUMMERY

Illustrated in colour on page 206
Cooking Time: 5–6 minutes   Serves 6–8   ✳✳✳

A Flummery and a Syllabub, also on this page, typify the light and delicate desserts that have been popular for generations. In a Flummery a small amount of gelatine is used to set the creamy mixture, so making it a little firmer than a Syllabub.

	Metric/Imperial	American
single (light) cream	300 ml/½ pint	1¼ cups
cinnamon stick, about 5 cm/2 inches in length	1	1
grated orange rind or orange flower water	2 teasp	2 teasp
caster sugar	50–75 g/2–3 oz	4–6 tbsp
almonds, blanched and chopped	100 g/4 oz	1 cup
sweet white wine	150 ml/¼ cup	⅔ cup
gelatine	2 *level* teasp	2 *level* teasp
brandy	1 tbsp	1 tbsp
double (heavy) cream	300 ml/½ pint	1¼ cups

Put the single (light) cream into a strong saucepan, add the cinnamon stick and orange rind or orange flower water. Heat slowly until the cream *reaches* boiling point but do not allow it to boil. Remove the cinnamon stick and add half the sugar and half the chopped almonds.

Meanwhile, put half the wine into a heatproof bowl or basin. Sprinkle the gelatine on top. Stand the bowl over a saucepan of boiling water until the gelatine has dissolved. Add gradually to the hot cream, whisking briskly as you do so. Add the remaining wine, the brandy and any extra sugar required; do not over-sweeten this dessert.

Allow the mixture to become quite cold and thicken slightly. Whip the double (heavy) cream until it just holds its shape, then fold into the jellied mixture. Spoon into individual glasses and chill well.

Toast the remaining almonds under the grill (broiler) until golden brown. Cool and sprinkle over the Flummery.

SYLLABUB

No Cooking   Serves 6–7   ✳✳✳

This is one of the oldest traditional desserts, still used today; although perhaps not in the original form. Some very old recipes (or receipts as they used to be called) recommended that the bowl was taken to the cow and freshly drawn milk mixed with wine and sugar; so the old syllabubs were very liquid. The syllabub today is still soft in texture but it can be eaten with a spoon.

	Metric/Imperial	American
double (heavy) cream	450 ml/¾ pint	scant 2 cups
single (light) cream	150 ml/¼ pint	⅔ cup
caster sugar	50 g/2 oz	¼ cup
lemon juice	2 teasp	2 teasp
brandy	2 tbsp	3 tbsp
white wine	150 ml/¼ pint	⅔ cup
To decorate: double (heavy) cream	150 ml/¼ pint	⅔ cup
crystallized flowers petals, optional	few	few

Whip the double (heavy) cream until it nearly holds its shape, then gradually whip in the single (light) cream. The mixture of creams is purely a matter of personal taste, but it does produce a less rich dessert. Gradually whisk in the sugar, lemon juice, brandy and wine. Some recipes pour the wine into the glasses, then put the brandy-flavoured mixture on top. Top with whipped cream and crystallized flower petals. Do not serve too large portions since it is a satisfying dessert. Chill well.

VARIATIONS
The decoration will vary; in Devon and Cornwall they often top this dessert with clotted cream and may add a sprinkling of cinnamon.
● The proportions of lemon juice and brandy may be altered to personal taste. Serve this dessert with ratafias or other small sweet biscuits.
● A syllabub is very delicious as an accompaniment to fresh pineapple. Cut the pineapple into rings, discard the centre core and peel. Put on rather large plates and serve small bowls of syllabub with the fruit.
● Use 600 ml/1 pint (2½ cups) whipping cream instead of the mixture of double and single cream.
● *Raspberry Syllabub:* Omit the brandy and reduce the wine to 4 tablespoons (5 tbsp). Use approximately 150 ml/¼ pint (⅔ cup) sieved uncooked raspberry purée. Other fruits could be used but always include the lemon juice.
● *Fruit Foule:* This could be termed a simple adaptation of a syllabub, for the texture should be soft and light. Nowadays, it is generally called a 'Fool' not 'Foule'. The richer recipe is made by blending equal amounts of a very thick sweetened fruit purée and whipped cream. This recipe can, however, be varied by using a thick sweetened custard instead of cream, or half custard and half whipped cream. Chill the dessert well before serving.

LEMON AND HONEY FANTASY

No Cooking   Serves 4   ❈

	Metric/Imperial	American
whipping or double (heavy) cream	450 ml/¾ pint	scant 2 cups
egg yolks	4	4
grated lemon rind	1 teasp	1 teasp
thin honey, warmed	2 tbsp	3 tbsp
milk	150 ml/¼ pint	⅔ cup
lemon juice	4 tbsp	5 tbsp
To decorate: grated lemon rind	2 teasp	2 teasp

Whip 150 ml/¼ pint (⅔ cup) of the cream until it just holds its shape. Cover and chill. Beat the egg yolks in a heatproof basin (bowl) until thick and light. Add the lemon rind and honey, beat again then pour on the remaining cream and milk. Stand the basin over hot, but not boiling, water and whisk or stir until the mixture forms a thick coating custard. Allow to cool; stir from time to time to prevent a skin forming.

Divide the lemon juice between 4 glasses, add the creamy honey custard. Top with the chilled whipped cream and extra grated lemon rind.

SWEET FANTASY

No Cooking   Serves 6–8   ❈❈

This name, or rather similar ones, occurs quite often in old recipes for creamy desserts. The interesting and unusual feature of this light gâteau is that hard-boiled (hard-cooked) egg yolks are used as a sweet decoration. The leftover egg whites can be chopped and added to sauces, sandwich fillings or salads.

	Metric/Imperial	American
light sponge, as page 164 made with	3 eggs etc	3 eggs etc
For the filling and topping: double (heavy) cream	300 ml/½ pint	1¼ cups
sweet white wine	150 ml/¼ pint	⅔ cup
raspberry jam	2–3 tbsp	3–4 tbsp
For the decoration: butter	25 g/1 oz	2 tbsp
icing (confectioner's) sugar	75 g/3 oz	⅔ cup
sweet white wine	½ tbsp	½ tbsp
eggs, hard-boiled (hard-cooked)	3	3

Allow the sponge halves to become quite cold. Whip the cream for the filling and topping. Put the bottom layer of sponge on to a serving dish, moisten with half the wine. Spread with the jam and half the whipped cream. Top with the second layer of sponge; moisten this with the remaining wine and top with whipped cream.

Beat the butter and sugar until soft and light. Gradually beat in the ½ tablespoon wine, then add the egg yolks. Do not over handle at this stage – the mixture should be crumbly. Rub the egg yolk mixture through a coarse meshed sieve over the top of the gâteau, making tiny golden 'balls'. Chill well before serving.

CHOCOLATE SOUFFLÉ

Cooking Time: few minutes   Serves 4   ❈❈❈

Soufflés were extremely popular in both the late Victorian and Edwardian eras. Good chocolate was becoming available and this was used to give a smooth texture as well as a good taste to the mixture.

The jellied soufflé should be well above the top of the dish, so that it looks rather like a hot soufflé that has risen well. Cold soufflés can be frozen, but tend to lose their light delicate texture. Use within a month.

The soufflé could be flavoured with a little Tia Maria (coffee liqueur) or Crème de Cacao (chocolate liqueur) in place of some of the water.

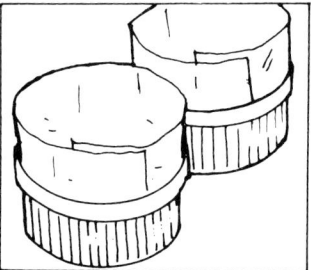

Prepare an 18 cm/7 inch soufflé dish by tying a buttered collar of paper around the dish to stand well above the top rim.

Break 100 g/4 oz plain chocolate (4 squares cooking chocolate) into pieces, melt in a basin (bowl) over hot water or in a microwave cooker.

Put 4 tablespoons (5 tbsp) cold water in a basin, sprinkle 15 g/½ oz (2 envelopes) gelatine on top, dissolve over hot water. Separate 4 large eggs. Beat the yolks with 50 g/2 oz (¼ cup) caster sugar and ¼ teaspoon vanilla essence (extract) until thick and creamy over a pan of hot water. Add the melted chocolate and dissolved gelatine to the egg yolk mixture.

Allow to cool and set to the consistency of a thick syrup. Whip 300 ml/½ pint (1¼ cups) double (heavy) cream in one bowl and 3 egg whites in a second bowl. Blend 25 g/1 oz (2 tbsp) caster sugar with the egg whites. Fold the cream, then the egg whites into the chocolate mixture.

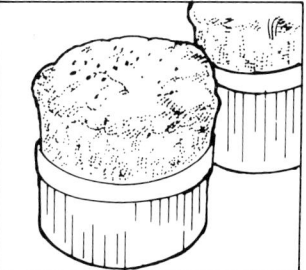

Spoon into the soufflé dish. Allow to set. Carefully remove the paper collar with the help of a palette knife. Decorate with more whipped cream and grated chocolate and/or hazelnuts.

Good Baking

There is a wealth of traditional recipes for interesting breads, scones, biscuits (cookies), cakes of all kinds, small tarts and other pastries in Britain. Many areas have their own local recipes for tea cakes or other specialities. The following pages give a selection of some of the older favourites together with recipes that have established a modern tradition of interesting ideas.

MAKING BREADS OF ALL KINDS

To make bread is one of the most satisfying of all cookery techniques. The sight of the dough rising dramatically is most encouraging and the smell of the freshly baked bread very tempting and appetizing.

There are certain points that ensure success:

The Ingredients

The choice of flour: Strong (hard wheat) flour gives a better rise and texture to plain loaves but plain (all-purpose) flour is recommended for richer mixtures.
The choice of yeast: Fresh baker's yeast (compressed yeast) is advisable. Once, only brewer's yeast was available to cooks. You can, of course, choose dried yeast instead. In this case, use only half the amount, i.e. for 25 g/1 oz fresh yeast (compressed yeast cake) use only 15 g/½ oz (1 tbsp) dried yeast.

When using fresh yeast simply cream this, then add the warm liquid. When using dried yeast, dissolve 1 teaspoon sugar, or as given in the recipe, in the warm liquid then add the dried yeast; leave until the mixture forms bubbles on the surface of the liquid, mix well and continue as when using fresh yeast.

Heating the Liquid

Do not overheat the water or other liquid. It should be blood heat, i.e. between 37 to 43°C/98 to 108°F.

Handling the Dough

Kneading: An important feature in yeast cookery, this means stretching the dough by pushing and folding the dough with the base of the hand (called the heel). This stage distributes the yeast evenly and helps to incorporate air into the mixture. Do not over knead. To test a bread or similar mixture, press firmly with a floured finger; if the impression comes out the dough is sufficiently kneaded. There are, however, softer doughs, like Barm Brack, which require special handling, pages 144 and 145.
Proving: Used to describe the way in which a yeast dough rises. The timing in the recipes assumes this is done at room temperature, but the process can be hastened or lengthened to suit your requirements, see White Bread.
Knocking back: Kneading the dough after it has risen.

Baking

Most yeast doughs are baked quickly or in a hot oven at the beginning of the cooking period. This destroys the action of the yeast. It may be necessary to reduce the temperature to complete the cooking; this information is given in the various recipes.

WHITE BREAD

Cooking Time: 45 minutes   Makes 1 loaf ❋❋

If you have never cooked with yeast before, it is a good idea to work with a small amount of flour and make one loaf. When you have become confident that making bread really is a simple operation, it is worthwhile making larger quantities and freezing the surplus, or using the bread dough as a basic recipe and adding other ingredients to this, as the suggestions on page 145.

	Metric/Imperial	American
fresh (compressed) yeast	15 g/½ oz	½ cake
water	300 ml/½ pint	1¼ cups
strong (hard wheat) flour	450 g/1 lb	4 cups
salt	1 teasp	1 teasp
lard or butter or margarine, optional	25 g/1 oz	2 tbsp

Cream the yeast. Warm the water, see the information on this page. Blend with the yeast. Sift the flour and salt into a large bowl. Rub in the fat, if using this. This small amount does improve the texture of the bread. Pour the yeast liquid into the centre of the flour mixture, blend well with a knife and then with your hands. The dough should be soft but sufficiently firm to leave the mixing bowl clean.

Turn on to a lightly floured surface, knead until smooth. Either return the dough to the bowl and cover with a cloth or lightly oiled sheet of polythene (plastic wrap) or put inside a very large and lightly oiled polythene (plastic) bag. Tie the bag loosely to allow room for expansion.

Allow the dough to prove until just double the original bulk. At room temperature, this will take approximately 1½ to 2 hours.

For quicker proving, put the dough into a warm, but not over hot, airing cupboard, or near a gentle heat. If more convenient, allow 12 hours in a really cold room or up to 24 hours in the storage (not freezing) compartment of the refrigerator. If using the refrigerator, allow the dough to return to room temperature for about 20 minutes.

Knock back the dough by kneading it until smooth again, then shape as desired.

Above: Tin Loaf, Twist and Rolls – see page 144. Below: Cottage Loaf

For a tin loaf: Grease and warm a 900 g/2 lb loaf tin. Press the dough into an oblong shape which should be the length of the tin, but 3 times the width. Fold the dough so the width fits the tin. Place in the tin with the join underneath.

For a plait: Divide the dough into 3 equal sized portions, make each into a long strip of matching length and thickness. Join the 3 ends together by moistening them slightly and then plait the dough. Place on to a lightly greased and warmed baking tray.

For a twist: Divide the dough into 2 equal sized portions then continue as a plait, but twist the strips instead of plaiting them. Place on to a lightly greased and warmed baking tray.

For a cottage loaf: Divide the dough into 2 portions, one consisting of two-thirds of the dough, the second remaining third of the dough. Form the large portion into a round and the small portion into a second round. Place the small round on top of the large one, press firmly in the centre with the handle of a wooden spoon to join the 2 balls. Place on to a lightly greased and warmed baking tray.

Cover the dough lightly with oiled cling film (plastic wrap). Allow to prove once again until nearly double in size. Remove the covering. Bake the loaf in the centre of a hot oven, 220°C/425°F Gas Mark 7, for approximately 45 minutes.

To test if cooked, knock on the bottom of the loaf, it should sound hollow.

The plaits and twists are more shallow than a tin or cottage loaf and could be cooked in 35 to 40 minutes.

VARIATIONS
Glaze the bread with beaten egg before baking, see page 144.
● Dissolve 1 teaspoon sugar or honey in the warm water, add 7 g/¼ oz (½ tbsp) dried yeast and allow to stand until frothy. Stir and blend, then continue as fresh yeast.
● *Speedy Proving:* Add a 25 mg ascorbic acid (vitamin C) tablet in the warm water. This enables the first proving to be reduced to about 10 minutes at room temperature. You need to increase the second proving of the loaf by about 10 minutes.
● *Brown Bread:* Use half wholemeal or wholewheat strong (hard wheat) flour and half white strong (hard wheat) flour. You will need a little more liquid.
● *Wholemeal Bread:* Use all strong (hard wheat) wholemeal flour. You will need about 390 ml/13 fl oz (1¾ cups) water. The dough will be very soft, so mix well with a wooden spoon or an electric dough hook on low speed until the dough feels springy and leaves the bowl clean. Put into the prepared tin, allow to prove for 25 minutes. Bake in a moderately hot oven, 200°C/400°F Gas Mark 6, for 45 minutes. This makes a beautifully moist loaf.

ABERDEEN SOFTIES

Cooking Time: 12–15 minutes   Makes 12   ✷✷

	Metric/Imperial	American
bread dough, as this page made with	450 g/1 lb flour etc	4 cups flour etc
butter, melted	75 g/3 oz	6 tbsp
caster sugar	25 g/1 oz	2 tbsp

Make the bread dough as the recipe on page 142. Allow the dough to prove for the first time, then knock back. Put into a large bowl, work in the butter and sugar. Knead well, divide into 12 portions, form into neat round bun shapes. Put on to a lightly greased baking tray. Allow to prove for 20 to 25 minutes or until nearly double the original size.

Bake towards the top of a hot oven, 220°C/425°F Gas Mark 7, for 12 to 15 minutes. Serve with butter and cheese.

TOPPINGS FOR BREAD

When the loaf is shaped ready for its final proving, brush the surface lightly with beaten egg, or the yolk of 1 egg mixed with 1 tablespoon milk or water. Another way to give a shine to the loaf, together with increased crispness, is to brush the loaf with a little oil before baking.

To give a soft floury look to bread or rolls, brush the loaf with a little milk and sprinkle with flour just before baking.

Rolled oats, wheat flakes, crushed wheat or caraway or poppy or sesame seeds can be sprinkled over the loaf before the final proving. Press the seeds gently into the dough.

HANDLING SOFT DOUGHS

Some yeast mixtures, such as the Wholemeal Bread on page 143, are too soft to knead. The mixture is then beaten to distribute the yeast and aerate the dough. Other mixtures are ultra soft, as the Crumpets on page 146, and are made into a very soft batter which should be well beaten. In the full recipe for Barm Brack on page 145 opposite, the basic recipe is for a rich cake-type bread which will appear too soft to handle. You can either beat the mixture or give it a modified kneading. Sprinkle about 15 g/½ oz (1 tbsp) flour on to a board. Add the dough; sprinkle another 15 g/½ oz (1 tbsp) flour over the dough and just try to work the soft mixture. The extra flour should stop your hands becoming too sticky. Do not try to knead as for bread, just be satisfied with mixing the ingredients well to distribute the yeast. If too much extra flour is added, the loaf still tastes good but loses its cake-like texture. The more economical recipe and Bara-brith, given under Variations, are kneaded in the usual way.

CORNISH SPLITS

Cooking Time: 12–15 minutes   Makes 12–16   ✽✽

In the past these teacakes, served with clotted cream and jam, were made with a yeast dough, rather like a rich bread. Nowadays light plain scones, such as those on page 147, are often served instead.

Devonshire Splits or Chudleighs are similar to Cornish Splits, except they are slightly smaller in size.

	Metric/Imperial	American
fresh (compressed) yeast	20 g/¾ oz	¾ cake
milk	300 ml/½ pint	1¼ cups
strong (hard wheat) flour	450 g/1 lb	4 cups
salt	1 teasp	1 teasp
butter	50 g/2 oz	¼ cup
caster sugar	50 g/2 oz	¼ cup

Cream the yeast. Warm the milk, blend with the yeast. Sift the flour and salt, rub in the butter. Add the sugar and the yeast liquid. Knead well then allow the dough to prove, as given under White Bread, until doubled in size. Knock back the dough and either divide into 12 to 16 rounds, or roll out lightly and cut into rounds. Prove again and bake as the recipe for rolls on this page. Serve cold, but freshly baked, with clotted or whipped cream and jam.

The photograph on page 143 shows small bread rolls; these are made from exactly the same recipe as the loaf of bread.

MAKING ROLLS
Cooking Time: 12–15 minutes   Makes 12–16   ✽✽

To make the rolls in the photograph on page 143, allow the dough to prove, then knock back. Divide nearly all the dough into 12 to 16 portions. Form into rounds.

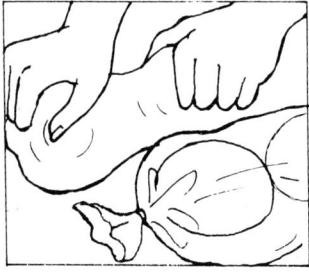

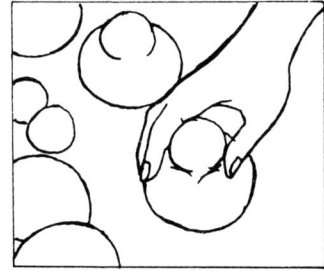

Take the remaining dough and make 12 to 16 tiny balls. Place these balls on top of the larger rounds and push down firmly so they are well joined to the bottom rounds.

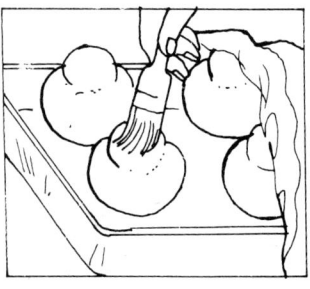

Place on to a lightly greased and warmed baking tray. Brush with beaten egg. Cover lightly with oiled cling film (plastic wrap).

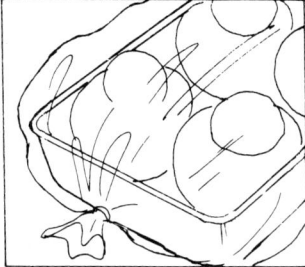

Allow to prove at room temperature for about 20 minutes until nearly double the original size.

Bake just above the centre of a very hot oven, 230°C/450°F Gas Mark 8, for 12 to 15 minutes.

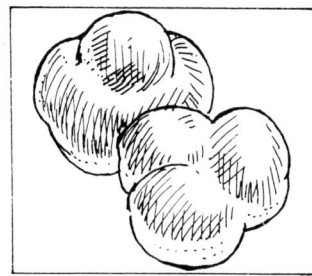

Rolls can be made into clover shapes by joining 3 small balls together, plaits and twists, as described for loaves under White Bread on page 143, and many other shapes.

BARM BRACK

Illustrated in colour on page 210

Cooking Time: 1¼ hours   Makes 1 loaf   ❋❋

This is the name of the famous Irish speckled bread; in the old days the spelling appears to have been Barm breac. This bread is generally served at Hallowe'en. Often a wedding ring, wrapped in paper, was baked in the cake; whoever had the slice of bread containing the ring would be engaged by the end of the year. Barm is the froth that forms on top of fermenting malt liquors and was used to leaven the dough, but today yeast is more likely to be used in this and similar breads. Recipes vary a great deal for Barm Brack (nowadays this is often given as Barmbrack). The proportions below provide a loaf that can be eaten as a cake when fresh or, after a day or two, may be sliced and spread with butter, as a bread.

	Metric/Imperial	American
fresh (compressed) yeast	20 g/¾ oz	¾ cake
milk	225 ml/8 fl oz	1 cup
plain (all-purpose) flour	450 g/1 lb	1 lb
grated or ground nutmeg	1 teasp	1 teasp
caster sugar	100 g/4 oz	½ cup
caraway seeds	2 teasp	2 teasp
butter, melted	175 g/6 oz	¾ cup
currants	225 g/8 oz	1¼ cups
raisins	225 g/8 oz	1¼ cups
crystallized (candied) peel, chopped	100 g/4 oz	¾ cup
eggs	3	3

Cream the yeast. Warm the milk until just tepid, then pour over the yeast. Add a sprinkling of flour and leave in a warm place for 15 minutes until the surface is covered with bubbles.

Meanwhile, sift the flour with the nutmeg, add the sugar, caraway seeds, melted butter, dried fruit and chopped peel. Blend in the yeast mixture with the eggs, and beat well with a wooden spoon. Turn out of the bowl on to a floured board and knead lightly, as explained on page 144. Flours vary in the amount of liquid they absorb and it may be necessary to work in a small quantity of flour in order to knead the mixture; on the other hand it could be slightly dry, in which case add a little extra warm milk before removing from the bowl. Return the kneaded dough to the bowl and cover with a cloth. Leave to 'prove' for approximately 1½ hours or until double the original size.

Knead once again, then press into a warmed and greased 23 cm/9 inch cake tin (spring form pan). Cover and 'prove' for the final time until the dough is well risen in the tin; this takes approximately 50 minutes.

Bake in the centre of a moderately hot oven, 190 to 200°C/375 to 400°F Gas Mark 5 to 6, for 30 minutes, then reduce the heat to very moderate, 160°C/325°F Gas Mark 3, for a further 45 minutes until firm to the touch. Turn out of the tin.

VARIATIONS

Use only 50 g/2 oz (¼ cup) butter and a little less fruit to make an economical loaf. In this case, strong (hard wheat) flour is better. Shorten the cooking time slightly.
● Use the same amount of barm as fresh yeast.
● If using dried yeast, see page 142.
● A richer loaf is made with 225 to 300 g/8 to 10 oz (1 to 1¼ cups) butter. This takes a little longer to cook at the lower temperature.
● *Bara-brith:* This Welsh 'speckled bread' is very like the Irish Barm Brack, although there are differences between the recipes. Bara-brith is more economical and therefore is baked differently; it has no caraway seeds. To make a large loaf, use the following ingredients:

Cream 20 g/¾ oz (¾ cake compressed) yeast. Warm 225 ml/8 fl oz (1 cup) milk or milk and water and blend with the yeast. Sift 350 g/12 oz strong flour (3 cups hard wheat flour) with ½ teaspoon salt and ½ teaspoon mixed spice. Rub in 25 g/1 oz (2 tbsp) lard, add 50 g/2 oz (¼ cup) caster sugar, 225 g/8 oz (1¼ cups) currants, 175 g/6 oz sultanas (1 cup golden raisins), 25 g/1 oz (1½ tbsp) chopped crystallized (candied) peel and the yeast liquid. Knead well and allow the dough to 'prove' until double in size. Knead again and form into an oblong shape to fit into a 1.15 to 1.35 kg/2½ to 3 lb well greased and floured loaf tin. Prove for approximately 35 minutes or until the yeast dough has risen well in the tin.

Bake in the centre of a moderately hot oven, 190 to 200°C/375 to 400°F Gas Mark 5 to 6, for approximately 45 to 50 minutes until firm.
Illustrated in colour on page 218

SIMPLE FRUIT BREADS

Use the basic bread recipe on pages 142 and 143 to make easy fruit breads. Simply blend about 100 g/4 oz (⅔ cup) dried fruit with the basic dough or follow the suggestions below.
Cherry Fruit Bread: Chop 50 g/2 oz glacé (¼ cup candied) cherries. Add to the basic bread dough with 50 g/2 oz (⅓ cup) seedless raisins, 50 g/2 oz (⅓ cup) chopped crystallized (candied) peel and 50 g/2 oz (½ cup) chopped walnuts (optional). Bake in one 900 g/2 lb loaf tin as the timing on page 143 or in two 450 g/1 lb shallow tins for about 30 minutes only as in the photograph on page 158.

Spiced Fruit Bread: Blend 2 teaspoons black treacle (molasses) with the water used to make the bread dough. Sift 1 to 2 teaspoons mixed spice with the flour. Add about 175 g/6 oz (1 cup) mixed dried fruit. Bake in one 900 g/2 lb loaf tin as the timing on page 143. This bread is shown on page 158.

TEACAKES AND SCONES

A teacake, such as a muffin or Sally Lunn or a light scone, has been a feature of British teas for a long time. Once all these would have been freshly made, but nowadays they can be prepared in larger quantities and frozen. It is a matter of minutes only to bring them from the freezer and reheat in the oven or microwave cooker, or allow them to defrost at room temperature. All the recipes on this and the next page can be frozen for up to 3 months.

ENGLISH MUFFINS

Cooking Time: see method   Makes 10   **

	Metric/Imperial	American
strong (hard wheat) flour or plain (all-purpose) flour or equal quantities of strong and plain flour	450 g/1 lb	4 cups
salt	1 teasp	1 teasp
caster sugar	1 teasp	1 teasp
fresh (compressed) yeast	generous 15 g/ ½ oz	½ cake
milk	300 ml/½ pint	1¼ cups
water	2 tbsp	3 tbsp
olive oil or melted butter	1½ tbsp	2 tbsp
rice flour, see method		

Sift the flour or flours with the salt, add the sugar. Cream the yeast. Warm the milk and water to blood heat, blend with the yeast, sprinkle with a little of the flour and stand for about 10 minutes until the surface is covered with bubbles. Blend in the olive oil or melted butter. Add to the flour and mix well. Beat for several minutes with a wooden spoon as the dough is too soft to knead at this stage. Cover the bowl with oiled polythene (plastic wrap) or a cloth and leave in a warm place for about 1¼ hours or until the dough rises to twice the original size. Turn out on to a lightly floured board, then knock back until a smooth soft dough. Divide into about 10 portions and shape these into rounds with a little rice flour on the board and your hands.

If baking the muffins: Press the rounds into lightly greased muffin rings placed on a lightly greased baking tray. Allow the dough to rise for about 25 minutes or until almost double the original thickness. Bake in the centre of a moderately hot oven, 190 to 200°C/375 to 400°F Gas Mark 5 to 6, for approximately 20 minutes.

If cooking the muffins on a griddle: Lightly grease and preheat the griddle over a low heat. To test the temperature of the griddle, shake on a little flour; it should turn golden in 1½ minutes. Place the rounds of dough (without the muffin rings) on to the griddle. Cook for approximately 8 minutes or until golden on the under side, then turn and cook for the same time on the second side.

To serve the muffins, toast on either side, then split through the centre and spread with butter.

VARIATIONS

Use 7 g/¼ oz (½ tbsp) dried yeast. Add 2 teaspoons sugar to the warm milk and water, add the yeast. Allow to stand until the mixture bubbles, mix well then continue as above.

● *Crumpets:* Follow the recipe above but use 600 ml/1 pint (2½ cups) milk to make a batter consistency. Blend well, allow to prove as above, then beat again to knock back the soft dough: it is too soft to knead. Allow to prove in the bowl for the second time. Grease and preheat the griddle. To test the temperature of the griddle, shake on a little flour; it should turn golden in 1 minute. Place the greased rings (these should be about 10 cm/4 inches in diameter) on the griddle, warm slightly. Spoon the batter into the rings. Cook for 3 to 4 minutes, then turn the rings containing the batter and cook for the same time on the second side.

Toast the crumpets on either side and serve hot spread with a generous amount of butter.

Note: The quantities above make a large number of crumpets. These become stale quickly so either reduce the proportions or freeze the cooked crumpets. Use within 3 months. Illustrated in colour on page 166.

● *Oatmeal Muffins:* Follow the basic recipe for English Muffins but substitute fine oatmeal for the flour or use half oatmeal and half strong (hard wheat) flour. It is better to bake oatmeal muffins, rather than cook them on the griddle.

SINGING HINNIES

Cooking Time: 8–10 minutes Makes 2 large or 8–10 smaller hinnies **

These teacakes have been given this name, often called a Singin' Hinnie, because the mixture makes a singing noise as it cooks on the griddle. The amount of mixture given above can be cooked as two large hinnies or a number of smaller ones.

	Metric/Imperial	American
plain (all-purpose) flour	450 g/1 lb	4 cups
salt	¼ teasp	¼ teasp
bicarbonate of soda (baking soda)	scant ¾ teasp	scant ¾ teasp
cream of tartar	scant 1½ teasp	scant 1½ teasp
lard	100 g/4 oz	½ cup
currants	175 g/6 oz	1 cup
milk	300 ml/½ pint	1¼ cups

Sift the flour with the salt, bicarbonate of soda (baking soda) and cream of tartar. Rub in the lard, then add the currants and blend with the milk.

Turn the dough on to a well floured board, pat or roll out gently until the dough is between 8 mm to 1.5 cm/ ⅓ to ½ inch in thickness. Cut into rounds, or divide the dough in half and form into 2 large rounds. Preheat and lightly grease the griddle. To test the temperature of the griddle, shake on a little flour; it should turn golden in 1 minute. Put the hinnies on to the griddle, cook steadily for approximately 4 to 5 minutes or until the bottom is golden brown. Turn and cook for the same time on the second side.

Serve when freshly baked; split and spread with butter.

SCONES

Illustrated in colour opposite and on page 163
Cooking Time: 10 minutes Makes 12 *

Scones have been traditional in Britain, especially in Scotland, for a very long time. They were frequently made fresh for breakfast as well as for tea. Although this habit no longer exists in most homes, you may well be offered scones with a mid-morning cup of coffee.

	Metric/Imperial	American
self-raising flour*	225 g/8 oz	2 cups
salt	pinch	pinch
butter or margarine or lard	50 g/2 oz	¼ cup
milk to mix	about 150 ml/ ¼ pint	about ⅔ cup

*or use plain (all-purpose) flour with ½ level teaspoon bicarbonate of soda (baking soda) and 1 level teaspoon cream of tartar. (If using sour milk, you need only ½ level teaspoon cream of tartar.) Or use plain flour with 2½ teaspoons baking powder.

Sift together the dry ingredients, rub in the butter or margarine or lard. Add sufficient milk to make a soft

Above left: English Muffins. Below left: Scones and Sally Lunn – recipe page 149. Above: Singing Hinnies

rolling consistency. This is one of the important secrets of a good scone – the mixture must be softer than a pastry dough.

Cut into rounds or triangles. Put on to an ungreased baking tray or sheet. Bake towards the top of a hot oven, 220°C/425°F Gas Mark 7, for about 10 minutes.

VARIATIONS
There are many ways in which the basic scone dough can be varied.
● Add 25 to 50 g/1 to 2 oz (2 to 4 tbsp) sugar for a sweet scone; add about 50 g/2 oz (⅓ cup) dried fruit.
● *Cheese Scones:* Add 50 g/2 oz (½ cup) grated cheese to the basic scone dough, and sift a good shake of pepper and pinch of mustard powder with the flour. Use an egg and milk to bind.
● *Treacle Scones:* The Scots are very fond of treacle scones. Add 2 tablespoons black treacle (3 tbsp molasses) (or to personal taste) to the dry ingredients before binding with the milk.
● *Oatmeal Scones:* Follow the basic recipe, but use 110 g/4 oz (generous ⅔ cup) fine oatmeal and 110 g/4 oz (generous 1 cup) self-raising flour with 1 level teaspoon baking powder, or plain (all-purpose) flour with 2 level teaspoons baking powder. Oatmeal Scones can be made sweet or savoury as the suggestions above. Bake as the recipe above.
● *Potato Scones:* These are popular in the North of England or in Devon and Cornwall. Use 175 g/6 oz (¾ cup) cooked sieved potatoes and 100 g/4 oz (1 cup) self-raising flour or plain (all-purpose) flour with 1 teaspoon baking powder. Add the salt to the flour, rub in the butter or margarine or lard, then mix with the potatoes and milk to bind. The scones can be made sweet or savoury, as the suggestions above. Bake as the recipe above.

MORE SCONES AND BREADS

The following recipes include some of the most delicious scones and special breads. Soda Bread is illustrated on page 210; Little Puddings are on this page and Scotch Pancakes on page 149. Bath Buns are included here because they are very similar to the famous Sally Lunn Teacake.

SODA BREAD

Illustrated in colour on page 211

Cooking Time: 14 or 30 minutes   Makes 1 loaf   *

There are many excellent breads in Ireland, but the basic soda bread is perhaps the most delicious of all. Although the bread can be made without buttermilk (the liquid left after making butter), it is buttermilk that helps produce the exceptionally light texture. If buttermilk is not available, use one of the alternatives given under Variations.

In the past, many British breads and teacakes were cooked on a griddle (in Ireland it would have been placed over a gentle turf fire). Much of the soda bread eaten today is still cooked on a griddle, but use an oven if more convenient.

	Metric/Imperial	American
plain (all-purpose) flour	450 g/1 lb	1 lb
salt, amount depends upon personal taste	½-1 teasp*	½-1 teasp*
bicarbonate of soda (baking soda)	½ teasp*	½ teasp*
cream of tartar	½ teasp*	½ teasp*
buttermilk, approximate amount	300 ml/ ½ pint**	1¼ cups**

* measure level spoons with great care
** different makes of flour vary in the amount of liquid they absorb

Sift all the dry ingredients together. Gradually add sufficient buttermilk to make a soft dough, but one that can be kneaded. Turn on to a lightly floured board and shape into a round, see below for the thickness. Mark into quarters (these are called farls) but do not cut right through the bread round.

To cook on a griddle: The round of dough should be approximately 2 cm/¾ inch in thickness. Heat the griddle; there is no need to grease this. To test the temperature of the griddle, shake on a little flour; this should turn golden in 1½ to 2 minutes. Put the dough round on the griddle. Cook for 6 to 7 minutes, then turn and cook on the second side for approximately the same time.

To bake in the oven: Make the round of dough 2.5 to 3.5 cm/1 to 1½ inches in thickness. Bake just above the centre of a hot oven, 220°C/425°F Gas Mark 7, for 30 minutes; reduce the heat slightly if the bread is becoming too brown, for soda bread should be pale in colour.

To test if cooked, knock the bread on the bottom, it should sound hollow.

VARIATIONS
If buttermilk is not available, use skimmed milk and increase the amount of cream of tartar to 1 teaspoon.
● A mixture of wholemeal and white flour can be used;

the dough should be slightly softer than for all white flour and the baking time may be longer.
● Another traditional method of cooking bread in Ireland is to put it into a saucepan. This must, however, be the kind of pan that does not have a long handle as it has to go into the oven, so a strong casserole could be used or a strong cake tin covered with foil. Grease the sides and bottom well. Form the dough into a shape to fit the pan, put it in and cover with the lid. Bake as in the recipe left, but allow a little longer cooking time. The bread will brown on top but have a soft crust; if a crisper crust is required, remove the lid for the last 5 to 10 minutes.

LITTLE PUDDINGS

Cooking Time: 12–15 minutes   Makes approximately 12   **

These may be said to be the British equivalent of a French brioche. They are really a bread, but are sufficiently light and sweet to be served as a cake or even served hot with jam or fruit as a pudding.

	Metric/Imperial	American
fresh (compressed) yeast	15 g/½ oz	½ cake
water	2 tbsp	3 tbsp
strong (hard wheat) or plain (all-purpose) flour	225 g/8 oz	2 cups
salt	pinch	pinch
caster sugar	50 g/2 oz	¼ cup
double (heavy) cream	5 tbsp	½ cup
large eggs	2	2
finely grated lemon rind	1 teasp	1 teasp

Cream the yeast. Heat the water to blood heat, blend with the yeast. Sift the flour and salt, add the sugar, the yeast liquid, cream, eggs and grated lemon rind. Beat well to give a smooth batter-like consistency. Cover the bowl and leave in a warm place for approximately 1 hour or until the dough is light and double the original size. Beat the mixture well to knock back.

Grease approximately 12 dariole moulds (often called castle pudding tins) with a generous amount of butter. Half fill with soft dough, do not over fill for the mixture rises well. Place the tins on to a baking tray so they are easy to handle in the oven. Put a sheet of oiled cling film (plastic wrap) over the tins and leave for approximately 20 to 30 minutes or until the dough has risen to the top of the tins.

Bake in the centre of a moderately hot oven, 200°C/400°F Gas Mark 6, for 12 to 15 minutes or until well risen and firm. Allow to cool in the tins for 2 to 3 minutes, then turn out on to a wire cooling tray.

VARIATIONS
Add grated orange rind instead of lemon rind.
● Use 1 teaspoon dried yeast and follow the method of using this given on page 142.

BATH BUNS

Cooking Time: 12–15 minutes   Makes 12   ❋❋

	Metric/Imperial	American
fresh (compressed) yeast	scant 20 g/¾ oz	¾ cake
milk, approximate amount	150 ml/¼ pint	⅔ cup
strong (hard wheat) or plain (all purpose) flour	350 g/12 oz	3 cups
salt	pinch	pinch
butter or margarine	100 g/4 oz	½ cup
caster sugar	100 g/4 oz	½ cup
mixed dried fruit	100 g/4 oz	¾ cup
crystallized (candied) peel, chopped	50 g/2 oz	⅓ cup
small eggs	3	3
loaf sugar	8 lumps	8 lumps

Cream the yeast. Heat most of the milk until tepid, add to the yeast, blend well. Add a sprinkling of the flour and leave in a warm place for 10 to 15 minutes until the surface is covered with bubbles.

Meanwhile sift the flour and salt, rub in the butter or margarine, add the sugar, dried fruit, chopped peel and the yeast liquid. Mix lightly then add the eggs and mix well. The mixture should feel very much softer than bread and most bun doughs. If necessary, add any of the remaining milk to obtain this soft texture.

Knead the dough on a floured board until smooth. Return the dough to a large bowl. Cover with a cloth and leave at room temperature for about 1½ hours or until the dough has risen to about double the original size.

Knock back the dough (this means kneading once again), then divide into 12 portions. Form each portion into a round, place on two lightly greased baking trays; allow adequate space for the buns to spread as well as rise. Lightly crush the loaf sugar with a rolling pin to make small lumps; sprinkle over the top of the buns and press into the dough with the back of a spoon. Allow the buns to prove for 20 to 25 minutes or until nearly double in size.

Bake just above the centre of a hot oven, 220°C/425°F Gas Mark 7, for 12 to 15 minutes.

VARIATION Illustrated in colour on page 146
Sally Lunn: This yeast cake is also attributed to the Roman city of Bath. The proportions are similar to the buns above but the fruit and peel should be omitted. A true Sally Lunn yeast cake should be mixed with the eggs and with double (heavy) cream instead of milk.

Form proven dough into a large, fairly flat, round on a lightly greased baking tray. Bake in the centre of a moderately hot to hot oven, 200 to 220°C/400 to 425°F Gas Mark 6 to 7, for nearly 30 minutes. Split and serve hot with butter, or cold with clotted cream.

SCOTCH PANCAKES

Illustrated in colour on page 214
Cooking Time: 4–5 minutes Makes 12–18   ❋

The pancakes, also known as Drop Scones, can be cooked in a heavy frying pan (skillet) if a griddle is not available. The secret of success is to have the griddle or frying pan sufficiently

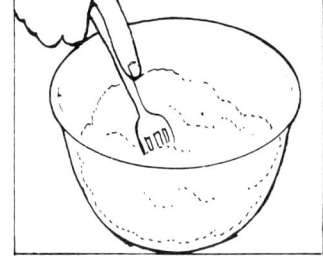

Sift the ingredients plus a pinch of salt into a mixing bowl.

Add 1 egg and gradually beat in 150 ml/¼ pint (⅔ cup) milk. If you like the pancakes sweet in flavour, add 1 tablespoon caster sugar. Add the 25 g/1 oz (2 tbsp) melted butter to the batter, mix.

hot so that the batter mixture sets quickly, and to add 25 g/1 oz (2 tbsp) melted butter to the batter just before cooking. Cover the pancakes with a cloth as soon as they are cooked, so they keep soft.

You can use 100 g/4 oz (1 cup) self-raising flour *or* plain (all-purpose) flour with 1½ teaspoons baking powder or ½ *level* teaspoon bicarbonate of soda (baking soda) and 1 *level* teaspoon cream of tartar.

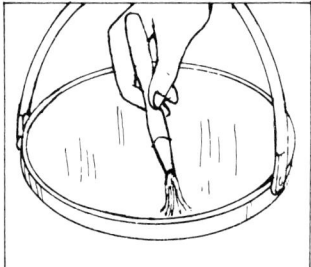

Lightly grease a griddle or heavy frying pan, heat steadily. To test if the right heat, drop on a small spoonful of the batter, this should set and turn golden brown on the bottom in 1 minute.

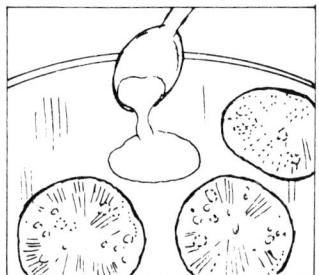

Drop spoonfuls of the batter from the tip of the spoon, making them a good round shape. Cook for 2 minutes or until there are bubbles on the top of the batter.

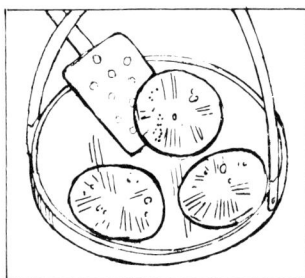

Put a palette knife under each pancake, turn and cook on the second side. To test if cooked, press firmly with the back of a knife, if no batter oozes out from the sides the pancakes are ready.

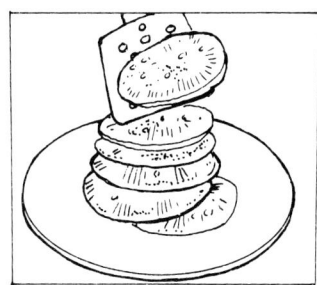

Place a clean teacloth on a wire cooling tray. Place the pancakes on this and cover. Eat when freshly made with butter and/or jam.

INTERESTING BISCUITS

Some of the most interesting biscuits (cookies) are based on traditional recipes. Many of these would be sold at the fairs, which were a feature of country life in the past.
Honey Snaps: Many years ago, honey was the only form of sweetening available to cooks. It is an excellent ingredient in making biscuits like the Brandy Snaps. Substitute thin honey for the golden (light corn) syrup in the recipe on this page below.

These Honey or Brandy Snaps can be filled with whipped cream just before serving.

Illustrated in colour below and on page 206

BRANDY SNAPS

**Cooking Time:
8–12 minutes
Makes 14–16 ❊❊**

These crisp biscuits (cookies) have been made in Britain for many centuries; they date back to the days of 'fairings' (fairs), which were originally established for the sale of horses and other cattle but soon became places of gaiety and amusement as well. These fairs took place throughout Britain, so one could say that brandy snaps are fairly universal. As the name suggests, a small amount of brandy was included in the recipe in the old days – this seems to be forgotten today.

	Metric/Imperial	American
golden (light corn) syrup	50 g/2 oz	3 tbsp
butter	50 g/2 oz	¼ cup
caster sugar	50 g/2 oz	¼ cup
plain (all-purpose) flour	50 g/2 oz	½ cup
ground ginger	½-1 teasp	½-1 teasp
brandy	1 teasp	1 teasp

Put the golden (light corn) syrup, butter and sugar into a saucepan. Heat steadily until the butter has melted; do not boil for any length of time otherwise some of the mixture will evaporate. Sift the flour and ginger together, add to the ingredients in the pan, then stir in the brandy.

Grease 2 or 3 baking trays. Put teaspoons of the mixture on to the trays; these will spread a great deal in cooking, so leave plenty of space between spoonfuls of mixture. In order to roll the brandy snaps, it is advisable to put one baking tray in the oven first then put in another as you take the first one out. If this is not done, all the brandy snaps will be ready to roll at the same time and will harden on the trays. (If this should happen, warm the biscuits again for 1 to 2 minutes only.)

Bake just above the centre of a very moderate oven, 160°C/325°F Gas Mark 3, for 8 to 12 minutes until the edges become firm. Cool for 1 to 2 minutes or until the biscuits can be removed from the baking trays with a palette knife. During this time, grease the handles of 1 or 2 wooden spoons. Lift the first brandy snap from the tray with a broad-bladed knife, then press the biscuit round the handle of the wooden spoon; put the flat side that touches the baking tray round the spoon, so you have the more attractive side uppermost. Hold in position for a few seconds to allow the biscuit to harden slightly and set, then put on to a wire cooling tray. Continue like this until all the biscuits are rolled. Put into an airtight tin immediately the biscuits are quite cold, for exposure to the air makes them soften again.

MACAROONS

Cooking Time: 20 minutes   Makes 12–18 biscuits ❊❊

	Metric/Imperial	American
egg whites	2	2
almond or ratafia essence (extract)	few drops	few drops
ground almonds	150 g/5 oz	1¼ cups
caster sugar	175 g/6 oz	¾ cup
rice flour or cornflour (cornstarch), see method	1 teasp	1 teasp
rice paper		
To decorate: glacé (candied) cherries, see method		
almonds, blanched, see method		

Whisk the egg whites until just frothy. Do not overwhisk. Add the essence (extract), then blend in the ground almonds and sugar. You should be able to handle the mixture; if it is a little stiff add a few drops of water, if too moist add a teaspoon of rice flour or cornflour (cornstarch) or a little more ground almonds.

Place sheets of rice paper on ungreased baking trays. Form the mixture into balls. The ingredients given will make 18 medium sized macaroons or about 12 of average size. Put the biscuits on to the rice paper, allowing room for the balls to flatten. Top with pieces of glacé (candied) cherry or whole or flaked almonds, the size depends upon the size of the macaroons.

Bake in the centre of a moderate oven, 180°C/350°F Gas Mark 4, for 20 minutes or until pale golden and firm. If you like sticky macaroons, place a bowl of water in the oven on a shelf below the biscuits. Cool sufficiently to handle, then cut around the rice paper. Macaroons are better freshly eaten; they do harden with keeping which is quite satisfactory for Ratafias, see below.

Ratafias: Make 48 to 60 miniature balls of the macaroon mixture and bake for 10 minutes only. These can be stored for months.

GINGERBREAD MEN

Cooking Time: 12–15 minutes   Makes 10–12   ❋❋

	Metric/Imperial	American
golden (light corn) syrup	75 g/3 oz	¼ cup
butter or margarine	75 g/3 oz	6 tbsp
caster sugar	75 g/3 oz	6 tbsp
plain (all-purpose) flour	225 g/8 oz	2 cups
ground ginger	1–2 teasp	1–2 teasp
milk	to bind	to bind
To decorate: icing (confectioner's) sugar, sifted	3–4 tbsp	4–5 tbsp
water	few drops	few drops
coloured sweetmeats, cut into small shapes		

Put the golden (light corn) syrup, butter or margarine and sugar into a saucepan. Heat gently until the ingredients have melted. Allow to cool. Sift the flour and ground ginger together. Add to the ingredients in the pan, mix well with a wooden spoon. Add just enough milk to bind to a firm rolling consistency. Knead very well and roll out to about 5 mm/¼ inch in thickness.

Cut out the shapes with a biscuit (cookie) cutter, or cut out and use a cardboard man. Put on to lightly greased baking trays. Bake in the centre of a moderate to moderately hot oven, 180 to 190°C/350 to 375°F Gas Mark 4 to 5, for 12 to 15 minutes until firm to the touch. Do not allow to become too hard as the biscuits harden as they cool.

Make a little glacé icing by blending the icing (confectioner's) sugar with a few drops of water. Use this to make the features on the men and stick the small portions of sweetmeat on to the biscuits.

Above left: Brandy Snaps. Right: Gingerbread Men

VANILLA RINGS

Cooking Time: 15 minutes   Makes 12–14 biscuits   ❋❋

	Metric/Imperial	American
butter	100 g/4 oz	½ cup
caster sugar	100 g/4 oz	½ cup
vanilla essence (extract)	¼ teasp	¼ teasp
egg yolk	1	1
plain (all-purpose) flour	225 g/8 oz	2 cups
To decorate: icing (confectioner's) sugar, sifted *or* Glacé Icing: icing (confectioner's) sugar, sifted	2–3 tbsp 100 g/4 oz	3–4 tbsp 1 cup
water	to mix	to mix
To fill: apricot jam	2 tbsp	3 tbsp
raspberry jam	2 tbsp	3 tbsp

Cream the butter, sugar and vanilla essence (extract) until soft and light. Add the egg yolk and flour. Blend the mixture together with a knife, then with your fingers. Knead lightly and roll out the dough until 5 mm/¼ inch in thickness. Cut into rounds, then stamp out the centres of half the rounds to make rings.

Place the biscuits (cookies) on ungreased baking trays. Bake in the centre of a very moderate to moderate oven, 160 to 180°C/325 to 350°F Gas Mark 3 to 4, for approximately 15 minutes. Allow to cool on the baking trays.

Dust the rings with a generous amount of icing (confectioner's) sugar or coat in glacé icing made by blending the icing sugar and water to a spreading consistency, allow to set. Place the rings on to the biscuit rounds, fill the centres with apricot, raspberry jam or with butter cream and chocolate vermicelli.

VARIATION
Vanilla Biscuits (Cookies): Use the same dough to make fancy shapes. Bake as above.

CRISP AND SHORT

The traditional shortbreads of Scotland are given below, followed by Princess Biscuits and a crisp type of shortcake on page 153. The texture of this shortcake makes a pleasing contrast in texture to the soft strawberries or other fruit served with it. Do not add the fruit until just before serving. The Princess Biscuits on page 153 are a piped shortbread type biscuit (cookie). Do not exceed the amount of sugar in this recipe, for the proportions are particularly important when piping biscuit dough.

The Saffron Cakes have been included under this heading for they should have a pleasantly crisp firm outside, while being soft and cake-like in the centre.

SHORTBREAD

Illustrated in colour on page 214

Cooking Time: 40–50 minutes   Makes 1 round **

Surely there is no biscuit (cookie) with a better flavour than the 'buttery' shortbread of Scotland. A delightful name for shortbread, rarely used today, is 'dreaming bread'; this is because shortbreads, often decorated specially with peel or a sugared almond, once were used for wedding celebrations as the bride's cake. The 'dreaming bread' was broken over the head of the bride and small portions given to her guests, who put it under their pillows and presumably dreamed. Very rarely today does one see fruit filled shortbreads, but these are delicious and suggestions are given, right.

	Metric/Imperial	American
butter, free from moisture, see method	150 g/5 oz	5/8 cup
plain (all-purpose) flour	175 g/6 oz	1½ cups
rice flour or ground rice or cornflour (cornstarch)	50 g/2 oz	½ cup
caster sugar	50–75 g/2–3 oz	4–6 tbsp

Two factors contribute to the success of shortbread, the first is to extract surplus moisture from the butter and the second is to add the sugar in two batches. To prepare the butter, put slightly more than the amount given in the ingredients list into a clean cloth and squeeze this very hard; so extracting the liquid. Weigh or measure the required amount of butter after doing this.

Sift the flour and rice flour or ground rice or cornflour (cornstarch). Add half the sugar, then rub in the butter. Knead the mixture well, then add the remaining sugar and knead again.

Brush a 19 cm/7½ inch wooden shortbread mould with a few drops of oil, coat in a little flour. Press the shortbread mixture into the mould, make sure it is of even thickness. Leave for 10 to 15 minutes, then invert on to a layer of greaseproof (waxed) paper on an ungreased baking tray or sheet. The mixture will have the attractive design from the mould on top. Prick very lightly at even intervals with a fine skewer.

Bake in the centre of a slow to very moderate oven, 150 to 160°C/300 to 325°F Gas Mark 2 to 3, for 40 to 50 minutes until very pale golden and firm. Allow to cool for about 5 minutes, then mark into 6 to 8 portions. Lift off the tray when cold; store in an airtight tin.

VARIATIONS
Dust the shortbread with 1 tablespoon caster sugar before baking.

● *Ayrshire Shortbread:* Use only 100 g/4 oz (½ cup) butter with the same proportions of flour and rice flour above. Increase the amount of sugar to 100 g/4 oz (½ cup). Add ½ tablespoon double (heavy) cream and 1 tablespoon beaten egg yolk to bind. This mixture can be made into one large shortbread round as before or made into small biscuits (cookies). To prepare these, roll out the mixture to about 1.5 cm/½ inch in thickness, cut into 5 cm/2 inch rounds or neat fingers. Place on to an ungreased baking tray or sheet. Prick lightly and bake in the centre of a very moderate oven, 160°C/325°F Gas Mark 3, for 15 minutes.

● *Fruit Shortbread:* Chop 25 g/1 oz glacé cherries (1½ tbsp candied cherries), 25 g/1 oz (¼ cup) blanched almonds and 25 g/1 oz (1½ tbsp) mixed crystallized (candied) peel. Blend with the shortbread mixture, form into a neat shape.

● *Petticoat Tails:* Follow the basic recipe but work in a little extra flour so that the shortbread can be rolled out until 5 mm/¼ inch in thickness. Form into a large round, then cut as the line drawing on this page. Place on a lightly greased baking tray. Bake in the centre of a very moderate oven, 160°C/325°F Gas Mark 3, for 15 minutes. Cool on the baking tray, then dredge with caster sugar.

TO SHAPE PETTICOAT TAILS

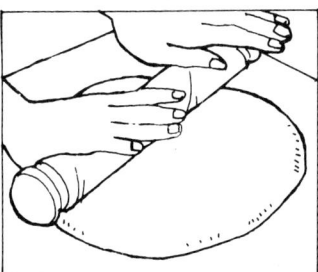

Roll out to the large round and put on the greased baking tray as described in the recipe on this page.

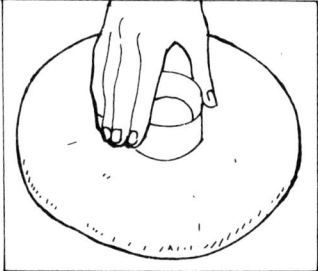

Press a 5 cm/2 inch cutter into the centre of the round, press lightly to cut half way through the dough.

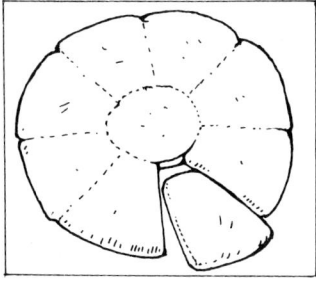

Cut lightly into wedges around the circle. Bake as above. When cooked, separate into portions.

PRINCESS BISCUITS

Cooking Time: 17 minutes　Makes 14–16　✹✹

	Metric/Imperial	American
butter	100 g/4 oz	½ cup
icing (confectioner's) sugar, sifted	25 g/1 oz	¼ cup
grated lemon or orange rind	1 teasp	1 teasp
plain (all-purpose) flour	100 g/4 oz	1 cup
To decorate: apricot jam, sieved	2 tbsp	3 tbsp
For the glacé icing: icing (confectioner's) sugar, sifted	75 g/3 oz	¾ cup
lemon or orange juice	1 tbsp	1 tbsp

Cream the butter, sugar and lemon or orange rind very well. Add the flour and blend thoroughly. Put the mixture into a large piping (pastry) bag with 1.5 cm/½ inch pipe (nozzle). Pipe finger shapes on to an ungreased baking tray. Chill well for 1 to 2 hours.

Bake in the centre of a very moderate oven, 160°C/325°F Gas Mark 3, for 15 minutes or until firm and golden in colour. Allow to cool. Brush the top of the biscuits (cookies) with the jam.

Blend the icing (confectioner's) sugar and lemon or orange juice. Brush this very thin icing over the apricot jam. Immediately put the biscuits back into the oven for 2 minutes only to harden the icing.

CRISP SHORTCAKE

Cooking Time: 20–25 minutes　Serves 4–6　✹✹

	Metric/Imperial	American
butter or margarine	175 g/6 oz	¾ cup
caster sugar	175 g/6 oz	¾ cup
plain (all-purpose) flour	225 g/8 oz	2 cups
baking powder	1 teasp	1 teasp
For the filling and topping: fruit, see method		

Cream the butter or margarine and sugar until soft and light. Sift the flour and baking powder, add to the creamed mixture. Divide between two 15 to 18 cm/6 to 7 inch greased and floured sandwich tins (layer cake pans) or flan rings on upturned baking trays.

Bake in the centre of a moderate oven, 180°C/350°F Gas Mark 4, for 20 to 25 minutes until just firm. Cool for about 15 minutes in the tins then lift out on to a wire cooling tray. When cold, sandwich together and top with strawberries or other fruit.

Serve with cream.

VARIATIONS
Sandwich and top with whipped cream and fruit.
● Cut one shortcake into triangles as soon as it is baked. Arrange with the fruit on the round of crisp shortcake, see the photograph on page 163.

● *Softer Shortcake:* Add 1 egg to the creamed mixture and use self-raising flour. Bake as before.
● *Date Shortcake:* Use 100 g/4 oz (⅔ cup) moist brown sugar instead of caster sugar. Add 175 g/6 oz (1 cup) finely chopped dates to the shortcake mixture. Bake in the centre of a very moderate oven, 160°C/325°F Gas Mark 3, for about 40 minutes.

SAFFRON CAKES

Cooking Time: 12–15 minutes　Makes 12　✹

In Cornwall, you will be offered various saffron cakes and probably each cook will claim that their produce is the most traditional and the best. These small cakes are quickly made.

The price of saffron (which comes from a special crocus) has increased a great deal in past years and you may hear a Cornish inhabitant grumbling about rising prices saying, "It is as dear as saffron". It is believed the Phoenicians brought saffron to Cornwall; certainly it is one of the specialities of this lovely part of Britain.

	Metric/Imperial	American
self-raising flour*	225 g/8 oz	2 cups
saffron powder	¼ teasp	¼ teasp
ground cinnamon	pinch	pinch
butter	100 g/4 oz	½ cup
caster sugar	100 g/4 oz	½ cup
caraway seeds	½ teasp	½ teasp
mixed dried fruit	100 g/4 oz	⅔ cup
crystallized (candied) peel, chopped	50 g/2 oz	⅓ cup
egg	1	1
milk	to bind	to bind
For the topping: caster sugar	25 g/1 oz	2 tbsp
caraway seeds	½ teasp	½ teasp

*or plain (all-purpose) flour with 2 teaspoons baking powder

Sift the flour, saffron powder and cinnamon. Rub in the butter, add the sugar, caraway seeds, fruit and peel. Bind with an egg and enough milk to give a 'sticky' consistency, i.e. so the mixture holds its shape.

Put spoonfuls on greased and floured baking trays; allow adequate space between the cakes. Sprinkle with the sugar and seeds. Bake above the centre of a hot oven, 220°C/425°F Gas Mark 7, for approximately 12 to 15 minutes. Eat when freshly made.

VARIATIONS
Put about 8 to 10 saffron strands into 1 tablespoon milk. Allow to stand for 30 minutes, strain and use the saffron-flavoured milk to bind the mixture.
● *Cherry Date Cakes:* Omit the saffron, caraway seeds and mixed dried fruit in the cakes and topping. Add 100 g/4 oz (⅔ cup) stoned (pitted) chopped dates and 75 g/3 oz chopped glacé (⅓ cup chopped candied) cherries instead. Top each cake with the sugar and half a cherry before baking.

PASTRIES

The following recipes are based upon various pastries. Most classic pastries have been a feature of cooking in Britain for many years. Some of the basic recipes are incorporated into various recipes.

Puff Pastry, which can be used in the Strawberry Horns recipe on this page, and those on page 155, is also on page 155.

FLAKY PASTRY

Cooking Time: as the particular recipe ❈❈

This pastry is used for both savoury and sweet dishes, for example, steak and kidney pie and fruit pies.

	Metric/Imperial	American
strong (hard wheat) or plain (all-purpose) flour	225 g/8 oz	2 cups
salt	pinch	pinch
butter or fat*	175 g/6 oz	¾ cup
lemon juice	good squeeze	good squeeze
water	to bind	to bind

*can be two-thirds butter or margarine and a third lard or cooking fat

Sift the flour and salt together. Put the butter or mixed fat on a plate and divide into 3 parts. Rub in the first part until the mixture looks like fine breadcrumbs. Bind with the lemon juice and water to an elastic dough.

Roll out to an oblong shape. Halve the remaining butter or mixture of fats. Put the one portion over the top two thirds of the dough in small pieces. Bring up the lower portion of the dough, so you have the effect of an opened envelope. Bring down the top portion. Turn the pastry at right angles so the open end is towards you. Seal the ends, then 'rib' the pastry with a rolling pin – this means depressing it at regular intervals.

Roll out carefully to an oblong shape again and repeat the above process. Turn, seal the ends, 'rib' the pastry. The dough is then ready to use, but it is advisable to wrap the dough in cling film (plastic wrap) and allow it to stand in a cool place if possible before the final rolling and shaping.

STRAWBERRY HORNS

Cooking Time: 8–10 minutes   Makes 10–12 ❈❈

	Metric/Imperial	American
Flaky Pastry, made as above with	175 g/6 oz flour etc	1½ cups flour etc
egg white	1	1
caster sugar	2 teasp	2 teasp
For the filling: double (heavy) cream	150 ml/¼ pint	⅔ cup
caster sugar	1 tbsp	1 tbsp
strawberries	8–10	8–10

Strawberry Horns

Make the flaky pastry as the recipe on this page, but use the slightly smaller proportions given in the recipe. Roll out very thinly and cut into 2.5 cm/1 inch strips; do not stretch the pastry. Lightly grease the outside of 10 to 12 cream horn tins and wind the pastry around these, starting from the base and making sure the edges overlap. Put on to an ungreased baking tray.

Brush with the egg white and sprinkle with the sugar. Bake just above the centre of a very hot oven, 230°C/450°F Gas Mark 8, for 8 to 10 minutes or until firm. Allow to cool.

Whip the cream, fold in the sugar and spoon into the horn cases. Top with the strawberries.

PUFF PASTRY

Cooking Time: as the particular recipe ❈❈

Puff Pastry is a very old type of pastry, although methods of making this have changed. In some old recipes the flour is mixed with eggs, in others just with egg whites, but today the flour is blended with water and lemon juice. This gives a very excellent result, particularly if strong (hard wheat) flour is used.

Roll out the dough once again to form an oblong, then fold as in Stage 1, and repeat Stage 2. It will be necessary to chill the dough; wrap in cling film (plastic wrap) and put into the refrigerator for at least 1 hour.

Repeat stages 1 and 2, seven times, putting the pastry to chill when it becomes slightly sticky.

MAIDS OF HONOUR

Illustrated in colour on page 206
Cooking Time: 30 minutes   Makes 12–15   **

This recipe is said to have originated in the time of Henry VIII and was a favourite of his ill-fated Queen Anne Boleyn (mother of Elizabeth I). It is said that she and her maids of honour made these for the King, and that is why the cakes were given this particular name.

	Metric/Imperial	American
Puff Pastry, see left made with	175 g/6 oz flour etc	1½ cups flour etc
For the filling: egg	1	1
egg yolk	1	1
caster sugar	50 g/2 oz	¼ cup
finely grated lemon rind	½ teasp	½ teasp
orange flower water or lemon juice	1 teasp	1 teasp
brandy	1 teasp	1 teasp
ground almonds	100 g/4 oz	1 cup
fine plain cake crumbs	25 g/1 oz	½ cup
To decorate (optional): icing (confectioner's) sugar, sifted	1–2 tbsp	1–3 tbsp

Make the pastry, see left. Roll out to just about 3 mm/⅛ inch thick. Cut into rounds to fit 12 to 15 fairly large round patty tins (patty shells). Press the pastry well down in the tins and put into the refrigerator while preparing the filling.

Put the egg and egg yolk into a bowl or bowl of an electric mixer. Add the sugar and whisk until thick and creamy. Add all the other ingredients. Spoon the filling into the pastry cases.

Bake just above the centre of a hot to very hot oven, 220 to 230°C/425 to 450°F Gas Mark 7 to 8, for 10 minutes, then reduce the heat to very moderate, 160°C/325°F Gas Mark 3, for a further 20 minutes or until the pastry and filling are firm; allow to cool. The cakes can be topped with sifted icing (confectioner's) sugar.

VARIATION
To give very crisp light pastry, bake the tartlets blind (without a filling) for 10 minutes in the hot to very hot oven, as given above, then add the filling and bake for a further 10 to 12 minutes in a moderately hot oven, 200°C/400°F Gas Mark 6.
Note: In order to keep the pastry a good shape while being baked without a filling, put a small piece of greaseproof (waxed) paper in each small pastry case, top with a crust of bread or a few plastic baking beans.

	Metric/Imperial	American
strong (hard wheat) or plain (all-purpose) flour	225 g/8 oz	2 cups
salt	pinch	pinch
lemon juice	good squeeze	good squeeze
water	to bind	to bind
butter	225 g/8 oz	1 cup

Sift the flour and salt into a mixing bowl. Add the lemon juice and sufficient cold water to make an elastic soft rolling consistency. Roll the dough out on a lightly floured board to a neat oblong shape. Place the butter in the centre of the dough. Bring up the bottom part of the dough to cover the butter, then bring down the top part of the dough, so the butter is completely enclosed and the dough has made an envelope shape. This is *Stage 1*, which is repeated 7 times with Stage 2, although the butter is incorporated in the first instance. For *Stage 2*, turn the dough at right angles, seal the open ends, then 'rib' the pastry. This means depressing it at regular intervals with the floured rolling pin.

TRADITIONAL PASTRIES AND CAKES

Shortcrust pastry, as given in the Yorkshire Curd Tarts below, is used to make a variety of tarts. Jam or Lemon Curd Tarts are a general favourite. Make the pastry and line patty tins (patty shells). Fill with jam or curd and bake in a hot oven, as the temperature given below.
Fruit Tarts: Cook the pastry cases without a filling, bake blind, then allow to cool. Fill with whipped and sweetened cream and top with seasonal fruit, such as strawberries; see the photograph on page 163. Small pastry cases take approximately 15 minutes to cook whether empty or filled with jam or curd.

YORKSHIRE CURD TARTS

Cooking Time: 30 minutes   Makes 8–10 saucer-shaped tarts   **

This dish originated when modern refrigerators and methods of processing milk were unknown; it was an excellent way of using sour milk. Nowadays fresh milk and rennet should be used.

	Metric/Imperial	American
For the filling: milk	900 ml/1½ pints	3¾ cups
rennet	2 teasp	2 teasp
butter, melted and cooled	50 g/2 oz	¼ cup
caster sugar	50 g/2 oz	¼ cup
salt	pinch	pinch
small eggs	2	2
currants	100 g/4 oz	⅔ cup
crystallized (candied) peel, chopped	50–75 g/2–3 oz	½ cup
ground or grated nutmeg	pinch	pinch
For the shortcrust pastry (basic pie dough): plain (all-purpose) flour	225 g/8 oz	2 cups
salt	pinch	pinch
butter or margarine or half margarine and half lard or cooking fat (shortening)	110 g/4 oz	½ cup
water	to bind	to bind
For the topping: ground or grated nutmeg	pinch	pinch

Heat the milk until just blood heat, stir in the rennet. Pour into a bowl, allow to become cold and to 'clot'. Strain through fine muslin (cheesecloth). Put the curds into a bowl and blend with the melted, but cooled, butter. Add the rest of the filling ingredients.

To make the pastry; sift the flour and salt, rub in the butter or other fat then add sufficient water to bind. Roll out thinly and line either flat saucer-shaped patty tins (patty shells) or smaller deeper patty tins with the mixture. The saucer-shape was traditionally used. Spoon in the curd mixture and top with the nutmeg.

Bake the tarts just above the centre of a hot oven, 220°C/425°F Gas Mark 7, for approximately 10 minutes to set the pastry, then reduce the heat to moderate,

180°C/350°F Gas Mark 4, for a further 20 minutes or until the filling is firm and golden and the pastry crisp.

VARIATIONS
If preferred, this amount of filling and pastry could be used to fill an 18 to 20 cm/7 to 8 inch really deep flan or pie plate. Use exactly the same proportions for the filling, but to give a slightly more moist filling add 2 tablespoons milk or double (heavy) cream. Bake for 15 minutes in a hot oven then for 30 to 35 minutes in a moderate oven, temperatures as before.
● Many family recipes for curd tarts include 1 or 2 teaspoons rum or brandy in the ingredients or a more modern addition is ½ teaspoon finely grated lemon rind.
● Vinegar can be used to sour the milk but this gives a less delicate curd.

ECCLES CAKES

Cooking Time: 20 minutes   Makes 12–15   **

These small pastries with a filling of dried fruit etc. are extremely popular in Lancashire. Up to the time of Elizabeth I, 'wakes' (the Lancashire name for holidays) were celebrated in the town of Eccles, with bull-baiting and cockfighting as the amusements of the day. These holidays were abolished by Queen Elizabeth I, but started once again in the reign of James I and continued up to the 19th Century; so it is quite likely that these pastries were sold at the 'wakes'.

	Metric/Imperial	American
Puff Pastry, as page 155 made with	175 g/6 oz flour etc	1½ cups flour etc
For the filling: butter, slightly softened	50 g/2 oz	¼ cup
caster or light brown sugar	50 g/2 oz	¼ cup
sultanas (golden raisins)	50 g/2 oz	⅓ cup
currants	50 g/2 oz	⅓ cup
crystallized (candied) peel, finely chopped	2 tbsp	3 tbsp
finely grated lemon rind	1 teasp	1 teasp
lemon juice	½–1 tbsp	½–1 tbsp
mixed spice	½ teasp	½ teasp
To glaze: milk	2 tbsp	3 tbsp
caster sugar	25 g/1 oz	2 tbsp

Make the pastry as page 155, wrap in cling film (plastic wrap) and chill in the refrigerator while preparing the filling.

Mix the ingredients for the filling together. Roll out the pastry to approximately 3 mm/⅛ inch thick. Cut into 12 to 15 rounds, about the size of an ordinary saucer. Place a little filling in the centre of each pastry round; brush the edges of the pastry with a little water then gather these together to form a ball.

Turn this ball with the joins underneath and roll gently, but firmly, to make a round again of about 6–7.5 cm/2½-3 inches in diameter.

Make 2 or 3 slits on top of each round; lift on to ungreased baking trays. Brush with the milk and sprinkle very lightly with the sugar.

Bake in the centre of a hot to very hot oven, 220 to 230°C/425 to 450°F Gas Mark 7 to 8, for 20 minutes. Reduce the heat slightly for the last 6 to 7 minutes if the pastry is becoming too brown.

VARIATIONS

Banbury Cakes: Make the pastry as before. Prepare the filling but add 50 g/2 oz (1 cup) fine plain sponge cake crumbs or Macaroon Biscuit crumbs, made as page 150. The cakes are made in an oval shape instead of a round one.
● *Shropshire Cakes:* Make the pastry as before. To prepare the filling, mix together 175 g/6 oz (1 cup) currants, 25 g/1 oz (1½ tbsp) finely chopped crystallized (candied) peel, 50 g/2 oz (¼ cup) sugar, 25 g/1 oz (2 tbsp) softened butter and 1 tablespoon finely chopped mint. Prepare and bake as Eccles Cakes.
● *Coventry Godcakes:* Use 300 g/10 oz (1¼ cups) mincemeat, made as page 195, instead of the filling in the Eccles Cakes. These cakes were presented to godparents by their godchildren, and by the godparents to the children on New Year's Day.

MERINGUES

Cooking Time: 1½-3 hours ❖❖

To make 8–10 large shells (4–5 complete meringues) as the photograph on page 163, use 110 g/4 oz (½ cup) caster sugar and 2 egg whites. This amount makes 24 small meringues.

Whisk the egg whites until stiff. Gradually beat in half the sugar then fold in the remainder, or you can gradually beat in all the sugar for a firmer meringue. Use a low speed with an electric mixer. A few drops of vanilla or other essence (extract) can be added.

Prepare the baking tray or sheet by brushing this with a few drops of oil, or use silicone (non-stick) paper on the trays or silicone baking trays.

Either spoon the meringue mixture on to the trays or put into a piping (pastry) bag fitted with a star nozzle and pipe the shape required.

Bake the meringues in a very slow oven, 90–110°C/ 200–225°F Gas Mark 0–¼, for 1½-3 hours, depending upon their size, or until firm and easily removed.

Store in an airtight container. Fill just before serving so the meringues retain their crisp texture.

CREAM PUFFS

Cooking Time: as the particular recipe ❖❖

I have given the name by which choux pastry buns were, and still are, often known in Britain. There is no record of this being one of the older traditional recipes, but it certainly can be called a modern favourite, especially in the form of profiteroles (small choux buns).

	Metric/Imperial	American
water	150 ml/¼ pint	⅔ cup
butter or margarine	50 g/2 oz	¼ cup
sugar	pinch	pinch
plain (all-purpose) flour	65 g/2½ oz	generous ½ cup
eggs	2	2
For the filling: double (heavy) cream	150–300 ml/ ¼-½ pint	⅔-1¼ cups
sugar	to taste	to taste
icing (confectioner's) sugar, sifted	1–2 tbsp	1–3 tbsp

Put the water, butter or margarine and sugar into a saucepan, heat until the butter or margarine has melted. Remove from the heat, sift the flour, add to the pan, return to a very low heat and stir until the mixture forms a dry ball. Take the pan off the heat once again and gradually beat in the eggs to make a sticky mixture. The pastry is then ready to use.

For large Cream Puffs; Spoon the mixture into 8 to 10 large rounds on a lightly greased baking tray.

For small Profiteroles: Spoon the mixture into about 24 small rounds on a lightly greased baking tray or make about 40 very tiny Profiteroles as a garnish for soup, see page 30.

Bake the pastry in the centre of a moderately hot oven, 200°C/400°F Gas Mark 6. Large bun shapes take at least 25 minutes, smaller ones from 10 minutes onwards. The pastry should be firm and golden in colour. Cool away from a draught.

Whip the cream, add the sugar to taste and fill the buns. Dust with the icing (confectioner's) sugar.

Profiteroles are served with a chocolate sauce. There is a recipe for this on page 126.

VARIATIONS

Pipe, rather than spoon, the mixture on to the baking trays.
● Fill the small choux buns with savoury ingredients as suggested on page 177, in which case omit the sugar in the pastry.

APPLE CAKE

Cooking Time: 1¼ hours　Makes 1 cake　✳✳

It is quite traditional to have cheese with apple cake and in Lancashire they still serve cheese with apple pie, for, as the saying goes:

> *'An apple pie without cheese*
> *Is like a kiss without a squeeze.'*

	Metric/Imperial	American
self-raising flour*	350 g/12 oz	3 cups
butter or margarine	150 g/5 oz	⅝ cup
caster sugar	175 g/6 oz	¾ cup
brown sugar	25 g/1 oz	2 tbsp
ground cinnamon	½ teasp	½ teasp
apples, peeled and diced, weight when prepared	225 g/8 oz	2 cups
egg	1	1
milk (if necessary)	little	little
For the topping: caster sugar	25 g/1 oz	2 tbsp
ground cinnamon	pinch	pinch

*or plain (all-purpose) flour with 3 teaspoons baking powder

Sift the flour, rub in the butter or margarine, add the caster sugar. Blend the brown sugar with the cinnamon, toss the diced apple in this, then stir into the flour mixture. Add the egg, blend very thoroughly then stir in just enough milk to make a sticky consistency, i.e. so the mixture stands up in peaks in the bowl when handled with a knife. Line a 20 cm/8 inch cake (spring form) tin with greased and floured greaseproof (waxed) paper. Put the cake mixture into the tin, smooth flat on top, sprinkle with the sugar and cinnamon.

Bake in the centre of a moderate oven, 180°C/350°F Gas Mark 4, for approximately 1¼ hours; reduce the heat after 50 minutes if necessary.

The traditional way of serving this cake was to cut it while warm, top each slice with a knob of butter and serve with cheese.

VARIATIONS
Use a mixture of butter or margarine and lard or clarified dripping in the cake.
● *Cider Apple Cake:* Use a small egg and 3 tablespoons (4 tbsp) sweet cider to mix the cake. This makes a softer textured cake, but bake as above.
● *Crisp-topped Apple Cake:* Make the cake as above. Rub 25 g/1 oz (2 tbsp) butter or margarine into 50 g/2 oz (½ cup) plain (all-purpose) flour, 25 g/1 oz (2 tbsp) brown sugar and a little ground cinnamon. Sprinkle over the top of the cake before baking.

GINGERBREAD

Cooking Time: 1¼ hours　Makes 1 cake　✳✳

A gingerbread is one of the oldest cakes although in the past it was, as the name suggests, a ginger flavoured bread which was spread with butter. Once gingerbreads were baked in the most elaborate moulds, some of which are still retained on show in a museum in Yorkshire. One of the most usual expressions we use in this country to denote a disappointment is that 'it has removed all the gilt from the gingerbread', i.e. all the pleasure (or profit) has gone. This originates from the fact that gingerbreads for very special occasions were often covered in gilt.

	Metric/Imperial	American
plain (all-purpose) flour	350 g/12 oz	3 cups
bicarbonate of soda (baking soda)	1½ level teasp	1½ level teasp
mixed spice	1 teasp	1 teasp
ground ginger	2 teasp	2 teasp
moist brown sugar	75 g/3 oz	½ cup
butter	175 g/6 oz	¾ cup
black treacle (molasses)	225 g/8 oz	⅔ cup
golden (light corn) syrup	75 g/3 oz	¼ cup
eggs	2	2
milk	3 tbsp	4 tbsp
water	150 ml/¼ pint	⅔ cup

Sift the flour, bicarbonate of soda (baking soda) and spices together, do this very thoroughly. Add the sugar.

Simple Fruit Breads – recipes page 145. Apple Cake

Meanwhile, melt the butter with the treacle and syrup in a saucepan. Cool very slightly, pour over the flour mixture and beat well. Add the eggs and milk and beat.

Heat the water in the pan in which the butter, treacle and syrup were melted. Bring just to the boil, but do not boil for any length of time as some of the liquid will evaporate. Stir well to make sure no treacle left in the pan is wasted. Pour over the other ingredients and beat.

Line a 25 x 18 cm/10 x 7 inch tin with greased and floured greaseproof (waxed) paper. Spoon in the mixture. Bake in the centre of a cool oven, 150°C/300°F Gas Mark 2, for approximately 1¼ hours. Do not open the oven door until well after 1 hour's cooking, as moist gingerbreads fall in the middle if there is a sudden draught.

Cool in the tin as the weight of the treacle could make the cake break. Take off the paper immediately the cake is removed from the tin, as this hardens on the cake with storage and can be difficult to remove. When quite cold, wrap in fresh paper or foil and put into an airtight tin. Do not cut for 2 or 3 days.

DOUGHNUTS

The photograph on this page shows a selection of doughnuts. These are made from the basic bread dough on pages 142 and 143. The dough should be made in the usual way, allowed to prove then divided into small portions.

To make round doughnuts: Form the dough into balls, make a deep impression with your finger, put in a little jam or very thick sweetened fruit purée. Re-roll the ball to cover the jam or fruit purée. Place on a baking tray and allow the doughnuts to prove for about 25 minutes. Fry as the Jersey Wonders on page 160 but allow an extra 2 minutes cooking time as the balls of dough are thicker. Coat in caster sugar.

To make ring doughnuts: Roll out the dough, cut into rings. Prove as the method above. Fry as the Jersey Wonders on page 160.

DUNDEE CAKE

Cooking Time: 2 hours Makes 1 cake ✷✷

This is probably one of the best liked of all British cakes. It is not as rich as a traditional Christmas cake, but has sufficient fat and fruit to keep well. The essential 'hallmark' of a Dundee cake is the topping of glossy brown almonds.

It is believed that the original Gaelic name for Dundee, the Scottish city from which this cake takes its name, was Tun Taw (the fort of the Tay River); this became Dundee.

	Metric/Imperial	American
butter or margarine	175 g/6 oz	¾ cup
caster sugar	175 g/6 oz	¾ cup
large eggs	3	3
plain (all-purpose) flour	225 g/8 oz	2 cups
baking powder	1 teasp	1 teasp
dry or sweet sherry or milk	2 tbsp	3 tbsp
mixed dried fruit	450 g/1 lb	1 lb
glacé (candied) cherries, chopped	50 g/2 oz	¼ cup
crystallized (candied) peel, chopped	50 g/2 oz	⅓ cup
To decorate: almonds, blanched	50 g/2 oz	scant ½ cup
egg white, see method		

Cream the butter or margarine and sugar until soft and light. Gradually beat in the eggs, but save a little egg white in the shells to glaze the topping of almonds. Sift the flour and baking powder, fold into the creamed mixture together with the sherry or milk. Add the fruit and peel. Spoon the mixture into a greased and floured or lined 20 cm/8 inch cake tin; smooth absolutely flat on top. Arrange the almonds in a neat pattern on top of the cake and brush with the remains of the egg white in the shells.

Bake in the centre of a very moderate oven, 160°C/325°F Gas Mark 3, for 30 minutes, then reduce the heat to slow, 150°C/300°F Gas Mark 2, for a further 1½ hours or until the cake is firm to the touch and has shrunk away from the sides of the tin. Allow the cake to cool for 3 to 4 minutes in the tin, then turn out on to a wire cooling tray. Store in an airtight tin. This keeps well for 3 to 4 weeks.

VARIATION

Orange Walnut Cake: Omit the dried fruit and cherries in the Dundee Cake above and the almonds on top of the cake. Cream 2 teaspoons grated orange rind with the butter or margarine and sugar; mix the cake with orange juice instead of sherry or milk.

Increase the amount of crystallized (candied) peel to 100 g/4 oz (⅔ cup) and use all orange peel if possible. Add 175 g/6 oz (1½ cups) coarsely chopped walnuts to the cake mixture. Bake as above.

Doughnuts

JERSEY WONDERS

Cooking Time: 5–6 minutes   Makes 12–15   *

These are one of the interesting old recipes to be found in the Channel Islands. The mixture can be formed into strips, circles or made into a bow shape (see line drawings). The fried cakes are light and crisp, and could have originated from Continental Crullers or even the French Beignets Soufflés. This is one of the fantastic aspects of eating in Jersey and indeed all the Channel Islands, you can enjoy a combination of food from France and England.

	Metric/Imperial	American
For the cakes: self-raising flour*	225 g/8 oz	2 cups
ground ginger	½ teasp	½ teasp
ground nutmeg	½ teasp	½ teasp
butter	50 g/2 oz	¼ cup
caster sugar	50 g/2 oz	¼ cup
small eggs	2	2
milk, see method	little	little
To fry: deep oil or fat		
To coat: caster sugar		

*or plain (all-purpose) flour with 2 teaspoons baking powder

Sift the flour and spices together, rub in the butter and add the sugar. Bind with the eggs and enough milk to give a soft rolling consistency. Roll out the dough until approximately 5 mm/¼ inch in thickness; cut into strips or rings or bows which are a favourite shape, see the line drawings on this page.

Heat the oil or fat to 175°C/350°F, drop in the cakes gently, so their shape remains good. Fry steadily for approximately 5 to 6 minutes until crisp and golden brown. Lift out, drain on absorbent paper (kitchen towels). Roll in caster sugar. Eat when hot or on the same day they are made. These cakes are very like a doughnut, but much easier to prepare.

TO MAKE A BOW

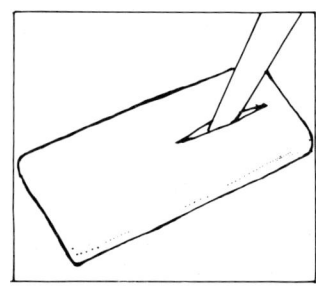
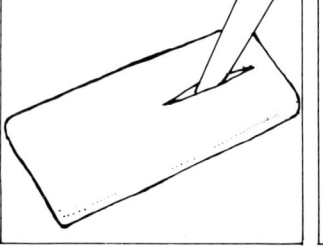
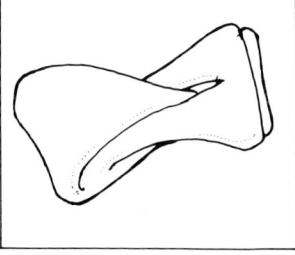

Cut a long strip. Make a slit towards one end.

Insert the other end of the dough through this.

POTATO APPLE CAKE

Illustrated in colour on page 210
Cooking Time: 30 minutes   Makes 1 cake   **

This traditional Irish cake used to be cooked in a heavy frying pan (skillet) over a slow burning fire. All the ingredients for the cake were formed into a round to fit the greased pan. The cake was topped with the apples and other ingredients, covered with a saucepan lid and cooked for about 30 minutes or until the apples were tender. The cake was cut in portions while in the pan, then lifted out and served hot. The modern method of baking produces a more attractive looking cake, but the old-fashioned way may well be convenient if you are on holiday and camping.

	Metric/Imperial	American
For the cake: old potatoes, weight when peeled	450 g/1 lb	1 lb
salt	pinch	pinch
self-raising flour	100 g/4 oz	1 cup
butter	50 g/2 oz	¼ cup
caster sugar	50 g/2 oz	¼ cup
egg	1	1
For the topping: large cooking (baking) apples	2	2
butter, melted	25 g/1 oz	2 tbsp
cloves, optional	4–6	4–6
ground cinnamon	½-1 teasp	½-1 teasp
caster or brown sugar	2 tbsp	3 tbsp

Cook the potatoes carefully in a saucepan of salted water so they remain 'floury'. Strain and mash. Sift the flour, rub in the butter, then add the sugar and potatoes. Work together to give a pliable dough, adding as much egg as needed. Shape into a 20 cm/8 inch round and put on a greased baking tray.

Peel, core and cut the apples in neat slices of even thickness. Put on top of the cake, brush with melted butter. Arrange the cloves at even intervals. Blend the cinnamon and sugar, sprinkle over the apples.

Bake in the centre of a moderate to moderately hot oven, 190 to 200°C/375 to 400°F Gas Mark 5 to 6, for approximately 30 minutes or until the apples are tender. Serve when fresh.

CHELSEA BUNS

Illustrated in colour on page 206
Cooking Time: 15–20 minutes   Makes 12   **

It is difficult to imagine Chelsea as a small village some distance from London but, of course, this was long before the borders of London spread. The original Chelsea Bun shop dates back to the 15th Century. The shop may have been small but the quality of the buns baked there became famous, and people travelled from London to sample them.

	Metric/Imperial	American
fresh (compressed) yeast	15 g/½ oz	½ cake
milk or milk and water	150 ml/¼ pint	⅔ cup
strong (hard wheat) or plain (all-purpose) flour	350 g/12 oz	3 cups
salt	pinch	pinch
butter or margarine	50 g/2 oz	¼ cup
caster sugar	25–50 g/1–2 oz	2–4 tbsp
egg	1	1
For the filling: butter or margarine, slightly softened	50 g/2 oz	¼ cup
caster or light brown sugar	50 g/2 oz	¼ cup
ground nutmeg or cinnamon	½ teasp	½ teasp
mixed dried fruit	100 g/4 oz	⅔ cup
To glaze: water	2 tbsp	3 tbsp
caster sugar	50 g/2 oz	¼ cup

Cream the yeast. Warm the milk, or milk and water as described under Bath Buns on page 149. Blend with the yeast. Sift the flour and salt, rub in the butter or margarine, then add the sugar, yeast liquid and egg. Knead the dough until smooth. Cover and allow to 'prove', as described under Bath Buns, until double the original size.

Knead the dough once again until smooth and a soft rolling consistency. Roll out on a lightly floured surface to a neat oblong measuring approximately 30.5 to 35.5 cm/12 to 14 inches x 25 to 28 cm/10 to 11 inches. Spread with the softened butter or margarine then with the sugar, nutmeg or cinnamon and dried fruit. Roll the yeast dough loosely as shown below, cut into 12 portions. Place these on a lightly greased baking tray or sheet or into a square cake tin measuring approximately 23 cm/9 inches as shown in the second line drawing. It is important to allow adequate space for the buns to rise and yet pack them sufficiently tightly to keep a good shape.

Cover the buns with lightly oiled cling film (plastic wrap) and allow to 'prove' for approximately 25 minutes or until *nearly* double in size.

Bake just above the centre of a hot oven, 220°C/425°F Gas Mark 7, for approximately 15 minutes or until firm to the touch. Heat the water, blend with the sugar. Brush over the buns to glaze as soon as they come from the oven. Eat when fresh.

VARIATIONS
Plain buns can be made by using bread dough. Take approximately 450 g/1 lb of the proven dough, made as page 142, work in a little extra flour to make a rolling consistency. Spread with the filling ingredients and continue as above.
● Top the buns with caster sugar when cold instead of a glaze.

GINGER MERINGUE CAKE
Illustrated in colour on page 218
Cooking Time: 1 hour 20–25 minutes   Makes 1 cake ❋❋

The Welsh cake below is rather unusual for it has a ginger flavoured shortcake base, topped with meringue. The Welsh name is Teisen Sinsir.

	Metric/Imperial	American
ground ginger	1 teasp	1 teasp
plain (all-purpose) flour	225 g/8 oz	2 cups
baking powder	1 teasp	1 teasp
butter	100 g/4 oz	½ cup
caster sugar	100 g/4 oz	½ cup
egg yolk	1	1
For the topping: apricot jam, sieved	3 tbsp	4 tbsp
egg whites	2	2
caster sugar	100 g/4 oz	½ cup

Sift the ginger, flour and baking powder together, rub in the butter, then add the sugar and bind with the egg yolk. Knead very well and form into a 20 cm/8 inch round. Place on an ungreased upturned baking tray (this makes it easy to slide off when cooked). To make a perfect shape, put the mixture into a sandwich tin (layer cake pan) or in a flan ring on the baking tray or sheet. Prick with a fine skewer.

Bake in the centre of a moderately hot oven, 200°C/400°F Gas Mark 6, for approximately 20 to 25 minutes until golden in colour. Cool slightly then spread with the jam.

Whisk the egg whites until very stiff, gradually whisk in half the sugar, then fold in the remainder. Pile or pipe over the jam covered shortbread. Return to a very slow oven, 120°C/250°F Gas Mark ½, and leave for 1 hour until set. Cool and serve when fresh.

VARIATION
Ground cinnamon may be used instead of ginger.

TO SHAPE CHELSEA BUNS

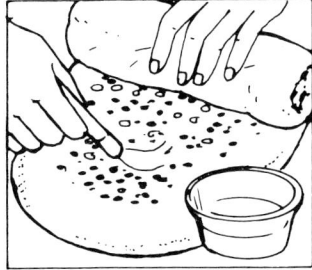

Cover the oblong dough with the butter and other ingredients as in the recipe, roll firmly but not too tightly.

Cut into 12 portions, place these on a baking tray or into a tin. Bake as the instructions on this page.

Traditional Teas

The delicious teas that were a regular feature in many homes in the past are now generally reserved for special occasions or when the family have leisure time to enjoy this most relaxing meal. If you have visitors from abroad, do give them an opportunity to sample this very British repast.
An elegant afternoon tea should consist of:
A plate of small sandwiches, made with wafer-thin brown or white bread and butter, filled with cream cheese or scrambled egg and cress or pâté or smoked salmon or salad ingredients such as cucumber. Brown Bread and butter rolled around asparagus tips were a favourite savoury food.
Hot toast or toasted teacakes in cold weather or a plate of wafer-thin bread and butter with home-made jam or other preserves.
Small scones and butter. The scones can be split and spread with butter or topped with whipped or clotted cream and jam, see page 147.
A selection of cakes. A light sponge cake, as the recipe below, a fruit cake like the Dundee Cake on page 159 and a rather more elaborate gâteau, as page 163, would give a good choice. You could include a selection of biscuits and/or pastries, see pages 150 to 157.
Many people prefer China tea with lemon at this meal, rather than Indian or Ceylon tea and milk.

SEASONAL TEAS

Make good use of seasonal soft fruit at teatime, as well as at other meals. The photograph on this page shows some of the ways to provide a Strawberry Tea.

The recipe for the Crisp Shortcake, which is topped with strawberries and decorated with triangles of shortcake, is on page 153. Meringues and small tartlets are an excellent way to serve strawberries and whipped cream; the recipes are on pages 156 and 157.

The photograph also includes Scones, made as page 147, and a Victoria Sandwich, the recipe for which follows.

VICTORIA SANDWICH

Illustrated in colour opposite and on page 206

Cooking Time: 20 minutes   Makes 1 sponge cake **

This light sponge cake became a favourite during the reign of Queen Victoria, as it was reputed to be one of her favourite cakes. It was during the 19th Century that elaborate afternoon tea menus were an accepted part of gracious living.

Although we tend to weigh or measure the ingredients these days, the old-fashioned method of ensuring one had correct amounts was to use the eggs as the weight, and have the weight of the eggs in fat, sugar and flour. This is an excellent procedure.

	Metric/Imperial	American
butter or margarine	175 g/6 oz	¾ cup
caster sugar	175 g/6 oz	¾ cup
large eggs	3	3
self-raising flour*	175 g/6 oz	1½ cups
To fill: jam or lemon curd	4 tbsp	5 tbsp
To decorate: caster sugar	to taste	to taste

*or use plain (all-purpose) flour with 1½ teaspoons baking powder

Cream the butter or margarine and sugar in a bowl until soft and light in texture and in colour. Stand the bowl on a folded teacloth so it will not slip. If using an electric mixer, choose a low speed.

Gradually beat in the eggs; if the mixture shows signs of curdling (separating), beat in a little of the flour.

Sift the flour, or flour and baking powder, and fold into the creamed mixture with a metal spoon.

Divide the mixture between two greased and floured or lined 19 to 20 cm/7½ to 8 inch sandwich tins (layer cake pans). Place both tins on the shelf just above the centre of a moderate oven, 180°C/350°F Gas Mark 4 (in some ovens you need a slightly higher setting, i.e. 190°C/375°F Gas Mark 5, so check this carefully). Bake for approximately 20 minutes or until firm to a gentle touch. Cool in the tins for 1 minute then turn out on to a wire cooling tray.

Sandwich the cakes together with the jam or lemon curd and top with the caster sugar.

Note: There is no need to flour or line silicone treated (non-stick) tins, use a very little oil or melted fat (shortening) to grease them.

The basic Victoria Sandwich or the lighter Sponge on the next page both freeze well for up to 3 months.

DECORATED CAKES

The simple gâteaux on this and the next page reflect modern tastes, for these are the kind of cakes that can be served as a dessert or for tea; this makes them a practical choice for a small family.

Make and bake the Victoria Sandwich. Make rather small sized Brandy Snaps; bake as in the recipe on page 150, but instead of rolling 10 to 12 of the biscuits round the handle of a wooden spoon, roll them round the oiled base of cream horn tins to form narrow horn shapes. The remaining biscuits can be kept flat, cooled and crushed.

Sandwich the two layers of sponge with 3 tablespoons (4 tbsp) jam and spread half the remainder in a thin layer over the sides of the cake. Whip the cream, pipe a little into each Brandy Snap shape. Spread half the remainder over the sides of the cake and then coat with the crushed biscuits. Top the cake with the last of the jam and then the cream. Arrange the small horn shapes on top. Serve as soon as possible.

Above: Strawberry Tea. Below: Brandy Snap Gâteau

BRANDY SNAP GÂTEAU

Cooking Time: see method   Makes 1 cake   ✳✳✳

	Metric/Imperial	American
Victoria Sandwich, see left made with	3 eggs etc	3 eggs etc
Brandy Snaps, as page 150, but see method below		
To fill and decorate: apricot jam, sieved	5 tbsp	½ cup
double (heavy) cream	300 ml/½ pint	1¼ cups

HIGH TEAS

This meal is probably unique to Britain. It may be found in those countries where some residents had British ancestry. It is a meal that is very practical when children are part of the family, as it gives them a satisfying meal when they return from school, for a high tea is generally served at about 5 pm (17.00 hours). It is a meal that combines savoury foods, cake, tea and possibly a dessert as well.

Some of the savoury dishes in the chapter that follows would be a good choice for this meal. Other favourites are boiled eggs or any dishes based upon eggs; fried fish or poached haddock, see pages 35 and 43; cooked bacon and/or sausages (British sausages are prime favourites with most people). Cold meats and salad are another usual main dish for this meal. Fried potatoes are quite likely to be served with many of the dishes.

The kind of desserts offered at this meal would be ice cream, or fruit salad, or cooked fruit, or the light sundae type of dessert shown on page 166. Instead of a dessert, one could have a rather special gâteau, such as those following and on page 163.

CHOCOLATE CREAM GÂTEAU

Illustrated in colour on page 166

Cooking Time: 50–55 minutes   Makes 1 cake   ✲✲✲

	Metric/Imperial	American
plain (semi-sweet) chocolate	150 g/5 oz	5 squares
rum or Curaçao	1 tbsp	1 tbsp
butter	150 g/5 oz	⅝ cup
icing (confectioner's) sugar, sifted	150 g/5 oz	1 cup
eggs	5	5
self-raising flour*	150 g/5 oz	1¼ cups
cornflour (cornstarch)	25 g/1 oz	¼ cup
For the filling: butter	50 g/2 oz	¼ cup
icing (confectioner's) sugar, sifted	75 g/3 oz	generous ½ cup
plain (semi-sweet) chocolate	50 g/2 oz	2 squares
For the coating: double (heavy) cream	300 ml/½ pint	1¼ cups
caster sugar	1 tbsp	1 tbsp
rum or Curaçao	½-1 tbsp	½-1 tbsp
For the topping: plain (semi-sweet) chocolate, grated	25 g/1 oz	1 square

*or use plain (all-purpose) flour with 1¼ teaspoons baking powder

Line a 20 to 23 cm/8 to 9 inch cake tin with greased greaseproof (waxed) paper. Melt the chocolate with the rum or Curaçao. Cream together the butter and sugar.

Beat in the melted chocolate. Separate the eggs and gradually blend the yolks into the chocolate mixture. Sift the flour and cornflour (cornstarch) together; fold into the creamed mixture. Finally, whisk the egg whites until they just hold their shape, but do not overwhip. Fold gently and carefully into the other ingredients.

Spoon the mixture into the prepared tin. Bake in the centre of a slow oven, 150°C/300°F Gas Mark 2, for 50 to 55 minutes or until firm to a gentle touch. Cool in the tin for 5 minutes then turn out very carefully and allow to cool.

Cream the butter and sugar together for the chocolate filling. Melt the chocolate, add to the creamed mixture. Split the cake through the centre, sandwich with the filling.

Whip the cream. Add the sugar and rum or Curaçao, whip again. Use most of the cream to coat the cake but save a little to pipe around the cake edge. Top with the grated chocolate.

VARIATION
The cake has such a good flavour that the filling can be omitted if desired.

FLUFFY SPONGE

Cooking Time: 12–15 minutes   Makes 1 sponge   ✲✲

This light, delicate type of sponge has always been a favourite. It is an excellent basis for teatime or it can be filled with jam or fruit and cream. Modern electric mixers make it very easy to whisk the eggs and sugar until light.

	Metric/Imperial	American
large eggs	3	3
caster sugar	100 g/4 oz	½ cup
flour, see method	75 g/3 oz	¾ cup
For the filling: jam, or see method	3–4 tbsp	4–5 tbsp
For the topping: caster sugar	1 tbsp	1 tbsp

Grease and flour or line two 19 to 20 cm/7½ to 8 inch sandwich tins (layer cake pans) with greased greaseproof (waxed) paper. Put the eggs and sugar into a bowl and whisk until thick and creamy.

Sift the flour at least once; plain (all-purpose) flour can be used as the egg mixture is so aerated, but self-raising flour ensures a good rise to the sponge. Fold the flour into the egg mixture very carefully and gently.

Spoon into the prepared tins. Bake just above the centre of a moderate to moderately hot oven, 190°C/375°F Gas Mark 5, for 12 to 15 minutes or until firm to a gentle touch. Cool for a few minutes in the tins, then turn out and allow to cool.

Sandwich together with jam, or as suggested above. Top with the sugar.

VARIATION
Melt 25 g/1 oz (2 tbsp) butter, fold into the mixture with the flour.

Vanilla Cheesecake

Cooking Time: 1–1¼ hours   Makes 1 cake   ❖❖

As cooks in most countries would agree, a modern cheesecake is one of the most popular of all desserts and an excellent gâteau for tea. The basic recipe can be varied in many ways, as given below. Cheesecakes freeze well for up to 3 months.

	Metric/Imperial	American
For the biscuit crust: butter, melted	50 g/2 oz	¼ cup
caster sugar	25 g/1 oz	2 tbsp
digestive biscuits (Graham crackers), crushed	100 g/4 oz	1 cup
For the cheesecake: butter	50 g/2 oz	¼ cup
caster sugar	75 g/3 oz	6 tbsp
vanilla essence (extract)	¼–½ teasp	¼–½ teasp
eggs	3	3
cream or curd cheese	450 g/1 lb	1 lb
double (heavy) cream	5 tbsp	⅓ cup

Grease the sides of a 20 to 23 cm/8 to 9 inch cake tin with a loose base (preferably a spring form tin), as shown on this page. Blend the butter, sugar and biscuit crumbs together. Press into the base of the tin.

Cream the butter, sugar and vanilla essence (extract) together. Separate the eggs, beat the yolks into the creamed mixture. Add the cheese and beat thoroughly. Whip the cream in one bowl and the egg whites in a second bowl. Mix 1 tablespoon egg white with the cheese mixture to soften this. Fold in the cream, then the egg whites.

Spoon into the tin over the biscuit-crumb base. Cook in the centre of a slow oven, 150°C/300°F Gas Mark 2, for 1–1¼ hours until firm but still light in colour. Allow to cool in the oven with the door ajar. When cold, remove from the tin and decorate as desired.

VARIATIONS

Fruit-topped Cheesecake: Top the cheesecake with whipped cream and fresh fruit.

● *Lemon Cheesecake:* Omit the vanilla essence (extract) and add 1 teaspoon grated lemon rind to the butter and sugar; whip only 3 tablespoons (4 tbsp) cream. Add 2 tablespoons (3 tbsp) lemon juice to the cheese mixture before adding the cream and egg whites.

● Other fruit juice could be used instead of lemon juice.

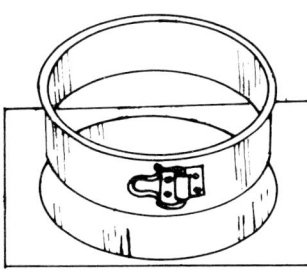

A springform cake tin (pan) is ideal for cheesecakes and any delicate cakes. The sides unlock and the tin has a loose base as shown.

Grape Cheesecake

Illustrated in colour on page 166

No Cooking   Makes 1 cake   ❖❖

The cheesecake pictured on page 166 is made by setting the cheese mixture with gelatine.

	Metric/Imperial	American
For the biscuit crust: butter, melted	50 g/2 oz	¼ cup
caster sugar	25 g/1 oz	2 tbsp
digestive biscuits (Graham crackers), crushed	100 g/4 oz	1 cup crushed
For the cheesecake: white wine	4 tbsp	5 tbsp
gelatine	15 g/½ oz	2 envelopes
large eggs	2	2
caster sugar	75 g/3 oz	6 tbsp
curd or cream cheese or cottage cheese, sieved	450 g/1 lb	1 lb
black or white grapes, deseeded and halved*	225 g/8 oz	½ lb
double (heavy) cream	150 ml/¼ pint	⅔ cup
To decorate: double (heavy) or whipping cream	150 ml/¼ pint	⅔ cup
whole grapes, deseeded	to taste	to taste

*the grapes can be skinned if wished

Prepare the tin, as in the recipe left. Blend together the butter, sugar and biscuit crumbs. Press into the base of the tin.

Put the wine into a heat-resistant bowl, sprinkle the gelatine on top. Place over a pan of hot water until the gelatine has dissolved. Separate the eggs. Beat the egg yolks and sugar over the pan of hot water until thick and creamy. Whisk in the warm gelatine mixture. Allow to cool, but not stiffen. Gradually beat the gelatine and egg mixture into the cheese, add the prepared grapes.

Whip the cream in one bowl and the egg whites in a second bowl. Fold the cream and then the egg whites into the cheesecake mixture. Spoon over the biscuit crumb crust and allow to set.

Whip the cream for decoration, pipe on top of the cheesecake. Decorate with the whole grapes.

A SIMPLE HIGH TEA

A satisfying meal, combining sweet and savoury foods, need not be too complicated to prepare. The menu illustrated overleaf consists of Cheese Scones, made as the recipe on page 147, filled with sliced tomatoes and smoked ham; hot buttered Crumpets, the recipe for which is on page 146; followed by a very luxurious Meringue Gâteau and light, refreshing Layer Sundaes, the recipes for which are given overleaf.

The Grape Cheesecake, which is also illustrated on page 166, would be a pleasant alternative to the gâteau and/or dessert.

MERINGUE GÂTEAU

Cooking Time: 3–3½ hours   Makes 1 cake   ***

	Metric/Imperial	American
egg whites	4	4
caster sugar	225 g/8 oz	1 cup
cornflour (cornstarch)	1 teasp	1 tcasp
white malt or wine vinegar	1 teasp	1 teasp
For the filling and decoration: whipping or double (heavy) cream	300-450 ml/ ½-¾ pint	1¼-scant 2 cups
fruit	as desired	as desired

Above: Grape Cheesecake. Below: Chocolate Cream Gâteau – recipe page 164

LAYER SUNDAES

Cooking Time: 10–15 minutes   Serves 4–6   *

	Metric/Imperial	American
cornflour (cornstarch)	50 g/2 oz	½ cup
milk	750 ml/1¼ pints	generous 3 cups
caster sugar	50–75 g/2–3 oz	4–6 tbsp
butter	25 g/1 oz	2 tbsp
whipping or double (heavy) cream	300 ml/½ pint	1¼ cups
oranges	4	4
grated orange rind	1–2 teasp	1–2 teasp
vanilla essence (extract), optional	to taste	to taste
coffee essence (extract)	1 tbsp or to taste	1 tbsp or to taste

Blend the cornflour (cornstarch) with the cold milk. Put into a saucepan, add the sugar and butter. Stir over a low heat until thickened and smooth. Pour into a bowl, cover to prevent a skin forming and allow to cool.

Whip the cream and fold most of this into the cornflour mixture. Cut the peel from the oranges, cut out the segments of fruit. Spoon one third of the creamy mixture into a bowl, add the finely grated orange rind and spoon into 4 to 6 tall sundae glasses. Top with the orange segments, then with one third of the creamy cornflour mixture (this could be flavoured with vanilla). Blend the coffee essence (extract) with the remaining creamy cornflour and spoon this into the glasses. Top with the remaining cream.

Simple High Tea – see page 165

Either brush 2 or 3 baking trays or sheets with a few drops of oil or use silicone (non-stick) paper or silicone baking trays or cut rounds of greaseproof (waxed) paper, put on to baking trays and oil lightly. It is advisable to oil silicone trays lightly when baking large meringue rounds.

Whisk the egg whites until stiff, add the sugar as described on page 157 and incorporate the cornflour (cornstarch). Fold in the vinegar. Form 3 equal sized rounds with the meringue mixture. Bake in a very slow oven, 90 to 110°C/200 to 225°F Gas Mark 0 to ¼, for approximately 3 to 3½ hours. Remove from the baking trays, cool slightly, take off the paper if this has been used. Allow to become cold.

Whip the cream, prepare the fruit (canned fruit must be well drained). Sandwich the rounds of meringue with some of the cream and fruit. Use the remaining cream and fruit to decorate the top of the gâteau.

Savouries

The recipes given on the pages that follow are for a wide variety of occasions. The first recipes are for classic savouries, and adaptations of these, that have been a feature of formal dinner party menus for a considerable time. This course is served after the dessert, or chosen by some people instead of a dessert.
The portions are small, as this is correct, but by following the recipe and making it serve 2 instead of 4 persons you will have a savoury that can be served for a light luncheon or supper. A salad or vegetable would make the meal more satisfying. On pages 176 and 177 are ideas for savouries to serve with pre-dinner drinks.

WELSH RAREBIT

Cooking Time: 10 minutes   Serves 4–6   *

This cheese dish is undoubtedly the best known of all British savouries. It often is called 'Welsh Rabbit' and there is mild controversy as to which title is correct. The recipe below is one of many versions of this dish, which obviously evolved from toasted cheese, see under Variations. The combination of milk or cream and beer or ale produces a piquant flavour and creamy texture.

	Metric/Imperial	American
butter	15 g/½ oz	1 tbsp
flour	15 g/½ oz	2 tbsp
milk or single (light) cream	2 tbsp	3 tbsp
beer	1½ tbsp	2 tbsp
salt and pepper	to taste	to taste
made mustard	½-1 teasp	½-1 teasp
cheese, grated*	225 g/8 oz	2 cups
large slices of bread	2–3	2–3
To garnish: parsley	few sprigs	few sprigs

*vary the cheese, it can be Double Gloucester (a favourite for this dish), Cheddar, Cheshire, Lancashire (crumble rather than grate this). Stilton makes a wonderful rarebit

Heat the butter in a saucepan, stir in the flour then blend with the milk or cream and beer. Stir over a very low heat for a few minutes to cook the flour. Add the salt, pepper, mustard and finally the cheese. Do not cook again in the pan for the cheese will be melted under the grill (broiler).

Toast the bread (some people prefer it to be toasted on one side only). Spread with the cheese mixture, this would go over the untoasted side. Heat under a preheated grill for 2 to 3 minutes or until the cheese melts and turns golden brown. Cut away the crusts from the toast and halve each slice for a savoury at the end of a meal. Top with parsley and serve with made mustard and/or Worcestershire sauce.

VARIATIONS
An easier mixture is made by blending 25 g/1 oz (2 tbsp) butter, ½ to 1 teaspoon made mustard, 225 g/8 oz (2 cups) grated cheese, 1 tablespoon beer or ale or milk and seasoning to taste.

● *Toasted Cheese:* Cut slices of Cheddar, Cheshire, Stilton or other good cooking cheese, put on to buttered toast and heat until melted. If preferred, the cheese can be grated and blended with a knob of butter.

● *Buck Rarebit:* This makes a sustaining light supper dish. Make the Welsh Rarebit as before and top each portion with 1 or 2 poached eggs.

● *Kent Rarebit:* Fry thin slices of peeled dessert or cooking (baking) apples in hot butter until just soft. Put on to hot unbuttered toast. Cover with the Welsh Rarebit mixture or grated cheese and heat under the grill (broiler) as the basic recipe.

● *York Rarebit:* York has long been famous for its smoked and cooked ham. In this recipe, a slice of cold cooked ham is put on the hot buttered toast then topped with the Welsh Rarebit mixture and heated as in the basic recipe.

Welsh Rarebit

EASY SAVOURIES

Some of the best liked after-dinner savouries are extremely simple as the following recipes show.

Angels on Horseback: Allow 1 large or 2 small oysters per person. Season lightly with pepper, add a squeeze of lemon juice. De-rind half a rasher (slice) of bacon, stretch with the back of a knife. Roll around the uncooked oyster(s) and secure with a wooden cocktail stick (toothpick). Cook under the grill (broiler) for a few minutes until the bacon is crisp and the oyster(s) lightly cooked. Serve on a small square of buttered toast or fried bread.

Now that oysters are expensive, cooked halved scallops or cooked mussels could be substituted.

Devils on Horseback: This is similar to the recipe above but stoned (pitted) cooked and well-drained prunes are used instead of oysters. The prunes can be filled with a little pâté or a tiny portion of cream cheese.

Marrow Toasts: Ask the butcher to crack large marrow bones. Remove the marrow, cut into tiny neat pieces. Simmer in seasoned water for 1 to 2 minutes, then drain through a fine sieve. Meanwhile, fry a small finely chopped onion or shallot in a little hot butter. Blend with the marrow. Serve on hot buttered toast and top with chopped parsley. The shallot or onion could be omitted, but it makes the savoury more interesting.

Mushrooms on Toast: Fry or grill (broil) small button mushrooms. Serve on hot toast, top with chopped parsley or a sprinkling of finely grated cheese.

Sardines on Toast: Serve boned canned or cooked fresh sardines on toast. Heat for 2 to 3 minutes under the grill (broiler). Top with chopped parsley and grated cheese. If preferred, bone and mash the sardines and blend with a squeeze of lemon juice, a few drops of Worcestershire sauce and a pinch of cayenne pepper.

CHEESE SOUFFLÉ RAREBIT

Cooking Time: 6–7 minutes   Serves 4–8   *

	Metric/Imperial	American
Cheshire red or white cheese, finely grated	225 g/8 oz	2 cups
mustard powder	1–2 teasp	1–2 teasp
light ale or milk	1 tbsp	1 tbsp
salt and pepper	to taste	to taste
eggs	4	4
large slices of bread	4	4
cayenne pepper or paprika	to taste	to taste

Blend the cheese with the mustard and ale or milk, add a little seasoning. Separate the eggs, whisk the whites until very stiff. Beat the egg yolks into the cheese mixture, then fold in the egg whites.

Meanwhile, toast the bread. Cut the slices into halves if serving as a savoury for the end of a meal. Spoon the fluffy cheese mixture on the toast, keep this away from the edges of the toast as the soft mixture spreads. It is quite a good idea to put the rarebit in a flameproof dish. Cook slowly under a preheated grill (broiler) until pale and golden in colour. Top with a very light dusting of cayenne pepper or paprika and serve at once.

CHEESE STRAWS

Illustrated in colour on page 175
Cooking Time: 7–10 minutes   Makes about 48   **

	Metric/Imperial	American
plain (all-purpose) flour	100 g/4 oz	1 cup
salt	good pinch	good pinch
cayenne pepper	shake	shake
mustard powder	1–2 teasp	1–2 teasp
butter	75 g/3 oz	6 tbsp
finely grated cheese, preferably Parmesan	75 g/3 oz	¾ cup
egg yolk	1	1
To glaze: egg white *or* egg yolk	1 1	1 1
To garnish: parsley	few sprigs	few sprigs

Sift the flour with the salt, pepper and mustard. Rub in the butter, add the cheese and bind with the egg yolk. If the egg yolk is small, a very few drops of water may be needed.

Roll out on a lightly floured board until about 5 mm/¼ inch in thickness and a neat oblong shape. Cut into fingers about 5 mm/¼ inch wide and 5 cm/2 inches long. Lift on to lightly greased baking trays and brush either with the egg white or egg yolk blended with a few drops of water.

Bake towards the top of a hot oven, 220°C/425°F Gas Mark 7, for approximately 7 to 10 minutes until crisp and golden brown. Cool for a few minutes before lifting from the trays, for the straws are very fragile and must be handled with care when hot. Arrange neatly on a dish to serve, garnish with parsley.

TO SERVE CHEESE STRAWS

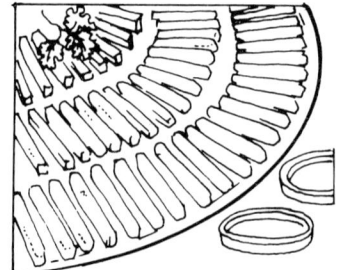

Cheese Straws can be served as in the recipe above, or use some of the cheese pastry dough to cut small rings.

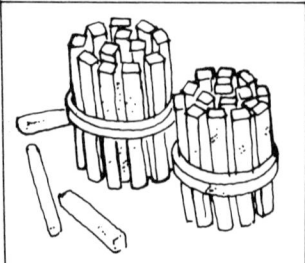

Bake the rings as the timing and temperature in the recipe above, then put several straws through each ring.

MAINLY EGGS

Eggs are an excellent food to make quick and nourishing meals. The basic methods of cooking eggs can be adapted in many ways.

Baked Eggs: Heat a little butter in an ovenproof dish. Add the eggs (allow 1 to 2 per person), top with a few tablespoons of seasoned cream. Bake towards the top of a moderately hot oven, 200°C/400°F Gas Mark 6, for 10 to 15 minutes.

Cooked asparagus tips, grated cheese, prawns (shrimp) can be added to the butter in the dish to make a more interesting meal.

Boiled Eggs: Hard-boiled (hard-cooked) eggs can be used in a variety of dishes; there are examples on this page. Hard-boiled eggs coated in a plain mayonnaise or one flavoured with grated cheese make an excellent hors d'oeuvre or supper dish. The cold eggs can be halved and the yolks removed and mashed with grated or cream or cottage cheese or with sardines or chopped anchovy fillets, and returned to the egg whites.

Fried Eggs: Fried eggs and bacon and/or sausages are not only one of the traditional breakfast dishes but a favourite meal in Britain for lunch or supper. Fried, or poached, eggs can be served on creamed spinach or other vegetables.

Poached Eggs: This is one of the most adaptable ways of cooking eggs. Break the eggs into steadily boiling salted water; move the water round the eggs with a metal spoon to set the whites in a good shape. Cook for 3 to 4 minutes or until set to personal taste. The eggs can be served on toast or coated with Cheese Sauce, see page 102.

Scrambled Eggs: If cooked scrambled eggs are served with smoked salmon or mackerel, they make a very satisfying dish.

Many other ingredients can be cooked with the eggs, such as chopped cooked prawns (shrimp) or other shellfish, or finely diced cooked chicken or ham or grated cheese. The secret of good scrambled eggs is slow cooking and the minimum stirring. If scrambling eggs for 2 people, heat 25 to 40 g/1 to 1½ oz (2 to 3 tbsp) butter in a saucepan. Beat 4 eggs with 1 to 2 tablespoons milk or, better still, use cream; season lightly, add to the hot butter. Cook slowly over a low heat until the consistency of thick cream. Stir very lightly as the mixture cooks. Serve as soon as cooked.

Scrambled eggs can be served cold as a filling for sandwiches. Cook lightly and, when cold, blend with a little mayonnaise. Chopped watercress leaves or finely chopped red or green pepper can be added to the cooked eggs.

Cheese Straws can be served with drinks or as part of a cheese board.

ANGLESEY EGGS

Cooking Time: 35–40 minutes   Serves 4–6   ✳✳

	Metric/Imperial	American
old potatoes, weight when peeled	450 g/1 lb	1 lb
salt and pepper	to taste	to taste
small leeks, cut into small pieces	6	6
butter or margarine	50 g/2 oz	¼ cup
flour	25 g/1 oz	¼ cup
milk	300 ml/½ pint	1¼ cups
eggs, hard-boiled (hard cooked)	6–8	6–8
Cheddar cheese, grated	75 g/3 oz	¾ cup
To garnish: chopped parsley	1 tbsp	1 tbsp

Cook the potatoes in boiling salted water for 15 minutes. Add the leeks and continue to cook for a further 10 minutes or until both vegetables are tender. Strain and mash well or sieve the vegetables if you want to pipe a border around the edge of the dish. Beat in half the butter or margarine. Spoon or pipe around the edge of a flameproof dish and make a deep border; keep hot.

Meanwhile, heat the remaining 25 g/1 oz (2 tbsp) butter or margarine in a saucepan, stir in the flour. Cook over a low heat for 2 to 3 minutes then blend in the milk. Stir as the sauce comes to the boil and thickens. Cut the eggs into thick slices, add to the sauce together with most of the cheese and heat for 3 to 4 minutes. Season well then spoon into the centre of the potato and leek ring. Top with the last of the cheese. Heat for a few minutes under a preheated grill (broiler), or in a hot oven, 220°C/425°F Gas Mark 7. Sprinkle the parsley over the vegetable border.

FRIED BOILED EGGS

Cooking Time: 12–13 minutes   ✳

This makes a quick and easy hot snack. Hard-boil (hard-cook) the eggs (allow 1 to 2 per person and 10 minutes steady cooking). Remove from the water. Gently crack the shells of the eggs; plunge the eggs into cold water – this prevents them from over-cooking (which is the reason for the dark line around the egg yolks). Shell the eggs. Coat in a little seasoned flour. Brush with beaten egg then thoroughly coat in crisp breadcrumbs.

It is better to deep fry the eggs, so heat oil or fat to 190°C/375°F and fry the eggs for 2 to 3 minutes until crisp on the outside. If shallow frying, turn several times. Drain on absorbent paper (kitchen towels).

Serve with a salad or hot vegetables.

LIGHT AND DELICATE

Soufflés have been a favourite dish in Britain for many generations. A Cheese Soufflé is frequently served as a savoury at the end of a meal. It is then usual to eat it with a dessert spoon and fork. Soufflés, like Cheese Pudding, make excellent light savoury dishes.

CHEESE PUDDING

Cooking Time: 30 minutes   Serves 4   **

	Metric/Imperial	American
milk	300 ml/½ pint	1¼ cups
butter	40 g/1½ oz	3 tbsp
soft fine breadcrumbs	75 g/3 oz	1½ cups
dry mustard	pinch	pinch
salt and pepper	to taste	to taste
single (light) cream	150 ml/¼ pint	⅔ cup
eggs	3	3
Cheddar, Cheshire or Double Gloucester cheese, finely grated	175 g/6 oz	1½ cups

Put the milk and butter into a saucepan. Heat gently until the butter has melted. Add the breadcrumbs, mustard, salt and pepper. Allow the mixture to stand for 20 to 25 minutes.

Beat the cream with the eggs, strain into the breadcrumbs mixture then add the cheese; stir to blend. Pour the mixture into a greased 1.2 litre/2 pint (5 cup) ovenproof pie or soufflé dish. Bake in the centre of a moderate to moderately hot oven, 180 to 190°C/350 to 375°F Gas Mark 4 to 5, for 30 minutes or until well risen and firm to the touch. Serve at once.

Cheese Soufflé

CHEESE SOUFFLÉ

Cooking Time: 40–45 minutes   Serves 4   **

Vary the cheeses used in the soufflé according to the particular flavour required. If you like a soufflé that is soft and creamy in the centre, use the larger amount of milk given. For an equally light, but firmer, texture use the smaller amount. The little quantity of cream gives a particularly good taste.

	Metric/Imperial	American
butter	25 g/1 oz	2 tbsp
flour	25 g/1 oz	¼ cup
milk	150–200 ml/ 5–7 fl oz	⅔- generous ¾ cup
double (heavy) cream	2 tbsp	3 tbsp
eggs	3	3
cheese*, grated or crumbled	150 g/5 oz	1¼ cups
salt and pepper	to taste	to taste
made mustard	½–1 teasp	½–1 teasp
egg whites	2	2

*choose Caerphilly or Cheddar or Cheshire or Double Gloucester or Stilton cheese

Grease the sides of an 18 cm/7 inch soufflé dish. Heat the butter in a large saucepan, blend in the flour. Stir over a low heat for 2 to 3 minutes then add the milk and cream. Stir over the heat as the sauce comes to the boil and thickens. Remove from the heat. Separate the eggs, beat the yolks into the sauce. Add the cheese and seasonings. Whisk all the egg whites in a bowl until they stand in peaks, but do not overwhip. Fold into the cheese mixture with a metal spoon.

Spoon the mixture into the soufflé dish. Bake in the centre of a moderate to moderately hot oven, 180 to 190°C/350 to 375°F Gas Mark 4 to 5, for 30 to 35 minutes. Serve as soon as the soufflé is baked.

VARIATIONS

Add a little smoked cooked haddock or smoked cooked ham to the other ingredients in the Cheese Soufflé above. It is important, though, not to exceed a total weight of 225 g/8 oz (½ lb) for the flavouring ingredients, otherwise the soufflé cannot rise.

● *Chicken Soufflé:* Use finely diced cooked chicken instead of cheese, and chicken stock instead of milk in the recipe above. Turkey and game birds could be used instead.

● *Fish Soufflé:* Follow the recipe for the Cheese Soufflé, but use fish stock instead of milk and up to 225 g/8 oz (½ lb) finely flaked fish instead of cheese. Delicate white fish, such as pike or whiting, can be flaked without pre-cooking, but more solid fish should be lightly cooked. Shellfish should be finely chopped.

● *Vegetable Soufflé:* Use a vegetable purée (such as carrot, spinach or other vegetables) instead of the milk. Mushrooms can be lightly cooked in butter, finely chopped and added to the Cheese Soufflé.

BÉARNAISE EGGS

Cooking Time: 15 minutes   Serves 4   ❖❖

	Metric/Imperial	American
For the Béarnaise Sauce: white wine vinegar	2 tbsp	3 tbsp
small shallot or onion, finely chopped	1	1
tarragon	small sprig	small sprig
thyme	small sprig	small sprig
egg yolks	2	2
unsalted butter, warmed slightly	50 g/2 oz	¼ cup
salt and pepper	to taste	to taste
chopped chervil or parsley	1 teasp	1 teasp
chopped tarragon	½ teasp	½ teasp
button mushrooms	100 g/4 oz	¼ lb
butter	50 g/2 oz	¼ cup
large slices of bread	4–8*	4–8*
eggs	4–8*	4–8*

*depending upon personal requirements

Heat the vinegar with the shallot or onion, tarragon and thyme until reduced to 1 tablespoon. Strain and put into a heat resistant bowl with the egg yolks. Beat well to blend then stand over a pan of hot, but not boiling, water and whisk until thick and creamy. Beat the butter in very gradually, add a little seasoning and the herbs.

Meanwhile wipe, but do not peel, the mushrooms. Heat the butter in a frying pan (skillet), fry the mushrooms until tender. Toast the bread, top with the mushrooms and any butter left in the pan, keep hot. Poach the eggs in seasoned water (see page 169), drain and place on the toast with the mushrooms. Coat the eggs with the sauce and serve at once.

Note: This is the same recipe for Béarnaise Sauce as one would serve with steak or other savoury ingredients.

HERB OMELETTE

Cooking Time: 5–6 minutes   Serves 2   ❖

	Metric/Imperial	American
eggs	4	4
salt and pepper	to taste	to taste
water, optional	1 tbsp	1 tbsp
chopped herbs*	2 tbsp or to taste	3 tbsp or to taste
butter	40 g/1½ oz	3 tbsp

*use plenty of chervil or parsley and chives, but basil, rosemary, savory, tarragon and thyme should be used more sparingly

Blend the eggs with the seasoning, water (this makes a lighter omelette) and herbs. Heat the butter in a 15 to 18 cm/6 to 7 inch omelette or frying pan (skillet); take

Cheese Omelette

out about 1 tablespoon of the butter and add it to the eggs. This makes a great difference to the flavour of the omelette.

Pour the eggs into the hot butter. Wait about 30 seconds, or until the eggs have formed a lightly set layer on the bottom of the pan, then tilt and, with the help of a palette knife or fork, push the top liquid egg to the sides of the pan. Continue like this until the eggs are set to personal taste. Fold or roll the omelette away from the handle and tip on to a heated dish.

VARIATIONS
There are many other ingredients that can be used to flavour the omelette, e.g. blend diced cooked bacon or ham or chicken or chopped shellfish with the eggs.
● Fill the omelette with hot tomatoes or cooked mushrooms or other vegetables or with Cheese Sauce, page 102, and cooked vegetables before folding or rolling.
● *Cheese Omelette:* Blend about 50 g/2 oz (½ cup) grated cheese with the eggs before making the omelette or sprinkle this over the cooked omelette before it is rolled or folded.
● *Macaroni Omelette:* Blend about 2 tablespoons (3 tbsp) hot cooked macaroni with the eggs. Add 1 sliced tomato, 1 to 2 tablespoons (2 to 3 tbsp) diced green pepper and 1 tablespoon very finely diced onion, then cook as above. If preferred, lightly cook the tomato, pepper and onion in a little butter then blend with the eggs and macaroni; cook as above.

DISHES BASED ON FISH AND MEAT

The term 'bangers and mash' is well known in England, for it means sausages and mashed potatoes. The sausages can be beef or pork or a mixture of these meats. Other flavourings are often available too, such as game or turkey sausages. The sausages can be fried or grilled (broiled) for 15 to 20 minutes or baked in a moderately hot oven, 200°C/400°F Gas Mark 6, for a slightly longer period.

The recipe right uses sausagemeat in an interesting way.

KEDGEREE

Cooking Time: 25–30 minutes   Serves 4   **

This combination of rice and smoked haddock was obviously brought into Britain when trade flourished with the East India Company. It is a much simplified version of the Indian Khicharhi which included lentils and spices as well as fish and rice. In the days when a large menu was served at breakfast time, a kedgeree was frequently one of the dishes selected. It makes an excellent light savoury dish.

	Metric/Imperial	American
long grain rice	175 g/ 6 oz	scant 1 cup
water	350 ml/12 fl oz	1½ cups
salt and pepper	to taste	to taste
smoked haddock, weight when skinned and boned	350–450 g/12 oz-1 lb	¾-1 lb
butter	50 g/2 oz	¼ cup
small onion, finely chopped	1	1
eggs, hard-boiled (hard-cooked)	2	2
cayenne pepper	to taste	to taste
To garnish: chopped parsley	1 tbsp	1 tbsp

The method of cooking rice today is very simple. Use twice the weight or volume of water to the amount of rice. If using precooked rice, follow packet directions.

Put the rice, with the cold water and a little salt, into a saucepan. Bring the water to the boil, stir briskly, cover the pan and simmer for 15 minutes or until the rice is just tender and all the liquid has evaporated.

Cut the smoked haddock into portions. Put into a dish, cover with boiling water and allow to stand for 5 minutes. Remove the bones, skin and flake the fish coarsely, take care not to mash it.

Meanwhile, heat a little of the butter in a saucepan. Add the onion and fry until transparent, but do not allow to brown. Shell the eggs, chop the whites and sieve the yolks or chop finely. Stir the flaked fish, onion, egg whites and the rest of the butter into the cooked rice. Season rather highly, remembering that the smoked haddock gives a certain amount of salt to the dish. Heat through gently and pile on a flat heated dish. Make a large yellow cross over the top with the sieved or chopped egg yolks and top with parsley.

WILTSHIRE PORKIES

Cooking Time: 15 minutes   Serves 4   *

This simple combination of sausagemeat, flavourings and light crisp batter, with apple, makes an interesting supper dish, which is extremely economical.

	Metric/Imperial	American
For the Porkies: pork sausagemeat	450 g/1 lb	1 lb
chopped sage	½ teasp	½ teasp
chopped thyme	¼ teasp	¼ teasp
chopped parsley	2 teasp	2 teasp
egg yolk	1	1
For the batter: self-raising flour	100 g/4 oz	1 cup
salt and pepper	to taste	to taste
egg yolk	1	1
water	200 ml/7½ fl oz	1 cup
egg whites	2	2
To fry: deep oil or fat		
To garnish: dessert or cooking (baking) apples, peeled, cored and sliced	4	4
parsley	few sprigs	few sprigs

Blend the sausagemeat with the chopped herbs and egg yolk. Form into small balls. In Wiltshire, these are sometimes partially cooked before coating with the batter, but this stage should not be necessary if the fat is hot and the sausagemeat balls are fried carefully.

To make the batter, blend the flour with the seasoning, egg yolk and water. Whisk the egg whites until stiff; add to the batter just before coating the Porkies. Heat the oil or fat to 185°C/365°F. Dip the sausagemeat balls in the batter, lower into the hot fat and fry steadily for approximately 10 minutes until crisp and golden brown. Drain on absorbent paper (kitchen towels).

Coat the apple slices in the batter and fry for about 5 minutes until crisp on the outside. Arrange on a heated dish with the Porkies; garnish with parsley.

TO FRY ONION RINGS

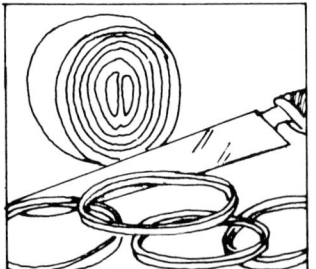

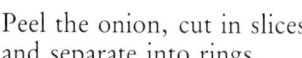

Peel the onion, cut in slices and separate into rings.

Dip the rings in a little milk then coat in flour.

Fry in hot oil or fat until crisp and brown. Drain on absorbent paper (kitchen towels).

LIVER TOASTS WITH PALOISE SAUCE

Cooking Time: 15–20 minutes   Serves 4   **

	Metric/Imperial	American
For the Paloise Sauce: egg yolks	2	2
lemon juice or white wine vinegar	1 tbsp	1 tbsp
salt and pepper	to taste	to taste
cayenne pepper, optional	to taste	to taste
unsalted butter, warmed slightly	50 g/2 oz	¼ cup
finely chopped mint	2 teasp	2 teasp
For the toasts: lambs' liver	225 g/8 oz	½ lb
butter	50 g/2 oz	¼ cup
small shallots or onions, finely chopped	2	2
bacon rashers (slices), de-rinded and finely chopped	2	2
large slices of bread	4–8*	4–8*

*depending upon personal requirements

Make the sauce before cooking the liver. Put the egg yolks, lemon juice or vinegar into a heat resistant bowl. Add a little seasoning. Stand the bowl over a pan of hot, but not boiling, water and whisk until thick and creamy. Gradually beat in the butter; do not add this too quickly, otherwise the sauce will curdle. Lastly stir in the mint.

Meanwhile, cut the liver into narrow strips. Heat the butter in a pan, fry the chopped shallots or onions and bacon until nearly tender. Add the liver and continue cooking for a few minutes only. Toast the bread. Spoon the liver mixture on to the toast and top with the sauce. *Note:* Paloise Sauce, made as above, is excellent with cooked lamb.

VARIATION
Kidney Toasts with Hollandaise Sauce: Use lambs' kidneys in place of liver and top with Hollandaise Sauce. This is made in exactly the same way as Paloise Sauce but without the mint.

CURRIES
A meat or poultry curry is generally served as a main course, but the Curried Eggs, right, makes an excellent light dish. The curry sauce given in the recipe is a good basic one, which can be used with all kinds of food.
Fish Curry: Use fish or chicken stock as the liquid. Make the sauce, add the portions of uncooked white fish. Heat for a few minutes, then allow the fish and sauce to stand for several hours away from the heat so that the fish absorbs the curry flavour. Reheat just before serving.
Cooked Meat or Poultry Curry: Follow the advice under Fish Curry. If using uncooked meat or poultry, brown this with the onions and garlic, remove from the pan. Make the sauce, but add an extra 300 ml/½ pint (1¼ cups) liquid. Return the meat or poultry to the sauce and simmer until tender; allow the same cooking time as if making a stew with the uncooked meat or poultry.

CURRIED EGGS

Cooking Time: 1¼ hours   Serves 4   **

Eggs, like many other foods, can be served in a curry sauce. This sauce freezes well for up to 3 months so it is useful to make a large quantity; divide into family-sized portions and freeze. This means it takes only a very short time to prepare a light meal. The range of modern curry powders and paste enables the cook to choose the strength most desired.

	Metric/Imperial	American
For the curry sauce: ghee (butter, clarified as page 17)	50 g/2 oz	¼ cup
small onions, finely chopped	2	2
garlic cloves, crushed	1–2	1–2
small dessert apple, peeled and finely diced, optional	1	1
flour	1 tbsp	1 tbsp
curry powder	1–2 tbsp	1–3 tbsp
curry paste, optional	1–2 teasp	1–2 teasp
stock* or water	450 ml/¾ pint	scant 2 cups
coconut milk, see below	150 ml/¼ pint	⅔ cup
sultanas (golden raisins)	1–2 tbsp	1–3 tbsp
chutney	1 tbsp	1 tbsp
lemon juice	½ tbsp	½ tbsp
salt and pepper	to taste	to taste
eggs, hard-boiled (hard-cooked)	8	8

*this must be well strained and chicken stock should be used with the eggs

Heat the ghee in a pan, gently fry the onions, garlic and apple (if using this) for several minutes. Stir in the flour, curry powder and paste and cook for several minutes, stirring well. Add the stock or water and coconut milk (see below), stir over a low heat until very slightly thickened. Put in the sultanas, chutney, lemon juice and seasoning to taste. Cover the pan and simmer for 1 hour.

Add the shelled eggs and heat for a few minutes. Serve with cooked rice and dishes of dried and fresh fruit, desiccated coconut, sliced tomatoes and green pepper and diced cucumber blended with yoghurt.

TO MAKE COCONUT MILK
Grate about 100 g/4 oz (1 cup) fresh coconut into a heat resistant bowl, or use 100 g/4 oz desiccated (1¼ cups shredded) coconut.

Add 150 ml/¼ pint (⅔ cup) boiling water. Leave for 2 hours; press the coconut several times to extract the maximum flavour. Strain and use as in the recipe above.

BASED ON PASTRY

The continental quiche (savoury custard tart) has become a great favourite in British homes. This is not surprising, for there are many traditional recipes for savoury tarts, flans and quiches requiring the same baking technique as the sweet custard tart which is so well liked.

The following recipes make excellent use of our products. The flans freeze well for up to 3 months. It is better to use single (light) cream, rather than milk, if you intend freezing the cooked flans.

Cheese pastry: The mixture used for Cheese Straws, given on page 168 and illustrated on the opposite page, is very often referred to as pastry. The dough is too brittle and rich to use for making a flan, it would break if you tried to mould it in any way.

If you would like to make a Cheese Pastry to line the flan cases, follow the recipe under Parsley Pie on this page.

Above: Egg and Prawn Tartlets – recipe page 176

PARSLEY PIE

Cooking Time: 55–60 minutes   Serves 4   **

	Metric/Imperial	American
For the cheese pastry: plain (all-purpose) flour	175 g/6 oz	1½ cups
salt	pinch	pinch
cayenne pepper	shake	shake
mustard powder	pinch	pinch
butter	50 g/2 oz	¼ cup
Cheddar cheese, finely grated	50 g/2 oz	½ cup
egg yolk	1	1
water or milk, see Note under recipe opposite	to bind	to bind
For the filling: small leeks, cooked and finely chopped	2	2
bacon rashers (slices), cooked and finely chopped	2–3	2–3
milk	150 ml/¼ pint	⅔ cup
eggs	3	3
chopped parsley	3–4 tbsp	4–5 tbsp
salt and pepper	to taste	to taste

Sift the flour and seasonings, rub in the butter, add the cheese, egg yolk and enough water or milk to bind. Roll out the pastry and line a 20 cm/8 inch flan dish or ring. Bake blind for 15 minutes as in the recipe opposite.

Arrange the well-drained leeks and bacon in the partially baked pastry case. Warm the milk, blend with the eggs and parsley, season. Pour over the leeks mixture.

Reduce the oven heat to slow, 150°C/300°F Gas Mark 2, and bake for a further 40 to 45 minutes or until both the pastry and filling are firm. Serve hot or cold.

VARIATIONS
Use shortcrust pastry (basic pie dough) as the pastry in Shrimp and Cheese Flan.

SHRIMP AND CHEESE FLAN

Cooking Time: 40–45 minutes   Serves 4   **

	Metric/Imperial	American
For the shortcrust pastry (basic pie dough): plain (all-purpose) flour	175 g/6 oz	1½ cups
salt	pinch	pinch
butter	85 g/3 oz	6 tbsp
water or milk, see Note		
For the filling: milk	150 ml/¼ pint	²/₃ cup
eggs	2	2
Lancashire cheese, crumbled	100 g/4 oz	1 cup
peeled (shelled) shrimps or prawns (American shrimp)	100 g/4 oz	¾ cup
salt and pepper	to taste	to taste
To garnish: peeled shrimps or prawns	4–6	4–6
parsley	few sprigs	few sprigs

Sift the flour and salt, rub in the butter and bind with the water or milk. Roll out the pastry and line a deep 20 cm/8 inch flan dish or flan ring placed on an upturned baking tray or sheet. By having the tray or sheet upside down and without a rim, it is very easy to slide the cooked flan on to a serving dish. Bake the pastry blind (without a filling) in the centre of a moderately hot oven, 200°C/400°F Gas Mark 6, for 15 minutes.

Meanwhile, warm the milk and blend with the eggs, cheese and shrimps or prawns (shrimp); larger prawns could be chopped. Season lightly and spoon into the partially baked pastry case. Reduce the heat to very moderate, 160°C/325°F Gas Mark 3, and bake in the centre of the oven for 25 to 30 minutes or until pastry and filling are firm. Serve hot or cold. Garnish with the extra shrimps or prawns and parsley.
Note: It is better to use milk rather than water to bind the pastry if you intend freezing this.

VARIATIONS
Use chopped cooked bacon or ham or chicken instead of the fish.
● Smoked salmon or other smoked fish is excellent as part of the filling. Use Cheddar rather than Lancashire cheese.
● If filling a deep flan ring or case, use 50 per cent more filling; the pastry should be adequate if rolled thinly.

Left: Cheese Straws – recipe page 168, Stilton Whirls – recipe page 176. Savoury Cheese Bites – recipe page 176

TO SERVE WITH DRINKS

There are many savoury dishes that can be served with drinks. These should be small and easy to pick up with the fingers.

The photograph on pages 174–175 shows a favourite savoury, Cheese Straws. The recipe is on page 168. The crisp biscuit-like savouries keep well when stored in an airtight tin. They do tend to become ultra-brittle when frozen.

The recipes that follow give a variety of easy savoury dishes. If these are made somewhat larger, they can be served as light savoury dishes. The two recipes on pages 174 and 175 also are excellent as cocktail snacks. Bake the flans in an 18 to 20 cm/7 to 8 inch square tin or dish to make it easier to cut the cooked hot or cold pastry dishes into 2.5 cm/1 inch squares.

EGG AND PRAWN TARTLETS

Illustrated in colour on page 175

Cooking Time: 15 minutes   Makes 12   ✺✺

	Metric/Imperial	American
Shortcrust Pastry (basic pie dough), as page 175 made with	175 g/6 oz flour etc	1½ cups flour etc
small peeled prawns (shelled shrimp)	100 g/4 oz	¾ cup
mayonnaise	4 tbsp	5 tbsp
anchovy essence (extract)	few drops	few drops
eggs, hard-boiled (hard-cooked)	6	6
To garnish: parsley sprigs	12	12

Roll out the pastry and line 12 shallow patty tins (patty shells). Bake blind just above the centre of a moderately hot to hot oven, 200 to 220°C/400 to 425°F Gas Mark 6 to 7, for about 15 minutes. Allow to cool.

Put 12 small prawns (shrimp) on one side for garnish (halve 6 large ones if necessary). Chop the remainder and put into the pastry cases. Blend the mayonnaise and anchovy essence (extract). Halve the eggs and put with the cut side downwards into the pastry cases. Carefully spoon the flavoured mayonnaise over the eggs and prawns. Garnish with the prawns and parsley as shown in the photograph.

VARIATION

For a cocktail savoury, use the pastry to fill 24 to 30 tiny pastry cases. Bake for 8 to 10 minutes as the temperature above. Chop the prawns and 3 to 4 hard-boiled (hard-cooked) eggs. Bind with a little anchovy flavoured mayonnaise. Fill the pastry cases.

STILTON WHIRLS

Illustrated in colour on page 175

Cooking Time: 15 minutes   Makes 20–24   ✺✺

	Metric/Imperial	American
Puff Pastry, as page 155 made with	100 g/4 oz flour etc	1 cup flour etc
For the filling: Stilton cheese, crumbled	100 g/4 oz	1 cup
cream cheese	50 g/2 oz	¼ cup
cayenne pepper	to taste	to taste
Worcestershire sauce	1 teasp	1 teasp

Roll out the pastry to a rectangle about 27.5 x 15 cm/11 x 6 inches. Blend the ingredients for the filling together, spread over the pastry. Roll up the pastry, starting from one long edge. Cover the roll very lightly with cling film (plastic wrap). Chill for 1 to 2 hours so the roll can be easily handled.

Cut into 20 to 24 slices. Place these on to a lightly moistened baking sheet or tray. Bake just above the centre of a hot to very hot oven, 220 to 230°C/425 to 450°F Gas Mark 7 to 8, for 15 minutes or until firm and golden brown. Serve when freshly baked.

SAVOURY CHEESE BITES

Illustrated in colour on page 175

No Cooking   Makes 30–36   ✺

	Metric/Imperial	American
Cheddar cheese, finely grated	100 g/4 oz	1 cup
cream cheese	75 g/3 oz	6 tbsp
cocktail onions, well-drained and finely chopped	10–12	10–12
gherkins (sweet dill pickles), well-drained and finely chopped	2 tbsp	3 tbsp
salt and cayenne pepper	to taste	to taste
Tabasco (hot pepper) sauce	2–3 drops	2–3 drops
To coat: nuts, finely chopped	50–75 g/ 2–3 oz	½-¾ cup

Blend the cheeses with all the other ingredients except the nuts. Roll into 30 to 36 small balls. Put the nuts on to a flat dish or sheet of paper and coat the tiny balls. Store in the refrigerator or freezer until ready to serve.

CANAPÉS

The base for canapés can be fried bread, pastry, toast or small rounds of bread and butter. Toast is the least successful base for interesting toppings since it becomes over-soggy and soft within a very short time. Small shapes of bread can be fried in shallow or deep fat or oil until brown and crisp, drain, allow to cool. The bread remains crisp for a number of hours.

The rich cheese pastry used for Cheese Straws makes a good base for canapés. Follow the recipe on page 168 but cut the pastry into small rounds, squares or diamond shapes. Bake as for Cheese Straws, then allow to cool.

Brown or rye bread is firmer than white bread and therefore better for cutting into small shapes. Miniature Scotch Pancakes, made as the recipe on page 149, can be used. They are particularly good spread with a flavoured butter before the topping, see right.

Topping for Canapés
Cheese: Choose cream cheese or blend finely grated Cheddar or Cheshire or mashed Stilton cheese with a little whipped cream. Pipe on to the bases.
Eggs: Put teaspoons of lightly scrambled egg or thin slices of hard-boiled (hard-cooked) egg on to the bases. Top with caviare or anchovy fillet or twist of smoked salmon.
Fish: Spread the bases with a little flavoured butter. Top with small pieces of sardine, anchovy fillet, smoked or cooked salmon, smoked eel or with prawns (shrimp).
Meat: Top the bases with pâté or salami or ham shapes.
Vegetables: Top the bases with Herb Butter then cooked button mushrooms or asparagus tips.

BARQUETTES

Cooking Time: 12–15 minutes   Makes 18–24 ❖❖

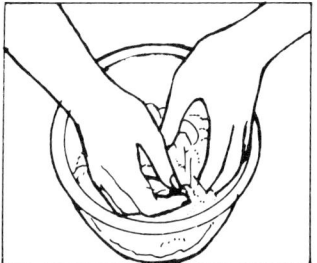

Make Shortcrust Pastry (basic pie dough) or Cheese Pastry made with 175 g/6 oz (1½ cups) flour etc. as page 174.

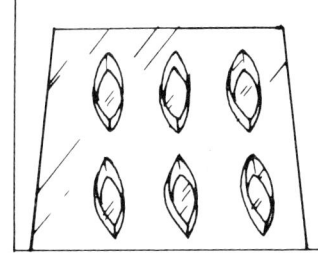

Arrange small boat shaped tins (patty shells) on a baking tray or sheet.

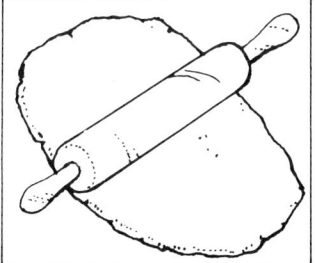

Roll out the pastry into a large oblong shape, sufficiently large to spread over all the boat tins.

Lay the pastry oblong over the shapes then press this down so it fits into each of the tins.

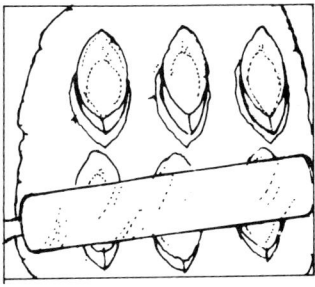

Take the rolling pin and roll firmly over the tins, so cutting off any surplus pastry. Re-roll the surplus and fill any remaining tins. Bake 'blind' just above the centre of a moderately hot to hot oven, 200–220°C/400–425°F Gas Mark 6–7, for 12–15 minutes. Cool and fill.

Fillings for Barquettes
Cheese: Spread a very little Herb Butter into each pastry case. Top with piped cream cheese or finely grated Cheddar or other cheese blended with a little whipped cream. Garnish with tiny pieces or red pepper and gherkin (sweet dill pickle).
Egg: Scramble eggs lightly, cool and blend with a little whipped cream or mayonnaise, then with very finely chopped smoked salmon or finely chopped shellfish or with chopped anchovy fillets. Put into the pastry cases. Garnish with tiny pieces of tomato.
Fish: Spread a little Anchovy, Herb or Lemon Butter into each pastry case. Top with Smoked Salmon Pâté, made as page 17, or with small peeled (shelled) shrimps or prawns or flaked cooked salmon or lobster blended with a very little mayonnaise. Garnish with tiny pieces of cucumber.
Meat and Poultry: Spread a little Herb, Lemon or Mustard Butter into each pastry case. Top with minced (ground) chicken or cooked ham or cooked tongue blended with mayonnaise. Garnish with paprika.

Fill the pastry cases with soft pâté and garnish with very small cocktail onions and/or pieces of gherkin (sweet dill pickle).
Note: These fillings are excellent in small savoury choux buns, page 157.

FLAVOURED BUTTERS

No Cooking ❖

	Metric/Imperial	American
butter*	50–75 g/2–3 oz	4–6 tbsp
flavourings, see method		

*this amount should be sufficient to filling 24 Barquettes

Cream the butter until soft. Add the flavouring as described below.
Anchovy Butter: Blend a few drops of anchovy essence (extract) or well-drained and very finely chopped anchovy fillets to the butter. Add a little pepper if desired.
Herb Butter: Add finely chopped fresh herbs to the butter. Allow approximately 1 tablespoon chopped herbs to 50 g/2 oz (¼ cup) butter, plus a squeeze of lemon juice and a little seasoning. Chervil, chives or parsley are the most suitable.
Lemon Butter: Add a little very finely grated lemon rind and juice to the butter. Season to taste.
Mustard Butter: Blend a little made English mustard or French mustard with the butter. Season to taste.
Watercress Butter: As Herb Butter, but use finely chopped watercress leaves. Season to taste.

Eating Out of Doors

To eat out of doors today can mean a simple picnic of fresh bread, cheese or cold meat, salad and fruit, or a really sustaining barbecue or sophisticated hot or cold meal.
Modern insulated boxes mean one can carry hot or cold meals (obviously not together) with great success. There are many festivities when a picnic meal is an ideal choice.

FOR A COLD PICNIC
Choose fruit juice or a simple hors d'oeuvre such as melon or a fish cocktail, see page 18, which can be prepared ahead, transported in plastic containers and kept well-chilled in the cold box. There are a selection of potted foods on pages 12 to 13 which would be easy to carry and serve with freshly baked rolls or crispbread. Smoked salmon or other smoked fish keep in perfect condition for a considerable period. If the weather is a little chilly, the first course could be an appetizing soup, see page 180 for special suggestions.

To follow the first course, choose a fairly sustaining cold dish, such as cooked game birds, chicken or duck. The Chicken Galantine, page 96, or Game Terrine or Pâté (a sustaining pie) on page 97 are ideal picnic fare. Rather more unusual jellied moulds follow on this and the next page. Tripe is a variety meat that is a great favourite in the North of England and the method of serving it in a mould is unusual, economical and appetizing. The second mould, made with cooked ham and parsley, is light in texture and full of flavour. Obviously these jellied moulds must be well-chilled before placing in the cold box.

Tripe Mould

Serve the main course with an interesting potato salad, recipe for which given on page 180.

The dessert could consist of fresh fruit and cheese, or one of the easy to transport tarts or cheesecakes on pages 132 to 135. The Chester Tart, a close connection with a Lemon Meringue Pie, would be most refreshing if it is possible to carry this carefully, so the delicate almond meringue topping is not spoiled.

Well-chilled white or rosé wines or fruit juice would complete a delicious picnic for hot weather days.

TRIPE MOULD

Cooking Time: 35 minutes   Serves 4 **

	Metric/Imperial	American
dressed (prepared) tripe	675 g/1½ lb	1½ lb
milk, see method	300 ml/½ pint	1¼ cups
medium onions, chopped	3	3
salt and pepper	to taste	to taste
carrots, sliced	450 g/1 lb	1 lb
grated nutmeg	to taste	to taste
gelatine	15 g/½ oz	2 envelopes
button mushrooms, neatly diced	100 g/4 oz	¼ lb
mayonnaise	1 tbsp	1 tbsp
To garnish: mint leaves shredded lettuce or cabbage heart		

Cut the tripe in strips, put into cold water in a saucepan. Bring the water to the boil, then drain. This process, known as 'blanching', whitens the tripe. Place the tripe, milk and onions into the saucepan, add seasoning to taste. Cover the pan and simmer for 30 minutes.

While the tripe is cooking, cook the carrots in boiling salted water, strain and mash with the grated nutmeg and seasoning to taste. Allow to cool.

Lift the tripe and onions out of the liquid, put into a food processor or liquidizer (blender) and switch on until just smooth.

Measure the milk, if less than 225 ml/8 fl oz (1 cup) add a little more. Heat this, sprinkle the gelatine on top and allow to dissolve. Blend the gelatine and milk with the tripe purée. Allow to cool and stiffen slightly. Taste and season well.

Blend the raw mushrooms and mayonnaise.

Take a 1.2 litre/2 pint mould (a shape similar to that in the photograph makes an easy-to-slice mould). Spread nearly all the half set tripe mixture on the base and sides of the mould. Fill the centre cavity with the carrots, then with the mushroom mixture.

Use the remaining jellied tripe to spread over the top of the ingredients. Allow to set, turn out and garnish with mint leaves and shredded lettuce or cabbage heart.

CHESTER PIE

Cooking Time: 1¼ hours Serves 4–6 **

	Metric/Imperial	American
flan case, made and lightly baked as page 132	1	1
For the filling: soft sponge or plain cake crumbs	100 g/4 oz	2 cups
egg yolks	2	2
lemon juice	2 tbsp	3 tbsp
grated lemon rind	2 teasp	2 teasp
caster sugar	1 tbsp	1 tbsp
almonds, blanched and chopped	50 g/2 oz	½ cup
For the meringue: egg whites	2	2
caster sugar	100 g/4 oz	½ cup
almonds, blanched and flaked	2 tbsp	3 tbsp

Prepare and bake the flan case as page 132, allow just 15 minutes cooking time. Mix the crumbs with the egg yolks, lemon juice and rind, sugar and almonds. Put into the partially baked pastry case.

Whisk the egg whites until very stiff. Gradually beat in half the sugar, fold in the remainder. Spoon or pipe over the lemon filling, cover this completely. Top with the flaked almonds. Bake in the centre of a very slow oven, 90 to 110°C/200 to 225°F Gas Mark 0 to ¼, for 1¼ hours.
Serve cold.

VARIATION
Increase the amount of lemon juice to personal taste.

Bacon and Parsley Mould

BACON AND PARSLEY MOULD

Cooking Time: few minutes Serves 4–6 **

	Metric/Imperial	American
stock from boiling bacon or chicken stock, well strained	450 ml/¾ pint	scant 2 cups
light sherry	150 ml/¼ pint	⅔ cup
gelatine	15 g/½ oz	2 envelopes
finely chopped parsley	5 tbsp	½ cup
cooked lean ham, coarsely minced (ground)	450 g/1 lb	1 lb
pepper	to taste	to taste
To garnish: small cucumber, sliced	¼	¼
parsley	2 sprigs	2 sprigs
mustard and cress	to taste	to taste

Pour the stock and sherry into a saucepan, bring almost to boiling point. Sprinkle the gelatine on top and allow to dissolve. Pour 3 tablespoons (4 tbsp) into the bottom of a 900 g/2 lb oblong or square tin (use one without a loose base) or a mould.

Place in the refrigerator or stand in a dish on ice cubes to set. Measure 150 ml/¼ pint (⅔ cup) of the remaining gelatine and liquid, blend with the parsley; allow to become cold and syrupy (so it will not run). When the layer has set on the bottom of the container, turn it on its side. Spoon half the parsley and gelatine mixture on to the one inside surface of the container. Allow to set, then repeat with the second side of the container, coating this with parsley jelly.

Meanwhile, blend the minced ham with the remaining gelatine liquid. Allow this to beome *cold*, add a little pepper to taste. Spoon carefully into the tin or mould. Allow to set, then turn out. Garnish with the cucumber, parsley and mustard and cress.

FOR A HOT PICNIC MEAL

A good warming soup will be appreciated, particularly if the weather is chilly. There are many interesting soups in the section that begins on page 20. Always warm the vacuum flask well before adding the hot soup. Vegetables tend to continue cooking in the flask, so undercook the soup slightly to compensate for this, particularly in a soup full of vegetables like the Scotch Broth on this page.

The main course can be hot cutlets or chops or sausages or a hot pie, such as the traditional Steak and Kidney Pie on page 74, or be a little more adventurous and make a dish en croûte, i.e. food covered with pastry as on page 181 with line drawings. One can claim that this very appetizing dish has become a truly modern fashion for it is universally popular. It can be carried in a deep baking tin for a meal out of doors.

Hot vegetables are not easy to carry, so serve a crisp green salad with the main course.

Casseroles can be transported in wide-necked vacuum flasks.

After a satisfying soup and main course, the dessert can be light. If you want to continue to have all dishes hot, then cooked seasonal fruit is ideal. Slices of home-made cake and cheese would be a pleasant ending to the meal or, if the main course does not include pastry, have hot Mince Pies, or hot Apple Dumplings (Apples in a Nightgown), see the recipes on pages 128 and 195.

A vacuum flask of really hot coffee or tea will ensure that all the diners feel warm and well-fed at the end of the meal.

SCOTCH BROTH

Cooking Time: 2¼ hours Serves 6 **

The vegetables in this soup can be varied according to the season and personal taste, but to be a traditional Scotch Broth the ingredients should include pearl barley with lamb or mutton.

The cooking time given can be shortened if the meat is tender lamb and the vegetables young. If using mutton, extend the cooking time before adding the vegetables. The cabbage can be lightly cooked to retain its firm texture, but if you prefer really soft cabbage cook for a longer time.

	Metric/Imperial	American
pearl barley	50 g/2 oz	generous ¼ cup
water for blanching the barley, see method		
scrag end of neck of lamb	450–675 g/ 1–1½ lb	1–1½ lb
water	1.5 litres/ 2½ pints	6¼ cups
salt and pepper	to taste	to taste
bouquet garni	1	1
medium onion, neatly diced	1	1
medium leeks, neatly sliced	2	2
medium carrots, neatly diced	3	3
small turnip, neatly diced	1	1
small swede (rutabaga), neatly diced	¼	¼
medium cabbage heart, finely shredded	¼	¼
chopped parsley	to taste	to taste

Put the barley into a saucepan with cold water to cover. Bring the water to the boil, strain the barley and discard the water. This process is known as 'blanching'; it whitens the barley and makes it a better texture.

Carefully remove all fat from the lamb. Put the meat into a saucepan with the prepared barley, 1.5 litres/2½

pints (6¼ cups) water, seasoning and bouquet garni. Bring the water to the boil, remove any grey scum that forms on the liquid. Cover the pan, lower the heat and simmer steadily for 1¼ hours.

Add all the vegetables, except the cabbage, and cook for 40 minutes. Check to see if the meat is tender, if so remove from the pan with a perforated spoon. Cut the meat from the bones. Dice the meat finely and return to the saucepan.

If the vegetables are almost tender when the meat is removed from the pan, turn off the heat under the pan so they are not overcooked.

Bring the soup to boiling point again, add the cabbage and cook briskly for 10 minutes.

Remove the bouquet garni, check the seasoning and serve the soup topped with parsley. When carrying the soup in a vacuum flask, sprinkle the parsley on to the soup in the flask; do not cook the herb.

VARIATIONS
Add several skinned and diced tomatoes with the cabbage.
● Fresh or frozen peas can be added to the soup towards the end of the cooking time. It is quite usual to include dried peas in Scotch Broth. These should be soaked overnight in water to cover. If using older mutton, which needs longer cooking then the soaked peas can be added to the saucepan with the meat and barley and cooked for 2½ hours before adding the vegetables. Increase the amount of water by 300 ml/½ pint (1¼ cups) to allow for the longer cooking period.

POTATO AND CARROT SALAD

Cooking Time: 25 minutes Serves 4–6 **

The method of serving this salad is very attractive. It is quite practical too if the well-washed red cabbage leaves are arranged in a large plastic container with the salad on the leaves. This could be made 12 to 24 hours before the picnic and left in the refrigerator. The flavours mature and improve.

	Metric/Imperial	American
For the dressing: mayonnaise	150 ml/¼ pint	⅔ cup
olive oil	1 tbsp	1 tbsp
white wine vinegar	1 tbsp	1 tbsp
garlic salt	pinch	pinch
celery salt	pinch	pinch
black pepper	shake	shake
For the salad: small new potatoes	450 g/1 lb	1 lb
new carrots, sliced	225 g/8 oz	½ lb
shelled peas	225 g/8 oz	½ lb
sugar	pinch	pinch
button mushrooms, sliced	100 g/4 oz	¼ lb
red cabbage (optional)	1	1

Blend the ingredients for the dressing so it is ready when the vegetables are cooked. Cook the potatoes in boiling salted water for 25 minutes or until just tender. Dice and blend with the dressing while warm. Cook the carrots and peas in boiling salted water with the pinch of sugar. Drain and add to the dressing while warm. Allow to cool. Add the raw mushrooms. Chill well. Serve in a bowl or on red cabbage.

VARIATION
Slice the mushrooms and cook very lightly in seasoned stock or a little hot oil.

PORK AND STILTON EN CROÛTE

Cooking Time: 1 hour Serves 6 **

	Metric/Imperial	American
Puff Pastry, as page 155 made with	175–225 g/ 6–8 oz flour* etc	1½–2 cups flour* etc
pork fillets, 350 g/12 oz (¾ lb) each	2	2
butter	25 g/1 oz	2 tbsp
made mustard	1–2 teasp	1–2 teasp
Stilton cheese, sliced	100 g/4 oz	¼ lb
thick apple purée	2 tbsp	3 tbsp
To glaze: egg, see line drawings	1	1

* the pastry for any dish 'en croûte' must be rolled out until it is very thin, but the amount of pastry made depends upon the quantity of decoration required

Make the pastry, chill well. Slice both pork fillets lengthways so the meat can be opened out flat, do not cut through the fillet completely. Heat the butter in a large frying pan (skillet), cook the pork steadily for 10 minutes until the meat is well-browned. Remove from the pan and allow to cool.

Spread the first fillet with the mustard, top with the Stilton cheese and then with the apple purée. Place the second fillet on top. Roll out the pastry and wrap the meat, as described in the line drawings on this page. Garnish with pastry leaves and use the egg to brush over the pastry. Bake in the centre of a hot oven, 220°C/425°F Gas Mark 7, for 50 minutes. The temperature can be reduced slightly after 30 minutes if the pastry is becoming too brown.

VARIATIONS
Beef Wellington (Boeuf en Croûte): Use approximately 900 g/2 lb fillet of beef (cut from the thickest end of the fillet) instead of the pork. Do not split the fillet of beef. Cover the meat with butter and roast as page 50 until almost tender; allow to cool. Spread a little liver pâté over the meat; the recipe on page 15 would be a good choice. Put the meat on to the pastry and continue as above, but allow only 40 minutes cooking time as the beef only needs heating through.

TO WRAP THE PORK

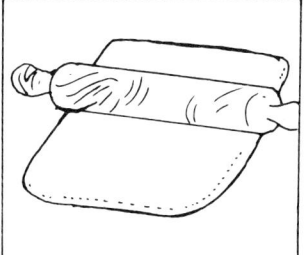

Roll out the pastry to a 30 cm/12 inch square or sufficiently large to wrap around the pastry.

Beat the egg and brush the centre panel (the area where the meat will be placed) with part of the egg. Place the pork over this.

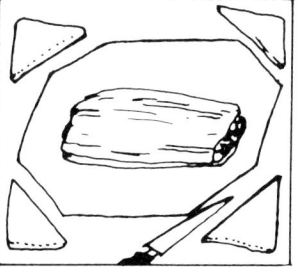

Make a cut from each of the 4 corners diagonally nearly up to the meat.

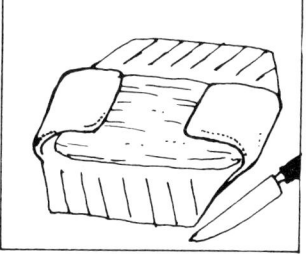

Take the flaps at each short end and fold over the meat.

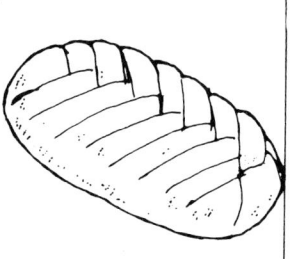

Make diagonal cuts through the side pieces of pastry at 2.5 cm/1 inch intervals, fold over the meat in a plaiting action. Brush with beaten egg.

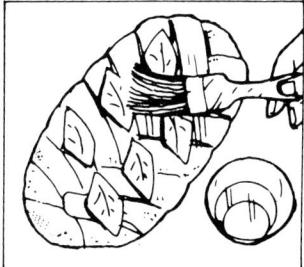

Decorate with pastry leaves, brush these with egg, press on to the pastry and bake as in the method above.

PLANNING A BARBECUE

Barbecues in Britain have not been as popular as in many other countries, due undoubtedly to the fact that people consider our weather is not sufficiently consistent to plan for outdoor eating regularly throughout the summer months. The development of relatively inexpensive barbecue equipment for summer has now encouraged households to invest in these, and to appreciate the fact that Britain does have many beautiful days.

Barbecued food should be satisfying, as everyone develops a good appetite. It can be simple, but should have an interesting flavour. A good basic Barbecue Sauce, with some variations, is suggested below. Never try cooking the food until the charcoal is red or the barbecue heater is really hot. Times for cooking joints and whole chickens are similar to those given in the meat and poultry sections. Always keep lean meat and poultry well basted with the sauce or with melted fat or oil.

FOODS FOR BARBECUES

The foods to be cooked over a barbecue must be similar to that selected for grilling (broiling) or frying, i.e. tender chops or cutlets of lamb, pork or veal and good quality steak. Young chickens can be halved or divided into joints. The cooking time is very much the same as when these foods are grilled or fried. Sausages are a prime favourite for a barbecue, they become beautifully brown and crisp on the outside.

The barbecue fire is very hot, so protect your hands when handling the food and turning it over. This is particularly important if cooking diced meats on long metal skewers for

Above: Meat Balls – recipe page 184. Below: Piquant Spare Ribs – recipe page 184

kebabs as the skewers become excessively hot.

If you do not want to make a sauce, which is also a basting liquid, for these foods, then brush them with plenty of oil before cooking.

Spare ribs are one of the most popular of all foods for a barbecue. It is better to prepare and cook these in the kitchen beforehand and just place the container over the barbecue fire for a short time to heat. The recipe is on page 184.

Barbecued Fish: Trout, mackerel, salmon steaks and small whole fish are delicious when cooked over a barbecue. Marinate the fish in the sauce given on page 183. Remove from the marinade; place each individual fish, or portion of fish, on to a square of well-oiled foil and cook over the barbecue. The fish can be stuffed before cooking. There are a number of dishes in the fish section which lend themselves to barbecue cooking.

Do not attempt deep frying of fish, or other food, over a barbecue fire, it is highly dangerous.

Jacket Potatoes: Wash the potatoes, rub the skin with a very little oil to encourage them to crisp, then place the potatoes on squares of foil. Wrap this around the potatoes and cook until tender. An average sized old potato takes 45 minutes to 1 hour. When cooked, the potatoes can be split and topped with cottage cheese and chopped chives or with soured cream or with plenty of butter.

182

Preparing for a Barbecue

This sauce can be used for marinating meat or poultry before cooking, so allowing the various flavours to penetrate into the food. Brush with the sauce as it cooks, see below. Serve the remainder of the sauce with the barbecued meat or poultry or fish.

Mix all the ingredients together and put into a shallow container. Marinate for 1 to 2 hours, turn if necessary.

Lift the food out of the sauce, drain over the container. Cook as the timings on page 184. Brush the top of the chops or steaks or chicken joints

BARBECUE SAUCE

Cooking Time: 5 minutes Serves 4–6 ❖❖

	Metric/Imperial	American
medium onions, finely chopped	2–3	2–3
garlic cloves, finely chopped	1–3	1–3
celery stalk, finely chopped	1	1
mustard pickle, chopped	2 tbsp	3 tbsp
tomato ketchup	2 tbsp	3 tbsp
red wine	3 tbsp	4 tbsp
red wine vinegar	1 tbsp	1 tbsp
olive oil	150 ml/¼ pint	²/₃ cup
chopped parsley	1–2 tbsp	1–3 tbsp
salt and pepper	to taste	to taste

with the sauce before turning them over. Tip the sauce into a pan and heat over the fire for 5 minutes. The onion and other firm ingredients should retain their crisp texture.

VARIATIONS
Barbecue Sauce for Fish: Use cider as the liquid instead of stock and wine. Add 1 tablespoon chopped fennel or dill leaves when heating the sauce.

● *Sweet and Sour Barbecue Sauce:* Use the ingredients as in the basic sauce but add 1 to 2 tablespoons (1 to 3 tbsp) brown sugar or honey.

Piquant Spare Ribs

Illustrated in colour on page 182
Cooking Time: 1 hour 5–10 minutes Serves 4–6 ✹✹

	Metric/Imperial	American
spare ribs of pork	1.5 kg/3½ lb	3½ lb
brown malt or red wine vinegar	3 tbsp	4 tbsp
water, see method		
olive or cooking oil	2 tbsp	3 tbsp
For the sauce: soy sauce	2 tbsp	3 tbsp
thin honey	2 tbsp	3 tbsp
plum jam	2 tbsp	3 tbsp
made mustard	1–2 teasp	1–2 teasp
tomato ketchup	1 tbsp	1 tbsp
tomato purée (paste)	1 tbsp	1 tbsp
salt and pepper	to taste	to taste

Trim any excess fat from the bones and cut these into 10 to 13 cm/4 to 5 inch lengths, or ask the butcher to do this.

Put the spare ribs into a saucepan with half the vinegar and water to cover. Bring the liquid to the boil, lower the heat and simmer for 25 minutes. Strain and discard the liquid. Leave the spare ribs on a dish for a short time so the excess liquid will evaporate.

Heat the oil in a large roasting tin, add the spare ribs and cook in a hot oven, 220°C/425°F Gas Mark 7, for 15 minutes.

Blend the remaining vinegar with the ingredients for the sauce, pour this over the spare ribs. Reduce the heat to moderate, 180°C/350°F Gas Mark 4, and cook for 20 minutes. Turn the spare ribs in the sauce to make sure they are evenly coated. Raise the oven temperature to hot once more, i.e. 220°C/425°F Gas Mark 7, for the final 5 to 10 minutes cooking time to crisp the meat.

WITH A CHINESE TOUCH

Chinese dishes are enjoyed in Britain as in most other countries. The dish with spare ribs is a popular one and our pork is excellent for this purpose. To make an attractive garnish, wash large spring onions (scallions), trim and cut down the stalks as shown.

Place in cold water until the stalks open out into a flower shape.

DRINKS FOR BARBECUES AND PICNICS

Rather robust drinks are popular with a barbecue, i.e. well-chilled beer, light ale and cider. A cold white or rosé wine would blend well with chicken and fish.

Use a vacuum flask to carry ice cold coffee for a picnic or use it for crushed ice to put into drinks. Check that the particular flask is recommended by the manufacturer for ice and crush it well before putting into the flask.

SIMPLE PICNIC DISHES

Sandwiches are the easiest of all complete meals to carry on a picnic and an ideal choice when travelling on foot. The origin of sandwiches is attributed to an Earl of Sandwich, who lived in the time of Charles II and is mentioned in the diary of Samuel Pepys. This gentleman enjoyed playing cards and gambling and was loathe to leave the card table for a meal. He conceived the idea of placing cooked meat, or other food, between slices of bread and butter. His friends called the al fresco meal 'a Sandwich' and the name persisted. There are some ideas for sandwiches on page 185.

Simple dishes for picnics which are extremely easy to pack are Scotch Eggs, the recipe for which is on page 185, and Meat Balls, below, served with coleslaw.

Meat Balls

Illustrated in colour on page 182
Cooking Time: 15–20 minutes Makes 15–40, see method ✹✹

	Metric/Imperial	American
For the meat balls: butter or margarine	50 g/2 oz	¼ cup
onion, finely chopped	1	1
topside (top round) of beef, minced (ground)	450 g/1 lb	1 lb
soft breadcrumbs	75 g/3 oz	1½ cups
carrots, grated	1–2	1–2
egg yolk	1	1
tomato purée (paste)	1 teasp	1 teasp
salt and pepper	to taste	to taste
To coat: flour	1–2 tbsp	1–3 tbsp
egg	1	1
crisp breadcrumbs	50–75 g/2–3 oz	¾ cup
To fry: oil or fat, see method		

Heat the butter or margarine in a frying pan (skillet), fry the onion until soft. Add the other meat ball ingredients to the pan and blend thoroughly. Allow to cool, roll into balls. The size can vary a great deal, for a cocktail snack make these the size of a small nut.

Add a little seasoning to the flour, coat the balls. Beat the egg, brush over the meat balls then coat in the breadcrumbs. Chill well before frying.

Deep fry for about 5 to 6 minutes or shallow fry for 10 minutes. If shallow frying, turn the meat balls with 2 spoons several times. Drain on absorbent paper (kitchen towels). These are equally good hot or cold.

Herb and Vegetable Pâté

Cooking Time: 1 hour 40 minutes Serves 4–6 ✳✳

This is an excellent vegetarian dish for a picnic. Take crispbread to serve with the pâté. If possible, transport in the tin. Slice thinly for a sandwich filling in rye or wholemeal bread.

	Metric/Imperial	American
butter	50 g/2 oz	¼ cup
spring onions (scallions), chopped	1 tbsp	1 tbsp
carrots, coarsely grated	225 g/8 oz	½ lb
mushrooms, thinly sliced	100 g/4 oz	¼ lb
courgettes (zucchini) or cucumber, grated or finely diced	225 g/8 oz	½ lb
eggs	4	4
cottage cheese, sieved	225 g/8 oz	1 cup
single (light) cream	150 ml/¼ pint	⅔ cup
chopped parsley	2 tbsp	3 tbsp
chopped lemon thyme or ordinary thyme	1 teasp	1 teasp
chopped chives	2 teasp	2 teasp
salt and pepper	to taste	to taste

Heat the butter in a large saucepan, cook the vegetables very gently over a low heat for 10 minutes; stir several times during cooking. Beat the eggs with the cottage cheese and cream. Add the herbs, then blend in the softened vegetables. Season well.

Line a 900 g/2 lb loaf tin with lightly oiled baking parchment. If this is not available, use greaseproof (waxed) paper. Spoon in the vegetable mixture. Cover the tin with oiled foil and stand in a bain-marie (container of cold water). Bake in the centre of a very moderate oven, 160°C/325°F Gas Mark 3, for 1½ hours or until firm to the touch. Allow to cool in the tin.

INTERESTING SANDWICHES

Choose fresh bread and spread with a reasonable amount of butter or margarine. As a pleasant change, you can use one of the flavoured butters given on page 177 to blend with the sandwich filling chosen.

Most breads can be used for sandwiches, for example sweet fruit bread, such as those on page 145, are excellent with a cheese filling; wholemeal or wholewheat bread with fish or fish pâtés or eggs.

Soft crustless brown bread and butter can be rolled round fillings, such as asparagus tips. If the bread seems too firm for this purpose, roll it first with a rolling pin, as though you were dealing with a pastry dough, this makes it pliable and easy to handle.

Nowadays the open-type of sandwich, a feature of Scandinavian cuisine, is very popular. If carrying these for a picnic, cover the topping with squares of grease-proof or waxed paper or cling film (plastic wrap) instead of the second slice of bread and butter.

Cheese Fillings
Choose grated Cheddar or Cheshire cheese and blend with grated raw carrots and mayonnaise or mix crumbled Stilton or Lancashire cheese with chopped nuts.

Cottage cheese makes an excellent filling when blended with finely chopped fresh or well-drained canned pineapple or with chopped dates or with chopped fresh herbs and/or watercress and seasoning.

Egg Fillings
Hard-boiled (hard-cooked) eggs can be slightly dry in a sandwich; if you like a fairly moist sandwich filling, chop the eggs and mix with the butter or margarine to spread over the bread or with Herb or Watercress Butters on page 177.

Scrambled egg can be mixed with grated, cream or cottage cheese or with chopped skinned cucumber, red or green pepper or diced tomatoes.

Fish Fillings
Choose shellfish and blend with lemon-flavoured mayonnaise or smoked fish blended with mayonnaise flavoured with a little horseradish cream or salmon and cucumber slices topped with mayonnaise and finely chopped fennel leaves.

Meat Fillings
Meat pâtés of most kinds make good sandwich fillings, for a pâté is more moist than sliced cold meat. Salted or cured meats, such as cooked ham, tongue, corned or salted beef, give plenty of flavour to the sandwiches. The meat can be spread with a little pickle or chutney. Minced (ground) or finely chopped meat is pleasant mixed with cottage cheese, finely chopped spring onions (scallions) and seasoning.

Vegetable Fillings
Most salad vegetables provide good sandwich fillings. If the ingredients are moist, like tomatoes, put between lettuce on the bread and butter, otherwise the bread will become soggy. The Herb and Vegetable Pâté is an excellent topping or filling for open or ordinary sandwiches.

Scotch Eggs

Cooking Time: 20–30 minutes, see method Serves 4 ✳

Hard-boil (hard-cook) 4 eggs. Shell these and coat the whites in a very little seasoned flour. This helps the moist sausagemeat coating to adhere to the eggs.

Divide 350 g/12 oz (¾ lb) sausagemeat into 4 equal sized portions. Press out the first portion into a flat shape, then completely cover the egg; seal the joins very firmly and form into a good shape. Repeat with the other 3 eggs.

Roll the sausage-coated eggs in a very little seasoned flour. Brush with beaten egg and coat in crisp breadcrumbs.

Deep fry the Scotch Eggs for 10 minutes or shallow fry for 15 minutes, turning them several times, or bake on a lightly greased baking tray in the centre of a moderately hot oven, 200°C/400°F Gas Mark 6. Serve hot or cold.

VARIATIONS
The hard-boiled eggs can be halved and the yolks blended with cream cheese or pâté.
● Instead of sausagemeat, use the mixture in the Meat Balls on page 184.

For the
—— Storecupboard ——

In these modern times the storecupboard may be less full than in the past, for the freezer has, to a certain degree, taken its place. Much of the fruit and vegetables that once would have been bottled is now frozen. Excellent advice on home freezing is given by the manufacturers of the appliances, so only brief hints are given in this section.
You will find a good selection of recipes for making home-made jams and other preserves in the following pages.

CHOOSING FRUIT FOR PRESERVATION
Whether the fruit is to be bottled or frozen, it should be ripe but not over-ripe. It should not be bruised in any way. When buying or picking fruit for jam or jelly, the fruit should be as fresh as possible, for the fresher the fruit the greater the amount of pectin (setting quality) it contains. The fruit should be ripe, although some gooseberries make an excellent jam or jelly if they are slightly under-ripe.

MAKING PRESERVES
It is important to have the correct proportions of sugar and fruit in a preserve. If too small a proportion of fruit to sugar is used, there is insufficient natural acid (pectin)

to make the preserve set properly. On the other hand, if too little sugar is used the preserves will not keep.

Unless the recipe states to the contrary, it is important to simmer the fruit slowly, to soften it before adding the sugar. This slow cooking extracts the pectin and makes certain that tough fruit skins are adequately softened. The skin will not soften once the sugar is added.

It is very important to stir well until all the sugar is dissolved. After this stage, allow the preserve to boil rapidly until setting point is reached. In order that the preserve *can* boil quickly, do not stir at this stage and make quite certain there is adequate space in the preserving pan for rapid boiling, without fear of the mixture boiling over.

Making Apricot Jam

Test for setting point early, see page 188, for, in some cases, this is a brief period only and if the preserve continues to boil the setting point can be passed and the preserve will not set. Always take the preserving pan off the heat while testing for setting point.

When the preserve has reached setting point it should be put into heated jars at once. If there are large pieces of fruit or peel, as in the case of marmalade, allow the preserve to cool and stiffen slightly then stir briskly to distribute the fruit or peel and put into the jars.

Always fill the jars to the top or within 5 mm/¼ inch, for preserves keep better if there is little air space. Put on the waxed and final coverings. Store in a cool dry place. If stored away from bright lights you will find the preserve keeps a better colour.

PROPORTIONS FOR JAM MAKING

Fruit used – 450g/1lb unless stated to the contrary. Weight when peeled or stoned* (pitted)	Preparations	Amount of water to each 450g/1lb of fruit	Amount of sugar to each 450g/1lb of fruit	Amount of lemon juice – where required to each 450g/1lb of fruit
Apples, cooking (baking) 450g/1lb with Blackberries 450g/1lb	peel, core, slice, wash and drain	4 tbsp (5 tbsp)	900g/2lb to the mixture of fruits	
Apple Ginger	peel, dice and sprinkle with the sugar and 1 teasp ground ginger, leave for 12 hours		450g/1lb	
Apricots, fresh	halve, stone (pit) if wished**	2 tbsp (3 tbsp)	450g/1lb	1 tbsp
Apricots, dried	soak in the water for 12 hours	1.8 litres/3 pints (7½ cups)	1.35kg/3lb	6 tbsp (good ½ cup)
Blackcurrants	stalk, wash and drain	450ml/¾ pint (scant 2 cups)	550g/1¼lb	
Cherries – Morello – black	wash and drain. See under method for Conserve	4 tbsp (5 tbsp)	450g/1lb	
Damsons	wash, stone (pit) during cooking or cook and sieve	4 tbsp (5 tbsp) if fruit is ripe up to 300ml/½ pint (1¼ cups) if under-ripe	400g/14oz 450g/1lb 550g/1¼lb	
Gooseberries	wash and 'top and tail' (clean)	as damsons	as damsons	
Loganberries and Boysenberries	wash and drain		450g/1lb	
Plums	as apricots			omit lemon juice if firm sour cooking plums
Quince, 450g/1lb with Apples, cooking (baking) 450g/1lb	peel, core and dice both fruits	200 ml/7½ fl oz (scant 1 cup)	900g/2lb	
Raspberries, also Blueberries (these are better in a jelly)	wash and drain		450g/1lb	
Strawberries	wash only if soiled		400g/14oz	1 tbsp

* if the fruit is not stoned (pitted), allow an extra 50g/2oz weight to compensate for the stones (pits)
** crack some of the stones and put the kernels into the jam when setting point is reached

TO MAKE CONSERVES

The term 'conserve' is used to describe a preserve where there are whole pieces of fruit. The Apple Ginger, given in the Jam Making table, might well be described as a 'conserve'.

To make a conserve, put the fruit into a container – it can be placed in the preserving pan. Add the amount of sugar recommended for the particular fruit; this would be exactly the same as if making jam. Turn the fruit in the sugar, so each piece is coated, then allow to stand for about 4 hours or even longer. During that time the sugar extracts the fruit juice and there is no need to add additional liquid.

Simmer the fruit with the sugar, stirring well until all the sugar has dissolved. Add lemon juice, if this is recommended in the Jam Making table or right. Boil steadily, rather than rapidly, until a light set. Cool until thickened slightly. Stir to distribute the pieces of fruit then put into jars as described under 'Preserves'.

Fruits that make first class conserves are: black cherries and small strawberries – use only 400 g/14 oz sugar to each 450 g/1 lb stoned (pitted) fruit (or just under 500 g/1 lb 2 oz fruit *with* stones) and 1 tablespoon lemon juice or 3 tablespoons (4 tbsp) redcurrant juice to each 450 g/1 lb fruit.

Ripe apricots or dessert plums (halved and stoned) or peaches (which should be skinned and sliced) – make excellent conserves. Use 450 g/1 lb sugar and 1 tablespoon lemon juice to each 450 g/1 lb prepared fruit.

Marrow (large zucchini) or pumpkin or rhubarb make good conserves too – proceed as the Apple Ginger in the Jam Making table.

SETTING POINT FOR JAMS AND JELLIES

There are 4 ways of testing whether jam or jelly has reached setting point. Three ways are outlined below. The fourth way is by weight. Jam that is adequately set should contain 60 per cent sugar, this makes sure it will keep. Every 450 g/1 lb sugar used should produce 750 g/1²⁄₃ lb jam.

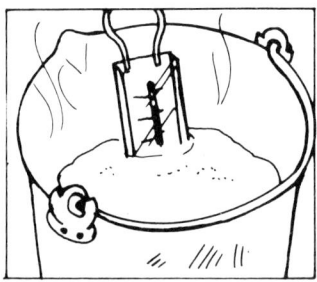

1 By temperature: Use a sugar thermometer, put this into the very hot jam or jelly. Stir it around gently in the preserve to give the overall temperature. The setting point for jams and conserves is 104–105.5°C/ 220–222°F and for jellies 104–105°C/220–221°F. The lower temperature gives a lightly set preserve. Never take the thermometer from the hot preserve and place it on to a cold surface, it will break.

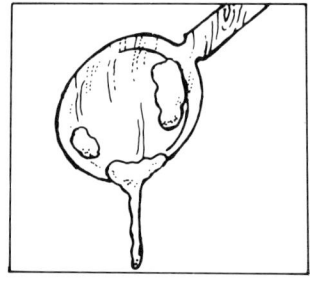

2 Forming a skin: Put a little preserve on to a saucer and allow to cool. Push it with your finger or with a spoon, it will wrinkle if setting point has been reached.

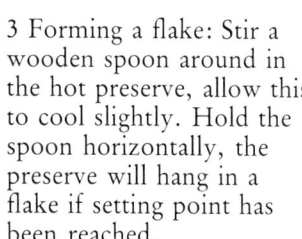

3 Forming a flake: Stir a wooden spoon around in the hot preserve, allow this to cool slightly. Hold the spoon horizontally, the preserve will hang in a flake if setting point has been reached.

TO MAKE JELLIES

Jellies are very much a favourite in Britain, they have been prepared for generations. Some jellies are considered an essential accompaniment with certain meats and game.

The procedure for making jellies is simple. Wash the fruit, there is no need to 'top and tail' (clean) or peel apples and other fruits; in fact the peel and cores of cooking (baking) apples or crab apples help to give colour, flavour and additional pectin to the jelly.

Simply dice large fruit, put into the preserving pan with the amount of water given below. Simmer very gently until the fruit is very soft. Put through a jelly bag – this is generally made of flannel, which strains the juice most thoroughly. If a jelly bag is not available, put several thicknesses of fine muslin (cheesecloth) over a hair sieve. Under the jelly bag, which is suspended by tapes or under the muslin and sieve, put a large bowl. Leave the purée dripping through the bag for some hours until all the juice has been extracted. Do not squeeze the bag or push the fruit through the muslin as this would result in cloudy liquid.

Measure the liquid and allow 450 g/1 lb sugar to each 600 ml/1 pint (2½ cups) juice. Put the liquid and sugar into the preserving pan, stir until the sugar has dissolved, add lemon juice if necessary. Boil rapidly until setting point is reached. Pour immediately into heated jars and seal, see the information on page 186 under Preserves.

Adding Extra Flavour to Jellies

The fruit juice in a jelly gives a good flavour but there are flavourings that can be added.

To Apple or Gooseberry Jelly: Add 1 tablespoon finely chopped mint leaves or 1 teaspoon finely chopped sage leaves.

To Redcurrant Jelly: Give the jelly a piquant flavour by adding a few drops of Tabasco (hot pepper) sauce.

Fruits to Choose for Making Jelly

Group 1 fruits high in natural pectin
Allow 300 ml/½ pint (1¼ cups) water to each 450 g/ 1 lb fruit.
Apples (cooking, baking and crab apples), blackcurrants, damsons, under-ripe gooseberries, rowanberries, redcurrants.

Group 2 fruits less rich in pectin
Allow only 150 ml/¼ pint (⅔ cup) water to each 450 g/1 lb fruit.
Blueberries, ripe damsons, ripe gooseberries, loganberries, plums, raspberries.

Group 3 fruits where lemon juice is needed
Allow 1 tablespoon to each 600 ml/1 pint (2½ cups) juice and water as stated below.
Quinces – allow 300 ml/½ pint (1¼ cups) water to each 450 g/1 lb fruit.
Strawberries – no water, simply simmer the fruit.

FREEZING FRUIT

Fruit can be frozen in several ways. One of the most useful methods is as a purée. This can be used for the basis of sweet sauces or, in the case of apples and cranberries, as the basis for sauces to serve with meat or poultry.

Cook firm fruit with the minimum of liquid, the purée can be diluted as desired when it has been defrosted. You can add sugar or other sweetening but do not add too much for this can be adjusted later according to the dish in which the fruit is used.

Pack the fruit into handy-sized containers. Allow a little headspace of about 1.5 cm/½ inch in a small container, for fruit contains a lot of juice which expands when frozen.

Tomatoes are a fruit, although generally treated as a vegetable. A purée of uncooked or cooked tomatoes is an excellent standby in the freezer.

Use these purées within 6 months.
Berry fruits, such as raspberries, loganberries, small strawberries, together with red and blackcurrants, are at their best when frozen whole, without any additional liquid. The fruit can be packed into containers with, or without sugar, but it keeps a better shape if frozen on flat trays first and then packed into containers. If adding sugar, gently toss the frozen fruits in dry sugar before packing.

All fruits can be frozen in a sugar and water syrup. Fruit tends to soften in freezing so if cooking firm fruits do not overcook these. Plums and fruits with firm skins should be pricked very lightly with a needle before poaching in the syrup. This makes sure the syrup penetrates the skins and they are not toughened with storage. Stones (pits) give a definite flavour to the fruit with prolonged storage, so you may like to remove any stones before cooking.

Any fruit that discolours, such as apricots, peaches and pears, are better poached in a lemon-flavoured syrup. Make sure the fruit is kept well covered with the syrup in the container in which it is to be frozen.

Fruits frozen as above can be stored for a year.

FREEZING VEGETABLES

There has been much discussion over the years as to whether vegetables need 'blanching', i.e. lightly cooking before freezing. In the opinion of experts, blanching ensures that harmful bacteria, that might be present in vegetables, are destroyed. Blanching also helps to retain the good colour and flavour of the vegetables.

Manufacturer's instruction manuals give full information about blanching and packing vegetables. As a basic guidance, the vegetables should be precooked for 1 to 3

minutes, cooled rapidly, drained well, then packed and frozen.

Vegetables can be stored in the freezer for up to 1 year.

BOTTLING FRUIT

The best way of bottling fruit is to pack it in a sugar syrup, then sterilize the filled jars in a deep container or proper sterilizer.

Prepare the fruit, i.e. peel and slice apples and pears, halve large peaches, stone (pit) fruit if wished.

Make a sugar syrup by boiling sugar and water together. Allow from 100 g/4 oz (½ cup) sugar to 600 ml/1 pint (2½ cups) water and up to 350 g/12 oz (1½ cups) sugar for an ultra heavy syrup. Allow the syrup to become quite cold.

Pack the fruit into the jars, cover with the cold syrup. Put on the lids and loosen any bands slightly as instructed by the manufacturer. Glass expands with heating and the glass could break if bands and clips are too tight.

Stand the jars on the rack (trivet) in the sterilizer or on a thick folded cloth in a deep saucepan. The glass jars should not be on the base of the metal pan.

Fill the sterilizer or container with cold water up to the necks of the jars or to cover the jars.

Take 1½ hours to bring the water to 75 to 80°C/165 to 175°F and hold at this temperature for 10 minutes.

For pears and tomatoes, bring the water to 82 to 87°C/180 to 190°F and hold at this temperature for 30 minutes.

Bring the jars out of the liquid, stand on a wooden or padded surface, tighten the screw bands or clips.

VARIATION
Bottling Vegetables: Vegetables must be bottled in a pressure cooker; it is unsafe to do this by any other method. Follow the full instructions in a pressure cooking book.

TO STONE CHERRIES

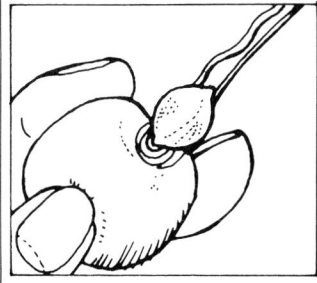

Insert the bent end of a fine hairpin into the cherry, feel this hook round the stone (pit) and pull firmly to bring out the stone.

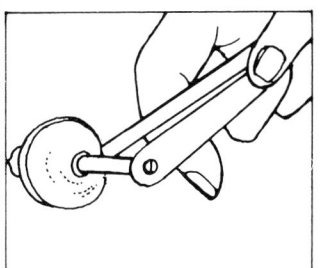

Use a proper cherry-stoner and insert this into the cherry and press firmly

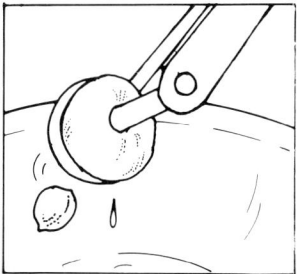

Stone cherries over a bowl or saucepan so no juice is wasted.

MARMALADE

Cooking Time: approximately 2 hours Makes nearly 1.8 kg/4 lb**

The story of how marmalade came to Scotland is an interesting one. Obviously, oranges were known in Scotland as well as in England in the 17th Century, but it was not until the early 18th Century that mention of real orange marmalade is given. Apparently, a ship from Spain had been unduly buffeted by high seas and docked at Dundee with a cargo of oranges. A local merchant decided to buy these cheaply and took the cargo, only to find that many of them could not be eaten as a fruit for they were so sour. Obviously, they were Seville or other bitter oranges. This gentleman had a thrifty nature and decided that they must not be wasted, so he took them to his wife who, like so many housewives then and now, was skilled in making preserves. She concocted the preserve we now call marmalade.

This marmalade recipe is particularly easy to make. The result is a pleasantly chunky preserve, such as might have been made by the enterprising housewife in Dundee.

	Metric/Imperial	American
Seville or bitter oranges	450 g/1 lb	1 lb
water	1.5 litres/2½ pints	5 cups
preserving sugar	1.2 kg/2½ lb	2½ lb
lemon	1	1

Wash the fruit, put into a preserving pan with the cold water. Cover the pan and simmer steadily until the fruit is so soft that it can be pierced with a wooden skewer or knitting needle. This takes about 1½ hours. Do not boil the fruit rapidly in the liquid at this stage. Allow to cool sufficiently to handle the oranges. Remove from the pan on to a board or plate. Halve the fruit and remove the pips. Return the pips to the liquid and boil for 20 minutes to extract the setting quality.

Meanwhile, cut the oranges into thin strips using the skin and pulp. Strain the pips from the liquid, put this liquid with the shredded oranges back into the preserving pan. Bring the pulp and liquid to the boil with the sugar; stir over a gentle heat until the sugar has dissolved. Halve the lemon, squeeze out the juice and add to the preserve. Boil rapidly until setting point is reached. If testing with a sugar thermometer, the preserve should reach 104°C/220°F; if testing without a thermometer, it should form a skin when a little is cooled on a saucer. Allow the marmalade to become fairly cool in the pan. Stir to distribute the peel, then put into warmed jars and seal.

VARIATION
If a slightly sweeter preserve is desired, use 1.75 litres/3 pints (7½ cups) water and 1.4 kg/3 lb sugar with 3 tablespoons (4 tbsp) lemon juice. For a truly bitter, thick marmalade, use 1.2 litres/2 pints (5 cups) water and 900 g/2 lb sugar and omit the lemon juice.

FINE CUT MARMALADE

The marmalade shown in the photograph on this page is finely cut. It is difficult to achieve this type of marmalade by the method described above. Use the proportions of fruit, water and sugar given in the basic recipe or the variation, depending upon personal taste. Allow the same amount of lemon juice.

Halve the oranges, squeeze out the juice, put on one side. Remove the orange pips, tie in a piece of muslin (cheesecloth). Shred the orange peel and pulp as finely as desired. Soak overnight in the water together with the bag of pips.

Simmer the fruit in the water with the pips until the peel is quite tender. Remove the bag of pips. Add the sugar and stir over a moderate heat until dissolved, then pour in the orange juice and lemon juice if needed. Boil rapidly until setting point is reached.

MORE FLAVOURS FOR MARMALADE
When making any of the following marmalades, use the Fine Cut Marmalade method.
Lemon or Grapefruit or Lime Marmalade: To 450 g/1 lb lemons or grapefruit or limes use 1.5 litres/2½ pints (6¼ cups) water and 1.2 kg/2½ lb sugar.

Sweet Orange Marmalade: To 450 g/1 lb sweet oranges use 1.2 litres/2 pints (5 cups) water and 900 g/2 lb sugar with 6 tablespoons (generous ½ cup) lemon juice.

Marmalade

MAKING PICKLES AND CHUTNEYS

Choose good quality malt vinegar and the full amount of sugar. Do not make the pickle or chutney in a copper, brass or iron pan, use aluminium or enamel.

Cover pickles and chutneys carefully, never put a metal container next to the contents of the jar. Use a round of thick paper under the metal or use a glass lid.

Kitchen salt is mentioned in recipes, this is cheaper than refined table salt and freshly ground pepper for pickles and chutneys.

PICKLED FRUITS

Cooking Time: see method ***

In the days when it was less easy to obtain exotic and interesting fruits out of season, pickling was used to make a delicious special occasion fruit relish to serve with cold meats.

	Metric/Imperial	American
fruit, see method, approximately	900 g/2 lb	2 lb
white malt vinegar	600 ml/1 pint	2½ cups
pickling spices	1–2 teasp	1–2 teasp
sugar	450 g/1 lb	1 lb

Choose whole small skinned peaches (or halve and stone (pit) these) or peeled and quartered firm dessert pears, crab apples (do not peel or core) and damsons or dessert plums.

Boil the vinegar with the pickling spices for 1 to 2 minutes. Strain and return the vinegar to the saucepan. Add the sugar, stir until dissolved then put in the fruit and simmer gently until just soft. Ripe fruit will need a few minutes cooking only.

Lift the fruit from the vinegar liquid with a perforated spoon so it is well-drained. Pack into heated bottling jars. Boil the vinegar, with the lid off the pan, for a few minutes, to make a thicker syrup. Pour over the fruit and seal down at once.

VARIATION
For a milder flavour, omit the pickling spices and just press a clove into each portion of fruit as shown in the photograph.

Above: Preserved Peaches

FLAVOURED VINEGARS

In the past, housewives used fresh herbs and spices to give vinegar an interesting flavour. Flavoured vinegars are used in salad dressings to give a more varied taste. Use either wine or malt vinegar according to personal requirements. The vinegar should be kept in the usual bottles.

Herb Vinegar: Any herbs can be put into vinegar for flavouring. The most suitable are dill, fennel, rosemary or tarragon. Wash and dry the leaves or sprigs. Bruise the leaves gently, this helps to extract the most flavour. Allow several sprigs, or equivalent in leaves, to each bottle of vinegar; put into the vinegar. Leave for 6 to 8 weeks, shaking the bottle from time to time. Strain and re-bottle the vinegar.

Spiced Vinegar: Put about ½ teaspoon mixed pickling spices into 600 ml/1 pint (2½ cups) cold vinegar and leave until required. For a stronger flavour, bring the vinegar and spices just to boiling point. Cool and return to the bottle. Do not strain the vinegar, leave the spices in. (Pickling spices are a mixture of various types of spice.)

MUSTARD PICKLES

Cooking Time: 20–25 minutes Makes approximately 2.25 kg/2½ lb *

	Metric/Imperial	American
For the brine: kitchen salt*	100 g/4 oz	scant ½ cup
water	1.2 litres/2 pints	5 cups
mixed vegetables**, diced	900 g/2 lb	2 lb
malt vinegar, brown or white	600 ml/1 pint	2½ cups
pickling spices	1 tbsp	1 tbsp
mustard powder	1 tbsp	1 tbsp
turmeric	1½ teasp	1½ teasp
cornflour (cornstarch)	2 teasp	2 teasp
ground ginger	1–2 teasp	1–2 teasp
caster sugar	50 g/2 oz	¼ cup

* this is the correct amount of salt, it is high but it is rinsed away
** choose a good selection, i.e. green beans, cauliflower (cut into florets), pickling onions, courgettes (zucchini), cucumber, tiny green tomatoes

Mix the salt and cold water, put into a china or glass bowl rather than a metal container. Add the prepared vegetables and leave soaking for 12 hours.

Drain the vegetables and rinse them well under running cold water. Dry and leave in the air for a short time to dry. Discard the brine.

Boil the vinegar with the pickling spices. The strength of different makes of spice varies so taste the vinegar after 1 to 2 minutes boiling and see if sufficiently well-flavoured; if not, boil for another 2 to 3 minutes or as desired.

Strain the vinegar and blend with the dry ingredients,

including the sugar. Put into a large saucepan and stir over a low heat until thickened. Add the vegetables, stir well to mix with the vinegar sauce. Cook steadily for 5 minutes, no longer, for the vegetables should keep a firm texture. Put into heated jars and seal.

Chutneys
Chutneys, based upon a mixture of fruits and vegetables, are a favourite relish. The following recipe is a good basic one that lends itself to simple variations.

APPLE CHUTNEY

Cooking Time: 45–55 minutes Makes 1.5–1.8 kg/ 3½–4 lb **

	Metric/Imperial	American
onions, weight when peeled and finely chopped	450 g/1 lb	1 lb
malt vinegar, white or brown	300 ml/½ pint	1¼ cups
pickling spices	1 teasp	1 teasp
cooking (baking) apples, weight when peeled, sliced	900 g/2 lb	2 lb
sugar, caster or brown	350 g/12 oz	1½ cups
salt	½–1 teasp	½–1 teasp
sultanas (golden raisins)	100 g/4 oz	⅔ cup
ground ginger	1–2 teasp	1–2 teasp

Put the onions, with half the vinegar, into a preserving pan and simmer for 10 minutes; this softens the onions and prevents overcooking the apples.

Tie the pickling spices in a muslin (cheesecloth) bag with long cottons so the bag can be removed easily.

Put the bag of spices and apples into the pan, add a little extra vinegar if this is necessary to prevent the apples sticking to the pan. Simmer gently until the apples make a soft pulp. Stir in the remainder of the vinegar and all the sugar, continue stirring until the sugar has dissolved. Add the salt gradually, tasting as you do so. Finally add the sultanas (golden raisins) and ginger. Boil steadily until the chutney has the consistency of a thick jam. Remove the bag of pickling spices, put the hot chutney into heated jars and cover.

VARIATIONS
Apple and Mint Chutney: Add 2 tablespoons (3 tbsp) finely chopped mint leaves just before putting the chutney into the jars. The ginger could be omitted.
● *Apricot Chutney:* Use apricots instead of apples and the grated rind of 2 lemons instead of the ginger.
● *Rhubarb Chutney:* Use rhubarb in place of apples.
● *Red Pepper Chutney:* Use half the amount of apples and 450 g/1 lb diced fresh red peppers. Omit the ginger and use mixed spice instead.
● *Tomato Chutney:* Green tomatoes are generally used for chutney. Use 675 g/1½ lb tomatoes and 225 g/8 oz apples.

Festive Food

The two festivals of Christmas and Easter have their own traditions of food, recipes for which are given on the following pages. The recipes on this page and page 194 are for savoury dishes for these holiday periods and on pages 195 to 201 for desserts and cakes.
Turkey is a good choice for Christmas and Easter. Salmon is one of the fishes that could be served at Easter time; methods of cooking it are on this page.

CHRISTMAS TRADITIONS

Christmas lunch or dinner is a very traditional meal. Turkey has become the choice for the majority of households, although chicken or duck or a joint of beef would be selected by a small family.

The turkey should be roasted as the timing on page 83 and served with various stuffings and sauces. The most popular accompaniments are Chestnut Stuffing and Parsley and Thyme Stuffing with Bread Sauce and Cranberry Sauce, see pages 105, 106 and 102. Many cooks however like to make slight alterations each year in the menu and the Tangy Lemon Sauce, given on page 100, is a delicious change from gravy. It blends well with the accompaniments given above.

Goose, which was so very popular some years ago, has been supplanted by turkey but a good plump goose makes a pleasant change. Follow the advice given on page 83 to ensure that the flesh is moist and free from excess fat.

The rich dark fruity Christmas Pudding is probably the most popular pudding of the year, although nowadays an interesting addition is appearing on the Christmas menu. With the ever-growing fondness for ice cream, and the ease with which this can be made at home, an Iced Christmas Bombe is becoming increasingly well-known, the recipe is on page 198.

The favourite accompaniments for the hot Christmas Pudding are Brandy Butter or Cumberland Rum Butter, the latter being more well-known in the North of England.

Mince pies are served at the Christmas meal. There is a legend that 'each mince pie eaten ensures a happy month in the year ahead', so at least 12 should be eaten over the Christmas period!

The traditional Christmas Cake is, like the pudding, rich and full of fruit. This should be baked several weeks before December 25th to make sure it has time to mature in flavour. The cake can be iced in various ways, but the simplest and most popular icing is given under the cake on page 196.

Cold desserts, such as the Trifle on page 136, would be a good choice for Boxing Day or make a Tipsy Cake instead. The recipe is on page 198.

Christmas is, of course, far less important in Scotland than it is in England, Wales or Ireland. It is New Year's Eve which is celebrated there. The rich Scotch Bun recipe to make for these celebrations is on page 201. A photograph of this cake is on page 214.

SALMON FOR EASTER

Although salmon is an oily fish, it dries very easily in cooking so care is needed to keep it moist. Salmon slices (known as cutlets or steaks) can be fried in butter or grilled (broiled). When grilling the fish, brush it with plenty of melted butter before and during cooking. Slices of salmon about 2.5 cm/1 inch in thickness take approximately 10 minutes to cook by frying or grilling.

If poaching portions of salmon, cut out squares of greaseproof (waxed) paper (one for each piece of fish). Brush the paper with melted butter if serving the fish hot, or with olive oil if serving cold; the oil prevents a film from forming on the fish.

Place the fish on the paper, top with a little butter or oil, salt and pepper and a squeeze of lemon juice. Wrap the paper around the fish and tie securely. Put into a saucepan with water to cover. Bring the water slowly to simmering point.

If serving the fish cold: cover the saucepan, remove from the heat and allow the fish to stay in the liquid until cold.

If serving the fish hot: allow the water to simmer for 8 minutes for portions that are 2.5 cm/1 inch thick. When poaching whole salmon, allow 10 minutes per 450 g/1 lb for a fish weighing up to 2.75 kg/6 lb and 6 minutes per 450 g/1 lb over this weight.

The fish can be cooked in a mixture of white wine and fish stock rather than water. Do not cover whole fish.

To Bake Salmon: Wrap the portions of salmon or whole fish in well buttered or oiled foil. The fish can be flavoured with a little salt, pepper and lemon juice and topped with butter or oil. Cook in the centre of a moderate oven, 180°C/350°F Gas Mark 4. Allow 30 minutes cooking time for individually wrapped portions of salmon, or a slightly shorter time, i.e. 20 to 25 minutes, if serving the fish cold, for it continues to cook as it cools. Allow 15 minutes per 450 g/1 lb for a fish weighing up to 2.75 kg/6 lb and 10 minutes per 450 g/1 lb over this weight.

Serve the fish hot with melted butter flavoured with lemon juice, or cold with mayonnaise.

SERVING THE GOOSE A NEW WAY

The instructions for cooking goose are on page 83. The photograph on this page shows the colourful effect of serving the bird with apples.

Press cloves (the number depends upon personal taste) into red and green dessert apples. Bake in the oven for about 40 minutes until just soft. Serve the red apples as they are, but cut a slice from the green apples and top them with Forcemeat Balls, made as page 92, and with Cranberry Sauce, given on page 100. Garnish with parsley.

Above left: Roast Goose.
Below left: Christmas Pudding and Mince Pies.
Right: Roast Turkey

GLAZES FOR BACON OR HAM

Instructions for roasting and boiling bacon (smoked ham) joints are given on pages 52 and 68. The bacon looks more festive if it is given an attractive glaze. Shorten the total cooking time by about 20 minutes, then remove the bacon from the oven or the liquid. Cut away the skin and lightly cut the fat in a definite design; this allows the glaze to penetrate. Coat with one of the following mixtures. Place the bacon with the glazed side uppermost into a moderate to moderately hot oven, 180 to 190°C/350 to 375°F Gas Mark 4 to 5, for 30 minutes to brown the topping.

The quantities given below are sufficient for a 2 kg/ 4½ lb joint.

Ginger and Sugar: Blend 175 g/6 oz (1 cup) brown sugar with 2 tablespoons (3 tbsp) syrup from preserved ginger and 1 to 2 teaspoons ground ginger. Put neat slices of preserved ginger on to wooden cocktail sticks (toothpicks) and press into the joint before serving.

Pineapple and Cherry: Blend 175 g/6 oz (1 cup) brown sugar with 1 teaspoon allspice, 1 tablespoon flour, 3 tablespoons (4 tbsp) pineapple syrup. Decorate the cooked bacon with pineapple rings and glacé (candied) cherries.

Treacle and Orange: Blend the finely grated rind of 2 oranges with 2 tablespoons (3 tbsp) black treacle (molasses), 2 tablespoons (3 tbsp) brown sugar, 1 tablespoon flour and 1 tablespoon orange juice. Decorate the cooked bacon with orange slices.

VEGETABLES FOR CHRISTMAS

There are many seasonal vegetables to serve with the Christmas meal; the following are particularly suitable:

Brussels Sprouts and Chestnuts: Slit the skins of the chestnuts and simmer in water to cover for 5 to 10 minutes. Shell while hot and remove the brown skins too. Put the chestnuts into fresh salted water and cook until tender but unbroken – this takes about 15 minutes. Cook the sprouts separately in boiling salted water. Drain the chestnuts and sprouts, mix together; toss in a little hot butter. Do not cook the chestnuts with the sprouts, this turns the green vegetable a blue colour. The chestnuts can be prepared ahead and simply heated in the butter before adding the sprouts.

Fennel Rings: Cut the fennel into thick rings. Cook in boiling salted water for about 8 minutes. Drain and toss in butter with chopped parsley and finely chopped canned red pepper.

Fennel is also good when served cold with turkey or goose. Cut the fennel into thin rings, toss in oil and vinegar dressing and then in the parsley and chopped fresh green and/or red pepper.

MINCEMEAT

No Cooking Makes 900 g/2 lb **

Most of the old original recipes for mincemeat, used as the filling for mince pies at Christmas time, included minced beef as an ingredient, so that one had the unusual mixture of meat and dried fruits flavoured with spices. Still another very old recipe, however, dating back to the 17th Century, was rather like a thick marmalade blended with dried fruits. Today, most mincemeat recipes are fairly similar – a rich blending of fruits, apple, spices, etc. When mixed with brandy, whisky or rum, according to personal taste, the mincemeat keeps very well.

	Metric/Imperial	American
mixed dried fruit	450 g/1 lb	3 cups
shredded suet	100 g/4 oz	scant 1 cup
cooking (baking) apples, peeled and grated, weight when prepared	100 g/4 oz	½ cup
brown sugar, preferably Demerara	100 g/4 oz	⅔ cup
crystallized (candied) peel, chopped	100 g/4 oz	⅔ cup
finely grated lemon rind	1 teasp	1 teasp
lemon juice	2 tbsp	3 tbsp
ground mixed spice	1 teasp	1 teasp
ground cinnamon	¼–½ teasp	¼–½ teasp
grated nutmeg	¼–½ teasp	¼–½ teasp
brandy, whisky or rum	4 tbsp	5 tbsp

Make quite certain the fruit is well dried; if it has been washed, allow to dry at room temperature for 48 hours. Mix all the ingredients thoroughly. Pot in dry jars and seal down firmly. Keep in a cool, dry place. Do not reduce the quantities of sugar, suet and spirits if you wish mincemeat to keep well.

VARIATIONS

Use melted butter instead of shredded suet.
● Add 50 to 100 g/2 to 4 oz (¼ to ½ cup) finely chopped crystallized (candied) cherries and 50 to 100 g/ 2 to 4 oz (½ to 1 cup) blanched and chopped almonds.

MINCE PIES

Cooking Time: 20 minutes Makes 18 to 20 **

These pies can be made with most kinds of pastry. Some people prefer them made with the richer puff or flaky pastries, recipes for which are on pages 154 and 155; other people with crisp shortcrust pastry, as on page 156, or the sweeter biscuit crust pastry used for flans and given on page 132.

You need a total weight of prepared pastry of approximately 450 g/1 lb to make 18 to 20 average sized mince pies, although the depth of tins as well as the width determines this.

Roll out just over half the pastry and cut into rounds to fit the base of the patty tins (patty shells). Put in a little mincemeat – do not be over-generous with the filling for an excess will boil out in cooking.

Roll out the remaining pastry and cut into slightly smaller rounds to fit over the filling. Moisten the edges of the pastry and seal very firmly. Make 2 slits on top of the pies. Brush with a little beaten egg white or egg yolk to give a shiny coating.

Bake in the centre of the oven. Use a hot oven, 220°C/425°F Gas Mark 7, if using flaky or puff pastry, a moderately hot oven, 200°C/400°F Gas Mark 6, for shortcrust pastry and 190°C/375°F Gas Mark 5 for the sweeter pastry. Allow approximately 20 minutes cooking time and reduce the heat slightly if the top pastry is becoming too brown.

Top with sifted icing (confectioner's) or caster sugar before serving. Mince pies freeze well, use within 3 months.

CHRISTMAS CAKE

Cooking Time: 3–3½ hours Makes 1 cake **

	Metric/Imperial	American
plain (all-purpose) flour	350 g/12 oz	3 cups
ground cinnamon	1 teasp	1 teasp
mixed spice	½–1 teasp	½–1 teasp
salt	pinch	pinch
butter	300 g/10 oz	1¼ cups
moist brown sugar	300 g/10 oz	1²/₃ cups
grated lemon rind	1 teasp	1 teasp
grated orange rind	1 teasp	1 teasp
treacle (molasses)	scant 1 tbsp	1 tbsp
large eggs	4	4
sherry or brandy or milk	4 tbsp	5 tbsp
currants	450 g/1 lb	2½ cups
seedless raisins	350 g/12 oz	2 cups
sultanas (light raisins)	350 g/12 oz	2 cups
glacé (candied) cherries, chopped	100 g/4 oz	½ cup
crystallized (candied) peel, chopped	100 g/4 oz	²/₃ cup
almonds, blanched and finely chopped	100 g/4 oz	1 cup

First prepare the cake tin. Line a 23 cm/9 inch round or 20 cm/8 inch square cake tin with brown paper on the base, then with greased greaseproof (waxed) paper over this at the bottom and inside the tin.

Sift all the dry ingredients together. Cream the butter, sugar, fruit rinds and treacle (molasses) together. Gradually beat in the eggs, then blend in the dry ingredients, the sherry, brandy or milk. Lastly add the dried fruit, cherries, peel and almonds. Spoon into the prepared tin. Smooth flat on top.

Tie a band of brown paper around the sides of the tin, standing up 2.5 cm/1 inch or more above the top level of the tin.

Bake the cake in the centre of a very moderate oven, 160°C/325°F Gas Mark 3, for 1½ hours. Reduce the heat to slow, 140 to 150°C/275 to 300°F Gas Mark 1 to 2, for a further 1½ to 2 hours or until the cake feels firm to the touch and ceases to hum. A fruit cake that is NOT cooked completely gives a definite humming noise. Allow to cool in the tin, the weight of fruit would cause the cake to break if it is turned out too early.

Store in an airtight tin until ready to ice. The cake can be given a more moist texture if it is pricked and soaked in sherry or brandy at intervals of 7 to 10 days.

TO ICE THE CAKE

	Metric/Imperial	American
For the Marzipan: ground almonds *	350 g/12 oz	3 cups
icing (confectioner's) sugar, sifted	175 g/6 oz	1 cup
caster sugar	175 g/6 oz	¾ cup
almond or ratafia essence (extract)	few drops	few drops
egg yolks	3	3
To roll the marzipan: caster sugar	1–2 tbsp	1–3 tbsp
For the Royal Icing: ** egg whites	4	4
icing (confectioner's) sugar, sifted	900 g/2 lb	5¹/₃ cups
lemon juice, depending upon personal taste	1–1½ tbsp	1–2 tbsp
glycerine	1–2 teasp	1–2 teasp

* a little less ground almonds could be used in which case increase the amount of sugar, so the total weight is the same
** this gives enough for a thick coating plus some piping. If omitting the piping then use slightly less icing unless you like a very thick coating

For the Marzipan

Blend all the ingredients together for the marzipan. Do not overhandle this. Brush the surplus crumbs off the cake and coat very thinly with the jam, see under Methods 1 and 2.

There are two ways of coating the cake with the marzipan. Both are satisfactory, it is just a matter of personal taste which method you use.

Method 1: Roll the marzipan out to a round or square sufficiently large to cover the cake. Coat both top and sides with the jam. Lower the marzipan over the cake and gently press it on to the cake surface to give a completely smooth flat layer.

Method 2: Use just over half the marzipan and roll this out to make a band which is exactly the depth and circumference of the cake, see line drawings, page 197. Brush just the sides of the cake with the jam then roll the cake along the strip until coated.

Roll out the remaining marzipan and cut to a round or square to fit the top of the cake. Brush the top with jam and place the marzipan layer in position. Neaten the join between the sides and top.

It is considered important to allow the marzipan to dry out for 48 hours before putting on the Royal Icing. This is to prevent the oil from the ground almonds seeping out and spoiling the colour of the icing. If you are very deft and handle the marzipan very lightly, you can put on the icing immediately after coating the cake. As an added precaution though, brush the marzipan with a very little egg white, this acts as a seal, before putting on the icing. The advantage of icing the cake without leaving it for 48 hours is that the marzipan is pleasantly moist in texture.

For the Royal Icing

Whisk the egg whites lightly, add the icing (confectioner's) sugar, lemon juice and glycerine. Beat until white and shiny and sufficiently stiff to stand in peaks. Do not over-beat the icing, particularly if using an electric mixer or food processor. Over-beating produces small air bubbles which makes it difficult to pipe the icing.

To give the 'snow effect' shown in the photograph on page 198, use most of the icing and coat the cake completely. Sweep the icing up in peaks, as shown in the line drawing on this page. Allow to harden.

Cover the small amount of icing left with a damp cloth or absorbent paper (kitchen towels) to prevent drying out. You then can pipe a border around the bottom edge of the cake or colour the icing and pipe greetings on the cake. In the case of the cake on page 198, all the icing was used for a snow effect, no piping was required.

TO COAT IN MARZIPAN

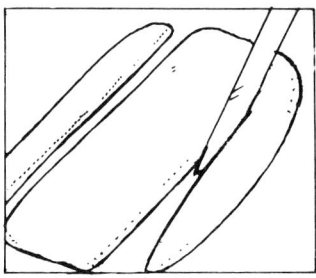 

Cut out the band of marzi-pan as described, page 196. | Roll the jam-coated cake along the band of marzipan.

Icing
To make the snow effect, lift up the icing in peaks with the tip of a knife.

SWEET SAUCES
The two kinds of butter below take the place of a sauce, but serve cream or custard with the Christmas Pudding and Mince Pies.

BRANDY BUTTER

No Cooking Serves 6 ✳✳

This is one of the best accompaniments to Christmas pudding. It is ideally suited to modern days and refrigeration, for Brandy Butter should be really hard and very cold, so giving a splendid contrast to the very hot rich pudding. Do not freeze the Brandy Butter though, for it loses flavour.

	Metric/Imperial	American
icing (confectioner's) sugar	150 g/5 oz	generous 1 cup
butter	100 g/4 oz	½ cup
vanilla essence (extract), optional	few drops	few drops
brandy	2 tbsp or to taste	3 tbsp or to taste

Sift the sugar. Cream the butter until it is light and fluffy; gradually beat in the sugar. Add the vanilla and gradually beat in sufficient brandy to give a good flavour. Continue to beat until the mixture is the consistency of whipped cream. Pile or pipe into a pyramid shape on a small dish.

VARIATIONS
A very little finely grated orange rind is a very pleasant addition; take just the top part of the peel, the 'zest' only.
● To make brandy butter an ornament for the table as well as a sauce for the pudding (its other name is hard sauce), decorate with nuts, glacé (candied) cherries and leaves of angelica if wished.
● If a little more icing (confectioner's) sugar is added to the butter to make a stiffer mixture, it is possible to incorporate more brandy.

CUMBERLAND RUM BUTTER

No Cooking Serves 6 ✳✳

This splendid flavoured butter is a 'rival' to Brandy Butter to serve with Christmas pudding; it is so much part of the Cumberland 'Scene' that it is made or bought to serve with bread, on plain cakes or in sponges, in pancakes etc. The butter keeps almost indefinitely if sealed down well, so a good quantity can be prepared at one time.

	Metric/Imperial	American
butter, preferably unsalted	100 g/4 oz	½ cup
Demerara or moist light brown sugar	175 g/6 oz	1 cup
ground cinnamon	pinch	pinch
grated nutmeg	pinch	pinch
rum	2 tbsp or to taste	3 tbsp or to taste

Cream the butter until very soft and light. Gradually beat in the sugar. The choice of sugar makes a great deal of difference to both flavour and texture – for Demerara gives a somewhat 'gritty' taste, whereas a light moist brown sugar produces a much smoother texture. Do not choose the dark brown moist sugar for this is too strong in flavour. The amount of sugar depends upon whether a softer and less sweet 'butter' is required. Add the spices and gradually beat in the rum; do this slowly so there is no fear of the mixture 'curdling'. Put into attractive pots and cover well.

When required, turn out on to a serving dish. Lightly whip the cream for coating and spoon this over the pudding. Decorate with holly, if desired.

VARIATION
For a darker pudding, add 2 teaspoons black treacle (molasses) as well as, or instead of, the honey.

TIPSY CAKE

No Cooking Serves 7–8 ***

Surely no recipe title could be more descriptive of a dish than a Tipsy Cake and certainly this is a very potent dessert, for the cake should be made very moist with brandy or brandy and sherry. It is not unlike a trifle except that a plain Madeira or sponge cake is used and the completed dessert has the shape of a cake.

	Metric/Imperial	American
Victoria Sponge or Madeira Cake, as pages 162 and 199		
raspberry jam	2 tbsp	3 tbsp
gooseberry jam	2 tbsp	3 tbsp
damson or other red or dark jam	2 tbsp	3 tbsp
brandy or brandy and sherry	approximately 200 ml/7 fl oz	scant 1 cup
sugar	to taste	to taste
double (heavy) cream	300 ml/½ pint	1¼ cups
single (light) cream	150 ml/¼ pint	⅔ cup
almonds, blanched	100 g/4 oz	1 cup

Cut the sponge or cake into 3 layers. Sandwich the first layers together with the raspberry jam, the second and top layers with the gooseberry jam, then spread the top of the sponge or cake with damson or another flavoured jam.

Warm the brandy or brandy and sherry, but do not boil. Add enough sugar to give a fairly sweet taste. Spoon the alcohol carefully and evenly over the cake. Whip the double (heavy) cream until it just holds its shape, then gradually whip in the single (light) cream. This gives a pleasantly light texture. Sweeten to taste. Pile the fluffy cream over the cake, decorate with the blanched almonds.

ICED CHRISTMAS BOMBE

No Cooking Serves 6–8 **

	Metric/Imperial	American
seedless raisins	100 g/4 oz	⅔ cup
sultanas (golden raisins)	100 g/4 oz	⅔ cup
sweet sherry	3 tbsp	4 tbsp
whipping cream	600 ml/1 pint	2½ cups
chocolate powder	2 tbsp	3 tbsp
thin honey	2 teasp	2 teasp
ground cinammon	½ teasp	½ teasp
ground nutmeg	½ teasp	½ teasp
glacé (candied) cherries, quartered	100 g/4 oz	½ cup
crystallized (candied) peel, chopped	50 g/2 oz	⅓ cup
almonds, blanched and chopped	50 g/2 oz	½ cup
eggs	3	3
icing (confectioner's) sugar, sifted	75 g/3 oz	⅔ cup
To coat: whipping cream	150 ml/¼ pint	⅔ cup

Put the dried fruits and sherry into a bowl, soak for at least 1 hour. Whip the cream until it almost holds its shape, then gradually blend in the chocolate powder, honey, spices, cherries, peel and nuts. The cream will continue to stiffen as you add these ingredients. Do not add the dried fruits and sherry at this stage.

Whisk the eggs and sugar until thick and creamy. Fold into the cream mixture. Spoon into a freezing tray or other container and freeze lightly.

Remove from the tray, blend the dried fruits and sherry into the mixture. Spoon into a well-chilled freezerproof basin or bowl. Freeze until firm. This dessert keeps well for several weeks.

A Tipsy Cake is rarely decorated in an elaborate fashion but if wished it can be topped with crystallized (candied) violet and rose petals, angelica, etc.

Basic Cakes

It is useful at holiday time to have plain cakes that can be served instead of the richer cakes or as a basis for a Tipsy Cake, page 198.

The Victoria Sandwich on page 162 is baked in 2 sandwich tins (layer cake pans). For the Tipsy Cake it is better to use a single 18 to 20 cm/7 to 8 inch cake tin and bake the cake for 1 to 1½ hours at the temperature given in the Madeira Cake below.

Madeira Cake: This is a cake that has been popular in Britain for a long time. It does not contain Madeira, but slices were once served with a glass of Madeira wine.

Cream 175 g/6 oz (¾ cup) butter with 175 g/6 oz (¾ cup) caster sugar until very soft and light. About 1 teaspoon finely grated lemon rind can be creamed with the butter and sugar. Gradually beat in 3 large eggs, then fold in 225 g/8 oz plain (2 cups all-purpose) flour sifted with 1½ teaspoons baking powder and 2 tablespoons milk or dry sherry. Put into a well-greased and floured 18 to 20 cm/7 to 8 inch cake tin. Sprinkle 1 tablespoon caster sugar over the top of the cake mixture.

Bake in the centre of a very moderate oven, 160°C/ 325°F Gas Mark 3, for approximately 1½ hours or until firm. After the cake has been baking for 45 minutes, open the oven door very carefully and place a large thin slice of crystallized (candied) peel on top of the cake. The peel can be omitted if using the cake as above.

Above left: Iced Christmas Bombe. Below left: Christmas Cake – recipe page 196. Above: Hot Cross Buns – recipe page 200

EASTER TRADITIONS

Good Friday is the day for Hot Cross Buns. These buns are very easy to make and freeze well for some weeks, so all you need to do is warm them in the oven for breakfast on Good Friday.

If following the usual practise of serving fish as a main course for lunch or dinner, you will find fresh salmon is in season. Suggestions for cooking salmon are on page 193. There are a number of other suitable fish dishes in the section that starts on page 32.

Easter Sunday means eggs for breakfast and chocolate eggs as presents.

Britain has not developed any special customs relating to decorating boiled eggs, but if you want to colour them use culinary tints in the water in which the eggs are boiled or onion skins to give them a yellow tint.

Lamb is the meat often chosen for the main meal, for spring lamb is in season. The Crown Roast on page 56 would give the meat a special occasion appearance.

Simnel Cake has become the traditional cake for Easter Sunday. It was originally the cake made for Mothering Sunday and, in households where maids were employed, the girls were allowed by their employers to bake this cake and take it home as a present for their mothers. The name 'Simnel' is believed to have originated from a combination of the names of a married couple called Simon and Nellie, who argued as how the cake should be cooked. A Simnel Cake is very like the Dundee Cake on page 159 but made richer with a marzipan layer through the centre and on top of the cake. If you find this cake rather rich and heavy, the lighter, but very delicious, plainer cake on page 201 is a good alternative.

HOT CROSS BUNS

Illustrated in colour on page 199

Cooking Time: 12–15 minutes Makes 12–16 ✳✳

These buns should be rather well-spiced; but the amount of spices can be reduced if desired.

	Metric/Imperial	American
fresh (compressed) yeast	15 g/½ oz	½ cake
milk	270 ml/9 fl oz	generous 1 cup
strong (hard wheat) flour	450 g/1 lb	4 cups
salt	¼ teasp	¼ teasp
ground cinnamon	½–1 teasp	½–1 teasp
allspice	½–1 teasp	½–1 teasp
ground nutmeg	½–1 teasp	½–1 teasp
butter or margarine	50 g/2 oz	¼ cup
caster sugar	50 g/2 oz	¼ cup
mixed dried fruit	100–175 g/4–6 oz	⅔–1 cup
egg	1	1
For the flour and water paste:		
flour	50 g/2 oz	½ cup
water	to bind	to bind
For the glaze:		
caster sugar	2 tbsp	3 tbsp
boiling water	2 tbsp	3 tbsp

Cream the yeast. Warm the milk and blend with the yeast. Sprinkle a very little flour over the top of the yeast liquid and allow this to stand until the surface is covered with bubbles.

Sift the remaining flour with the salt and spices into a bowl. Rub in the butter or margarine, add the sugar and the dried fruit. Add the yeast liquid to the flour mixture, together with the egg. Knead the dough until smooth, see the directions under White Bread on pages 142 and 143. Cover the dough and allow it to prove until double the original size. This will take about 1½ hours, although it can be adjusted to suit personal requirements, as explained on page 143.

Knead the dough again to 'knock it back' then divide into 12 to 16 portions. Roll into balls and place on to warmed and greased baking trays. Either mark a cross with a knife or make a more definite cross with a flour and water paste. To make this, blend the flour with enough water to give a firm rolling consistency. Roll out until very thin, cut into long narrow strips. Do not put on the buns until the dough has proved again. Allow the buns to prove for about 25 minutes or until well risen, then arrange the strips of dough on top to form a cross.

Bake just above the centre of a hot oven, 220°C/425°F Gas Mark 7, for 12 to 15 minutes or until firm.

Blend the sugar and water together. Brush over the top of the buns when they come from the oven to give an attractive glaze.

SIMNEL CAKE

Cooking Time: 2¼ hours Makes 1 cake ✳✳

	Metric/Imperial	American
ingredients as Dundee Cake on page 159 but omit the almond topping		
Marzipan, as page 196 made with	225 g/8 oz ground almonds etc	2 cups ground almonds etc
apricot jam, sieved	1 tbsp	1 tbsp
To glaze: egg white	1–2 teasp	1–2 teasp

As there is a layer of marzipan through the centre of the cake, it is advisable to use a slightly larger cake tin than given under Dundee Cake, i.e. either 21.5 cm/8½ inch tin or, if this is not possible, make quite certain the tin is sufficiently deep to take the increased amount of mixture. Grease and flour the tin.

Prepare the Dundee Cake mixture and the marzipan. Take just under half the amount of marzipan and roll out neatly to give a round that is just a little smaller than the tin size.

Put in half the cake mixture, add the round of marzipan then the rest of the cake mixture, smooth flat on top.

Bake in the centre of a very moderate oven, 160°C/325°F Gas Mark 3, for 30 minutes, then reduce the heat to slow, 150°C/300°F Gas Mark 2, for a further 1¾ hours or until the cake is firm to the touch. Cool in the tin for 20 to 30 minutes then remove on to a wire cooling tray.

Spread the top of the cake with the apricot jam. Roll out almost all the remaining marzipan to give a round and press this over the top of the cake. Make the last of the marzipan into 12 small balls (the number of apostles) and arrange round the edge of the cake. Brush the marzipan with the egg white. Place under a preheated grill (broiler) with the heat set to very low until the marzipan is pale golden.

Decorate the cake with little chickens, miniature Easter eggs or as desired.

MAKING THE CROSS
Another method of making a cross on the buns is to blend 50 g/2 oz (½ cup) flour with 1 tablespoon olive oil and enough water to make a soft piping consistency.

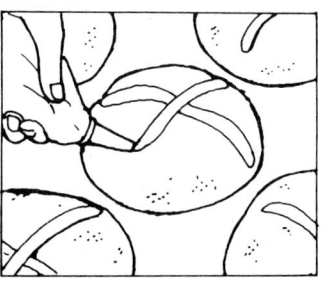

Put this into a piping (pastry) bag with a small writing pipe (nozzle) and pipe the cross on the yeast rounds *before* allowing these to prove prior to baking.

SCOTCH BUN OR BLACK BUN

Illustrated in colour on page 214
Cooking Time: 2½ hours Makes 1 cake ***

Scots all over the world will recall this rich cake which is baked for Hogmanay. It is sometimes called a Scotch Currant Bun, although this does not indicate the very interesting mixture of ingredients inside the crisp pastry crust. In spite of the fact there is no fat in the fruit filling, it keeps moist for a considerable time and should therefore be baked several weeks before the New Year.

	Metric/Imperial	American
For the filling: plain (all-purpose) flour	175 g/6 oz	1½ cups
bicarbonate of soda (baking soda)	½ teasp	½ teasp
cream of tartar	½ teasp	½ teasp
ground cloves	½–1 teasp	½–1 teasp
ground cinnamon	½–1 teasp	½–1 teasp
black pepper	pinch	pinch
moist brown sugar (Barbados if possible)	100 g/4 oz	⅔ cup
currants	550 g/1¼ lb	3⅓ cups
raisins, seedless or deseeded	350 g/12 oz	2 cups
crystallized (candied) mixed peel, chopped	100–175 g/ 4–6 oz	¾–1 cup
almonds, blanched and chopped	50–100 g/2–4 oz	½–1 cup
buttermilk or milk	4 tbsp	5 tbsp
egg	1	1
brandy	2 tbsp	3 tbsp
For the pastry: plain (all-purpose) flour	225 g/8 oz	2 cups
salt	pinch	pinch
butter	75 g/3 oz	6 tbsp
To glaze: egg	1	1
water	1 tbsp	1 tbsp

Sift all the dry ingredients for the filling together, then add the sugar, currants, raisins, peel and almonds. Bind with the buttermilk or ordinary milk, the egg and brandy, mix thoroughly. If wished, this fruit mixture may stand overnight before putting it into the lined tin.

For the pastry, sift the flour and salt together. Rub in the butter and bind with water. Roll out until very thin. Cut two rounds to fit a 20 cm/8 inch cake tin, one is for the base and one for the top. Next, roll out a strip the length of the sides of the tin, for it is advisable to have as few joins in the pastry as possible. If preferred, roll out the dough and make one round only for the top of the cake, and use the remaining dough to make a large round that may be moulded to fit the base and sides of the tin.

Lightly grease the tin. Line the bottom and sides with the pastry, press this down firmly and make sure all joins are moistened with water and firmly sealed.

Put the filling into the pastry, press down very firmly. Brush the edges of the pastry dough with water, then put on the top round. Do not press this down too firmly, for the dried fruit mixture swells during cooking and could break through the top covering. Beat the egg with the water, brush over the top of the cake to glaze. Make several holes at even intervals with a fine skewer or fork.

Bake in the centre of a slow to very moderate oven, 150 to 160°C/300 to 325°F Gas Mark 2 to 3, for approximately 2½ hours. Look at the bun after 1½ hours and, if the pastry is becoming rather brown, reduce the heat slightly. Cool for 1 hour in the tin, for the weight of hot fruit could break the pastry, then turn out carefully. When quite cold, store in an airtight tin.

APRICOT AND ALMOND SPONGE

Cooking Time: 25–30 minutes Makes 1 sponge ***

	Metric/Imperial	American
For the sponge: butter or margarine	175 g/6 oz	¾ cup
caster sugar	175 g/6 oz	¾ cup
large eggs	3	3
self-raising flour*	175 g/6 oz	1½ cups
ground almonds	50 g/2 oz	¼ cup
milk	1 tbsp	1 tbsp
For the filling and topping: butter or margarine	50 g/2 oz	¼ cup
icing (confectioner's) sugar, sifted	175 g/6 oz	1⅓ cups
ground almonds	50 g/2 oz	½ cup
double (heavy) cream	2 tbsp	3 tbsp
apricot jam, sieved	5 tbsp	½ cup
Ratafias, as page 151	12	12
almonds, blanched	12	12

* or plain (all-purpose) flour with 1½ teaspoons baking powder

Cream the butter or margarine and sugar until soft and light. Gradually beat in the eggs. Sift the flour and ground almonds. Fold into the creamed mixture with the milk.

Grease and flour or line two 20 to 23 cm/8 to 9 inch sandwich tins (layer cake pans). Divide the mixture between the tins. Bake in the centre of a moderate oven, 180°C/350°F Gas Mark 4, for 25 to 30 minutes or until firm to a gentle touch. Cool in the tins for 2 to 3 minutes, then turn out on to a wire cooling tray and cool.

To make the almond filling, cream the butter or margarine until very soft. Add the icing (confectioner's) sugar, ground almonds and cream, beat well until light.

Spread one sponge with half the jam and half the almond filling. Place the second sponge over the filling. Top with the remaining jam, then the almond cream. Decorate with the ratafias and blanched almonds.

The British Heritage

Throughout this book you will find a selection of the traditional recipes of Britain. In some cases the dishes are made in exactly the same way as they have been for generations. In other instances the dishes have been slightly adjusted to please the changing tastes of today.

There are many contrasting aspects of British food. For example, smoked salmon is a luxuriously simple dish; many British dishes are simple, because the quality of the food is so good that it needs little adornment.

There can be few countries that produce such an interesting variety of fish and high quality meat and poultry.

The homely rabbit stew and dumplings represents the many appetizing dishes in which inexpensive ingredients are used to create satisfying meals; for the British housewives of the past were highly inventive and skilled in cooking.

Well-spiced food may be an unexpected part of the British tradition; our merchant seamen roamed the world to bring back treasures, and these included spices and exotic foods from other lands. The simple recipe for Devilled Chicken on page 204 is typical of the liking for curried flavours.

There are several pies and dishes made with pastry in this section of the book; for a good pie has been appreciated since the time of Chaucer, who mentioned pies when he wrote in praise of a good cook;

'He could roste and sethe and broille and frye
Maken mortreux and wel bake a pie.'

Each country and region in Britain takes great pride in producing recipes for the interesting cakes that have been enjoyed for generations; there are several in this section, but many more in the chapter that begins on page 142.

Rabbit Stew – recipe page 204

Melton Mowbray Pie

Cooking Time: 2½ hours   Serves 5–6   ✳✳

This is one of the best known savoury pies. It was first made by a Leicestershire baker in the 1830's and has been popular for well over 150 years. Leicestershire is one of the counties in central England and it is famous for Stilton cheese as well as this savoury pie.

The kind of pastry used in this, and similar pies, is called 'hot water crust'.

	Metric/Imperial	American
For the pastry: plain (all purpose) flour	350 g/12 oz	3 cups
salt	generous pinch	generous pinch
water	150 ml/¼ pint	⅔ cup
lard or cooking fat (shortening)	100 g/4 oz	½ cup
For the filling: lean, boneless pork	675 g/1½ lb	1½ lb
fat, boneless pork	225 g/8 oz	½ lb
anchovy fillets, chopped	6–8	6–8
white stock✳	3 tbsp	4 tbsp
pepper	to taste	to taste
To glaze: egg	1	1
water	1 tbsp	1 tbsp
For the jelly: white stock✳	150 ml/¼ pint	⅔ cup
gelatine	1 teasp	1 teasp

Sift the flour and salt into a mixing bowl. Put the water and lard or cooking fat (shortening) into a saucepan and heat only until the lard or fat has melted; do not continue to heat longer, for some of the water will evaporate and give too dry a texture to the pastry. Pour the melted fat and water over the flour and salt and blend with a firm knife. Knead lightly while still warm. Put a third of the dough into a warm place to be used for the lid and decorations on the lid.

If you wish to roll out the pastry and line a tin (spring form pan), choose one that is approximately 18 cm/7 inches in diameter. Roll out the two-thirds of the dough and cut a round the diameter of the cooking tin; put this into the bottom of the lightly greased tin. Roll the remainder of this dough into a band the circumference and depth of the tin being used. Place this inside the tin and press the joins firmly together; if necessary, brush with a little water first to make sure they are firmly sealed.

Dice the pork neatly. Mix lean and fat together with chopped anchovies and pack into the pastry. Blend the 3 tablespoons (4 tbsp) stock with the pepper, pour over the meat; do not use any salt as the anchovies give sufficient. Turn the rim of the pastry down slightly to make a firm base for the pastry lid. Roll out the remaining pastry into the shape of the tin. Make 'leaves' and a 'rose' or 'tassel' from the trimmings, for traditionally this type of pie is fairly elaborately decorated. Put the pastry 'lid' over the filling, seal the edges firmly, but do not press down too hard on to the meat filling, for space must be left for the jelly which is added when the pie is cooked and cold. Make a definite 'hole' in the pastry lid; so the liquid jelly may be added. Moisten the decorations with a little water and press on to the pastry, placing the 'rose' or 'tassel' over the 'hole' but do not obscure this. Beat the egg with the water, brush over the pastry to glaze.

Bake in the centre of a very moderate oven, 160°C/325°F Gas Mark 3, for approximately 2½ hours; lower the heat slightly if the pastry is becoming too brown. Allow the pie to become quite cold.

Heat the stock and dissolve the gelatine in this. Cool until slightly thickened but do not allow it to set. Pour the jelly very gradually through a small funnel into the top of the pie. Lift carefully into a cool place so that the jelly will set before cutting the pie.

VARIATION

If you prefer to mould the pastry, put a third of the pastry on one side as before. Roll out the remainder into a large round. Lightly grease a 18 cm/7 inch jar or tin, stand it on the pastry. Mould the pastry around the jar or tin and press firmly. Hold in position until the pastry cools. Lift out the jar or tin and put the 'raised pastry' shape on to a lightly greased tin; hold in position with a double band of greaseproof (waxed) paper.

Fill the pie, cover the top with the reserved pastry and proceed as above. The baking time could be shortened by approximately 15 minutes as the heat penetrates through the pastry more easily this way.

✳Note: To make the stock for the pie and jelly, simmer chicken, veal or pork bones or a pig's trotter or calf's foot in approximately 600 ml/1 pint (2½ cups) water with seasoning to taste, a bay leaf and bouquet garni for approximately 1 hour. Strain then boil in an open pan until the amount of liquid, 3 tablespoons (4 tbsp) plus 150 ml/¼ pint (⅔ cup) remains. If using a pig's trotter or calf's foot, there is no need to use gelatine.

Negus

Illustrated in colour on page 206

Cooking Time: few minutes   Gives 8–10 glasses   ✳✳✳

This is one of the traditional drinks of England, and novelists (including Dickens) of the 18th and 19th Century often mention Negus as a warming winter drink.

	Metric/Imperial	American
port wine	1 bottle	1 bottle
water	300 ml/½ pint	1¼ cups
loaf (lump) sugar	12 lumps	12 lumps
lemon	1	1
ground or grated nutmeg	pinch	pinch
vanilla pod (bean)	1	1

Pour the port wine and water into a saucepan. Rub the lumps of sugar over the whole lemon to absorb the flavour of the lemon rind. Halve the lemon, squeeze out the juice. Add the sugar, lemon juice, nutmeg and vanilla pod (bean) to the pan. Stir until the sugar has dissolved then bring just to boiling point. Remove the vanilla pod. Serve in warmed glasses.

RABBIT STEW

Illustrated in colour on page 202

Cooking Time: 2 hours 35 minutes   Serves 4   ❊❊

This stew is excellent with wild rabbit or ones specially reared for the table. The combination of lemon and herbs gives the flesh a delicious flavour. The bacon dumplings blend well with the lean flesh of rabbit.

This is the kind of stew that you would be offered in the country districts of Britain, but town dwellers also appreciate the good flavour of rabbit.

	Metric/Imperial	American
large rabbit (with the liver), jointed	1	1
vinegar	1 tbsp	1 tbsp
water	900 ml/1½ pints	3¾ cups
flour	40 g/1½ oz	scant ⅓ cup
salt and pepper	to taste	to taste
butter or fat (shortening)	75 g/3 oz	6 tbsp
medium onions, diced	4-5	4-5
medium carrots, sliced	6	6
medium swede (rutabaga), diced	1	1
beer	300 ml/½ pint	1¼ cups
lemon juice	1 tbsp	1 tbsp
bay leaf	1	1
chopped parsley	2 tbsp	3 tbsp
chopped sage	½-1 teasp	½-1 teasp
For the dumplings: self-raising flour*	100 g/4 oz	1 cup
salt	pinch	pinch
shredded suet	50 g/2 oz	⅖ cup
bacon rashers (slices), cooked and finely chopped	2-3	2-3
chopped parsley	2 tbsp	3 tbsp
water	to bind	to bind
To garnish: paprika	to taste	to taste

*or use plain (all-purpose) flour with 1 teaspoon baking powder

Soak the rabbit for 2 hours in cold water with the vinegar, this helps to whiten the flesh. Meanwhile, simmer the liver of the rabbit in the 900 ml/1½ pints (3¾ cups) water for 45 minutes to make stock.

Lift the rabbit out of the water, dry it thoroughly. Blend the flour with the seasoning, coat the rabbit joints. Heat the butter or fat (shortening) in a large saucepan, fry the diced onions for several minutes; remove from the pan. Add the rabbit and fry gently for 10 minutes. Strain the liver stock, measure out 600 ml/1 pint (2½ cups) and pour it into the saucepan. Allow the liquid to come to the boil and stir well to give a thickened sauce. Add the root vegetables, the onions, beer, lemon juice and herbs.

Cover the pan and simmer gently for 1¼ hours or until the rabbit is almost tender.

Check there is adequate liquid in the pan and bring to the boil. Blend the ingredients for the dumplings together, roll into balls, as shown below. Add to the pan and cook for 20 minutes.

Top the dumplings with paprika and serve.

VARIATION

Chicken Stew: Use jointed chicken instead of rabbit. Beer could still be used in the sauce or substitute white or red wine. A young chicken would need a total cooking time of 1¼ hours only.

MAKING DUMPLINGS

Cooking Time: 15–20 minutes   Serves 4-6   ❊

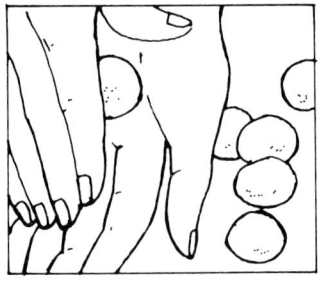 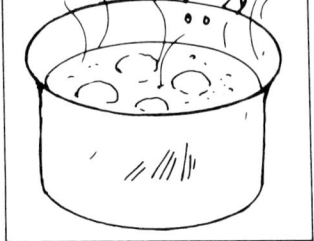

Prepare the dumplings as the particular recipe, see left. Roll in balls with floured hands.

Check there is sufficient liquid in the saucepan and that it has reached boiling point.

Drop in the balls, cook quickly for 10 minutes, then lower the heat and complete the cooking.

DEVILLED CHICKEN

Cooking Time: 8–10 minutes   Serves 4❊

The use of devilled mixtures, i.e. very hot butters containing curry and cayenne, was extremely popular during the Regency and Victorian eras. It may prove a surprise to learn that devilled game, see under Variations, was quite a usual dish to serve for breakfast. While this may not be popular now at such an early hour in the day, devilled poultry or game is excellent as a main dish and also as a practical way of reheating leftover poultry. The same mixture can be used with cooked meat or fish.

	Metric/Imperial	American
joints of cooked chicken, preferably leg joints	4	4
For the devilled mixture: butter	75 g/3 oz	6 tbsp
made English mustard	2 teasp	2 teasp
curry powder	1–2 teasp	1–2 teasp
Worcestershire sauce	few drops	few drops
cayenne pepper	pinch	pinch
salt	to taste	to taste
sweet chutney*	2 tbsp	3 tbsp

*if using a mango chutney, cut the large pieces of mango finely. The amount of chutney depends upon personal taste, the quantity recommended gives a pleasing sweetness to the dish

Make slashes in the chicken joints, this enables the devilled mixture to penetrate through the flesh. Cream the butter with the other ingredients. Spread evenly over the flesh of the poultry.

Place the chicken joints in the grill (broiler) pan. Cook steadily under the grill (broiler) until the flesh is very hot. Some of the butter will run off the chicken so it is a good idea to 'baste' the joints during cooking with this hot butter mixture. Serve with boiled rice and a crisp green salad.

VARIATIONS
50 g/2 oz (1 cup) fine soft breadcrumbs may be blended with the butter, etc. This gives a more interesting coating.
● *Devilled Game:* Halve cooked young grouse or pheasant, cover with the devilled mixture. Heat as the recipe above.
● *Devilled Turkey:* Cut thick portions of cooked turkey, cover with the devilled mixture. Heat as recipe above.

ENGLISH CHEESES

There are a number of English cheeses that can take their place among the great cheeses of the world. The best known is undoubtedly Cheddar. Although this is made in many other countries, the original home is Somerset in the West Country. The reason for the popularity of Cheddar cheese is that it is both an excellent dessert and cooking cheese. Derby cheese bears a distinct resemblance to Cheddar; one can also obtain Derby cheese mixed with chopped fresh sage leaves. Other splendid English cheeses are the blue veined Stilton, Double Gloucester, Cheshire (both white and blue veined), Yorkshire Wensleydale cheese (originally made from sheep's and goat's milk). There also is crumbly Leicester cheese and Lancashire, with its soft texture and strong flavour. The newest of the English cheeses is Lymeswold, a soft creamy blue veined cheese.

FISH PIES

Cooking Time: 50 minutes   Serves 4–6   ❋❋

Although fried fish is undoubtedly the most popular modern way of serving fish in England, there always has been a tradition of creating pies with fish as a filling. The great advantage of this dish is that the pie can be as economical or lavish as the cook desires. The following is a basic recipe that can be varied in a great many ways.

	Metric/Imperial	American
milk	450 ml/¾ pint	scant 2 cups
salt and pepper	to taste	to taste
bouquet garni	1	1
medium onion, halved	1	1
white fish, filleted and skinned	550–675 g/ 1¼-1½ lb	1¼-1½ lb
chopped parsley	1–2 tbsp	1–3 tbsp
eggs, hard-boiled (hard-cooked), sliced	2–3	2–3
peeled prawns (shelled shrimp) *or* cockles	100 g/4 oz	¼ lb
butter or margarine	40 g/1½ oz	3 tbsp
flour	25 g/1 oz	¼ cup
Shortcrust Pastry (basic pie dough), as page 175 made with	175 g/6 oz flour etc	1½ cups flour etc
To glaze: egg	1	1

Pour the milk into a deep frying pan (skillet) or large saucepan. Add the salt, pepper, bouquet garni, onion and the fish. Bring the milk to simmering point and cook for 10 minutes or until the fish is just tender, do not overcook. Divide the fish into 5 cm/2 inch pieces. Put into a 1.2 litre/2 pint (5 cup) pie dish with the parsley, eggs, prawns or cockles or any other flavouring required. Strain the milk.

Heat the butter or margarine in a pan, stir in the flour and cook for 2 to 3 minutes. Blend in the milk, bring to the boil and cook until thickened, stirring. Pour over the fish.

Roll out the pastry, cover the filling. Beat the egg and brush over the pastry to glaze. Bake in the centre of a moderately hot to hot oven, 200 to 220°C/400 to 425°F Gas Mark 6 to 7, for 25 to 30 minutes. Serve hot.

VARIATIONS
Cod's Roe Pie: Prepare fresh cod's roe as page 49 or buy ready-cooked roe. Slice the roe fairly thickly and use instead of the white fish.

Uncooked soft or hard herring roes could be used instead. Put the roes into the hot sauce and heat for 2 to 3 minutes. Place into the pie dish and add the various ingredients as above.
● *Cockelty Pie:* Use all cockles instead of a mixture of white fish and cockles. The hard-boiled (hard-cooked) eggs can be omitted, although they are a pleasant addition.
● *Eel Pie:* Sliced eel can be poached in milk as above and used as white fish, or poached in cider rather than milk. The cooking time will vary with the size and age of the eel. As the cider would be used to make the sauce, omit the eggs and other fish, but add 2 to 3 peeled and diced dessert apples instead.
● *Star Gazy Pie:* The most unusual of all pies from Cornwall. In the past pilchards were used, these are now less plentiful so small mackerel or herrings can be substituted. Use 8 herrings, 1 to 2 finely chopped onions, 2 to 3 tablespoons (3 to 4 tbsp) finely chopped mixed herbs (parsley, chives, fennel leaves, rosemary and thyme).

Slit the fish, do not take off the heads or tails, remove the bones as page 41. Fill the fish with the very finely chopped onions and herbs.

The amount of pastry should be doubled. Roll out the pastry, line an ovenproof pie plate or deep flan dish with very thin pastry.

Place the fish over the pastry, top with the finely chopped bacon. The heads should point outwards over the edge of the plate or dish.

Cover with a round of pastry, do not cover the fish heads. Decorate with pastry leaves and brush with beaten egg. Bake the pie for about 45 minutes at the lower setting in the recipe above.

THE FOOD OF ENGLAND

England, like the other three countries that make up the British Isles, may be small in size, but it has very clearly defined geographical areas that vary enormously in the scenery to be found. Each area has its own particular beauty spots, historical buildings and traditions of local dishes.

Visitors to England have heard about the industrial towns and cities of the north, but are captivated by the beauty of the Lake District, the magnificent scenery of the Yorkshire dales and the beaches of Northumberland. Good satisfying dishes come from these areas, such as stews and casseroles made from meat, poultry or game, with dumplings to make the family feel well fed. In the past, when meat was a luxury for many households, it

was customary to serve a Yorkshire Pudding or Dumplings with gravy as the first course of the meal, so that the appetites of the family were fairly satisfied before the meat course arrived on the table. Many interesting traditional breads and cakes come from these northern counties, too. These are included in the section on Baking that begins on page 142, together with up-to-date favourites.

In the midland areas, which includes the famous pottery towns where delicate china is produced, people enjoy savoury dishes such as the pie on page 203 and the Faggots on page 80.

In London and the counties around the city of London, the traditional food ranges from homely dishes like Steak and Kidney Pie and Pudding, both favourites in the eating

206

houses of the past, to sophisticated savoury and sweet dishes.

The southern counties have long been known for the excellent fruits and vegetables that are grown and harvested there. Kent, the county of hops and oast houses, is often known as the 'Garden of England'. Some of the light delicate fruit desserts originally came from the areas that include Kent, Sussex and Hampshire.

The south western part of England is a holiday maker's delight, with its winding lanes, small villages and lovely beaches. The well known cream teas of Devon and Cornwall are described on page 144. Excellent fish of all kinds is caught in these areas; the Star Gazy Pie given on page 205 is like the Cornish Pasty, page 76, a speciality of this region, which is still popular today.

From left to right: Flummery – recipe page 140. Sherry Trifle – recipe page 136. Chelsea Buns – recipe page 160. Maids of Honour – recipe page 155. Brandy Snaps – recipe page 150. Victoria Sandwich – recipe page 162. Negus – recipe page 203. Steak and Kidney Pudding – recipe page 73. Grilled Scallops – recipe page 45. Roast Duck.

CASSEROLE OF PORK

Illustrated in colour on page 210
Cooking Time: 1 hour   Serves 4   ✳✳

The Irish love of pork almost equals their liking for potatoes. Obviously there are many recipes for making a pork casserole, but this Irish recipe combines apples and herbs in an interesting way.

	Metric/Imperial	American
small cabbage	1	1
butter	50 g/2 oz	¼ cup
large onions, thinly sliced	3	3
salt and pepper	to taste	to taste
chopped sage	½ teasp	½ teasp
chopped parsley	2 teasp	2 teasp
grated nutmeg	good pinch	good pinch
large pork chops	4	4
sweet cider	300 ml/½ pint	1¼ cups
To garnish: medium cooking (baking) apples	2	2
butter	25 g/1 oz	2 tbsp
brown sugar	2 tbsp	3 tbsp

Cut all the outer leaves from the cabbage, so using just the centre heart. Shred the heart finely. Heat the butter in a saucepan, toss the cabbage and onions in this. Season well and put on the bottom of a shallow casserole. Add the herbs and nutmeg, arrange the pork chops on the vegetable mixture. Pour the cider over the top of the meat to flavour and keep it moist. Cover the casserole with a lid or foil.

Bake in the centre of a moderate oven, 180°C/350°F Gas Mark 4, for approximately 50 minutes or until the meat is very tender.

Meanwhile, peel the apples, core and cut into thin rings. Heat the butter in a large frying pan (skillet), cook the apple rings until just tender. Sprinkle with the sugar and arrange round the edge of the casserole before serving.

CORING APPLES

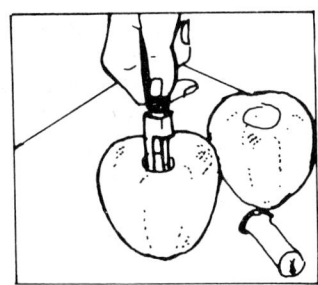

Place the whole apples on a chopping board. Press through the centre with a corer.

POTATO SOUFFLÉ

Cooking Time: 1 hour   Serves 4   ✳✳

It is said, indeed with great truth, that the potato is to Ireland what rice is to the Chinese or pasta to Italians; it provides a filling, sustaining and economical food. There is no doubt that potatoes have a very important place in Irish cooking. This recipe is a delicious dish of Irish origin, even though the word soufflé cannot be termed an Irish one.

This soufflé is an excellent accompaniment to the grilled Dublin Bay prawns, mentioned on page 211.

	Metric/Imperial	American
old potatoes, unpeeled	450 g/1 lb	1 lb
salt and pepper	to taste	to taste
ground nutmeg	pinch	pinch
butter	50 g/2 oz	¼ cup
eggs	4	4

Wash, boil the potatoes in their jackets in a saucepan of water and skin while warm: this makes sure the potatoes are floury. Return to the pan, warm gently and mash until smooth. Add salt, pepper, nutmeg and nearly all the butter, blend well.

Separate the eggs and mix the yolks with the mashed potatoes. Whisk the egg whites in a bowl until stiff, fold into the potato mixture. Use the remaining butter to grease an 18 cm/7 inch soufflé dish. Spoon in the light potato mixture. Bake in the centre of a moderately hot oven, 190 to 200°C/375 to 400°F Gas Mark 5 to 6, for 35 minutes until well risen and serve at once.

BOXTY PANCAKES

Cooking Time: 40 minutes   Makes 8 pancakes   ✳✳

These simple potato pancakes are often served in Ireland at Hallowe'en. They are excellent if topped with Brandy Butter, which can be found on page 197.

	Metric/Imperial	American
large old potatoes	3	3
plain flour	50 g/2 oz	½ cup
baking powder	1 teasp	1 teasp
salt	¼ teasp	¼ teasp
caraway seeds	1 teasp	1 teasp
milk, see method	about 150 ml/ ¼ pint	about ⅔ cup
To fry: fat (shortening)	100 g/4 oz	½ cup

Peel the potatoes and grate them fairly coarsely. Squeeze the grated potatoes very firmly with your hands over a bowl, then cover the grated potatoes. Keep the liquid that has been extracted, cover and allow to stand for at least 1 hour. Strain this through fine muslin (cheesecloth) and mix the sediment left in the muslin with the grated potatoes. The potato liquid should be discarded.

Sift the flour, baking powder and salt into a bowl. Mix with the grated potatoes and caraway seeds. Gradually add sufficient milk to make the mixture the consistency of a thick batter.

Heat 15 g/½ oz (1 tbsp) fat (shortening) in a frying pan (skillet); spoon in an eighth of the mixture. Fry steadily for about 2 to 3 minutes or until golden brown on the under side. Turn and cook on the second side. Lift on to a heated serving dish and keep hot in the oven while cooking the remaining pancakes.

Serve the pancakes hot topped with butter, sugar and a squeeze of lemon juice, or with well-spiced apple purée or with Brandy Butter, as the recipe on page 197.

CHAMP

Cooking Time: 30 minutes   Serves 4   ❋❋

This simple blending of vegetables is excellent with any meat, but particularly with grilled or fried gammon (smoked ham) slices (often called gammon steaks).

The potatoes must be really light and fluffy – the secret of successful mashed potatoes is to cook them carefully so they do not absorb too much water, to drain and dry them well, and to beat in the hot milk near an open window; the draught makes them very white.

	Metric/Imperial	American
old potatoes, peeled	675 g/1½ lb	1½ lb
salt and pepper	to taste	to taste
small spring onions (scallions)	about 24	about 24
milk	225 ml/8 fl oz	1 cup
butter, melted	75 g/3 oz	6 tbsp
To garnish: chopped parsley	1 tbsp	1 tbsp

Cook the potatoes in a saucepan of salted water until just soft. Strain and put over a very low heat to dry for 1 minute.

Meanwhile, chop the spring onions (scallions) using both the bulb and stem. Put in the milk in a pan with a little salt and simmer until tender. Strain the onions, put on one side.

Mash the potatoes thoroughly, then gradually beat in all the hot milk and 25 g/1 oz (2 tbsp) of the butter. Add the onions and pepper to taste. Pile into a heated dish, make a well in the centre and fill with the remaining melted butter. Top with the parsley.

VARIATION
Other cooked vegetables are sometimes used, such as peas, cooked cabbage or beans, instead of spring onions.

IRISH CHEESES

Although the Irish produce many of the English variety of cheeses superbly, they also make their own individual products; although you may have to hunt carefully to find shops selling these for they are not plentiful. Blarney is the cheese that the Irish lovers of Guinness would recommend. There is a special Cheddar-type cheese called Killarney, which is made for export. A newer Irish cheese is Wexford, which is very similar to Cheshire cheese. Many continental-type cheeses are also produced in Ireland.

IRISH COFFEE

Illustrated in colour on page 211
No Cooking   Serves 1   ❋❋

Until a few years ago, Irish (or Gaellic) coffee was virtually unknown, except in Ireland. It now is extremely popular throughout Britain. To enjoy the true flavour of Irish coffee, one should order Irish whiskey (spelt with an 'e', whereas Scottish whisky omits this). Some people like to whip the cream lightly, others to pour the thick cream on top – this is a matter of personal taste.

The Irish toast which might well be drunk with this coffee is worth repeating:
> *Health and long life to you,*
> *Land without rent to you,*
> *A child every year to you,*
> *And may you die in Ireland.*

	Metric/Imperial	American
whiskey	1 measure to individual taste	1 measure, to individual taste
sugar	to taste	to taste
strong hot coffee, see method		
double (heavy) cream	1–2 tbsp	1½-3 tbsp

Heat a stemmed whiskey glass. Put in the whiskey, add the sugar and fill with coffee to within 2.5 cm/1 inch of the top of the glass. Top with the cream, poured over the back of a spoon to prevent curdling. Do not stir the coffee as one should enjoy the hot coffee and whiskey through the cool cream.

THE FOOD OF IRELAND

The first impression one has of Ireland is the exceptional greenery of the country. The grass, hedgerows and trees all seem to be more colourful than in most other countries. This is due to the temperate climate and fairly generous rainfall.

The fact that the Irish enjoy potatoes is well known, but perhaps a lesser known fact is the way in which the potatoes are included in a great variety of dishes. Examples are given on this and the next page.

Bacon and pork are favourite foods in Ireland, although the most famous meat dish is probably an Irish stew. In the past this was made with mutton or even with goat's meat. Nowadays, as mutton has become less plentiful, lamb is used instead.

There is excellent fish to be caught in Ireland, including salmon and shellfish. The Irish enjoy cockles in various ways and make better use of these tiny fish than in other parts of Britain. A variation on a Fish Pie, using cockles, is on page 205.

The large prawns (shrimp) found in Dublin Bay are really not a prawn at all, they are a species of lobster, which often are referred to as 'scampi'.

These fish are so delicious that they do not need elaborate cooking. Put them into cold water, bring this steadily to boiling point and simmer until the fish are pink in colour, or plunge into boiling water and cook for a few minutes only. The prawns are then ready to eat. They look more interesting though if browned under the grill (broiler); keep the shells on the prawns. The fish can be split lengthways or grilled whole. Brush with melted butter, add a sprinkling of lemon juice and heat for a few minutes only under a preheated grill.

From left to right: Barm Brack – recipe page 145. Potato Apple Cake – recipe page 160. Grilled Dublin Bay Prawns. Casserole of Pork – recipe page 208. Roast Loin of Pork. Irish Coffee Pudding – recipe page 136. Mussel Stew – recipe page 44. Irish Coffee – recipe page 209. Soda Bread – recipe page 148.

BAKED HADDOCK

Cooking Time: 40 minutes   Serves 4

This recipe is only suitable for mildly cured haddock. Arbroath smokies (the tiny smoked haddock) are ideal. If you fear that the haddock may be too salty, soak in cold water for 1 hour before cooking, drain well.

	Metric/Imperial	American
tomatoes, skinned and chopped	450–675 g/1–1½ lb	1–1½ lb
water	3 tbsp	4 tbsp
pepper	to taste	to taste
chopped parsley	2 tbsp	3 tbsp
chopped chives	2 tbsp	3 tbsp
smoked haddock portions	4	4

Simmer the tomatoes with the water and pepper to taste. Add the parsley and chives. Spoon half the mixture into a casserole. Add the haddock portions then the remaining tomato purée.

Cover the casserole and bake in the centre of a moderate to moderately hot oven, 180 to 190°C/350 to 375°F Gas Mark 4 to 5, for 30 minutes.

HAGGIS

Illustrated in colour on page 215

Cooking Time: 3 hours   Serves 4   ✲✲

Scots all over the world revere the Haggis. This is served on Burns night with due ceremony. The true Haggis is difficult to make at home, for the various ingredients, which should include a sheep's pluck (i.e. the liver, heart and lights – sometimes spelt 'lites'), make a very large quantity. They are placed into a cleaned sheep's stomach bag, which is difficult to obtain.

It is, therefore, better to make a less traditional looking (but still pleasant tasting) mixture, or buy a Haggis from a shop. If you buy one, prick it gently to prevent the mixture bursting through the bag and simmer for about 2 hours, or as directed by the supplier for sometimes the Haggis is ready-cooked. The easy way to make Haggis is given below.

	Metric/Imperial	American
lambs' liver, sliced	225 g/8 oz	½ lb
lambs' hearts, sliced	2–3	2–3
medium onions, whole	2	2
salt and pepper (this can be cayenne)	to taste	to taste
stock, see method	300 ml/½ pint	1¼ cups
fine oatmeal (often called pinhead oatmeal)	100 g/4 oz	⅔ cup
beef suet, shredded or finely chopped	100 g/4 oz	⅘ cup
chopped sage	1 teasp	1 teasp
chopped thyme	½ teasp	½ teasp

Put the liver, heart, onions and water to cover into a saucepan. Add a generous amount of salt and pepper. Simmer for 35 minutes or until tender. Strain and save 300 ml/½ pint (1¼ cups) of the stock. Either mince (grind) the ingredients or put into a food processor.

Heat the oatmeal until it turns slightly golden in colour. Add to the liver with the suet, herbs and extra seasoning. Put into a 1.2 litre/2 pint (5 cup) greased basin and cook over gently simmering water for 2½ hours.

Turn out and serve with mashed swede (rutabaga), known as 'neeps' in Scotland.

FORFAR BRIDIES

Illustrated in colour on page 214

Cooking Time: 1½ hours   Serves 4   ✲✲

The Cornish Pasty on page 76 is so well-known that the fact that there is a similar Scottish pasty is often forgotten. The main difference between the Scottish pasty (called a Bridie) and the Cornish one is that extra fat is included with the meat and onion filling in Scotland, and a cheaper meat is often used, which necessitates longer cooking and therefore produces a very crisp crust pastry.

	Metric/Imperial	American
good quality stewing beef	450 g/1 lb	1 lb
onions, finely chopped	2	2
salt and pepper	to taste	to taste
shredded suet	75 g/3 oz	generous ½ cup
Shortcrust Pastry (basic pie dough), as page 175 made with	350 g/12 oz flour etc	3 cups flour etc

Cut the meat into very narrow strips, about 2.5 cm/1 inch in length and 5 mm/¼ inch wide. Mix with the onions. Add a generous amount of salt and pepper and the suet.

Make the pastry, roll out and divide into 4 portions. Shape these into ovals, about 18 cm/7 inches x 23 cm/9 inches; this is the traditional shape but if more convenient, cut into large rounds. Put the meat mixture in the centre of each pastry oval, damp the edges with water and press together firmly. Flute with your forefinger and thumb. Make a small hole in the centre of each bridie, to allow excess steam to escape, keep the pastry crisp and prevent the meat mixture breaking through the joins. Put on to a lightly greased baking tray.

Bake in the centre of a hot oven, 220°C/425°F Gas Mark 7, for 15 minutes, then reduce the heat to very moderate, 160°C/325°F Gas Mark 3, for a further 1 hour 15 minutes to make sure the meat is tender. Serve hot.

OATCAKES

Illustrated in colour on page 215
Cooking Time: see method   Makes 10–12 ✳✳

Although oatcakes are ideal for breakfast with marmalade, they are equally good with cheese and butter at the end of a meal. Oatcakes were originally cooked on a griddle, but they are easier to bake in the oven; both methods are given.

	Metric/Imperial	American
fine oatmeal	200 g/7 oz	generous 1 cup
plain (all-purpose) flour	25 g/1 oz	¼ cup
baking powder	½ teasp	½ teasp
salt	¼ teasp	¼ teasp
butter or fat, melted	50 g/2 oz	¼ cup
boiling water	up to 150 ml/¼ pint	up to ⅔ cup
To roll: fine oatmeal	2 tbsp	3 tbsp

Put the oatmeal into a bowl; sift the flour, baking powder and salt into the bowl, mix with the oatmeal. Add the melted butter or fat and gradually pour on the boiling water. Work this into the other ingredients with a firm knife. As soon as the mixture binds together, knead it well; this is the secret of a good texture.

Sprinkle a pastry board and rolling pin with oatmeal; roll out the mixture until 3 to 5 mm/⅛ to ¼ inch in thickness. Cut into rounds or triangles.

To bake the oatcakes: place on a very lightly greased baking tray and bake in the centre of a moderate oven, 180°C/350°F Gas Mark 4, for 20 to 25 minutes until firm. Cool on the baking tray.

To cook on a griddle: preheat the griddle, grease very lightly. To test if the right heat, shake on a little flour, it should take a minute to turn golden; no less a time. Place the oatcakes on the griddle. Cook for 5 minutes, then turn and cook for the same time on the second side. Lift the oatcakes off the griddle very carefully and place on to a wire cooling tray. When cold, store in an airtight tin.

VARIATION
Add 1 tablespoon caster sugar for sweet oatcakes.

ATHOLL BROSE

Illustrated in colour on page 215
No Cooking Makes 1.5 litres/2½ pints ✳✳✳

The first mention of Atholl Brose occurs in the 15th Century; it is that warming mixture of oatmeal, whisky and honey. Atholl Brose is the drink that celebrates the 'first footing' at Hogmanay, i.e. the first person to cross the threshold as the old year ends and the new year begins. As a winter drink, one would always blend the oatmeal and whisky with hot water and with a little cream if desired, but Atholl Brose is also very refreshing as a summer drink with iced water or soda water. Heather honey gives the best flavour according to most Scots.

	Metric/Imperial	American
fine oatmeal	4 tbsp	5 tbsp
water	to mix	to mix
honey	2 tbsp	3 tbsp
Scottish whisky	1.2 litres/2 pints	5 cups

Blend the oatmeal with enough cold water to make a thick paste. Very thoroughly mix in the honey and strain into a large bottle. Fill up with whisky. Shake well before using. Serve neat, or with hot or cold water or soda water.

SCOTTISH CHEESES

One of the most interesting Scottish cheeses is Caboc. This is sold as a small cylindered cheese and its attraction is the contrast between the creamy texture of the cheese and the nutty oatmeal coating. The islands in the north of Scotland produce Caithness, Orkney and Islay cheeses; all fairly mild in flavour. A delicious creamy cheese is called Crowdie. Dunlop cheese is the most universally popular Scottish cheese, it is not unlike Cheddar. Cheddar is, of course, made in Scotland as well as England.

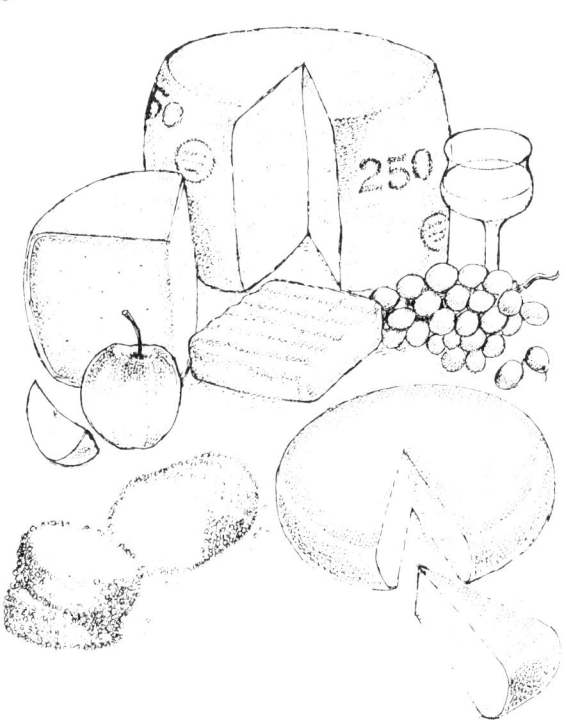

THE FOOD OF SCOTLAND

To summarize the scenery in Scotland is difficult, for it varies from high mountains to beautiful lakes (lochs) and moors, that in autumn are covered with purple heather, to the gentle scenery of the islands and the grandour of the cities like Edinburgh.

It is just as difficult to sum up the food and traditional dishes in just a few words, for Scottish fare ranges from the simple to the relatively sophisticated. It must be remembered that the French had an important influence on Scottish life and cuisine, particularly in the time of Mary Queen of Scots. One finds many French words,

or words of French origin, in the gastronomic vocabulary of Scotland.

The highest praise one can give beef is to say it is 'Scotch' but there is excellent lamb too. Good fish, including shellfish, abound round the coast of Scotland. Two of the most famous fish are economical herrings and luxurious salmon, although it is now possible to buy salmon quite inexpensively today, due to the development of salmon farms.

Game is still to be found in Scotland; this is generally cooked in fairly simple ways, see pages 86 to 97.

The soil in Scotland is very suitable for growing oats and barley, and both these cereals are used in many dishes. Soft fruit grows well too. It is, however, at tea-time where one will see Scottish housewives at their best. For the light scones, tea cakes, crisp shortbreads and fruit cakes, such as the Dundee Cake on page 159, are an everyday part of the meal. Anyone visiting Scotland should take care to have a light mid-day meal, so they can do justice to a good Scottish tea table.

From left to right: Forfar Bridies – recipe page 212. Floating Islands – recipe page 137. Roast Pheasant. Shortbread – recipe page 152. Scotch Pancakes – recipe page 149. Partan Bree Soup – recipe page 28. Scotch Bun – recipe page 201. Poached Salmon Cutlets – recipe page 193. Oatcakes – recipe page 213. Beef Collops – recipe page 57. Haggis – recipe page 212. Atholl Brose – recipe page 213.

SNOWDON PUDDING

Illustrated in colour on page 218

Cooking Time: 1¾-2 hours   Serves 4–6 ❉❉

This recipe, which is a Welsh speciality and known as Pwdin Eryri, typifies the kind of steamed pudding that is popular in Britain. Many people have the idea that these puddings are very solid and heavy: if a steamed pudding is well-made, it should be deliciously light and crumbly. The reason the pudding is called after one of the famous Welsh mountains is because it is topped with a lemon and white wine sauce just before serving, so looking like a snow-capped mountain.

	Metric/Imperial	American
butter	40 g/1½ oz	3 tbsp
raisins, seedless or de-seeded	175 g/6 oz	1 cup
fine soft breadcrumbs	175 g/6 oz	3 cups
cornflour (cornstarch)	25 g/1 oz	¼ cup
shredded suet	100 g/4 oz	⅘ cup
caster sugar	50 g/2 oz	¼ cup
salt	pinch	pinch
grated lemon rind	1 teasp	1 teasp
grated orange rind	1 teasp	1 teasp
orange marmalade	4 tbsp	5 tbsp
egg	1	1
For the sauce: large lemon	1	1
water	150 ml/¼ pint	⅔ cup
caster sugar	75–100 g/3–4 oz	scant ⅓-½ cup
cornflour (cornstarch)	25 g/1 oz	¼ cup
white wine	300 ml/½ pint	1¼ cups

Use most of the butter to coat the inside of a 1.2 litre/2 pint (5 cup) ovenproof basin or bowl. Take half the raisins and press against the butter coating. Mix all the remaining pudding ingredients, except the butter, together and put into the basin. Spread the remaining butter over greaseproof (waxed) paper and cover the pudding with this, then with foil. Either tuck in the edges of the paper and foil very securely or secure the covering with string. Put into a steamer over a pan of boiling water and steam for 1¾ to 2 hours.

While the pudding is cooking, prepare the sauce. Thinly pare the rind from the lemon, halve the fruit and squeeze out the juice. Put the lemon rind into a saucepan with the water, cover the pan and simmer gently for 10 to 15 minutes to extract the lemon flavour. Strain the liquid and return to the pan with the lemon juice and sugar. Blend the cornflour (cornstarch) with the wine, add to the pan and stir over a low heat until thickened; this should not be too thick a sauce.

Turn the pudding out of the basin, top with a little of the sauce. Serve the remainder of the sauce separately.

VARIATIONS
Add 25 g/1 oz (2 tbsp) butter to the sauce for a richer flavour.
● Use lemon marmalade in the pudding instead of orange marmalade.
● Use a rosé wine instead of white wine; obviously this will not give the snow-capped effect, but the flavour is excellent.
● Use melted butter or margarine instead of suet and brown sugar instead of caster sugar.

WELSH CAKES

Illustrated in colour on page 218

Cooking Time: 10 minutes   Makes 15–18 ❉

	Metric/Imperial	American
self-raising flour*	225 g/8 oz	2 cups
salt	pinch	pinch
butter or margarine	100 g/4 oz	½ cup
caster sugar	100 g/4 oz	½ cup
currants	100 g/4 oz	¾ cup
egg	1	1
milk	to bind	to bind
To decorate: caster sugar	to taste	to taste

*or plain (all purpose) flour with 2 teaspoons baking powder

Sift the flour and salt into a mixing bowl. Rub in the butter or margarine until the mixture resembles fine breadcrumbs. Add the sugar, currants and egg. Mix thoroughly, then slowly and gradually blend in sufficient milk to make a fairly firm rolling consistency.

Roll out the dough on a lightly floured board until just under 1.5 cm/½ inch in thickness. Cut into small rounds.

Preheat the griddle (often called a bakestone), grease lightly. To test if the right heat, shake on a little flour, it should take a minute to turn golden; no less a time. Place the cakes on the griddle. Cook for 4 to 5 minutes until golden brown on the bottom, turn and cook for the same time on the second side; watch the heat under the griddle and lower this if the cakes are browning too quickly. Lift off the griddle and place on a wire cooling tray. Dust with a little sugar.

VARIATION
The amounts of butter or margarine and sugar can be reduced slightly.

WELSH EVE'S PUDDING

Illustrated in colour on page 218

Cooking Time: 1 hour Serves 4–6 ❋❋

The name 'Eve's Pudding' is also used to describe a very pleasant dessert, i.e. a sponge mixture baked over apples. The Welsh pudding also uses apples, as one might expect, since Eve is associated with an apple. The mixture produces a particularly light, soufflé-like hot dessert.

	Metric/Imperial	American
cooking (baking) apples, peeled and sliced	675 g/1½ lb	1½ lb
water	150 ml/¼ pint	⅔ cup
caster or soft brown sugar	to taste	to taste
For the topping: butter	50 g/2 oz	¼ cup
flour	50 g/2 oz	½ cup
milk	300 ml/½ pint	1¼ cups
caster sugar	50 g/2 oz	¼ cup
vanilla essence (extract)	¼ teasp	¼ teasp
eggs	3	3
icing (confectioner's) sugar, sifted	1 tbsp	1 tbsp

Put the apples into a saucepan, add the water and sugar. Simmer until the fruit is soft. Spoon the fruit into a 1.2 litre/2 pint (5 cup) pie or other ovenproof dish.

Heat the butter in a saucepan, stir in the flour and cook over a very low heat for 2 to 3 minutes. Gradually blend in the milk. Stir as the mixture comes to the boil and thickens; add the sugar and vanilla essence (extract). Remove the pan from the heat.

Separate the eggs. Whisk the yolks into the hot, but not boiling, mixture. Whisk the egg whites in a bowl until stiff, then fold gently and carefully into the ingredients in the pan. Spoon the light mixture over the apples and spread flat.

Bake in the centre of a moderate to moderately hot oven, 180 to 190°C/350 to 375°F Gas Mark 4 to 5, for 40 minutes or until well-risen and just firm. Top with the icing (confectioner's) sugar and serve at once.

VARIATIONS
Use 1 to 2 tablespoons lemon juice when cooking the apples (omit this amount of water), then add the very finely grated rind of 1 lemon to the topping.
● *Apricot Soufflé Pudding:* Use apricots instead of apples.

MEAD

Illustrated in colour on page 219

This is one of the oldest drinks recorded. The choice of honey is important; experts each extol the virtue of their own favourite honey in making the drink. Soft water is frequently recommended for good mead. Although mead is made throughout Britain, generally by bee-keepers, it is more popular in Wales than elsewhere.

	Metric/Imperial	American
root ginger, amount depends on personal taste	25–50 g/1–2 oz	1–2 tbsp
large lemons, de-seeded and sliced	2	2
water, preferably soft	4.5 litres/8 pints	10 pints
light coloured thin honey	1.35 kg/3 lb	3 lb
mead yeast or brewer's yeast	25 g/1 oz	1 cake of compressed yeast
ground ginger, optional	to taste	to taste
lemon juice, optional	to taste	to taste

Bruise the ginger by crushing with a weight. Put the ginger and lemons into a piece of muslin (cheesecloth), tie tightly. Put the bag into a very large pan with the water. Bring the water just to the boil, boil for 2 minutes, then leave it to stand until the temperature drops to 55°C/130°F.

Meanwhile, warm the honey until it reaches the same temperature, blend with the water. Allow to stand again until the mixture is at 21°C/70°F. Crumble the yeast until it is very fine and stir into the liquid. When quite cold, remove the bag of ginger and lemons. Taste the liquid and if it is not sufficiently strong in flavour, add a little ground ginger and/or lemon juice.

Pour into a fermentation jar or cask. Leave for about 5 weeks, or until all fermentation ceases. After this, allow to stand in a cool place for 2 weeks, then strain or syphon into another clean cask or jar.

Store for at least 6 months, then strain into bottles. Wire on the corks. Mead matures well with several years storage.

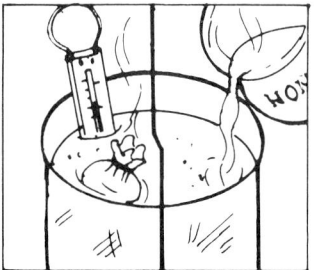 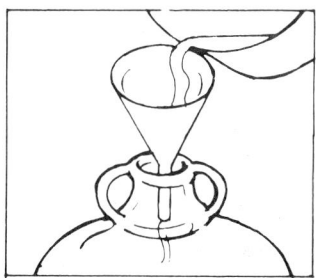

WELSH CHEESE

Caerphilly is often described as one of the best of British cheeses. It has a soft texture and a fresh flavour. It is both a good cooking cheese and a cheese that blends well with fruits, salads and biscuits at the end of a meal. This is the only Welsh cheese that is universally known.

THE FOOD OF WALES

Wales is a singularly beautiful country with a great variety of scenery, ranging from high mountains and wooded valleys to attractive coastal resorts, which are greatly enjoyed by holiday makers.

Often it is said that traditional Welsh cooking consists of plain fare. This fact may be true, but the food is extremely good, for Welsh farms provided an abundance of butter, cream and bacon in the past and still do today. Welsh lamb and mutton have always been recognized as some of the finest meat. The streams that come from the mountains and hills provide excellent trout and salmon trout, and there is excellent fishing around the coasts.

Oysters and other shellfish are available in the south-west of Wales, see the soup on page 28. Caerphilly is the name of the national cheese of Wales. Strangely enough this is rarely used in a Welsh Rarebit, see page 167; although it is a good cheese for cooking and, with its distinct yet delicate flavour, an excellent cheese to serve at the end of a meal. The leek is not only the national emblem of Wales, it is also an ingredient used a great deal in cooking.

Welsh Cakes are one of the easiest and quickest tea-time delicacies. These small crisp fruit cakes are cooked on a griddle (often called a 'bakestone'); they are excellent when freshly cooked.

From left to right: Leek Pie – recipe page 113. Oyster Soup – recipe page 28. Welsh Eve's Pudding – recipe page 217. Roast Lamb. Snowdon Pudding – recipe page 216. Ginger Meringue Cake – recipe page 161. Welsh Cakes – recipe page 216. Bara Brith – recipe page 145. Mead – recipe page 217.

Index